A Mayor's Life

A Mayor's Life

GOVERNING NEW YORK'S
GORGEOUS MOSAIC

David N. Dinkins

with Peter Knobler

PublicAffairs

NEW YORK

PublicAffairs books are available at special discounts for bulk purchases in the US by corporations, institutions, and other organizations. For more information, please contact the Special Markets Department at the Perseus Books Group, 2300 Chestnut Street, Suite 200, Philadelphia, PA 19103, call (800) 810-4145, ext. 5000, or e-mail special.markets@perseusbooks.com.

BOOK DESIGN BY JENNY DOSSIN

Library of Congress Cataloging-in-Publication Data

Dinkins, David N.

A mayor's life : governing New York's gorgeous mosaic / David N. Dinkins ; with Peter Knobler.— First edition.

pages cm

Includes index.

ISBN 978-1-61039-301-0 (hardcover)—ISBN 978-1-61039-302-7 (ebook)

1. Dinkins, David N. 2. New York (N.Y.)—Politics and government—1951– 3. Mayors—New York (State)—New York—Biography. I. Knobler, Peter. II. Title.

F128.57.D56A3 2013

974.7'043092—dc23

[B]

2013000769

FIRST EDITION

10 9 8 7 6 5 4 3 2 1

Contents

Foreword

Like many Americans, I have longed for the arrival of a heroic politician who could lead America to a better place—a true "servant leader" whose interest is only to serve those who put him in office and who cares little about the next election or the next rung on the ladder of his political career. A person who has the perfect blend of character and humility, who is plainspoken, who is incapable of telling a falsehood. A person like David Dinkins, the 106th mayor of New York City, about whom I am honored to write this foreword.

Since Mayor Dinkins has covered his life story and remarkable political career in the pages of this book, I would like to comment on the man I came to know and admire after he left office. So first, a little story.

It was 5:00 PM on Saturday, May 18, 2013, when David Dinkins presided at the wedding of my assistant, Jeannie Santos, soon to be Mrs. Frank Zammataro. At eighty-five, he was in full voice and soon had the entire audience spellbound by his masterful delivery. I watched in awe as the former mayor—gracious, respectful, and reverential—turned a civil ceremony into a spiritual event, reminding all in attendance that God's wishes are that we humans get along.

Before and after the wedding ceremony, Mayor Dinkins conversed with nearly all of the 120 guests, with a look of joy and love in his eyes, charming everyone. These were not the actions of a politician who was used to working a room, but of a human being who was born to lead.

Because I knew many of the people at the reception, and knew that most were Republicans, I could not help but marvel at how readily he won their hearts. Is it any wonder he became the first African American mayor of New York City—a city with a largely white population at that?

In 1993, several weeks after he lost his reelection bid, I had lunch with Mayor Dinkins in midtown. Although he was still smarting from his narrow loss, he seemed more concerned about how I was doing than interested in answering my questions about his future. "The only thing I know for sure," he said, was that, "on January 1, I'll be out of work, so I'll need a job to support my family." How could this be, I wondered? Didn't all ex-mayors and ex-politicians get "taken care of," and didn't many of them become fabulously rich after leaving office?

From then until now, I have spent a good deal of time with "Mr. Mayor," prodding him to write this important book and assisting him in the process. During this time I have become convinced that his portrayal in the mainstream media has been largely at odds with the facts.

To begin with, New York City was not the crime-infested capital of the world under David Dinkins, as has been proposed by his successor, Rudy Giuliani. This widely accepted myth, which was used by Giuliani as fodder for his presidential campaign, did as much to malign the law-abiding citizens of our great city as it did to damage the reputation of Mayor Dinkins.

The truth be told, crime had reached historic highs during the last term of Ed Koch, which carried over to Dinkins's first year in office. Racial tensions, too, had reached a boiling point well before Mayor Dinkins took the oath of office. Moreover, the entire nation experienced surging crime rates that ultimately resulted in what is popularly known as the federal "Crime Bill," which was signed into law in 1994 by President Clinton. Exacerbating the problem, weakening city finances and a national economic downturn conspired to cut social service expenditures at a time when they were needed most, and a tragedy such as the Crown Heights riot was an accident waiting to happen.

As I like to say, they didn't exactly lay out a welcome mat for this proud veteran of the United States Marine Corps. And yes, they also didn't know how tough he was.

As you will see as you read this book, two things David Dinkins does not tolerate are violence and lawlessness. While some in the media grudgingly regarded him as "courtly" and "civil," from his first day in office to his last, critics insisted he be tougher on crime, yet never gave him credit for actually doing something about it.

In point of fact, crime began dropping at a faster rate during Mayor Dinkins's tenure than during any other time in the history of New York City, and has continued to do so up to the present. In fact, it was Mayor Dinkins who hired five thousand new cops despite the budget deficit he inherited, and it was he who initiated the "Safe Streets, Safe City" program, which took police out of their cars and put them on the streets—the one policing strategy that many experts credit as actually being effective in combating crime. In fact, those initiatives combined to bring about a rapid drop of crime and put the city well on a path to being among the nation's safest.

Need I mention that it was David Dinkins who promoted Ray Kelly to the position of police commissioner?

In line with his abhorrence of crime and lawlessness, Mayor Dinkins also had zero tolerance for white-collar crime and political malfeasance of any sort. As a result, his administration did not have a single scandal or indictment handed down to any of its members, while those of his predecessor produced many. In fact, the team he put together to run the city government consisted of some of the most competent and public-spirited individuals ever assembled by any administration. And yes, they represented his "gorgeous mosaic," a blend of men and women, whites, blacks, Hispanics, Asians, Christians, Jews, and nonbelievers.

Perhaps the greatest disservice to Mayor Dinkins's reputation was the furor over building a new stadium for the US Tennis Open, which was named for one of the greatest tennis players of all time. How dare he spend millions of taxpayers' money? came the hue and cry. Why was it named after Arthur Ashe? Who other than Mayor Dinkins really cares about tennis?

Well, as it turns out, the investment has produced by some estimates more than $1 billion in revenue for New York City since the stadium was completed, and tennis is now widely recognized as a national sport. Arthur Ashe was the Jackie Robinson of tennis, his legacy lives on, and not solely because a black mayor chose to honor him. Yet we still haven't heard a single accolade for Dinkins's vision, and the stadium remains widely derided, most recently because we didn't spend even more money to include a retractable dome!

Sometime in the near future we may well build a new domed stadium. In my view, it should be named after David Dinkins. However, knowing him as I do, I can say that he would never consider such a gesture.

Today Mayor Dinkins is leading a wholesome and productive life. A professor of public policy at Columbia University and, as always, a man about town, he enjoys a popularity that speaks volumes about his place in New York City's history. He remains both thankful and humbled to have had the privilege to serve as mayor of the greatest city in the world.

He is equally thankful, perhaps, for the years he served as city clerk, about which he writes, "The part of the job I most enjoyed was presiding over the city's Marriage Bureau. The city clerk can preside over marriage ceremonies, and I took the opportunity as often as I could. I had a convocation ready to go at any moment, adaptable to whomever was celebrating their happy day:

> We are here to participate in and witness the sacred ceremony of marriage which has been, since the time of the first born, a means of establishing and continuing a home. For it is by this act that the community endures.

Mayor Dinkins made estimable yet largely overlooked contributions to the New York City community. It is time they were appreciated.

Thank you, Mr. Mayor.

LEONARD RIGGIO

A Mayor's Life

1

———

Trenton Makes, the World Takes

Trenton, New Jersey, where I grew up, was a major center of manufacturing in the Northeast. A working-class city, Trenton was home to a half-dozen rubber companies, Roebling Wire and Steel, and Lenox China; its factories made cigars, anvils, farm tools, steam turbines, aspirin, dolls, watches, bricks, linoleum, and felt-tip pens. Westinghouse, General Motors, Eastern Aircraft, American Standard—all called Trenton home. The world's largest bathtub was made in our fair city and was sent to President William Howard Taft. A sign on the side of the Lower Free Bridge over the Delaware River announced proudly, TRENTON MAKES, THE WORLD TAKES. Locals still call it the "Trenton Makes Bridge."

I was born in Trenton on July 10, 1927, and my first memories are of the Great Depression. None of these factories was doing very well. I didn't know it was the Depression, I thought this was just how life was.

My parents, William Harvey Dinkins Jr. and Sarah Lucy, met at Huntington High School in Newport News, Virginia. My mother, whom everyone called Sally, stood perhaps five-foot-two and was very proud to be co-captain of the girls' basketball team. They married young and came north.

My father went to beautician school in Newark, and my earliest memories of him are in the one-chair barbershop he ran on the ground floor of the row house in which we lived at 81 Spring Street. The street was wide, and the houses that lined it were two and three stories high, some made of brick, some of wood. My father did all the renovations himself; he was very good with his hands. I shined the shoes of the men who came for a cut and a shave. We didn't have a lot of money, but we got by.

When I was around six years old, my parents separated. I couldn't understand why and they didn't tell me, but I went with my mother and grandmother, Nora Bacon, to live in New York City. My younger sister, Joyce, came with us and later moved to Baltimore to stay with my father's sister. We lived in Harlem. The only apartment I remember must have been on Seventh Avenue, overlooking the subway yards. We never stayed in one place very long; we moved when the rent was due.

My mother and grandmother both worked as domestics, cooking and cleaning for white folks for a dollar a day. I don't remember ever being hungry, I never went to bed without dinner, and my clothes were clean. I had toys; when the children of the families for whom my mother and grandmother worked outgrew or got tired of theirs, they were given to me. We were poor as hell, but I didn't know that we were poor.

There were rules in my mother's house. If we were walking in the street and encountered an adult and I called that person by his or her first name, I would receive a stern rebuke. "This is *Mr.* Smith," I was informed. Propriety was important. And respect. I was an obedient child, and they didn't have to discipline me often. I do not mean to suggest that I was never bad, because I'm sure I got into as much trouble as the average kid, but I would not defy them. If I did something wrong, my mother or grandmother would simply talk to me. Whatever the infraction—perhaps my room was messy—they would say, "Today we worked so hard, why don't you pick up your clothes?" In about thirty seconds I would be in tears. They were loving, caring, hardworking women, and they never had to lay a hand on me.

With just one exception.

In the mid-1930s on the streets of New York, the latest in personal transportation was what we called skate scooters: wooden soapboxes nailed onto two-by-fours with metal roller-skate wheels affixed in the front and back. They made a racket in the street, and we would race them incessantly. Of course, if you wanted a really good-looking scooter, you'd nail on reflectors, the kind found mostly on license plates. We wouldn't buy reflectors; we didn't have the money or the inclination. We would liberate them. On one occasion, as a group of us were huddled over the back bumper of a particularly vulnerable automobile, a police officer—a black police officer in plainclothes—saw us and knew immediately that we were up to no good. We all took off and he chased us, and because I was the smallest he caught me. He could have taken me to the station house, but he did something he knew would be far worse: he took me home to my mother and grandmother. They took off all my clothes, stood me in the bathtub, and beat me with straps. I haven't stolen a reflector since.

When I was around seven years old, I used to sell shopping bags. At the corner of 125th Street and Eighth Avenue, men sold fruit and vegetables from pushcarts. This open-air marketing was the very personal way shopping got done in Harlem. And because nobody had any money, you didn't get a shopping bag in which to place your groceries, you had to buy one. Little entrepreneur that I was, I would buy bags from a wholesaler three for a nickel and sell them to shoppers at two cents apiece. It took quite a while, but when I finally made ten cents, I went to the five-and-dime and bought a present for my mother. It was one of the proudest moments of my life.

I was still in grammar school when I was sent back from Harlem to Trenton to live with my father. His name was Bill, but I called him Pop, and everybody else did too. If Pop had gone to college, he would have done quite well; he was a very smart, self-made man. By the time I got back, his barbershop was thriving. He had started with one chair and then expanded, renting space to other people. Ed Veldeen had a chair, and a man named Cox, and another fellow from nearby Philadelphia used to come over and cut hair. In the years I was away, Pop was certified as a real estate broker and insurance agent, and he managed his businesses from an office in back of the barbershop. He was making a better living than my mother, and apparently together they decided I would be better served living with him in Trenton.

I had responsibilities. In those days people didn't pay their bills by mailing in a check at the beginning of the month, they went to each office personally and paid in cash. Pop had a box with many compartments into which he would put aside some money each week—"This is the rent, this is the electric, this is the telephone"—and as each was due I would be dispatched to pay the bill. He didn't use these exact words, but he was teaching me the difference between "gross" and "net," he was teaching me that not all the money in the cash register was his. We had debts, and he was teaching me how to save. And he was demonstrating his faith in me.

There was a smattering of black families on Spring Street. We didn't live in a ghetto. From my father's barbershop all the way down a couple of blocks to the shoemaker was mostly white. There were two black families on the 200 block. Mrs. Hence, an African American, ran a little tearoom, but most of the families in the immediate vicinity were working- or lower-middle-class white folks. No one locked his door, not during the day, not at night. We all knew each other. It was mostly black in the stand-alone wooden homes on West End Avenue, a little mixed on nice, quiet Montgomery Place. There was not much crime to speak of. Once, a man opened the door of the neighborhood doctor's car, parked unlocked as it was in front of the doctor's home/office on Spring Street, and stole his medical bag. An hour later the same man drove by and tossed the bag on the sidewalk; he didn't want to deprive the doctor of his equipment, he just wanted the morphine the doctor was carrying. That is the sum total of crime I can recall.

Once back, I quickly rejoined a tight group of friends. There was

Frederick Schenck (pronounced *Skank*); Hilmar Ludwig Jensen Jr., also known as Junky Joe; and Aloysius Leon Higginbotham Jr. The Hayling brothers, Leslie and Hartley (known as Bill), lived across the street. Fred Schenck grew up to become the deputy undersecretary of commerce for the Jimmy Carter administration. Junky Joe became a teacher and school principal in Delaware. Leon Higginbotham became chief judge of the US Court of Appeals for the Third Circuit and was awarded the Presidential Medal of Freedom. Les Hayling was one of the Tuskegee Airmen—in 2007 they were honored with the Congressional Gold Medal—and became a successful dentist, and Dr. Bill Hayling delivered everyone's babies.

When we were little boys, we would play down by the canals that ran through Trenton, fed in part by the Delaware River and remnants of the horse-drawn barge system that served as a shipping lane from New Brunswick in north Jersey all the way down to Lambertville. My father had found an old piece of wood that was wide enough and long enough to stand on, and he had anchored it with rocks and dirt in the well-worn towpath out behind West End Avenue for us to use as a diving board. Trenton summers were hot, and it was a great treat to be able to jump into the water, even if some of us, myself among them, could not swim. One afternoon I trotted out to the end and started jumping up and down, singing, "This is my daddy's diving board! This is my daddy's diving board!" I slipped and fell. The first time my head got above water, I saw Junky Joe's heels rounding the corner of the alley, running. I was going down for the second time when Les Hayling walked into the water and pulled me out. Later that afternoon I saw Joe.

"You left me to drown!"

"No, I didn't," he said. "I went to *seek aid!*" Nine years old and he went to "seek aid"!

Not long after I returned to Trenton my father told me he was going to remarry. I thought I would die. All this time my parents had been very civil to one another—we were together at holiday times—and I was convinced that they would someday be a family again. I had built my vision of the world on that reunion, and when that future fell apart I was very distressed. I cried for a week.

The woman my father married, my stepmother, was named Lottie Lee Hargett, but everybody called her Sis. In my day there were no African American teachers at Trenton Central High School, but she started in the middle school and taught for forty years, and by the time she retired Sis was teaching English and drama at Central. She was a presence. The year she retired they dedicated the Trenton Central yearbook to her. On occasion we would encounter two generations of her students—say, mother and daughter—walking down the street. She was very helpful to me and my friends when we needed educational assistance. Whenever there was a school play or poetry recital, the participants always asked her to help. It didn't take long for me to learn to love her, and I ended up having two mothers who loved me. They were very much alike, and each of them thought there was nothing I couldn't do.

Sis was a trusting soul. My father would fill the gas tank in our car without telling her, and she never caught on. According to Les Hayling, she once said, as Pop winked at us around the dinner table, "This car gets good mileage. I've been riding all summer and haven't had to fill up once!"

I attended the Bellevue Avenue Colored School, later named the New Lincoln School, obviously an all–African American institution. Black students, black teachers, and a black principal, P. J. Hill, a no-nonsense educator whom kids used to call Pickle Juice. I was a decent student. Each of the adults in my life instructed me to pay attention, and I did.

In junior high school we studied Latin, and my very strict teacher, Ms. Bernice Munce, never gave me better than a B. However, I got to Trenton Central High School and proceeded to lead the class. On the other hand, my arithmetic teacher, who had earned his doctorate, never gave me less than an A–. The first day in high school the math teacher, Mr. Murphy, put a square root sign on the blackboard and referred to it as a "radical." I had never heard the term, didn't know what he was talking about. In the six math marking periods that year, I started with a D and by the end the best I could do was a B. Ever since that time I have felt that it is not the subject matter that is primary in the creation of a student, it is the quality of the teacher. I have had a handful of good teachers in my life, men and women who made an impression on me and who I think taught me well, and I am very thankful for them.

As we grew older Fred Schenck, Junky Joe, and I grew even closer. If you saw one of us, you saw us all. We were known in the neighborhood as the Three Musketeers. I wasn't an athlete. Although I was too little to play basketball, I loved to play baseball—second base or shortstop—but wasn't particularly good. We played football in the street as though we were competing for professional contracts. Our football, however, was old and beaten, and the bladder was dried out completely. We didn't have money to replace it, so we stuffed the leather shell full of leaves and continued our pursuit of athletic greatness. In fact, at age ten or twelve, we played a game against a team of white kids down the shore in Asbury Park. We arrived, and they couldn't have been nicer. They fed us sandwiches and cookies and ice cream, and we stuffed ourselves, and then they went out and ran all over us. We didn't know whether that was their plan, but it worked!

On Saturday mornings, Fred, Junky Joe, and I would investigate the alleys of the affluent neighborhood west of Spring Street, looking for soda bottles in rich folks' garbage. There was a nickel deposit on those bottles, which was big money. We would trade in what we found and head over to the local bakery, Pryor's Doughnuts on Edgewood Avenue. On any given day fresh pastries were too expensive for us, but a nickel would get you a baker's dozen of day-old doughnuts, and those we shared happily. Pryor's was right across the street from the Strand Theater, where we spent many Saturday afternoons. Starting at one o'clock, the price of admission got you four hours of a movie matinee, serials, cartoons, and an on-screen contest. If your ticket number came in, you'd win a candy bar. Fred Schenck swears he actually won one.

Of course we sat in the balcony. When we stepped up to the ticket window, that's where they automatically put us. I don't have any recollection of white and colored water fountains in Trenton, but I do know that I was never permitted a seat in the orchestra of the Strand Theater. Now and then we would ask for a downstairs seat, but these requests were never granted. (Maybe because that is where I sat during my formative moviegoing years, I have always felt that a seat in the mezzanine is superior to one in the orchestra. One, it is cheaper, and two, it has a better view.)

None of us was allowed to smoke, but that didn't stop us from buying cigarettes. Usually we would buy them loose for a penny apiece, but one day we gathered enough money to purchase an entire pack—we must have made off with a great haul of soda bottles. It was Joe's responsibility to take the pack home, and he got caught. In our neighborhood it wasn't hard to figure out who the other culprits were. There was no inquisition, no call to ask any of us, "Did you do this?" The assumption was that we were all co-conspirators, and that assumption was almost always correct. As we shared our successes, we shared our failures: whatever punishment was meted out to one of us the other two got as well, as a matter of course. And they did not spare the rod; this punishment was corporal.

We spent a lot of time at the colored YMCA. The white Y was downtown on Clinton Avenue, where we would occasionally get invited to shoot pool, but most of our time was spent at the colored Y, a townhouse at 105 Spring Street run by Junky Joe's father. Mr. Jensen had an assistant, Calvin Brown, who was a nice fellow with an excellent singing voice, and he was there to help make sure we kids didn't get unruly.

The colored Y was free. There would be fifteen or twenty boys and girls there almost every day—before dinner, after dinner, it was like a second home. We would play Ping-Pong, and if you backed up too far trying to hit a shot, you would bang your paddle against the wall and knock out some plaster. Years later, my father bought that house, and I found myself patching some of the holes I had helped create.

There was a gym in Les Hayling's basement built by an Indian man who worked for Les's father. He had taken a card table, turned it upside down, fastened it to the ceiling, and hung a punching bag from it. He had erected a platform to serve as a ring. We went down there and fought like cats and dogs. I would fight in the schoolyard; if you pushed me, I would push you back. My friend Alphonse Wheeler—"Fonz"—was not much bigger than I, but he was a tough cat who liked me because I refused to get pushed around; he kind of became my protector. He, too, later joined the Marine Corps. Still, since I was smaller than most of the other boys, I knew enough not to put on gloves and step into a ring.

The Y housed a number of colorful characters. We had a fellow named Ike Williams who ended up being lightweight champion of the world from 1945 to 1951. A fighter like Sugar Ray Robinson—he threw a thousand punches and you couldn't touch him. And we had at least one guy who could beat Ike! Jake Richardson, whose brother Percy became a cut man for Larry Holmes and Michael Spinks, was tougher than anyone. Jake wasn't tall—around five-foot-eight or -nine—but he was very strong, limber, and athletic. He could stand on the first step of my stoop, keep his legs straight, and put his palms on the pavement. He could throw a snowball halfway down the block and hit you dead in the head. He would throw a bolo punch and send people into the middle of next week. Les Hayling swears he saw Jake hit a guy with an uppercut and flip him 360 degrees onto his stomach. When Jake fought on the second floor of the Y, we had to station two boys in front of the window to keep him from knocking his opponents into the street.

Jake went into the service, and a sergeant who did not know with whom he was messing started picking at him. Jake hit the sergeant, knocking him out cold. The officer, who only a moment before had thought himself the toughest guy in the Army, could have put Jake in the brig. Instead, he put him in the ring. Jake said, "I'm not a boxer, I'm a fighter." They put him in anyway. Jake knocked out everyone he faced . . . in the first round! He wasn't one to throw a lot of punches and score points; he would just stand flat-footed, and when the time came he would hit you in the jaw and you were finished. He ended up an all-Army champ.

Junky Joe grew to be about five-foot-ten. He was a light-skinned handsome boy with a sharp nose who put his energy to good use. In high school he played the drums and organized a band, Junky Joe Jensen and his Jim Jam Jiving Jamboree, which, when World War II started, evolved into Junky Joe and the Jiving Jodys. ("Jody" was what soldiers called civilians—guys who stayed home and messed with people's wives and girlfriends.) You may have heard soldiers singing while marching in cadence; these are the lyrics for one of those songs:

> *Your baby was home when you left,*
> *You're right!*
> *Jody was home when you left,*
> *You're right!*
>
> *Ain't no use in going back,*
> *Jody's got your Cadillac.*
>
> *Ain't no use in calling home,*
> *Jody's got your gal and gone.*
>
> *Ain't no use in feeling blue,*
> *Jody's got your sister too.*

Les Hayling's father had gone to art school, so he painted a fancy JJJ on the bandstands for the professional touch. The very distinguished Aloysius Leon Higginbotham Jr., about six feet, four inches tall and possessed of a sonorous voice, played saxophone. I couldn't play anything, but I used to carry the instruments so I would get into the dances for free. We were underage, and our Jody status was tenuous, but we played it up anyway.

One summer during high school, Les Hayling, who was working at the Trenton Country Club as a waiter, got me a job there as a busboy. We weren't country club kind of guys, but we were happy to have jobs. When we got there, we learned how that world worked.

The headwaiter was a very short, very strict black man named Mr.

Nevius, who walked with his chin slightly raised, countenanced no non-sense from his people, and completely controlled the dining room. If members wanted a table of some stature, it behooved them to put some cash in his hand. The going rate was a dollar.

One of the regulars was Mr. Hindecamp, an insurance banker who often dined at the club with his wife. At one meal the man crossed Mr. Nevius's palm with two quarters. The headwaiter lowered his eyes and peered into his hand. "Mr. Hindecamp . . . can't very well fold this, can I?"

Mr. Hindecamp was not swayed. "Well, Nevius," he said, "takes little ones to make big ones," and went on and sat down.

Some members were certainly less appealing than others. One man, a doctor who wore black-and-white golf shoes every day and never seemed to go to work, carried himself with an excess of importance. He was approximately thirty-five years old, entirely imperious, and often in the company of an older lady who must have been seventy if she was a day. The woman had double chins and bags under her eyes, and to a teenager she was a prime example of what not to become when one aged. One afternoon, sitting in the second-floor grill room, she called me over.

"Young man," she intoned, "go down and tell the doctor I want him."

I found the doctor in the lounge. Others on the staff were waiting tables, serving drinks, folding napkins, going about their business. "Sir," I told him, "your mother wants you."

The guys just about fell down laughing. The man looked at me with cold steel in his eyes. Hell, I didn't know she was his wife!

From that moment forward, that man and I simply did not get along. He treated me with the disdain of the wealthy, and I just didn't care. One rainy day I was sitting around a table between meals, playing cards with some of the guys in charge of the locker room, when he came walking by. "What are you doing, young man?" He and his wife shared a wither-ing tone. I looked up from my cards.

"I'm playing poker."

The doctor shook his head and continued his promenade.

Country club employees lost their jobs all the time for all sorts of reasons. There was a long driveway that wound from the street to the clubhouse, and when someone got fired the phrase was "Hit the lane." One afternoon the club's manager, Mr. Donahue, stood in the bay window of the dining room with his hands behind his back, just looking. He had the air of a bird holding its place in the air stream, waiting for a fish to approach the surface and become a meal. Below him, a coworker named Nate was playing Ping-Pong with a little white girl at a table that had been set up near the pool. Mr. Donahue did not approve of such employee-member trans-racial fraternization. He told Leon Shepard, another member of the waitstaff, "Leon, go out there and tell Nate that as long as he's got the Ping-Pong paddle in his hand, he's got a job. But when he puts it down, tell him to hit the damn lane!"

I worked wherever I was instructed, but the bulk of my job was to bus tables during meal service. Busboys were responsible for setting the tables beforehand and removing dirty dishes, glasses, linen, and silverware afterward. Scut work. Still, a job was a job, and I performed adequately. We routinely loaded an aluminum tray with what must have been forty to fifty pounds of china and cutlery, hoisted it on one shoulder, and swept through the swinging doors into the busy confines of the kitchen, where through the din of orders and curses we would set the tray down and let the dishwashers have at the pile.

For some reason the geniuses who designed the Trenton Country Club's kitchen saw fit to place a small set of steps just inside these doors. As a result, bringing in a load successfully was a feat of considerable navigational difficulty. But we were young, strong, and coordinated, and after a while each of us developed his own personal rhythm and the operation became second nature.

The dining room was staffed by men only, except when we had a big function; then they would put on some women to help out. One of the classic waiter's rules is that you stack your own tray—it's just the way things are done—and at a midsummer banquet, when one of the temporary busgirls was about to lift this big tray, I said, "I'll take that for you." I had things well in hand as I shouldered through the entryway.

"Les," I called to my friend, "we're going to the tennis dance party up in north Jersey tonight, right? What time are we leaving for Shady Rest?" And as I was talking the plates began to fall. Maybe the tray wasn't stacked properly, maybe her sense of balance wasn't in line with mine. First one slid off the stack. It took an age. Then another. Of course, only a moment passed, but it seemed like two or three minutes before the last dish shattered on the concrete floor. And of course, at that very moment the doctor was passing through. He looked at me, looked at the wreckage at my feet, and said, "He's fresh and surly and everything unbecoming a busboy. Get him out of here!" It wasn't long before I hit the lane.

I got another job immediately, trucking freight at the Pennsylvania Railroad station. We worked in crews of five or six, and our job was to use heavy wooden carts to transport whatever was being shipped from the loading dock, down the platforms, through freight car after freight car connected by wooden walkways, to the car in which it would travel. You got paid extra for tonnage. If you were unloading lightbulbs, you were out of luck—you weren't going to make a lot of money. If you had the opportunity to cart stoves or appliances, you stood to make a good day's pay. I weighed about 125 pounds and stood in front of the wooden cart laden with freight several times heavier than I was, and every once in a while I'd miscalculate the leverage and it would lift me up in the air, right off my feet. If I had it balanced and I was moving, I was moving fast. Sometimes the weight would chase me. As was the custom, I'd yell out, "Makin' tonnage!" and everyone would clear out in front because I had a runaway train behind me.

Scrappy Manny ran a bar in Trenton and was one of the best pool shooters in the world. He didn't get a lot of action outside the local community because he was black, but when the Haylings bought a pool table, he came down to their basement and showed Les how to make trick shots. More to the point, Scrappy Manny was a gambler with connections in the world of horse racing. Scrappy sent his nephew, Killer Manny, to Trenton to watch over his action and run the numbers racket. As time passed Killer Manny tried to go legit. He married a schoolteacher, donated to the church, and got involved in politics. As part of his civic beneficence, he fixed it so some of us could take the civil service test and get work at the post office sorting mail.

At the post office, I worked one summer under a little man who enjoyed using his power to the fullest, an assistant supervisor who took pleasure in intimidating his workers by throwing them out and docking their pay. Losing a day's pay was a significant deprivation; no one who worked at the post office could afford it. He would tell that day's transgressor, "Get your card and stand by the clock," which meant he or she should take his time card from its assigned slot and cool his heels before the assistant supervisor arrived for the ritual humiliation of punching him out. This became my catchphrase for the summer. Whenever anyone anywhere did anything of which I disapproved—at the pile of mail next to me, in the street, at the poker table—I would tell him, "Get your card and stand by the clock!"

One morning I arrived after the 9:00 punch-in.

"You're late," he told me.

I didn't like this man at all. "That's obvious," I said.

"Where were you?"

"Clearly, I was elsewhere."

"Get your card and stand by the clock!" I was out a day's pay, but talking back was worth it. There are some abuses one ought not stand for.

I was seventeen years old in the summer of 1944, heading into my senior year of high school. World War II was in full force. My friends and I would go to the Strand and watch the newsreels of soldiers hitting the beach. No one thought of *not* going to war. Everybody went. Only a physical disability or a job in an essential occupation like the police or fire department could keep you from defending your country overseas. I knew I was going to fight, and I knew a lot of people were dying. People I personally knew were dead—young men from across the street and around the corner. I figured the way to stay alive, or at least to increase my chances of survival, was to be well trained. There were the Army Rangers, who were an elite fighting corps, and the Navy Seals, who were equally tough and well prepared. I had never heard of either of them. But I knew about the Marines.

I liked the way the Marines looked. My friend Everett Mills's brother Julius looked good in his dress blues with the red stripe they called the "bucket of blood" running down the side of the pants leg. But more than that, even though I was only seventeen years old and around 125 pounds, like a lot of young people I was determined, I was bad, and I was ready, willing, and able to fight for my country.

These were Jim Crow days, and as I grew older I found that people in the United States were still being murdered because of their color. I heard things like, "You Negroes shouldn't be so pushy, they only lynched five last year." By this we were supposed to understand that things weren't so bad, by God, they were getting better. I was not intimidated by white folks, and I wasn't angry at white folks. But the armed forces were segregated. If a black man was drafted and went to the induction center and asked to be placed in the Army, they would put him in the Navy. If he wanted the Navy, he'd get the Army. In the experience of the young men in my Trenton neighborhood, nobody got what he asked for. Clearly, the way to be inducted into the branch of service you preferred was to enlist. The object then became to enlist in the armed forces before you turned eighteen, when you were required to register for the draft and it was too late. So began my sojourn to the Marine Corps recruitment offices.

The Marine Corps was an elite unit, "a Few Good Men," and prior to 1942, there were no black men *at all* in the Marines. It took an executive order from President Franklin D. Roosevelt to begin the integration of that armed service, which was done grudgingly at best.

First, I found there was no recruitment station in Trenton, so I went to Newark and presented myself. I was turned away cold. "We have our quota of Negro Marines," the officer-in-charge informed me. A few days later I pushed on, traveling to the recruitment center in Jersey City. "We have our quota of Negro Marines." Camden, the same. I took the bus to New York City and tried to enlist at the recruitment station in Manhattan. They asked me where I lived. I told them Trenton. They turned me away. "You have to go to the state in which you reside." But I had done that, I said, to no avail. That wasn't their problem. I took the train to Philadelphia, only to be told the same thing. I came home, then returned to Philadelphia. "I want to be a Marine. That's all there is to it. I just want to be a Marine." I told the story of my quest and hounded the recruitment officer so intensely that he allowed me to take the armed forces physical and fill out the necessary forms. I was five-foot-seven, 130 pounds. They said I had high blood pressure and turned me away.

I knew I didn't have high blood pressure; this was just another way of discouraging black men from joining the Marines. I found a doctor's office nearby and had my pressure taken. Normal. I went home to Trenton and visited my family doctor, Dr. Granger, who had been an Army surgeon. Normal. I went back to Philadelphia, and they took the pressure in my left arm. Too high. Right arm. Too high. Lying down, standing up—according to them, always too high. (Later I concluded that I had what's known as "white coat syndrome," in which one gets nervous in front of doctors because one wants to pass the test so badly. At the time I didn't know what was going on.) But by now I was a regular . . . and an annoyance. The officer prepared a letter for my draft board and gave me a copy. It said, in substance, "This man passes the physical and selects the Marine Corps. Put him in the Marine Corps." I was in.

I don't remember much about my senior year of high school. All I wanted to do that year was finish and enlist. Everybody was going to war, it was the natural order of things, and I was going to be a Marine! On July 10, 1945, I turned eighteen. I signed up for the draft that day and requested immediate induction. About two weeks later I was on my way. My parents did not gnash their teeth that their son was going to war; I think they were impressed with my persistence. Of my friends from home, Junky Joe was never in the service and Schenck and Everett Mills served in the Navy.

The black Marines were trained at Montford Point, Camp Lejeune, North Carolina; the white troops trained separately at Parris Island, South Carolina. We left as a group via train out of Jersey City, about twenty-five white kids and two African Americans. Since the other black inductee was a year older than I, they gave him both our orders to present.

I was so proud. I bought a stack of postcards and began writing everyone I knew, telling them where I was, where I was going, what I was going to do. We were going by train to Washington, DC, and from there making several stops through Virginia and into North Carolina, where we would get on a bus to the base. I wrote the itinerary so many times that I memorized it.

Good thing too, because the clown I was traveling with missed the connection in Washington, DC, never got on the train, and all of a sudden I was on my own—without my orders. The conductor came through to take our tickets, and I pointed to the white Marines and said, "I'm with them! I'm with them!" That worked until I had to get off in North Carolina and take the bus. Fortunately, I had some money in my pocket and knew my destination. I stepped up to the ticket window.

"Around back, boy."

This was my first real experience with Jim Crow in the Deep South. It felt different from what little I had encountered in New Jersey. It felt significantly more threatening. There was an unyielding physicality to it. I had no more chance of getting a ticket from this person than I did of moving the building. I went around back.

Finally, I arrived at the little town of Jacksonville, North Carolina, took another transport to the base, and thought I would enter Camp Lejeune with a story to tell. I got off the bus, and a great big black sergeant said, "Where are your orders, boy?!" I started to launch into an explanation of how the Marine I was traveling with had my orders but missed the train and I had to—

The sergeant hit me. Knocked me down. I bounced up, and that was my introduction to the United States Marine Corps.

We were taught to obey the commands of whatever officer was directly in charge. If a sergeant or corporal was drilling us and a lieutenant or even a general were to come by and say, "Platoon halt!" we would keep on marching. The idea was to teach us discipline, and we learned it well. They ran us through the "manual of arms," porting foot-lockers instead of weapons. "Right shoulder . . . locker box!" If you were cited for an infraction and were disciplined, the drill sergeant would hang wet clothes on a pole and tell you, "Now run around them until they dry." Guys would run until they dropped. I saw grown men cry, but I was young and fit and I could run all day. I wanted so much to be a Marine, I wasn't going to quit no matter what.

Obedience to command was completely ingrained in us. In fact, not in my time but later, two Marines in battle gear were marched into water and didn't make it out. They drowned following orders. I still take my service in the Marines very seriously.

Our drill instructors, the DIs, taught us the basics. All of them were black. Our gunnery sergeants taught us to use bayonets and the M1 rifle. All of them were white. The gunnies would show up and say, "All right, niggers, fall in!" And we would fall in. They treated us that way right up until we were issued live ammunition; then their attitude became differ-ent. Vastly different.

Now, that's the way I remember it. However, in real life it doesn't sound likely that battle-tested Marine gunnery sergeants would change their tune for anything, least of all a platoon of black recruits, which brings me to this story my father used to love to tell:

There was a man who said he had a horse. He did not have a horse, but he said he had a horse, and he would tell stories of his horse and all the adventures he and his horse had together. These adventures were thrilling, and everyone admired him for his horse and his adventures, this man who had no horse. This man who had no horse said he had a horse so often that one day he went out . . . and bought himself a saddle!

Maybe the gunnery sergeants did not change their tune, but in our minds something big had changed, and maybe that's what they were aim-ing for.

There were no black commissioned officers in our experience, that's for sure. We used to joke that the only way one of us would become an officer would be to get commissioned one day, hold the march and parade the next, and get discharged the third. Segregated as we were, we heard stories from black Marines under fire who told us how warmly they were greeted by white Marines who had been pinned down and were running low on ammo when our men hit the beach bringing fresh supplies. We liked those stories.

We recruits didn't get much liberty, but every once in a while we would get sixty-two hours off base—the other branches of service got seventy-two hours, I have no idea why ours was ten hours shorter—and I would either try to get home or go to Kingston or Wilmington, North Carolina, just to get out of there.

It was no picnic being black in the armed forces during World War II. The Tuskegee Airmen served with distinction and were denied credit and respect for more than fifty years. These men were heroes. They begged to be taught how to fly but were initially told, "No, you black folks are not smart enough." When they won the battle to be trained, they were denied combat duty because they were thought to be cowards who would turn in the face of the enemy. And when they were allowed to fly escort for bombers, they never lost a single one. In fact, the white bomber pilots requested their cover. When their commander, Benjamin O. Davis, attended West Point, he had been shunned for four years, and no one spoke to him outside of the line of duty. This was the world in which we were serving.

I knew several Tuskegee Airmen personally: besides Les Hayling, there was Dr. Roscoe Brown, a fighter pilot who was the first in his group to shoot down a jet while flying a propeller plane; Percy Sutton, who was a stunt pilot before enlisting and became a very influential presence later in my life; and Lee Archer, who rose to the rank of lieutenant colonel and was an ace, which is to say he had five confirmed kills.

On one of their liberties, as several black airmen were heading north, the train stopped to pick up a group of Italian and German prisoners of war who were being transported from one prison to another. They had not been riding in the best of seats to begin with—this was the Deep South, after all—but the conductors, guided by the military officers in charge, told the airmen that they had to relinquish even those seats to the prisoners. These men were prepared to give up their lives to protect our country, and here they were being told to give up their seats for our enemies. Captured on the battlefield, these POWs were treated better than black soldiers. They had been taught to respect the command of our officers, and they did so, moving forward to seats behind the engine filled with smoke and soot. I found this to be un-American in the extreme, and I've never forgotten it.

I had been in the Marines for less than a year when a drill instructor gathered our platoon, number 547—some things you remember!—in the barracks and said, "Get on your knees. Thank God the war is over!" We couldn't believe it. "Now get up!" he said. "Nothing's changed."

And nothing had changed. We drilled, we went about the business of being Marines, but we never saw combat. I was honorably discharged on August 21, 1946.

In August 2012, the nation's highest civilian honor, the Congressional Gold Medal, awarded to persons "who have performed an achievement that has an impact on American history and culture that is likely to be recognized as a major achievement in the recipient's field long after the achievement," was awarded to all African American Marines who served in the Corps between 1942 and 1949 and were trained at Montford Point. Twenty thousand black men had come through there. We were Montford Point Marines and said the name with pride, deserving the same place in history as the Tuskegee Airmen and the post–Civil War Buffalo Soldiers. Those of us still surviving were presented with replicas of the Gold Medal in a ceremony held at the Capitol Building and the following day at the Marine Corps barracks in Washington, DC. I was proudly among them. I had been a teenager when I enlisted, and although I was eighty-five years old when I accepted the medal, I was almost the youngest Montford Point Marine in attendance. They called me "kid."

2

The Education of a Ditch Digger

I had never thought of going to college, but the GI Bill made education affordable, and clearly an educated man would advance more quickly than one without a diploma in the postwar world. However, because I was discharged from the Marines in August and most schools started in September, I thought, *Too late, can't get in.* Then my stepmother, Lottie Lee, changed my life. She was a college classmate of the fellow in charge of veterans' affairs at Howard University, Dr. Carroll Miller, and she insisted that I apply to Howard immediately. "I can get you in," she said, and I believed her. My grades were good enough to gain entrance into that esteemed institution, and Lottie Lee got it done in three weeks, which I thought was a miracle.

I was not the only young person she helped. In fact, there was strong support from many men and women in my Trenton neighborhood who, though not necessarily our teachers, were friends of the family—the extended family—and helped counsel us toward higher education. At one point in time there were nearly forty students at Howard from Trenton. Successful students were a source of great community pride.

This surely was different from the attitude of our high school counselors, who most often directed African American students toward service jobs. The most enlightened of them encouraged some few of us to be nurses or teachers, but college and then medical or law school was outside their idea of reasonable career paths for black youth. Every generation preceding mine—and I am not just talking about the high school counselors in Trenton—was directed away from higher education. The result was that many people who might have thrived intellectually and economically never had the opportunity to succeed. Nor did their children, or their children's children, have that opportunity; the effect was exponential. Most of my friends went to college, but there were some left behind, and they did not fare as well as their intelligence might have allowed. Hilmar Ludwig Jensen Jr. (Junky Joe) had entered Howard University a year before I arrived. Les and Bill Hayling mustered out of the service earlier than I and were there already as well. Fred Schenck, who was younger, arrived a year later.

The GI Bill took care of tuition and books and provided a $75 monthly stipend for room and board and other expenses. I planned to live on campus, referred to as "the Hill," in Cook Hall, where the rent was $17.50 a month. However, the administration, in its infinite wisdom, decided that because I was a veteran I was too old to live with freshmen and therefore had to reside in one of three vet dorms—Wake, Guam, or Midway—out in northeast Washington, DC, off Benning Road. The fact that I was nineteen didn't seem to factor into their thinking. My rent in Wake Hall was $30.50, and a trolley pass, which I now needed to reach the Howard campus, cost $4.50, so my monthly total was $35—or precisely twice the amount I thought I was going to be paying. This and other factors caused me to have month left at the end of my money.

Money was an issue throughout college. I had a roommate junior year whose father was an undertaker in Americus, Georgia. I figured he was very wealthy, for he wore a suede sport jacket. Most of us were dirt poor. A few of us were coming home one day when we saw my roommate in a little convenience store playing pinball. Now, you don't win anything playing pinball. If you do real well, they let you play an extra game or two, but it's a money-taking, not a money-making, venture. So there he was playing pinball. And eating cashew nuts! We raised hell. We were eating pancake batter and water, poor as hell, and he's eating cashew nuts!

I developed a taste for representative democracy while at Howard. Because we were more mature, or had faced enemy fire, or had already lived outside our parents' homes, the veterans' concerns differed slightly from those of the rest of the student body. There seemed to be a constant rift between the veterans and the regular matriculants, and the student council was the forum in which it was adjudicated. I appeared before them several times with three or four sheets of paper rolled into a baton that I waved extravagantly. "I have in my hand," I'd proclaim, "the proxies of seventy-five veterans!" and then would proceed to browbeat the council until I made my point or got my way. Now, the pages were blank—I had no proxies whatsoever. What I did have was the informed sense of the men in my dormitory; I knew what people had been discussing, I knew what we wanted, and I was determined to do right by them. I was relatively successful.

My time at Howard wasn't devoted entirely to rhetoric and student government. When I was lucky enough to study freshman English under Alice Jackson Houston, my world changed. Alice Jackson Houston was a Virginia woman who was intensely serious about the English language, its grammar and usage. She tolerated no deviance from the proper form. Subjects were to fit their predicates, tenses were to be consistent and inviolable. She was mathematical in her precision and eloquent in her diction, her speech was impeccable, and I responded to her every word as if it were the gospel. I had been a reasonably good conversationalist until then. I wasn't given to excessive use of street slang or wild linguistic invention, and I wasn't so formal that anyone made fun of the way I spoke, but under Ms. Houston's tutelage I became a true traditionalist.

Her bible was *The Macmillan Handbook of English*, a highly detailed primer. Chapter 2 in particular, "The Sentence," with its components

"Grammatical Patterns" and "Rhetorical Patterns," held my commandments.

> One might say that correct grammar is like a pair of trousers: when a man has them on, no one notices him, but when he does not, he will be painfully conspicuous and embarrassed among people whose opinion he values.

From that time on I have been supremely aware of what is correct and what is incorrect English. One would get drummed out of Alice Jackson Houston's class if one said, "between you and I"; the preposition "between" takes the objective case personal pronoun "me," not "I." When I hear this mistake coming from newscasters or public figures or anyone who can influence popular usage—when I hear it from friends!—I cringe. When I hear someone say, "Everyone is entitled to their opinion," I know—because Alice Jackson Houston taught me—that the correct usage is "his opinion" (or more recently "his or her opinion"), and I am very apt to correct the error. I understand that language is a fluid thing, changing with the times and generations. When one knocks on a door and is asked, "Who's there?" the answer now is "It's me." You will find only one in five thousand who will say, "It is I." However, since the first day I set foot in Alice Jackson Houston's class, I have also understood that this fluidity should not be confused with a lack of standards. There are rules!

More than fifty years later I spoke to Alice Jackson Houston's son on the phone. He was a judge in the Washington, DC, area, and he seemed hesitant, as if asking, "Why are you calling me?" She had died in 2001, and I wanted to pay my respects. I said, "I just want you to know what your mother did for me."

Whether or not it was stated directly, Howard students all knew that to succeed in a white world one would be required to present and comport oneself in accordance with white community standards. African American culture, then and now, has its own unique and expressive outlook and lexicon that stand outside the white mainstream. My generation had integrationist, not separatist, aspirations. Speaking unimpeachable English, I felt, offered not only the rewards of intellectual propriety but the added benefit of easier entrance into the halls of wealth, power, and respect. These were the goals of a college education, and I pursued them.

Which is not to say I was a grind. For the first year and a half on campus my motto was "Don't let your education interfere with your recreation!" My sophomore year I roomed with Fred Schenck and James Roderick Purdy at 2222 First Street. We called ourselves "the Three Aces at the Four Deuces," and we were a partying crew. If it was wet, we drank it. Freddy in particular liked to put it away. We had the music going, there was dancing. You hadn't been to Howard if you hadn't partied at 2222 First Street.

Fred was a lot of fun, and he could cook. We were still living on the $75 a month provided us by the GI Bill, and Fred managed it brilliantly. Aside from bacon and eggs and the occasional steak, he usually found some corner of the food budget for enough sugar and flour to make a coconut layer cake. (His summer working at a bakery was paying off.) I was an appreciative eater and taught Fred the glories of the cake sandwich—two pieces of cake with another piece of cake in the middle!

The next year we lived at 52 Seaton Place with Les and Bill Hayling, who were in professional school. By that time I had discovered mathematics. The precision and structure of the discipline appealed to me, and I was good at it. I spent a lot of time on the telephone, solving problems with other math students. Fred says that if there was any social value to having a telephone in our room, it was lost by my study habits. When I discovered that one had to have a concentration in some area in order to graduate, I found I had more math credits than any others, so I continued on that path. I did not have a strong idea of what career I might choose. I did not seem to have the vision or foresight required to be an engineer or architect; I just wasn't that good. I liked order and the need and ability to find creative but concrete solutions to specific problems, so I became a math major. Dr. David Blackwell, the head of the Howard math department, was an inspiration. He had received his PhD from the University of Illinois at age twenty-two and was a brilliant and wonderful man.

I always had a job in the summertime, not because I was very eager to work but because I needed the money. One summer I was so late applying that the only job I could find was washing dishes in a place called Mammy's that served hotcakes and such on the boardwalk. I lasted one day. I said, "Let me get the hell out of here!"

I spent another summer digging ditches. Les Hayling took a picture of me and a fellow named Jesse Pone down in a ditch. He said, "I'm gonna take this back to Howard and show 'em what you all were doing!" I also worked for the New Jersey Department of Agriculture out around Heightstown, doing surveys and looking into issues involving the many African American farmers who had emigrated to our state from the South. Bill Hayling, who was in medical school by then, spent the summer working on their health care.

Rural southern Jersey encompassed a lot of farmland and produced large crops of apples, apricots, beets, blueberries, peas, and peppers, among others. Its residents were also remarkably conservative and hidebound. As elsewhere, workers were often exploited and preyed upon. For example, a salesman would sell a farmer a wristwatch for $10 down and $1 a week. But this was outright price gouging: the watch would only be worth $5, and the payments would last forever. If he never saw another nickel, that salesman had made a killing. The farmers were unsophisticated and needed protection from such swindlers. These farmers led a tough life.

One thinks of New Jersey as a northern state, but we used to say that Jersey was the first cousin of Georgia. The Ku Klux Klan was active as far north as Red Bank. There were cross burnings in Heightstown and Hamilton Township. They had separate schools for colored folks in Salem County until around 1958, even after *Brown v. Board of Education,* and neither blacks nor Jews were allowed to stay in some Salem hotels even into the 1960s. When I was younger, I recall that in Cranberry a migrant farmer and his wife were stripped naked and painted white.

That same summer I spent digging ditches, Fred and I went to the

Lincoln Theater in Trenton to see a movie. It was a hot night, and we were thirsty when we got out. We came to a drinking establishment on Hanover Street called Jack's Rathskeller, but when we got about two steps inside the proprietor stepped from behind the bar and said, "I'm not serving you. You've had enough. You've had too much. You can't drink here!" We had no intention of hanging out and listening to the jukebox, and we weren't going to ask any of the women to dance; all we wanted was a glass of beer. Having been a Marine, I took umbrage, but the man completely refused us. I was faced with many choices. I could cause a scene, I could slink away, or I could try not to let this happen again.

Out we went. I was furious, but what recourse did we have?

We filed a complaint with the New Jersey Civil Rights Bureau, a small but fervent independent organization that tracked and protested just such incidents. The Bureau had no teeth to speak of, but after several months it negotiated a mediated settlement: we could go back to Jack's Rathskeller and be served. I suppose we should have been elated: we had, against long odds, integrated a de facto segregated drinking establishment. But this was New Jersey—it was supposed to be integrated in the first place! And we certainly had no interest in going back there; bartenders were known to spit in glasses, if not worse.

I was by no means the only one among us who made a point of being treated fairly. Les Hayling and our friend Sam Dorsey emerged from a community dance one evening around midnight and went looking for something to eat. Les was wearing a shirt and tie, as was his fashion, and Sam, who was in the Air Corps, had on his leather bomber jacket. They found the Lenox Restaurant on Perry Street across from the Catholic church, went in, and ordered a ham-and-cheese sandwich. The man behind the counter refused to serve them. Les said, "Man, we're going to have to sue him!" He brought the case to a lawyer of the National Association for the Advancement of Colored People.

In the hall outside of the courtroom, the owner of the Lenox Restaurant tried to settle. He still wasn't going to let Les or any of us eat in his establishment, but he offered $500 to drop the case. Les said, "Oh no, I'm not making any money out of this. The NAACP is suing you, and they'll get the money."

A Judge Volpe presided. "How many stools were at the counter?" he asked Les.

"I don't know, Your Honor."

"How far were you from the tables or booths?"

"I don't know, Your Honor."

"How many booths were there?"

Les had had enough. "I don't usually take a tape measure with me when I go to get a ham-and-cheese sandwich at twelve o'clock at night!"

Judge Volpe responded, "*I hold you in contempt of court!*"

Les changed his attitude, but only slightly. He wasn't jailed for contempt, and he did win his case. The money for damages went straight to the NAACP.

.   .   .

I saw a young lady with great legs reading a book while strolling down Howard's Senior Walk and took immediate notice.

"Hey, freshman!"

She looked up, surprised to be interrupted.

"Don't you know you young folks aren't supposed to be here?" By tradition, Senior Walk was reserved for seniors. Permission to set foot on this hallowed ground had to be earned; if one had matriculated to senior year, one had proved some semblance of worth and promise. And here this pretty young woman was treading blithely. This was as good a reason as any to strike up a conversation.

When she found that I was reading a calculus text, she was impressed. It turned out that she had only recently come to campus. I kicked her off the Walk and asked her out on her first Howard date. It didn't take long for her to tell some of her New York friends about me. They had heard about the Three Aces at the Four Deuces and said, "Him?!" Her name was Joyce Burrows. We began dating and simply never stopped.

I was a member of Alpha Phi Alpha, the oldest black fraternity in the United States, among whose distinguished members were Dr. Martin Luther King Jr., Jesse Owens, and Justice Thurgood Marshall. Its guiding principles were "manly deeds, scholarship, and love for all mankind." As the APA dean of probates—the "big brother" responsible for recruiting new fraternity brothers—I brought in Andrew Young, who went on to become mayor of Atlanta and US ambassador to the United Nations. We used to call him "Little Andy" Young.

Howard was also home to several sororities, including Delta Sigma Theta, of which Joyce Burrows was a member, and Alpha Kappa Alpha, of which my sister Joyce was a member. Whereas DST was affiliated with the fraternity Omega Psi Phi (known as the Q's), AKA was affiliated with Alpha Phi Alpha. I was an Alpha. Joyce was the Q Queen. This meant trouble.

There was a serious rivalry between the Alphas and the Q's, and now here you had this rival Alpha taking out the Q Queen. This did not sit well with a lot of the brother- and sisterhood. Sometimes Joyce would go to a Q party, and because I was not invited, I had to wait for her to be brought home before she'd go out with me. She felt it was her duty to preside over the sorority's official functions. I used to raise hell about it, but to no avail.

I graduated cum laude from Howard University in 1950 and did sufficiently well in my mathematics studies that I won a fellowship to continue at Rutgers University graduate school. I didn't quite know what I would do with a degree in mathematics; although I continued to feel that I did not have the vision or foresight to become an engineer or an architect, I was good at the pure math and decided to pursue it.

That summer I lived in Trenton. I saw Willie Mays play for the Trenton Giants his first year in the minor leagues—not the Negro Leagues, but regular white folks' baseball, a Class B team—the year before the Giants called him up to play at the Polo Grounds. The story about "Say Hey Willie" was not his hitting but his arm: they'd say he could back up to the wall in center field and throw a strike across the plate.

I worked in a rock wall factory making insulation. The idea was to save enough money over the summer to go the whole school year without working and be able to concentrate on my studies. I manned one machine that shot granular material into burlap bags, and then another that I stepped on to stitch the bags shut. I didn't ask what this material was or what effect it might have on me; I didn't have that luxury because I needed the paycheck. The work was stultifying and grueling, and two or three times a week I put in a double shift—not overtime but sixteen hours straight. My second-shift boss didn't care that I might be tired or bored, he just wanted me to produce, and I had to oblige.

After a summer of factory labor, I had amassed the necessary funds to quit working. One night I stayed up damn near half the night solving a math problem. I arrived at what I thought was the correct answer, took a quick nap, went to class, and asked the smartest student, who was a woman, "Did you get the answer to number two?" "Yes," she said, and told me what it was. I agreed. "That's what I got."

As an afterthought, elated as I was that I had the correct answer, I said, "How long did it take you?"

"About twenty minutes."

It had taken me several hours. I knew then I could not succeed. I told my father, "I'm dropping out of school."

"You can't do that! What are you going to do?"

"I don't know, Pop, but I know what I'm not going to do." I dropped out and got a job selling insurance.

Life was not easy in the African American community of Trenton after the war. People had jobs, but not many were prospering. At the same time, the tradition of supporting one's family was strong, and people were proud to be able to put away something to make their loved ones' lives better after they passed away. Life insurance provided this opportunity.

I sold "industrial insurance," which is to say, policies the face value of which was $1,000 or less—poor people's insurance, which fit the budgets of the people I knew and the people I was meeting going door to door.

African Americans. I worked for Progressive Life Insurance Company, home office in Red Bank. The premiums were small: ten cents a week, fifty cents a month, or two dollars a quarter. There was usually a little card hanging somewhere in the house, and with each visit the salesman would collect the money and mark the card "paid." On a term policy, people could pay a dime a week forever. Salesmen were compensated based on collections as well as net increase. How was I to succeed?

I studied the habits of the insured. One man got paid on Thursday, another on Friday. One got paid every other week and brought his check straight home to his wife; another stopped at a bar, cashed his check, and drank it. A good salesman had to know where to be the moment his customers had money in their pockets.

I started wearing a hat so I could take it off. I would knock at a single-family home and wait until the lady of the house answered. As soon as she opened the door I would remove my hat with one hand and introduce myself. "Mrs. Smith," I would say, "how are you today? My name is David Dinkins, I'm from the Progressive Life Insurance Company . . ." and launch into my presentation. It was important that she see me take off my hat. I was showing respect to people who received very little of it. People pay respect to those who give respect, and besides, whether or not it was reciprocated, I felt that was the way one ought to behave. I had always been taught to be polite, and I found it to be good business.

I was also aware that the white agents from the Metropolitan Life Insurance Company, my competition, treated these same women quite differently. They would breeze in to collect their premiums, step through the door, and say, "Hi, Suzie, how're you doing?" With their big smiles and air of assumed familiarity, these men were entirely unaware of the resentment they were creating. This was the plantation mentality brought north, and in their smug certainty, the agents didn't even know it. *This woman is your client,* I'd think. *She is paying your salary, and she is entitled to better than being called by her first name. "Suzie" is a girl, "Mrs. Smith" is a woman; there is a profound difference.* I found their behavior disrespectful, and of course it was racial. I resented it, and my presentation was in clear contrast. Apparently my approach was appreciated. Within a year I was leading Progressive in both collections and new business.

As I began to move in new financial circles I met an agent who sold ordinary life insurance—policies with a face value of more than $1,000 whose premiums were paid monthly, quarterly, sometimes annually. For a salesman, selling ordinary life insurance meant less time spent on collection rounds, higher premiums, and higher fees. This fellow took clients to lunch and sent flowers to them on their birthdays. I said to myself, *Man, this guy knows how to live. I'm in the wrong end of this business!* My success at Progressive got me a job with his general agent in Philadelphia. I lived and worked there for six months and then moved to New York.

As I established myself in the insurance business I waited for Joyce Burrows to graduate. I had received my diploma in 1950, and she was in the class of '53. Boat rides were the big thing in New York during those summers, and I was pleased to escort Joyce on one of these excursions sponsored by a Howard fraternity. What I didn't know was that the fellow she had dated before me and his cohorts were lying in wait. Apparently they had decided they would get me drunk and steal my girl. So all night long these guys came up to me with flasks and said, "Hey, Dave, want a drink?" We'd step into the head for a nip. What they didn't realize was that I had driven my daddy's new car up from Trenton and no way was I going to be drinking! Certainly not to excess. Sure enough, when the night was over, they carried the other guy off the boat, stoned, and I drove home with Joyce.

Joyce and I were partners. She had a very vague sense of direction, and I used to kid her that she'd get lost if she couldn't see the flag on top of the Howard library! We used to go to a little place with red checkered tablecloths and get a pitcher for seventy-five cents and sit and drink beer and plan our future.

Joyce has always had my number. Still does. I often tell this story:

I am mayor of New York. I'm riding in the car with my wife, and I see a fellow with a shovel, digging a ditch. I say, "Joyce, isn't that a fellow you used to date?" I say, "Nothing wrong with a fellow digging ditches. I've dug ditches." I used to work for a general contractor digging ditches. I've worked in factories, waited tables, shined shoes, washed dishes, washed cars, all kinds of jobs. So I'm not knocking them, I'm just commenting on my wife's good fortune. "That is a fellow that you used to date, isn't it?"

She says, "Yes, as a matter of fact it is."

I say, "See, if you'd have married him, you'd be the wife of a ditch digger."

She says, "No, if I'd married him, he'd be mayor."

3

Home in Harlem

After Joyce graduated from Howard that spring, we got married on August 30, 1953. While waiting for an apartment to become available in the Riverton, the Metropolitan Life Insurance Company's uptown development, she and I moved in with her mother and father in an apartment on 149th Street and Convent Avenue in Harlem.

I married well. Joyce's mother, Elaine Burrows, was terrific. At those rare times while Joyce and I were courting when we had a dispute, my future mother-in-law was, more often than not, on my side. She loved me and was convinced that I would be able to support her daughter. I tell Joyce that the reason she never learned to cook was that her mother thought she'd be having a maid. I have been very fortunate; in a way, I've had three very loving mothers!

My father-in-law, Daniel L. Burrows, was a self-made, rough-and-tumble kind of man, beginning with his middle name, L. It didn't mean a damn thing; he gave it to himself because he thought that he should have a middle initial, that it added stature. He was a man who liked these kinds of gestures. Mr. Burrows dabbled in politics and was one of the first African Americans to serve in the New York State Legislature. He had been a significant presence in the New York City Democratic Party, a prominent member of the State Assembly in the 1930s, and a successful real estate and insurance executive. The *New York Times* reports that in 1939, during an Assembly debate on a bill to "classify as dangerous weapons those typically used by warring gangsters … Assemblyman Burrows suddenly brandished a switchblade knife, snapped its catch and swished its four-inch blade through the air." End of discussion. Flashing metal in the Assembly was sufficient to scare the members into passing the bill 140 to 0.

Mr. Burrows was politically well-connected and he had interesting friends. I was in Frank's Restaurant on 125th Street joking around with some guys, and I made a comment that apparently offended Bumpy Johnson, who was also in Frank's at the time. Now, I didn't know Bumpy Johnson personally, but I knew of him: Bumpy Johnson was alleged to be the gangster who ran organized crime in Harlem, he was an enforcer for the Genovese crime family, and he was known to do whatever it was he wanted to do to whomever he wanted to do it. He was not a man to cross, and without knowing quite how, I had crossed him. I had pissed off Bumpy Johnson! Under normal circumstances, I would have been in big trouble—people died for less—but someone said, "No, no, no, no, leave him alone, he's all right, that's Danny Burrows's son-in-law."

Mr. Burrows saw a future for me in the Democratic Party and encouraged me to go back to school and get a law degree. I was more than pleased to oblige. I enrolled in Brooklyn Law School in September 1953. Money continued to be an issue. I went to school full-time during the day and at night worked over at St. Nicholas Avenue and 148th Street at St. Nicholas Wines & Liquors, which was owned by my father-in-law.

Living with my in-laws while we were on the Riverton waiting list was not a situation I encouraged, but it was an acceptable short-term solution. While we were in this circumstance, Joyce and I visited a store and picked out furniture for our future abode. Despite the fact that we did not yet have a place to put it, Joyce wanted the suite delivered and stored in the liquor store basement. "Honey," I said, "if we have them deliver it now, we'll have to pay to have it shipped again to the apartment where we're going to live." She argued and argued, but there was no logic to her position, and I would not capitulate. Finally one day she said, "But it's my first furniture. I just want to look at it!"

Ah! "Why didn't you say that?!" I asked. "Now I understand!" And that's exactly what we did.

Law school was rigorous, but I learned a lot about negotiating by selling alcohol in Harlem. If a person came into the store and requested a bottle of Canadian Club, and we didn't have any in stock, I couldn't very well just stand there like a fool and say, "I don't have Canadian Club. Is there anything else you'd like?" The sale was very apt to walk out of the store. What I learned was to step to the shelves, grab a bottle of Seagram's VO, a Canadian whiskey, in one hand and MacNaughton, another Canadian whiskey, in the other, turn, set the two bottles firmly on the counter in front of the customer, and say, "Out of Canadian Club." And wait. Let the sale make itself. Automatically, the person's mind had moved from what he or she had wanted to what I was offering and would start concentrating on those choices. Rather than being disappointed, the buyer would try to choose between two attractive alternatives. And instead of being a person who said no, I became someone with the good sense and goodwill to present two satisfactory solutions. This technique works in other endeavors as well, the law and politics among them. Options are beautiful.

When my bride and I found we were going to have a child, we knew it was going to be a boy. In those years one could not determine the gender in advance, as they do today, but we just sort of knew. Bill Hayling was a resident at Lincoln Hospital in the Bronx. Joyce loved and trusted Bill, so she delivered there. I had always loved kids—I still do—and now we had one of our own. We eliminated what could have been a nasty clash of grandfathers by naming him after me. David Jr.—Davey—was our joy.

We moved into the Riverton, located from 135th to 138th Streets, from Fifth Avenue to Madison. Its resident manager was a man named

Cliff Alexander, whose son later became secretary of the Army, the man to whom the list of promotions to general was handed. He handed the list back because there were no blacks on it. When a new list was produced, it included the name of Colin Powell.

The Riverton was Stuyvesant Town North, so to speak. The apartment was very small, and the rent was very low. I was paying the rent, but not much more.

We surely did love our boy. What a wonderful child! My bride was a very protective mother and would allow only her mother or mine to take care of our son. When Davey was an infant, we received a visit from Joyce's childhood friend Joan Carter, who had attended Howard with us. Some women think children are like dolls or toys, and Joan wanted to give him a bath. When Joyce went out, she hid the bassinette, so Joanie gave him a bath in a salad bowl!

I tried to instill a sense of responsibility and accomplishment in our son. He was Daddy's Little Fella. (He's in his fifties now, but he's still Daddy's Little Fella!) One morning when he was five or six years old (my wife swears he was three or four, and by now there's no way of knowing), I decided it was time for him to go outside and get the Sunday paper. This is a New York child's rite of passage: take the money, buy the paper, and bring home the correct change. My bride disagreed. What if he gets lost?! What if he gets hit by a car?! What if he gets stolen by a stranger?! I told her, "He knows how to stop on red and walk on green." We discussed the pros and cons, but I was resolute: this was a good life lesson, and he might as well learn it now.

From where we lived, Davey would have to cross Fifth Avenue and then Lenox Avenue to the far, westerly side. While Fifth Avenue at 135th Street was not particularly broad, Lenox Avenue was a boulevard, a six-lane transit hub with a grass median in the middle, filled with cars and trucks and all manner of speeding vehicles. I told our five-year-old, "Cross half at a time. Cross to the median, wait until the light changes, and then cross the next half. Do the same coming back. You will be fine." I sent him on his way.

Joyce set about taking a bath. When I walked in, I found her sitting up in the bathtub, crying. Tears were pouring down her cheeks. She raised so much hell that I got dressed and ran out after him. Davey didn't know I was following, he was just running along, skipping and whistling, having a grand old time, and I was a half-block behind, making sure no harm came to him. Which, of course, it did not. Davey returned successfully, as I had great faith that he would.

From the beginning our son was smart and inquisitive. Davey grew up to be an active, athletic boy, always passionate about sports.

.   .   .

I passed the bar the first time I took the exam, in the fall of 1956, because I had to—I didn't have the luxury of playing around, for I needed a job. To become a lawyer in New York in 1956 you were required to submit papers to the Committee on Character and Fitness of the Appellate Division of the First Department for Manhattan and the Bronx. These papers had to contain a letter or affidavit from every employer you had ever had, which for me included summer job bosses, post office supervisors, all kinds of people. I don't believe I asked for one from Mr. Donahue at the country club or from my favorite postal worker, but I rounded up almost everyone else. I had been a stock boy in the shoe department of a department store and was very proud to go back there and say, "I'm going to be a lawyer, I need this letter."

In addition to the employment references, you had to present an affidavit from someone on the committee who knew you. To be a lawyer you had to know a lawyer. The law profession was a chain, a network; one needed to be vouched for. The Committee on Character and Fitness consisted of eleven men, and if you were not personally acquainted with a member of the committee, it was customary to obtain an affidavit from someone who knew you and also knew one of them. For the majority of New York's black lawyers, that person was Thomas Benjamin Dyett. Upon my acceptance to the New York bar, I was fortunate to get a job in the law offices of Mr. Dyett, Fritz Alexander, and Kenneth McArthur Phipps. Law school admission was dominated by quotas, and there was no abundance of jobs at white firms for those black lawyers who graduated. There were very few African American law offices in the 1950s, but the association of Dyett, Alexander, and Phipps was one of them.

Thomas Benjamin Dyett was the dean of black lawyers. He was also an old-fashioned gentleman. If he were to meet a woman in the street during a light rain, he would take off his hat because one simply did not converse with a lady while covered. So it would be raining on his bald head while he stood there talking. Similarly, Mr. Dyett would no more remain seated when a woman approached a table than he would fly. (To this day I follow his lead. If I am seated for dinner and rise as a woman comes to greet me, she will often say, "Don't get up, I just want to say hello." My rejoinder always is, "Either you've got to sit down or I've got to stand up, because I can't sit while you are standing and talking to me. It's just not done." I learned that from Mr. Dyett. I never called him Tom to his face. He was Mr. Dyett, or more often, Mr. D. Everyone stands on someone's shoulders, and I stood on Mr. D's. I frequently say to women, "I always rise for royalty." It always gets a rise out of them.)

Unlike today, when young associates just out of school earn over a hundred thousand dollars when they join a practice, Messrs. Dyett, Alexander, and Phipps paid me $25 a week, and each partner lectured me on how I should be paying them for the privilege of learning the practice of law. Actually, they were quite generous. If I happened to bring in a client, whether I worked on the case or not, I always shared in the fee. Because the office consisted of only the four of us, I filed papers, helped write briefs, and was intimately involved in most areas. One might think of law offices as moneymaking machines, and perhaps they were elsewhere, but in our office times were tight. Though each attorney had a sterling reputation, none of us was making a lot of money. We attended to business with great acumen, but we were hungry for dollars.

Mr. Dyett's specialty was wills and estates, and I followed in his footsteps. He had written wills for many people in the community. When they died, the family would find the document, come to the office, and say, "Daddy died," and we would handle the estate. It didn't take long for me to become familiar with the surrogate judges and the head clerk for the probate section; on occasion, when someone died intestate, we would be handed the business.

I continued to work two jobs. Each morning I put on a shirt and tie, picked up my briefcase, and went to the law office on Broadway, but at night I took the subway up to St. Nicholas Avenue and the liquor store.

In 1958 Ken Phipps, who had been a member of the State Assembly representing Harlem, was appointed to the criminal court bench by Mayor Robert Wagner. Mr. Phipps was in Hulan Jack's political club— Hulan Jack, New York's first black borough president, not only lost his job but was indicted for having his property renovated for free by a developer. (An indictment related to similar behavior was brought against NYPD commissioner Bernard Kerik many years later.) One of three judges who presided in the obscenity trial of comedian Lenny Bruce in 1964, Mr. Phipps died only four years after that at the age of fifty-one.

After Mr. Phipps's appointment, Mr. Dyett, Fritz Alexander, and I formed the firm Dyett Alexander & Dinkins. We helped create Allied Federal Savings & Loan Association, a black institution based in Queens, and I spent a considerable amount of time representing the bank while closing mortgage loans. Frequently, the black folks coming in to get those loans had white lawyers. This wasn't difficult work—we were not arguing before the Supreme Court of the United States, and the actions of all the attorneys in these proceedings were largely pro forma—so one wondered why these white lawyers were in the room when there were black lawyers to be had. The answer was simple: there was a widespread sense in the black community that in order to obtain a favorable result you needed a white lawyer.

We encountered this all the time. "White folks run everything," the reasoning went. "They have power, access, they all know each other. If I'm going to get anything done, I need a big downtown white lawyer." These weren't necessarily the facts, but as is so often the case, perception clouded reality. Our own offices were downtown at 401 Broadway, a block below Canal Street in the Foley Square area near the courts—and there were some very fine lawyers with offices in Harlem—but we were faced with a perverse and pervasive prejudice. We spent a lot of time trying to counter it, and the best way to do that was to do good work and hope the word got out. It was a very big day in my life when, in 1958, I was making enough money to stop working at the liquor store and devote myself full-time to the law.

How did a lawyer get clients? Word of mouth and personal contacts. Only a handful of men of color were in my law classes. If the white student sitting next to me had a business client, he might be someone who owned a string of muffler shops, because these were the people whom that white student knew. Any business client of mine was more likely to be leasing a corner candy store, because these were the people whom I knew. I might have been far brighter or more capable than my fellow student, but clearly he was going to make more money. This is the self-perpetuating nature of class. How did anyone go about breaking this barrier? You had to meet people to know people, and the perfect avenue for such networking was the local political club. In Harlem the place to be was the George Washington Carver Democratic Club.

·   ·   ·

The Democratic Party has ruled Harlem politics for almost a century because it has made the African American community part of its constituency. The Republican Party has for the most part abdicated any role in Harlem politics; the GOP is not a significant presence there because it has never evinced a great concern for black New Yorkers, and we are simply not part of its equation. The Republican Party has not made our needs a priority, or even in any large way a talking point, and black folks are well aware of this disregard. Harlem is a Democratic enclave because we support those who support us.

The general structure of the Democratic Party begins at the top with the Democratic National Committee. Beneath it stands the state committee, then the county committees with one county committeeperson per election district. These committee people are members of the local Democratic club, and they are the ones who organize the petition drives and get candidates on the ballot for public office. They elect district leaders. The president of the Carver Democratic Club was my law partner, Fritz Alexander, but the more powerful leader of the district that included Harlem was a man named J. Raymond Jones, known throughout New York political circles as "the Fox." My father-in-law had been active in the Carver Democratic Club, and he introduced me.

The Carver club was on what old-timers called Sugar Hill. Central Harlem was to the south, down in what was called the Valley, and the neighborhoods were separated from one another by St. Nicholas Park. One must climb a mountain of steps to get from the Valley to City College or St. Nicholas Avenue. During the Harlem Renaissance, Sugar Hill residents included W.E.B. Du Bois, Thurgood Marshall, Adam Clayton Powell, and Duke Ellington. But times had changed, and if Sugar Hill had ever been an affluent part of town, it wasn't now.

The Carver club had enormous clout. First and foremost, it got people jobs, particularly in civil service. The post office was a convenient conduit, and the regional postmaster could be counted on to be helpful when someone with the Carver club imprimatur came looking for employment. We used to love to tell the story of a guy who was "casing" mail, taking individual letters from the huge piles sprawled on the industrial tables and putting them into slots from which they would be delivered to each street. Amsterdam Avenue from number 1 to number 99, Amsterdam from 100 to 199 . . . this was a tedious business, but this guy was very good, very fast. Instead of standing in front of the slots and placing the letters in them one by one, he stood a couple of yards away and tossed mail behind his back, between his legs. The guy was putting on quite a show. The Harlem Globetrotter of mail distribution. All he needed was a soundtrack of "Sweet Georgia Brown." The letters zipped through the air and slapped into the boxes with accuracy and certainty. Someone said, "Damn, you're good!" "It's nothing," he replied. "Wait till I learn to read!"

Located at 145th Street and Amsterdam Avenue, the Carver Democratic Club was the place where the wheels of government and industry were made to glide smoothly. People in the community looked there when they needed more help than their friends or neighbors could give; it was the place where people who didn't know anybody knew somebody. The club did more than hand out Thanksgiving turkeys, though it did that too. We had lawyers in the club twice a week to help attend to the needs of the people. "I'm out of work, I need a job" was a recurring problem in Harlem in the 1950s, and the club often could be counted on to provide a solution. Yet one of the Fox's favorite sayings was "Nobody does anything for nothing." In return, the community could be counted on to vote consistently and convincingly Democratic.

At one point in my career I was approached by some West Side politicians who asked me whether I wanted to become a judge. When I declined, they asked, "What about Fritz?" It didn't appear to me that being a judge was among the aspirations of my law partner, so I said, "I doubt it, but ask him." They asked Fritz, and he said, "What time?!" Fritz Alexander was elected to the New York Supreme Court and went on to sit on New York's highest court, the Court of Appeals.

James L. "Skiz" Watson, a member of the Carver Democratic Club, became a federal judge in the US Court of International Trade, appointed by President Lyndon Johnson. He got to be a judge because Ray Jones had a relationship with LBJ. From then on, Judge Watson carried some weight and ultimately became the first African American to head a federal court in the South since Reconstruction.

We were sitting around one Saturday afternoon waiting for the start of a meeting of a committee that was making plans for a community center in Harlem, of which Judge Watson was chairman. Someone among us got impatient and said, "Man, let's go, let's get started, we have enough people."

He was shot down. "No, we're waiting for the chairman, waiting on the judge."

In the door walked Herb Evans, who was a judge on the State Supreme Court. The impatient fellow said, "There's the judge now!"

Not good enough. "No, man, I mean the *heavy* judge!"

From that moment on, Skiz Watson was "the Heavy Judge."

Esteemed civil rights attorney Constance Baker Motley (she wrote the 1950 complaint that became the landmark civil rights case *Brown v. Board of Education* and was the first African American woman to argue before the US Supreme Court) became borough president of Manhattan out of the Carver club in 1965. She later moved on to become a federal judge, raising the question of who was going to succeed her. Percy Sutton wanted to be that person. Ray Jones single-handedly had the power to make that selection: the vacancy was filled by the county committee, and Jones controlled that committee. Jones had a record for assisting people of quality (your humble servant excluded). For example, Kenneth Clark, the psychologist so influential in the *Brown v. Board of Education* case, became the first African American appointed to the New York Board of Regents with Jones's support. So every Monday on our ride together to Albany Percy would ask me, "What's Ray saying?" One possible rival was Herb Evans, who was also in the Carver Democratic Club but did not appear to want the job. Ultimately, much to his pleasure, Percy Sutton did succeed Constance Baker Motley as borough president. The BP's offices and the federal buildings were almost next to each other. I asked Connie, "How do you like it? What's the difference?" She said, "When I was borough president, I'd come to work in a limo. Now I ride the subway."

As in the black churches, the backbone of the club was its women. They were reliable, they were committed, they turned out in large numbers to participate in the petition drives, and they did the scut work that maintained the club's power. For decades women performed these functions without taking leadership positions. In recent years, however, they began to say, "It's time. We supported you men all those years; now we want to lead." In the past few years several women have successfully sought elective office from Central Harlem: Virginia Fields became borough president of Manhattan and Inez Dickens a member of the City Council, who may become speaker.

I met many people and became a known quantity at the club, bringing clients to Dyett Alexander & Dinkins while also working to elect local Democratic candidates. I managed to get Ray Jones's attention. One day someone there said, "Ray wants to see you." His office was in back, and the door was closed, so I sat outside at 9:00 at night and waited. Nine o'clock passed, then ten. Finally, at around a quarter past eleven, Ray walked out, big cigar in his mouth. "Hi there, boy," he said and kept on going.

But over the course of several years I made an impression. I started as a worker and grew to become captain of an election district. My job was to get to know the people, personally and as a voting bloc, and to be responsive to their problems. I spent time in the street handing out flyers and introducing myself, and I would meet with the individuals who came to the clubhouse with situations to be resolved. My experience selling insurance had taught me a valuable lesson in recognizing the need for respect—both giving and earning it.

Harlem was sufficiently congested that an election district could consist of one square block. In the old days a good captain was supposed to know all the people in his district, and I knew mine. I'd stand near the polling site, hand out literature in the period leading up to the contest, and say, "Be sure to vote for John Brown," or whomever I had on the ballot. I learned how to motivate my workers to get out the vote, and on election day I delivered my district.

.　　.　　.

Ray Jones decided he wanted to run for a seat on the City Council, which brought the council seat into play in Harlem because the Valley's New Era Democratic Club in Central Harlem was supporting a different candidate, Henry Williams. Jones recruited a young man named Charles Rangel, who was very dissatisfied with New Era's leadership, to run in a club election against its chief, Lloyd Dickens. Rangel thought his own smartness and brilliance had attracted this attention, but in fact Jones was trying to dethrone a rival district leader. It was simple addition by subtraction. Another New Era activist, Percy Sutton, was also running a candidate against Dickens, and Jones wanted to undermine him. At first, Percy and Charlie were fighting between themselves much of the time. Percy called Charlie "Pretty Boy," which drove Rangel up a wall. Despite Jones's efforts, both Williams and Rangel were defeated and Dickens was reelected. Even the Fox couldn't win every time.

Though he lost, Rangel's run earned him Ray Jones's ear. "I had my club in Central Harlem," Charlie says, "but I didn't have any J. Raymond Jones or anyone who won anything citywide. If I had to lose, it didn't hurt me too badly politically, since I was able to set the impression that I was a pretty important guy from the Valley. Who the hell knew the Valley? And I was the only connection that the City Council and the county elite had with the Valley. I had a lot of meetings with J. Raymond Jones at his home, and I wanted to be perceived as being his right-hand man, but no, J. Raymond Jones really was his own right-hand man."

Rangel and Sutton had met during the campaign and sooner or later found that they liked and thought like each other. They agreed that whoever won would reach out to the other. After they both lost, they began working together despite the fact that, as Charlie says, Percy "had never won anything. . . . [He] nevertheless was very well known." Rangel was valuable to Ray Jones because he knew what was going on inside New Era's operation. Jones, however, despised Percy Sutton, not because of his personality but because Percy had chosen to identify himself with what was referred to as the "reform movement" and against the regular organization, which was J. Raymond Jones.

To an outsider, the term "reformer" might indicate someone who wants good government, honesty among politicians, and candidates with high qualifications, someone who is against corruption. But the reformers were all white folks, and to those of us on the ground being led by a black county leader, "reform" meant a whole bunch of whites who were anxious to overthrow the regular organization only for the purpose of obtaining political jobs.

The reformers' basic platform was "Politicians shouldn't hold public-service jobs." District leaders should not be City Council members. It was clear what their intentions were: run for office, win, quit the Democratic clubs, and leave the neighborhoods without personal representation. It was just the title "reformer" that would make it sound so aboveboard; in actuality, it was a power grab. So when it came to picking candidates, it was us against them.

The reformers attacked Ray Jones, and because there were no blacks in the reform movement, they jumped at the opportunity to land Percy Sutton. He, seeing a chance to advance himself and have an effect, grabbed them right back. When Jones found out that Rangel and Sutton were allies, he told Charlie, "Those Sutton brothers are gonna eat you up alive." Percy had a brother, Oliver, with whom he practiced law. They didn't look that much alike, but they were very close and were together so often that when I first met Percy I wasn't sure which one he was. Charlie told Ray, "I'd rather be eaten up in the Valley than be ignored on the Hill. I don't have a lot of choices. I don't have a lot of problems with these reformers. They don't know me, I don't know them."

"They'll know you soon, and you'll be subject to attack."

"Hey, there's nothing to attack. They'll attack *you;* you're the county leader. But I will be irregular."

After much discussion, Ray Jones was persuaded to at least meet Percy Sutton, and there in Jones's living room, sure enough, he fell in love with Sutton and Rangel both, and as a result of that friendship they never looked back. As a result of Jones's support, Charlie became district leader and Percy was elected assemblyman. When Percy went on to become borough president, Charlie took his Assembly seat. When Charlie ran for Congress, Ray Jones supported him in a very contentious race against the incumbent, the legendary Harlem figure Adam Clayton Powell, Jr.

I got to know both Charlie and Percy much better during the height of this controversy. I looked up to Percy Sutton, whose reputation preceded him. He was polished, well groomed, soft-spoken, knowledgeable, articulate, influential. A major presence in Harlem, Percy was involved in all its main organizations, both political and civic. It wasn't so much his politics that was impressive—he was a smooth lawyer, and we and many others got to know one another through the Harlem Lawyers Association—as the fact that in many ways Percy was a visionary. Who but Percy Sutton would have dreamed that a black could own a radio station in New York City? Who but Percy would have decided that a black could run for mayor of New York and that he would be that person? Percy was active in the NAACP. For years there was competition among Percy, Basil Paterson, Charlie Rangel, George Miller, and some others for that organization's district leadership positions. Percy succeeded spectacularly. One of the accolades he was most proud to receive was the Spingarn Medal, the NAACP's highest award for outstanding achievement, previously bestowed upon W.E.B. Du Bois, George Washington Carver, Paul Robeson, Mary McLeod Bethune, Thurgood Marshall, and Jackie Robinson. Percy was our leader, a man undeterred by the fact that something had never occurred before. He had a vision that one day New York City could have a mayor of color. He was prepared to make it happen. Percy Sutton was a pioneer.

Charlie Rangel was my brother. We saw the world the same way, we saw our community the same way, and we saw individual people the same way. Sometimes we didn't even have to talk about an issue; we knew what we stood for, we knew where we wanted to go, and we knew how we wanted to get there. Neither Charlie nor I can recall more than a few times in our lives when we had a difference of opinion over politics.

It takes a lot to get a candidate on the ballot in New York City. Whether you're running for the position of district leader, a seat in the Assembly, or a spot on the City Council, any office requires first and foremost that you have a petition signed by the requisite number of duly registered voters in your district stating that they want you to run. Those people you see in the street, sitting at tables or standing in the middle of the sidewalk with clipboards and lined paper? They are out there using up shoe leather, talking to their neighbors, making democracy work. (If you are not registered to vote, let me encourage you strongly to do so immediately.)

The petition is spelled out at the top of a single sheet of paper, with space for signatures underneath. Sometimes there are duplications, typographical errors, illegible signatures, or errors of fact in these petitions—wrong election district, wrong assembly district. Sometimes people are not who they say they are, which is why we routinely collected many times more signatures than the law deemed necessary. If your petition is defective, you have no candidacy, but once the qualifying number has been reached it is valid. Petitions run hundreds and hundreds of pages and become literally worth their weight in gold! The candidate or his staff collects these sheets—stacks from one location combined with stacks from another and another—and binds them in a book or secures them with rubber bands or gathers them with twine, and then guards them with his life. The term of art is "wrapping the petition."

The Board of Elections is the governing body that decides who gets on the ballot. For the sake of security, the Board of Elections accepts only original signatures; carbon copies (then) or photocopies (now) are impermissible. If you lose the petition, not only have days and months of people's time and effort been rendered useless, but you as a candidate will be denied ballot placement, your election becomes impossible, and your career may die before it is born. Why? Because the Board of Elections doesn't care what happened; if you don't have your petition, it's over.

There were all sorts of political stories running around the Carver Democratic Club and every other political club in New York City about a candidate getting a call in the middle of the night—"Can't imagine how that fire started. . . . The whole damn house burned down."

"The house burned down? And my petitions?!"

"I had just put them inside. I was returning shortly. When I got back, *they burned the house to the ground!*"

Even though accidents do happen and petitions have been known to get legitimately lost, there's a certain amount of healthy skepticism among the people on the Board of Elections, because they have heard every "the dog ate my homework" story in the book. "The clubhouse burned down." "I left them in the trunk of the car." "Don't you remember? I gave them to Jerry."

Jerry shrugs, and your political career is gone. Security is therefore at a premium, and you will as much as sleep with that petition under your pillow. This may sound silly to outsiders, but to the people involved the degree of trust you put in the person who wraps your petition is extraordinary. Fritz Alexander and I wrapped Charlie Rangel's petition. It's the kind of thing you do for your brother.

.   .   .

Our daughter Donna was born in Newark because Dr. Bill Hayling had moved his practice to New Jersey. Early in the pregnancy, I was driving Joyce to an examination with Bill. The New Jersey Turnpike had yet to be created, so we were on either the Pulaski Skyway or Route 1.

When we started our road trips, Joyce, like many wives, would routinely get in the car and lean over and say, "Are you sure you have enough gas?" This was a constant. I would respond by giving her a lecture. "Honey, if the tank holds twenty gallons, and if it's on a quarter, that means it has a fourth of twenty, or five gallons, and if you can get fifteen miles per gallon, that's seventy-five miles."

So we started off, and we were on the Skyway and—*putt, putt, putt*—the car sputtered to a halt. A police car came along almost immediately and pulled up behind us. "What's the trouble?" the officer asked.

I said, "I don't know, but it's not out of gas."

The officer used his patrol car to shove our vehicle fifty yards, a hundred yards, to an exit. We coasted down the ramp, and at the bottom was a gas station. The attendant came and lifted the hood.

"What's the trouble?" he asked.

"I don't know," I said, "but it's not out of gas."

He checked the spark plugs and everything, and he finally said, "Why don't we put a little gas in and see?" Put some gas in and—*vroom!*—it kicked right over. It took a long time for me to live that down.

.   .   .

We just knew our second child was going to be a girl, because we already had a boy. Seemed logical. Sure enough, it was a girl. I wanted to name her Dawn. "Dawn Dinkins," I said. "That's cool!" Joyce wanted to name her Deborah, so she could call her Debbie. She thought that was cute, Debbie. I said, "If you want to call her Debbie, you should name her Debbie." We debated and argued, and I was almost holding my own until I made a big mistake. I said, "Can't you see, she's lovely, she's sixteen, she comes to the prom, the trumpets blare, and the announcer says, 'Comes the Dawn!'" Joyce said, "That's it. Never!" So our daughter's name is Donna.

Donna was a sweet and lovely child, as was her brother Davey. She was bright and inquisitive, as we found out early in her infancy. Sometime shortly after she learned how to stand, she managed to get on top of a chair and reach some hair tonic, which she drank. We found her crying next to the open bottle. There were no ingredients on the label, so we were truly frightened. I scooped up our baby and ran to the Harlem Hospital emergency room, which fortunately was on Fifth Avenue almost directly across the street from our home.

The place was crowded, of course. I came running in, cradling our baby, and was told something like, "Take a number, take a seat." I said, "You don't understand, this is our daughter! You've got to do better than that!" I raised a little hell, and whether my anger made a difference is hard to determine, but the doctors examined her and decided they had to pump her stomach. It hurt me more than it hurt her. Donna was crying, but I was just about to die. Oh, my God.

Apparently, when the ER receives a case such as this, they file a report with the appropriate city agency. Much to our embarrassment, Poison Control arrived at our door to interview Joyce. She was mortified. "They think I'm a bad mother!" Joyce was exactly the opposite: she was the most loving, protective, almost overly protective parent one could imagine. For a long time she would not let anyone, except her mother or mine, take care of the kids, and when we had only one, certainly no one else was going to take care of Davey. Davey used to fall down from time to time, nothing serious, but the scare with Donna, boy, that was something.

I was the taskmaster, I suppose. It wasn't quite "Wait until your father gets home," but I did feel the need to establish order. Davey to this day thinks I was a pretty stern dad. He recalls the following incident, which I do not:

One morning when he was under the age of ten, we gave our son a quarter to buy an ice cream cone. Walking in the street, Davey carelessly dropped the coin down a grate on the sidewalk. The money was irretrievable, the ledge on which it sat was too deep for either of us to reach. As far as I was concerned, the case was closed; we had given him the opportunity to have a treat, and he had not been sufficiently responsible to accept it. Davey started crying, but I would not give him another quarter; I felt there was an important lesson to be learned here.

We happened to be standing in front of his grandfather's liquor store, and my father-in-law heard the boy's crying and walked outside. He reached into his pocket, gave his grandson a coin, and said, "Go get some ice cream." Davey ran on his way, and the grown-ups proceeded to have a serious father-in-law/son-in-law talk.

Davey had a monkey—like a rag doll, but it was a monkey. He loved this stuffed animal, just loved it; it was his security blanket. Once, when we were perhaps twenty or thirty miles from home, my father-in-law driving, we realized we had left this monkey behind. I must not have been entirely severe: we turned around and went all the way back home to get the damn monkey.

This animal was filthy, just disgusting. Finally, when we could not stand it anymore, when the monkey was approaching the status of an environmental hazard, Davey's mother put it in the washing machine. After it emerged all nice and clean from the wash, rinse, and spin cycles, that was the end of the monkey. Davey didn't want it anymore.

Donna was "Daddy's Angel." Our children were equally bright, but Donna was a better student, more attentive, less likely to be outside playing ball than attending to her studies. I tell Joyce all the time, "You did a good job."

It is my contention that the mothers get together in the playground with the baby carriages and strollers to plot and scheme and conspire. Daddies do not have a clue. God bless mothers! Because Joyce told me that, after talking to these other women about New York's educational opportunities, she had decided that we ought to send our children to private school. I said, "You must be out of your mind. There's a brand-new school across the street at 135th and Fifth, and it's free!"

But she was insistent and eventually convinced me that she'd made the right decision. Education is the foundation of civilization, and in order to progress satisfactorily all children need to be given full opportunity to develop their minds. In the early 1960s in New York City, we felt that the best education available to our children was in private school. The tuition was estimable, and we had very little money, but through grants-in-aid and some personal sacrifices—Joyce and I rarely exchanged gifts or dined out or indulged in holiday travel—we were able to send Davey and Donna to the Ethical Culture and Fieldston Schools all the way through high school.

Joyce and I felt it was important to expose our children to life outside Harlem as well as in it. At Ethical Culture and Fieldston, they met a group of people whom they might not otherwise have encountered. Central Park was their playground, and when they went to museums and on other field trips, they interacted with people from very different backgrounds and cultures than their own. "You know," I told Davey, "everybody's not the same as people you see in the neighborhood. The people whom you meet at school are not necessarily of the same background as those in Harlem." We did not want our children cloistered in one neighborhood with only one culture, and it was important to us that they not develop misconceptions about people with whom they were not familiar. Davey came home one day and told me, "The Jewish kids don't celebrate the holidays that we celebrate." He kept me informed when he learned about his Asian friends' unfamiliar history and culture.

"People are different," I told him. "They're just different. They're still people!"

But this was not a Hallmark card education either. Joyce and I were keen on making certain that our children did not become narrow-minded or have prejudices engrained in them at an early age. When Davey or Donna would come home from school and tell us an inappropriate joke they had heard among their classmates—we were extremely pleased, but not at all surprised, that they would share their stories with us—I recall Joyce saying, "That's not right, and here's why. You don't use those kinds of names to talk about other people."

At the time our children were growing up, I was developing my law practice and becoming increasingly involved in politics. My job was not a conventional nine-to-five one, and often my time was limited by my professional responsibilities. Joyce was juggling part-time work as a bookkeeper in her father's liquor store with being a homemaker and a full-time mother. Nevertheless, I tried to make it clear to our children that they could always find me. In the summer we would occasionally visit my in-laws' summer home in Belmar, New Jersey, which is south of Asbury Park, by driving down the shore early Saturday morning and spending the weekend there. We would swim and have lunch, and I would read the paper, and we would all relax together. Our talks in the car on the way down and back were precious. Sometimes, because of my schedule, the family would have to travel without me, and I would join them late at night or early the next morning; Davey now informs me that the fact that I made the time to get away made a powerful impression on him. I was a husband, a father, and a man with a career, and I tried to make those occasions special.

.   .   .

My baby sister, Joyce, is three years younger than I. We called her Boots, though I don't recall why. She was smart and a lot of fun. She was my kid sister and also went to Howard University. On campus I didn't exactly try to avoid her, but whenever they told me, "Your sister's looking for you," I knew she wanted money. Joyce stayed in Trenton and became a teacher in the school system. She has four great kids, three daughters and a son. One day she went to school and developed a headache so severe that she had to be driven home. It turned out that she had a brain aneurysm; she ended up in the hospital, partially paralyzed on one side. In middle age, Joyce had to relearn how to talk—"That's a window, that's a door"—and she remains affected to this day. Her son, a psychologist separated from his wife, is now living with her, which is a great benefit. But she's a good kid and a tough cookie, and I love her.

4

"Walk in My Shoes"

In 1966, as a result of a lawsuit brought in federal court, the New York State Assembly was expanded from 150 to 165 members. This was known in political circles as "Republican Plan A," because it was the first of several compromises in that lawsuit presented by the New York GOP. Most of us didn't think the court would ever go for that because it flew in the face of the state constitution, which established the number at 150, but the court resolved that the expansion was acceptable for a single one-year term. So there were fifteen new Assembly seats to be had.

J. Raymond Jones, and undoubtedly my father-in-law Danny Burrows, had plans for me. Jones asked whether I wanted to run. I don't think he was asking me a question so much as telling me it was something I should do if I wanted to move forward. I agreed.

The general election didn't mean anything—the Democratic candidate was going to win the Assembly seat, and that's simply the way it was. In the 78th Assembly District, running along the overwhelmingly liberal West Side of Manhattan from 108th to 150th Streets, roughly from Amsterdam Avenue to the Hudson River, Republicans didn't stand a chance. The primary was winner-take-all.

The first order of business was to create an outstanding piece of campaign literature. Never having run for public office, I was an unknown quantity. My opponent was a progressive and a good guy named Franz Leichter who was running with the stamp of approval of the Riverside Independent Democrats, a truly liberal bastion that included notable activist congressman William Fitts Ryan. My mandate was to show that I was something other than a clubhouse hack.

Dr. Kenneth Clark, the noted psychologist whose work had figured prominently in the *Brown v. Board of Education* Supreme Court decision desegregating the nation's schools, had been a client of mine and also a friend. I represented him in the incorporation of Harlem Youth Opportunities Unlimited (HARYOU), a social activism organization that taught people in the community how to deal effectively with government agencies. He became the chairman of my citizens' committee, which gave me solid liberal bona fides.

Nobody had money to run television or radio ads; we had to marshal our funds carefully, which meant putting a memorable piece of paper into the hands of as many potential voters as we could find. Our technology was minimal. We didn't have computers, we had mimeograph machines, and it was literally a cut-and-paste job putting together the most important political statement I had ever made. I enlisted my law partner Fritz Alexander and law school classmate Bernie Jackson to help me, and my father-in-law to lend his expertise. We were up half the night when I showed Mr. Burrows what I had. His response was, "You must have a family picture." To win in Harlem a candidate needed to be a family man, and it helped to be verifiably African American. (In Texas, even into the 1980s, black candidates almost uniformly did the opposite: they produced campaign literature with no photos of themselves whatsoever to avoid being rejected out of hand by white voters.)

My wife and children were down at the seashore in Belmar, so we drove down there early in the morning and took a family photo. Once we pasted that into our masterpiece, Bernie took a step back, looked at our handiwork, and said, "This is common and ordinary and pedestrian, and I don't want to have anything to do with it." We tore the thing up and started all over again. Ultimately we came up with something we were proud to distribute. It was considered one of the best in that political year, as indeed it was.

On the ticket with me, running for state senator, was Andrew Tyler, who later became a judge. His opponent was Basil Paterson; I was friendly with Paterson, but did not know him well. Also on the Democratic ticket, running for Manhattan borough president, was the widely popular Constance Baker Motley, the NAACP trial attorney. Connie came out of the Carver Democratic Club, and when Andy and I circulated a piece of campaign literature picturing him and me and Connie together and calling ourselves "the Team," Franz Leichter hit the ceiling. "That's not true!" he wailed. "She's not part of your team, she's a reformer!" Franz and the Riverside Independent Democrats felt that they had more claim to Connie's political affections than I did. However, I respectfully disagreed and proceeded to campaign hard. I did a lot of work at the busy corner of 125th Street and Broadway and outside the subway station at 110th and Broadway, handing out literature and buttonholing people. I was largely unknown, but I enjoyed talking to folks, and the more I felt I knew what they wanted, the more I felt I could help.

It was a big surprise to me when I won. Ray Jones had made a practice of winning elections, but his imprimatur was not a guarantee of success. What pushed me over the line was the Grant Houses, a working-class public housing project where what I had to say about getting the state to pay attention to New York City had some resonance. A little to the west and south, in the more affluent middle-income cooperative of Morningside Gardens, I got killed. But with a combination of message, organization, and determination, I'd won my first elected office.

.   .   .

The Assembly did not meet twelve months a year in Albany, only a fraction of that. It was a life to learn. We freshman legislators weren't making any money to speak of, but we went to almost nightly receptions and parties thrown by lobbyists. We would frequently read the papers the next day to find out what we had done the day before in session. Sometimes the process was so complex and convoluted that we didn't know what the hell we were doing. The Speaker and his staff ran the lawmaking business.

A year before I was elected, in 1965, the Democrats held the majority in the State Assembly and in the opening days of the session were preparing to vote for Speaker. In those days the Speaker had even more authority than he has today—no legislation saw the light of day if the Speaker said no, and he appointed the chairs of all committees and hired and fired all Assembly employees. His power was enormous. The Speaker was chosen by all Assembly members, but things being as partisan then as they are now, Democrats caucused and voted for Democrats, Republicans did the same for Republicans, and the reigning party prevailed by simple force of numbers.

The contest in 1965 was between two Brooklynites, Anthony J. Travia and Stanley Steingut, and the Democrats could not decide which man they wanted. Whatever differences in policy they might have had, the contest was more about which man was going to run this fiefdom, and it was an utter deadlock. The debate went on for weeks while everything else stood still. The Assembly was rudderless, bills floundered, and the people's business did not get done.

Nelson Rockefeller, a smart politician, was governor of New York at the time. With his own agenda held hostage to the deadlock, Rockefeller convinced several Republican members of the Assembly to cross the aisle and vote for Tony Travia. Presumably this unheard of but effective gesture of electoral beneficence did not go unnoticed by the new Speaker.

Skip ahead a year to 1966. The fifteen new Assembly members elected under Republican Plan A had been seated, and the legislature was about to organize. A Speaker once again had to be elected. Travia and Steingut were in the same position as the previous year, and the same conflict was brewing. Now, for the purpose of illustration, I'll take some poetic license with the numbers. Let's assume that of the 165 members there were 90 Democrats, 9 of whom were black. If you subtract those 9 votes from 90, you are left with 81, fewer than the one-half of 165 (83) needed to win that election. In other words, without those black votes, the Democrats would not have a majority, and the party and the Speaker would be faced with exactly the same deadlock as the year before, which would be terribly embarrassing. The New York State Democratic Party did not need to be run by Nelson Rockefeller. Certainly not twice.

So eight or nine of us black members of the Assembly, led by Percy Sutton and Brooklyn's Shirley Chisholm, went to see Tony Travia in his room at the DeWitt Clinton Hotel in Albany. Some called it "the Midnight March." We did not ordinarily have or wield significant power. In fact, our concerns and those of our constituents were largely bypassed in the day-to-day world of the New York State Legislature. It was widely known then and remains true now that New York City delivered significantly more in taxes than it received in services from the state. But here we saw an opportunity, and this was exactly the kind of power play in which Percy Sutton was willing to engage. He had assessed the vote count and come to the very logical conclusion, as regards Speaker Travia, that "he can't do it without us!" It might not have occurred to many others of us in that day. Today some of the dumb stuff they are doing in the State Senate will drive you crazy, but at that time it was unheard of for black legislators to go to the mighty Speaker and bargain for their constituents and themselves. We were sitting on the floor, on the radiator, on the side of a bed—all crowded into Tony's small hotel room. "Mr. Speaker," we said, "we're politicians too, and we've got to go home with something."

This was a pretty drastic action we were taking, and I had been in Albany for only a week. If I had been more politically astute, that fact might have occurred to me. But it didn't—this just seemed to be the right thing. Days later someone said to Ray Jones, "Do you know what Dave is doing up there in Albany?!" He responded, "The kid knows what he's doing."

Whether I did or not, that's how the SEEK program was born. Search for Education, Elevation, and Knowledge (SEEK) provides grants and educational assistance to low-income students in the State of New York and is responsible for bringing a good portion of our young people into the higher education system. It came into existence in exchange for our support, and I am credited as one of its founders. We also got some semblance of a seat at the table. A fellow named Bertram "Bert" Baker, a black old-timer out of Bedford-Stuyvesant in Brooklyn, was made deputy whip. A deputy whip is not much, but it was an official office, the first party position given to a person of color, and we were proud of the accomplishment.

Also born of this effort was the Council of Black Elected Democrats. Percy Sutton was our leader, aided by Shirley Chisholm. Sometimes we African American legislators would meet in Percy's office, sometimes in Shirley's. I didn't understand why we couldn't agree on a single meeting place. It was explained to me that while we from Harlem thought we were trying to be broad and inclusive, the people from Brooklyn felt that we thought we were better than everybody else. (Now, Harlem is the best-known black community in the world. You go to Africa, they know where Harlem is. As the black population in Brooklyn increased it was said that Brooklyn had the numbers and Harlem had the brains.) But Percy recognized the need for territorial compromise and acceded to it gracefully.

Percy used to say, "You can't dance every set." The State Legislature was very much an old boys' club, and if you could not get in the door, you could not get anything done. Percy would pick his battles. One of his areas of concentration involved the state's voluntary fire departments, which were notoriously segregated and discriminatory organizations no matter where you went in New York. This was where white firefighters would gather to cook hamburgers, drink beer, and perpetuate associations in which black folks could not participate. We adopted the position that if you're going to use public money, you will not be permitted to discriminate. We would attach such an amendment to various bills being brought before the Assembly by legislators seeking funds for fire departments from around the state, giving our bloc of votes to whatever they were seeking, and now and then we'd win.

Percy held seat number one in the well of the Assembly room, down front and near the Speaker's desk. There were no microphones on the floor of the Assembly; one had to use the power of one's own voice to be heard. Way up in back sat a fellow named Ken Brown, a former Queens County assistant district attorney with a very sonorous voice. He would call down, "Mr. Speaker, will the member yield to a question?" Of course, it was legislative etiquette for fellow Assembly people to yield and encourage debate. Assemblyman Brown would then proceed to begin his questioning with an antagonism. "You mean to tell me. . . ." He was as unpleasant as an elected man could be, and his tone was unceasingly withering, as if we were all liars and he was the sole possessor of the truth. When Brown got through roughing up the member, Percy Sutton would rise and say softly, "Mr. Speaker, will the member yield for a question?" He would be recognized.

Percy spoke gently. He was polite in response to provocation. "Walk in my shoes," he would tell Mr. Brown or any of our detractors. "I come from the village of Harlem. Let me tell you what really goes on in the lives of my constituents. Walk in my shoes." His gentility was perfect.

These were long conversations. Percy would not simply reject an argument—he would explain its flaws and turn argument into understanding. "Walk in my shoes" was not so much a rhetorical flourish as a philosophical outlook, and it often carried the day.

One of the major successes that year was our founding of the New York State Black & Puerto Rican Caucus. Previously, we had neither the size nor the power to exercise significant influence over the course of legislation, and we were not sufficiently adept to combine our communities' needs and desires into a single legislative agenda. Ours were both largely working-class constituencies with what should have been compatible objectives, but we had been divided by ethnicity and ego. Now, however, things were beginning to change in New York State, and we made a concerted effort to combine ideas and resources in pursuit of a common goal.

When the legislature was in session, I spent Mondays through

Thursdays living out of a small room at the DeWitt Clinton Hotel (the Albany home of the Democrats) and carpooled to and from New York City. Percy had a small Chevy registered in his wife Leatrice's name, and one morning four of us—Percy, Charlie Rangel (who was working in the Office of Counsel), a fellow named Jenkins, and I—were headed for Albany when a tire blew. Percy struggled mightily to keep control of the car to prevent it from crossing the median into oncoming traffic and getting us killed. The Chevy flipped over on its roof and came skidding to a rest, but none of us was seriously injured. Only Jenkins had to go to the hospital. When we walked into the Assembly chamber the next day, all the members stood and applauded. We told everyone with whom we came in contact what a great job Percy had done in saving us.

Then Charlie and I consulted our lawyers . . . and decided Percy was negligent as hell! Sued the crap out of him and settled for a couple thousand dollars, which was big money at the time. One sues an insurance company, not an individual, so he didn't take it personally.

I spent the year working for my constituency, trying to get bills passed. Very quickly I became hopelessly hooked on public service. The concept that an idea, if presented properly and negotiated with other representatives, could be transformed into law and affect millions of people for the better . . . that was heady stuff indeed. Idealism does not last long in Albany, but it was the quest to do good work that sustained me.

Unfortunately, after the year went by the expanded Assembly was reduced to the 150 districts that had existed prior to my arrival. My time in Albany was over. I was elected a delegate to the 1967 New York State Constitutional Convention, where I made a lot of friends. Bill vanden Heuvel, one of Senator Robert Kennedy's confidants, was among them. I sat in close proximity to the co-founders of the Liberal Party, International Ladies' Garment Workers Union president Dave Dubinsky, American Hatters' Union president Alex Rose, and Community Church minister and American Labor Party state chairman Donald Harrington. This was back when the Liberal Party was liberal. They were about to help elect New York's Mayor John V. Lindsay on the Liberal ticket.

.   .   .

It was the 1960s, and all hell was breaking loose. The Black Panthers were active, SDS (Students for a Democratic Society) was fomenting revolution, and before he was murdered in 1965, Malcolm X was heard on many Sunday evenings on radio station WADO debating all comers. "Black Power" was a phrase and an idea whose time was coming. These were highly active, semi-violent political times. I never felt the need or urge to join activist civil rights groups like the Student Nonviolent Coordinating Committee (SNCC) or the Congress of Racial Equality (CORE). I believed that the system worked and that if we—and I'm talking about everybody, the black community, the white community, working-class, middle-class, wealthy—worked within the system, we all had a better chance of succeeding.

Bobby Kennedy was elected senator from New York in 1964. His organization was active and effective in the city, and because of his progressive politics and integrationist image, my neighborhood was his natural constituency. Once elected, he delivered on his promise. We were all impressed when he visited apartheid South Africa and said, "Each time a man stands up for an ideal, or acts to improve the lot of others, or strikes out against injustice, he sends forth a tiny ripple of hope." His assistance in the attempt to redevelop the Bedford-Stuyvesant section of Brooklyn, his activity to advance the War on Poverty, his support of the Voting Rights Act of 1965 and antipoverty social programs to increase education, his call for desegregated busing and the integration of all public facilities—all these positions brought him directly into Harlem's heart. The Kennedys were icons in the black community.

In 1968, when Bobby ran for president of the United States, Harlem was behind him. Several years before the businessman Earl Graves would found *Black Enterprise* magazine, he was among Kennedy's administrative assistants. Fresh off his assignment to bring the body of Dr. Martin Luther King Jr. home to Atlanta after King's assassination in Memphis, Earl recruited four or five New York community representatives to fly to Los Angeles for a last-minute get-out-the-vote effort. I was happy and proud to be included. It was the night before the election in the California primary, and the race against Senator Eugene McCarthy was close. The cross-country flight was long, we got very little sleep, and at five o'clock in the morning I arrived at headquarters and was put in charge of turning out the town of Long Beach. I had never been to Long Beach.

I was a former assemblyman, which didn't sound important enough, so I became "Senator Dinkins" from New York. It had resonance, and we needed it. There were all sorts of problems: the phones had been cut off; the troops, such as they were, were unorganized; leadership was nonexistent. The staff was enthusiastic but untrained and undirected. The lessons learned in a decade on the streets of Harlem were put to good use. I made more promises than you could shake a stick at. I told the staff, "When we get to the White House...." I guess these southern Californians hadn't seen a New Yorker in action before, because they got out and got the job done. We turned out voters, brought people to the polls, and helped Bobby Kennedy win.

When the polls closed, I was exhausted. I wasn't in the Kennedy inner circle—I was just some guy from New York doing his part—and I was in a hotel across the street from the Ambassador Hotel, eating a steak and drinking some red wine, when Bobby came down from his suite and addressed the crowd to announce his victory. I was all alone watching the television when I saw him shot. I was stunned, shocked. The family had sure seen a lot of hardship, and I felt for the Kennedys as they were undergoing it again. The rest is a blur. I have no recollection even of coming back to New York. The city, state, and world were unalterably changed for the worse that night.

Black Panther Eldridge Cleaver was on the Peace and Freedom Party ballot for president in 1968, the Yippies were running a pig named Pigasus, and there was talk in some circles of sitting out the election altogether, thereby electing Richard Nixon and "making the contradictions manifest." I voted for the Democrat, Vice President Hubert Humphrey.

.　　.　　.

I returned to my law practice and pursued politics through the Carver club and rose through the Democratic Party organization. I was happy to do the work and take on more responsibility. In 1972 I was selected for a seat on the Board of Elections, a job one received through the machinations of party politics. In those days the board consisted of four commissioners, two Democrats and two Republicans. We always thought the law was unconstitutional—What about the Liberal Party? What about the smaller parties? What about independents?—but the City of New York saw it differently. Which left the board with a conundrum each year: with two commissioners each, how were we to decide on a president?

A fellow commissioner who was a Republican agreed with me that, politics aside, the efficient running of the Board of Elections was paramount; someone had to actually push the buttons and do the work of managing New York City's elections. The president's main job entailed dealing with the five Republican and five Democratic county leaders, and it turned out that I got along better with some of his folks than he did. In a display of bipartisan amity that might not be possible today, I was elected. I was the first person of color to hold this position in New York City. I steeped myself in election law and made sure that the petitions were all in order, the poll sites open, and the machines operative, that records were up to date, and that voters were registered and educated and welcomed.

I was a member of the Harlem Lawyers Association and the Urban League. I was chosen to a position on the executive committee of the Association of the Bar of the City of New York. I was a lifetime member of the NAACP and a founder of a civic organization we named 100 Black Men. I was becoming part of the fabric of New York politics.

.　　.　　.

My children participated in those important times in ways that suited their personalities and strengths. Davey was not an excellent high school student, but he was a bright young man and an enthusiastic athlete who would play anything in season. I attended his Little League games, where he always seemed happiest. But we often came to loggerheads over his studies. Nor did he inherit my passion for politics. Although, as a teenager, he enjoyed helping me campaign—obtaining petition signatures, leafleting on street corners, putting flyers under apartment doors—he was not a natural, and I did not push him to pursue the family business. I felt that if both my children were happy in their vocational pursuits, they would be productive human beings and things would take care of themselves. I knew that my job and lifestyle made me happy, and I believed that Donna and Davey would find comfort if they followed their passions.

Which is not to say I did not raise my voice when my son came home with a less than stellar report card. Education is important, and when presented with the opportunity to increase one's knowledge and understanding, one ought to seize it. I tried everything I could think of to motivate him, without much success. At one point we discussed his future. "You should do something you like," I said. "Otherwise, it's a job and it's real work. You should make sure that you're happy in those choices." Often in youth one hears advice from one's parents and it is water over a rock, while sometimes the words are meaningful and are absorbed. Even as a loving parent, you don't know how deeply your advice penetrates or how it will affect your children in later life. You hope you are providing nourishment, but often it takes time to tell. With our son it took years, but ultimately he got it.

Davey attended Case Western Reserve University in Cleveland, Ohio, and did not immediately excel. His first report card was indeed one of those "Wait till your father gets home" types. Clearly I had not reached him in our previous conversations, so this time I took a different tack. He was now a young man, living away from home for the first time; perhaps the distance had begun to alter his perspective. Instead of raising my voice or yelling or losing my temper—"What are you doing, you're under-achieving!"—as I had done in the past, I remained very quiet. I was no longer angry, I told him, I was disappointed. He had an agile mind, I said, he was now out of our house and out in the world, and he was not taking full advantage of the opportunity to move forward. It was time to grow up and be a man. Davey was aware of our sacrifices. Was he willing to make some of his own? He remembers my silence as deafening.

Davey's grades and participation improved dramatically. He made the dean's list! Whether by design, luck, lack of patience, or simple resignation, my improbable use of silence with my son worked remarkably well.

My daughter Donna was every bit the student that my son was not. Although they are equally bright, she was the more studious, and Davey saw his kid sister as the golden child. Donna breezed through the Ethical Culture and Fieldston Schools, which is not to say I did not expect great things from both of my children. When Donna brought home report cards filled with As, she remembers me saying, "You didn't get an A+?" I loved my kids abidingly, but I must have been a difficult dad to satisfy.

Fieldston was an excellent, progressive school that taught its students to think independently. The education process worked so well that when Davey was in tenth grade and Donna was in seventh, the students occupied the administration offices in protest of the school's perceived lack of African American faculty and students. When Donna called Joyce to say that she was one of the occupiers, her mother told her firmly, "You're too young. Come home."

"I'm going to stay with Davey. He's here too!"

"No, no, no. You're coming home."

When I heard of the uprising, I was not at all concerned. There were plenty more dangerous places to occupy than the Fieldston offices. In addition, I thought the students were on the right side of the argument. I called Davey to tell him to call his mother so she would not worry and would be assured of his safety. The phone rang in the administration office, and some kid answered. I told him who I was and that I wanted to speak to my son. The young man put me on hold. Sooner or later, Davey came to the phone. He was very amused.

"Ha, ha, ha, Dad, they put you on hold!" He thought that was funny as hell.

Of course the issue was ultimately resolved and the kids went back to class.

Donna took a job as a counselor in the Fieldston summer program, working with younger children. The full-time employees, who were unionized, went on strike over a set of grievances that I cannot now recall and put up a picket line. This presented Donna with a dilemma: she had a job and a contract; should she cross the picket line? Our daughter had never been faced with this situation before. I was pleased when she sought my advice.

I did not instruct her as to her actions. I felt it was her own ethical decision, an early one of many she would face in her lifetime, and I did not want to usurp her authority. We did, however, sit down and discuss the matter. What were those folks and their union fighting for? I asked. I reminded her that anytime she decided to cross a picket line she was affecting the workers' ability to negotiate, and that as a result it was important that she be informed and understand what each side stood for. What was her own position in regard to the participants? She was a part-time employee, while the people who were striking depended for their livelihood on these jobs. She would have to determine the relative values of her contract and the needs of the people around her. I was pleased but not surprised when she decided not to work until the strike was settled. She has never since been faced with the decision of whether to cross a picket line, but she says she never would.

.   .   .

America didn't get any better under Nixon. The Vietnam War went from bad to worse, civil rights took a step backward, and black folks remained largely disenfranchised and underemployed. In March 1972, eight thousand African Americans convened in Gary, Indiana, for the National Black Political Convention. Why Gary? Because Gary's mayor, Richard Hatcher, and Cleveland's Carl Stokes were the first black mayors of major American cities. The convention's purpose was to develop a unified strategy for African Americans from that time forward. On the steering committee were Mayor Hatcher, Michigan congressman Charles Diggs, and writer Amiri Baraka. Attendees included people from a variety of political persuasions, among them Congressman Ron Dellums, actor Richard Roundtree (still basking in the glory of *Shaft,* which had been released the year before), Black Panther Bobby Seale, political activists Barbara Jordan and Julian Bond, Nation of Islam minister Louis Farrakhan, Reverend Jesse Jackson, Mayor Carl Stokes, and his brother, Congressman Louis Stokes.

I was one of eight vice chairs of the New York delegation, which stood approximately four hundred people strong. Several days prior to the convention, we caucused at a Chicago YMCA, where one of our major tasks was to establish the mechanism for the selection of alternates; if an elected delegate was for whatever reason unable to participate, we needed to be certain that another would be immediately credentialed and available. This was of significant importance because a group of black nationalists, led by a hothead Brooklyn street activist named Sonny Carson, wanted to seize control of our delegation.

Two slates were running: an integration slate, consisting of me and many city and state politicians, and what they were calling a separatist slate, run by radicals. Basil Paterson was on both. Basil, who was my friend and law partner, had run for lieutenant governor in 1970 and knew everybody. He was well respected by people in the professional political world for his intelligence, vision, and wit. At the same time, the separatists thought that Basil was advocating for the integration of the schools only because he figured that was how to get more money into Harlem. That was not untrue. Dr. Kenneth Clark had testified in the *Brown v. Board of Education* case that having white children sitting next to black children in school was advantageous for both.

The chair of the New York delegation was State Senator Waldaba Stewart. His had been the decisive vote in eliminating abortion in New York State. (We called him "A Bad Law," his name spelled backward.) He did not last long at the job. Following the first night's session, he got sick; his brother came in and told us that A Bad Law was so exhausted he practically fainted and that we would have to find a new chair. Basil was asked to accept the position. He refused, didn't want any part of it. Harlem state senator Carl McCall also turned it down. Both felt that this was a no-win situation, with each side ready for battle. I was asked to accept the post. I didn't know Carl and Basil had rejected the offer. I said, "Of course I will." The opportunity to preside over such an important event seemed too good to turn down. Basil encouraged me, told me he had my back.

Things did not take long to turn contentious. There were significant disagreements between the integrationists and the separatists over issues and approach, and both saw accommodation as acquiescence. At some point, as I was trying to maintain order, Sonny Carson tried to make it physical. Basil remembers that "Carson, with these little riffraff people he's got with him, starts charging the stage" and approached me directly. According to Basil, I said, "I'm trying to be fair, Sonny, I'm trying to be fair."

"You're selling out!" He was right in my face and shouting.

"You want this damn gavel?!"

It looked like I was about to have a physical confrontation with Sonny and his underlings when someone said to Basil, "Isn't Dave your law partner?" Basil had a way with Carson, a way of carrying himself, a means of handling these guys.

"Yes."

"Whatever you're ready to do, we're with you."

Basil and several New York City cops, men of strength, walked to the front of the stage and stood beside me. Helen Marshall, a delegate then, now Queens borough president, said, "It was straight out of Hollywood. That was a Western."

After a certain amount of jawing, the good guys prevailed. Carson stopped his charge and the event proceeded.

The National Black Political Convention created an element of difficulty for New York congresswoman Shirley Chisholm. In 1969 she had defeated CORE-founder-turned-Republican James Farmer in her first run for Congress. She was one of the founding members of the Congressional Black Caucus. In 1972 Shirley was running for president of the United States. She was the first major-party African American to do so, and the first woman of any color to run for the Democratic nomination. She was widely respected by the African American community, yet she chose not to attend because the event was unsettled, swinging between the integrationist and separatist slates, and if the outcome did not go well, she felt she might lose all her white support. As a result, she lost some significant black support. Such are political calculations.

The convention began with an extraordinary idea: in a presidential election year, as African Americans, we needed to represent ourselves before we could bestow our representation on others. We spent several days crafting a statement of purpose, an inclusive "black agenda" that would lift our people while maintaining unity with the rest of America. When most of us New Yorkers boarded a jet home, we thought we had done good work, but we were outflanked. Once we were out of town, the separatists commandeered the convention and issued "The Gary Declaration," a provocative document that characterized America as a place of "single-minded dedication to profits for some and white supremacy for all. . . . Meanwhile, the officially approved epidemic of drugs threatens to wipe out the minds and strength of our best young warriors." Electoral politics was "the pointless question of who is to preside over a decaying and unsalvageable system." White America, it said, "moves toward the abyss created by its own racist arrogance, misplaced priorities, rampant materialism, and ethical bankruptcy."

"The Gary Declaration" was separatist in the extreme. It not only opposed busing to integrate the country's public schools but essentially opposed the entire concept of integration. It also included a plank that condemned Israel's part in the Six-Day War of 1967 and excoriated the country and its people for its "expansionist policy and forceful occupation of sovereign territory of another state." One proposal discussed before being omitted from the final document called for a "dismantling of Israel."

The NAACP membership walked out. A majority of the Michigan delegation, led by state legislator and later Detroit mayor Coleman Young and consisting of many United Auto Workers activists, did the same. A great gulf became apparent between the radicals—the black nationalists who felt America was beyond saving and needed to be torn down—and those of us who wanted to work with the best of all Americans and lead the country in a better direction. I chose to work within the system because I believed then and believe now that the system works. Still, when the New York delegation walked off the plane, we had a lot of explaining to do. Perhaps Shirley Chisholm was right to have avoided this convention, notwithstanding what it might have cost her in black votes, if any.

5

_____

From Sugar to Shit
in a New York Minute

Pursuing my own agenda, I threw myself into political work as well as my law practice. In 1967 Ray Jones stepped down as district leader, timing his retirement so as to be able to choose his successor. Ray let it be known that he chose me. I ran … and lost. I had no business losing, they just stole it, and I was such an electoral neophyte that I allowed it to happen. I was so inexperienced and unsophisticated in the ways of New York City politics that I neglected to place poll watchers in every polling place. The voting booths at the time were fitted with a large sliding handle that controlled both the curtain to the booth and the entering of the vote itself, and in one or two crucial election districts someone got in there and slid that handle over and over, cranking out votes for my opponent in sizable numbers. As a result, I lost an election I was predetermined to have won. I learned my lesson and in the next district leader election was a lot smarter and won.

In 1973 many in Harlem and in the African American community citywide worked extremely hard for the election of Abraham "Abe" Beame as mayor. Abe came out of the Democratic clubhouse. He was trained as an accountant and had been New York City's budget director from 1952 to 1961. He had lost a mayoral election in 1965 to Republican John V. Lindsay, and in 1969 he was elected city comptroller. After Lindsay was reelected, changed his party affiliation, and ran unsuccessfully for the Democratic presidential nomination in 1972, the mayor's seat was available and Abe seized the opportunity. The race against Republican state senator John Marchi looked like it was going to be tight, and in order to win the support of Harlem, Beame promised Percy Sutton, who by this time had been elected Manhattan borough president, that he would not run for reelection, leaving the presumed nomination in 1977 to Percy and essentially paving the way for New York to elect its first black mayor. Beame won handily.

Abe was a sweetheart, a guy who cared about the city and had an accountant's attention to detail. He was also a diminutive man; like New York's legendary Mayor Fiorello LaGuardia, he stood five foot-two. Abe hated to make speeches, and on the stump and in the transition period there were many speeches to be delivered. This gave him the opportunity to make a personal contribution to New York's political landscape. Abe's press aide traveled with what was known to the entourage as a "Beame Box," a small platform along the lines of an extended milk crate for the candidate and now mayor-elect to stand on when he spoke at a podium. (I'm no giant at five-foot-six, and I once had the occasion to speak in public with the actress Ruby Dee, herself a petite woman. We arrived and found the microphone placed at an inconvenient height. "Don't worry," I told her, "they'll have a Beame Box." I do not know whether New York's current mayor, Michael Bloomberg, avails himself of this political advantage.)

Abe Beame was New York's first Jewish mayor, a significant milestone in a city of such ethnic and religious variety. New York's mayors were traditionally WASPs or Irish or Italian, and the Jewish community was thrilled with his victory. I come from a generation that found great parallels in the Jewish and African American experiences in America.

We were peoples who had to overcome prejudice to obtain opportunity, and it is no exaggeration to define both groups' progress as a struggle. Jews were active and highly appreciated participants in the civil rights movement and were welcomed as brothers in black churches, in progressive lawsuits, and on picket lines. Neither Mayor Beame nor I was a proselytizer, but Abe recognized the chance to provide opportunity to all. Traditionally, there had been only two deputy mayors in each administration. Mayor-Elect Beame expanded that number to four, and he was determined to name one a person of color.

Thirty-five years later we elected an African American president, but in 1973 a black mayor of New York City was unthinkable, and the installation of a black man as deputy mayor signified a mighty step forward. We had never had an official of that scope, and for a community that was large and compactly located and only just beginning to believe that its members could take the reins, the fact that we had a voice—that we were being defined as worthy of attention—was extremely important. My nomination for this post was a very, very big deal, almost as if I had become mayor myself.

Of course, this was politics, so there was controversy. The job as originally conceived was to be deputy mayor for community affairs, with responsibility for smaller agencies and programs such as the Office of the Aging or the Office of the Handicapped. This was not acceptable—many people read the position as "deputy mayor for black people." The *Amsterdam News*, an influential weekly newspaper published in Harlem, warned on its editorial page against the creation of a "'Spook Mouse' . . . the appointment or selection of a Black to sit outside the door, so to speak, in a Mickey Mouse job, while real municipal power is exercised elsewhere." Percy Sutton was also particularly critical, and as the idea grew even more public it was met with such resistance that Mayor Beame was forced to reconsider.

A new post was created—deputy mayor for planning of the city of New York—and I was nominated. With Judah Gribetz as deputy mayor for government relations, James Cavanagh as deputy mayor of operations, and Melvin Lechner as budget director, the new mayor's inner circle covered the racial and cultural waterfront.

The position of deputy mayor is of vital importance to the running of New York City. Deputy mayors do not create policy—that is done by the mayor himself—but they are consulted, they advise the mayor, and they are responsible for implementing the administration's ideas. In fact, deputy mayors are delegated significant decision-making authority, and their power to affect real life in the city and to effect real change is estimable. The mayor is responsible for guidance, direction, and vision; the deputy mayors put that guidance, direction, and vision into practice. In the history of New York City, no black man or woman had been entrusted with this responsibility. The highest elective office any black had ever held prior to that was borough president. The fact that I would be the first black deputy mayor was extremely significant. The new Beame administration called a press conference to make the announcement, and it was well attended. Many reporters and camera crews were on hand to memorialize this momentous civic occasion.

I was thrilled. My areas of responsibility would include oversight of the city's hospitals, the Off-Track Betting Corporation, and the planning and development offices. Mayor-Elect Beame's team assured me that I would be reporting directly to the mayor, which was vital to my ability to get things done. My first assignment, even before my confirmation, was to draft a plan to combat the city's energy crisis. Clearly, important tasks were going to be handed to me, and I was looking forward with great enthusiasm to the opportunity to help move the city forward.

The Beame transition office was in the same building, the Municipal Building on Centre Street, that housed Abe's office as comptroller. At the close of each day, after all the city workers had gone home, my good friend Judah Gribetz and I would walk across the street to the empty offices of City Hall and see how we might redesign the space to fit us all. We tried to cut small offices into even smaller ones. There were many city-owned office spaces down the block on Broadway where I could have worked and been effective, but even if the carpet was an inch thick and the walls were papered with mayoral invitations, the people in Harlem would never understand. The first black deputy mayor had to be within shouting distance of the mayor himself. Access was key—I didn't want to design programs and have them waylaid before the mayor could review them personally—and I found it extremely important, for both managerial and symbolic reasons, to have an office in City Hall on the same floor as the mayor's.

There are disclosure forms one must sign in order to work in city government. Among the questions on these forms was, "Have you filed all your income tax returns for the past three years?" Upon my return from the State Assembly, I became a partner in the law firm Paterson, Michael, Dinkins and Jones. The firm's accountants prepared our taxes, and they routinely filed a "Request for Extension of Time to File" on the partners' returns. These requests were always granted, and once the deadline passed, the sense of urgency passed as well and we all went about our business, comfortable in the knowledge that we had informed the government of our good intentions: we would pay our taxes in the fullness of time. As a result, these extensions were rolled over, and I had not paid in three years. This was not a crime; there had been no intent to evade or avoid payment of our taxes. We had simply delayed it. Still, the answer to the question "Have you filed all your tax returns for the past three years?" was "No, I have not." I always thought of paying my taxes as something that could be done tomorrow. I wish it had been done.

I signed the form, recognized the problem, and immediately set about correcting it. I stayed up all night with accountants and lawyers while we computed the taxes, interest, and penalties for city, state, and federal returns for the years in question. Got all of it together.

I owed approximately $15,000 and had to borrow from my father and several other people to pay it. All overnight. I showed up at the IRS office the next morning with the signed returns and check in hand. I thought I had worked a miracle.

I hadn't.

Here's the way politics works. The failure to pay taxes may or may not be a disqualifying issue, depending on the person involved and the circumstances in which the issue arises. Failure to pay withholding taxes on a housekeeper's salary doomed Lani Guinier's appointment to head President Bill Clinton's Civil Rights Division as well as Zoe Baird's nomination as Clinton's attorney general; Republicans, mightily displeased by the Clintons in general and the results of the 1992 election in particular, were out to make trouble for the new president, and they succeeded. Sixteen years later, however, with the economy in dire straits, the same error did not derail Timothy Geithner's acceptance as President Barack Obama's secretary of the Treasury. His failure to pay a housekeeper's taxes was referred to by the White House as an "honest mistake," and Senate Finance Committee chairman Max Baucus announced, "We have to roll up our sleeves and get this economy moving again for the American people, and Tim Geithner has the right combination of experience and skill for these difficult economic times."

Now, as it happened, the day before I was to be sworn in as deputy mayor, Beame's former campaign manager and nominee for director of special programs, Seymour Terry, had been found to have sent a letter on official stationery to six hundred clients of his one-man insurance firm promising "greater benefits" because of his "new circumstances." This was an outrageous breach, and the conflict-of-interest charges, once brought to light, caused him immediately to withdraw his nomination. Now here I came with my problems.

It appeared that although I had filed all the necessary returns to federal, state, and city offices and made full payment, the various agencies involved would take months to sign off on my submissions. Mayor Beame, already embarrassed by Terry, was facing more of the same from me. I was mortified. Still, I wanted to keep my job; I was about to have the opportunity to do a lot of good, and I could not simply walk away.

I asked for and was granted a meeting with the mayor; I wanted this information to come directly from me. Also in the room were Abe's close adviser Howard Rubenstein, Commissioner of Investigations Nicholas Scoppetta, Judah Gribetz, and the incoming first deputy mayor, Jim

Cavanagh. They laid out the case against me: they knew me to be an honorable man, and they trusted me personally, but I had to understand how this would look to the press and the people. Facing a second ethical question mark in an administration not even yet inaugurated, they could not allow me to assume my post.

To argue my case I brought my law partner and good friend Basil Paterson. Basil is a spellbinder, a storyteller, and an old-school verbal acrobat. He is also an able negotiator with an ability to satisfy his adversaries by putting himself "in the other person's suit." Asking what, from the mayor's point of view, would save me, that day Basil was Clarence Darrow, Thurgood Marshall, and Johnny Cochran all rolled into one.

"David Dinkins has not committed a crime," he said. "There will be no legal action against him. What he has done here is something a lot of people do: he got so busy he forgot to pay his taxes. They're paid up now. With interest and penalties, he's paid much more than he ever owed. He is not a man of means trying to protect his wealth. When he started in our program, he wore the same sports coat every day!

"Here's a man, you know him, he's been devoted to you, he will work hard for you. He has stumbled here, but if you stay with him you will earn political points you're never gonna imagine." Basil was not just an orator and an attorney; at the time he was vice chairman of the Democratic National Committee. "Mr. Mayor," he said, "Hubert Humphrey remained for many years a viable political candidate for one reason: wherever he ran, he had the black vote." (Black folks had indeed been very partial to Senator Humphrey because of his record in civil rights and his other humanitarian efforts.) "There's great sympathy for Dave, not just in the black community but throughout. He's an outstanding person, he's a highly *respected* person, and for you as mayor to lend a helping hand will put you in the first rank. You will be remembered!"

Mayor Beame looked as though he understood. He was about to begin an incumbency that he no doubt hoped would provide him with a favorable niche in New York City history. What better way to begin than to demonstrate personal trust and forgiveness?

Nick Scoppetta looked like he might be leaning. The idea arose of leaving my position unfilled until the tax matter was resolved.

Jim Cavanagh was a numbers guy: he read polls, he did not have an understanding of the community goodwill for which Basil was reaching, and Basil's argument meant nothing to him. He saw an administration with a second question of ethics, projected the headlines, and left it at that. He said very firmly, "We can't do it!"

Cavanagh was about to become first deputy mayor because he had been Beame's first deputy in the comptroller's office and was the man to whom Abe had consistently turned, for many years, for advice and counsel. Unfortunately, he was adamant. And ultimately, he prevailed. The Beame administration, as represented in that room, could not or would not take the public relations hit that my appointment as deputy mayor would undoubtedly bring. Politically, it was deemed just too damaging.

Now someone in the room said, "Don't worry, Dave. We'll just issue a statement saying that you've withdrawn." I am certain they were trying to spare my feelings. When my appointment had been announced, we had held a big press conference, with tons of cameras and lots of reporters in attendance. "Oh, no," I said. "We'll have a press conference again. I want to go out the same way I came in." I wasn't going to put my tail between my legs and sneak into the night. I had made a mistake, a significant mistake, but this wasn't tax evasion and I hadn't shot anybody. I was determined to stand up and face the cameras, and I did. I also knew that if no one was there to defend me, I would go undefended. I needed to meet the press.

I was very emotional when I withdrew my name from designation as deputy mayor. Facing a battery of cameras and reporters, I read a prepared statement and then answered questions. The *New York Times* reported that my eyes filled with tears, and they were right. I felt the loss of something great—the capacity to do good work for the city. I apologized for the embarrassment I had caused Abe and his new administration. "To my wife and children, my partners and my many friends and supporters," I said, "please know that while I take this action with a heavy heart, it is to me the only honorable course."

Mayor Beame said that I was "a very talented person" and "would have made a great deputy mayor." To his credit, he appointed another African American, Paul Gibson Jr., to the position I was to have filled. The *Times* editorial page praised my "outstanding accomplishments" as president of the Board of Elections and my "impressive qualifications," but like all the news reports, the *Times* editors also mentioned Seymour Terry, despite the fact that his case and mine had nothing to do with one another, and said I should go. Apparently Jim Cavanagh's political barometer was correct. State tax commissioner Mario Procaccino, who had lost to John Lindsay in the previous mayoral election, grabbed a headline by saying that his department was "looking into" my tax situation, though of course I had not willfully evaded payment and my explanations were completely correct. It went nowhere. Reporters asked the IRS whether I had committed a crime and asked me whether I might be disbarred, and although my actions certainly had not risen to that level, the mere mention of the issue showed the amount of misunderstanding and hostility I was facing. My friends were stunned; none of them thought of me as a risk-taker or financial miscreant. To a person they were supportive, even though this incident was a significant embarrassment to me and to the cause of black empowerment.

Not everyone, however, had my back. Roy Wilkins of the Urban League was quoted as saying I had "let down the Negro race." My wife will never forgive him for that. Jack Greenberg, who worked on *Brown v. Board of Education* and succeeded Thurgood Marshall as director-counsel of the NAACP Legal Defense Fund—and who should have known better—was similarly unkind.

Personally, I was devastated. I had risen through the ranks to take the most significant job with which a black man in New York City government had ever been entrusted, and then I had plummeted as though I were in a garbage chute. All the pundits were throwing dirt in my face and writing my epitaph. *This is the end of Dinkins.* I went from the penthouse to the outhouse, from sugar to shit, in a New York minute.

·   ·   ·

I had hit a political dead end. What was I going to do? I couldn't go back to political work; with no career path to follow, I could never rise to a position of authority. I could practice law, but with this cloud over me, what clients could I attract? I was faced with the truly unpleasant and unsettling fact that I had nowhere to go.

Fortunately, throughout my political career, even going way back, I had made more friends than enemies. There didn't appear to be a groundswell murmur, "Oh, I'm glad it happened to him." This is not always the case in politics.

I was sitting in my office one day after the New Year, in 1974, when Paul O'Dwyer called. A silver-haired Irish lawyer, he was a lifetime progressive with a passion to protect the oppressed. I used to call him Uncle Paul. He had been active in the National Lawyers League, had run several times for citywide office, and in something of an upset had just been elected New York City Council president. Paul was a supremely decent man. Apparently he had been conferring with Percy Sutton.

"Dave," he said, "Percy and I have been discussing your situation. There's a vacancy at the city clerk's office, and we think it would be good for you to take it. It's well within your abilities, and it will rehabilitate your career."

"Paul," I asked, "what's the city clerk? What does the city clerk do?" I had no idea.

"Look it up. Then call the mayor."

I came to find that the Office of the City Clerk is one of the oldest in New York City government, with its beginnings traceable to the inception of the Town of New Amsterdam. The original role of the clerk was to record the proceedings of the town's legislative body and attest to and affix the town seal on official documents.

As the office itself describes it, historically the city clerk has played a dual role as the clerk of the City Council and the clerk of the Municipal Corporation known as the City of New York. As the clerk of the City

Council, the main function is to attest to all laws enacted by the council. The clerk also attests to all legislation desired by and affecting the city that requires concurrent action by the State Legislature. The clerk of the City Council is also responsible for keeping the transcripts of the council's proceedings.

The city clerk attests to the leases and deeds of city property, grants, agreements, bonds, tax notes, and other forms of obligations of the city. The city clerk also has charge of all papers and documents of the city that include executive and administrative orders of the mayor, certificates of judicial appointments by the mayor, oaths of office of city employees, city Marshall bonds, and referendum petitions. Other duties include the qualification of the commissioners of deeds and the certification to the Board of Elections of all judicial vacancies. Aside from these functions, the city clerk's office maintains two separate and important bureaus under its jurisdiction: the Lobbying Bureau and the Marriage Bureau.

The city clerk was nominated by the mayor and appointed by a vote of the full City Council. It was a political plum. I picked up the phone and called Abe Beame. "Mr. Mayor, I understand there is a vacancy in the city clerk's office. I just want you to know that I am interested in that position."

"Okay, David."

Mayor Beame and I had no further conversation on the matter, but he must have communicated my interest to City Council majority leader Tom Cuite. The only problem I had at my hearing before the council was the perception that I was overqualified. The general thrust was: "You're a lawyer, you were deputy mayor-designate; do you not have too many qualifications"—and by that perhaps they meant too much ambition— "to perform this job?" I assured them that I would be pleased to serve to the best of my abilities and pointed out that having more than the necessary attributes to perform the job successfully should not disqualify me from doing so. Several council members were not ready to vote for me, perhaps thinking I wanted this position to further my political career. In fact, I wanted the job, as Paul O'Dwyer and Percy Sutton were suggesting, as an opportunity to "cleanse myself," as it were. I am perplexed as to why any council members would not have wanted me to do so. In an effort to overcome their reservations, I agreed not to practice law during the time I held the position. I told them, "I'm just going to do my job." There were thirty-five council members, and because New York was an overwhelmingly Democratic city, most were Democrats. I was appointed with close to thirty votes; the two Republicans voted against me, and two members of the Liberal Party, one of whom was Henry Stern, abstained. Bobby Wagner, a Democrat and son of former New York City mayor Robert Wagner, also abstained. Their stated reason was that I was overqualified. That was bullshit, but that's politics.

I enjoyed my ten years as city clerk. I was party to all the inner workings of city government; the paperwork had to come across my desk sooner or later. The city clerk's office consists of five offices, one in each borough, with deputies who perform the city's ceremonies and keep its records. I met a significant number of New Yorkers from all walks of life who had to do business with the city. The city clerk also personally attends the City Council meetings, which soon gave me a deep familiarity with the intricate ways in which our government actually worked.

It was a political job with a great amount of freedom. I had the opportunity to attend functions every night of the week if I so chose. As an experienced Carver Democratic Club hand, I knew the value of personal contact. I made every event; I was everywhere. And I enjoyed that too. I developed a reputation. Basil Paterson used to say, no matter who was doing what, "it's not official until the city clerk shows up!"

The part of the job I most enjoyed was presiding over the city's Marriage Bureau. The city clerk can preside over marriage ceremonies, and I took the opportunity as often as I could. I had a convocation ready to go at any moment, adaptable to whomever was celebrating their happy day:

> Marriage is a supreme sharing of experience and adventure
> in the most intimate of human relationships. Marriage is not a rit-
> ual or an end. It is a long, intricate, intimate dance together, and

nothing matters more than your own sense of balance and your choice of partner. Marriage is the joyous uniting of two people whose comradeship and mutual understanding have flowered into love.

Love is a canvas furnished by nature and embroidered by imagination. Love is patient; love is kind and envies no one. Love is never boastful, nor conceited, nor rude; never selfish, nor quick to take offense. Love keeps no score of wrongs; does not gloat over a person's mistakes but delights in the truth. There is nothing love cannot face; there is no limit to its faith, its hope, and its endurance.

Today, [bride and groom] proclaim their love to the world, and we who are gathered here rejoice with them and for them in the new life they now undertake together. We who are witnessing your marriage trust that, despite the stresses inevitable in any life, your love and respect for each other, your trust and understanding of each other, will increase your contentment and heighten your joy in living.

We are here to participate in and witness the sacred ceremony of marriage, which has been, since the time of the first born, a means of establishing and continuing a home. For it is by this act that the community endures.

Until 2009, the Marriage Bureau's office was on the second floor of the Municipal Building, a massive structure at 1 Centre Street in Lower Manhattan that was designed by the renowned architectural firm McKim, Mead and White. Completed in 1914, the floors were old-fashioned ceramic tiles that had been worn slick by decades of brides and grooms, some in their finery, some in work clothes, some walking in to apply for marriage licenses, and some getting married. One day my longtime adviser Barbara Fife came to me and said, "You know, you get off the elevator or walk up the stairs, and there's rice all over. I mean, people throw rice at each other, and it's like walking on a skating rink. Especially for someone like me in high heels. You go to maneuver down those few steps to the office, you could fall on your nose!"

Now, Barbara is a fine woman with a great heart, and she wasn't complaining—she was pointing out a safety hazard and potential civic liability. "I know," I told her. "They wanted to make a rule that people could not throw rice here at their weddings. I said no. People who get married at City Hall mostly don't have money to spend on a wedding. They have very little they can do to make it feel like a special occasion. I don't want to take that away from them. We should just sweep more often." The cost to the city in dollars was minimal, but the benefit to its citizens in joy was substantial. This was my vision of government: do not create rules that make life more difficult for people, but create opportunities that make life easier and better for people.

It was a city requirement that the bride and groom appear in person to apply for a marriage license. If for some reason one could not—perhaps because he or she was ill or bedridden or hospitalized—a letter of explanation was required. It didn't have to come from a physician, but often it did. The letter would read "The applicant can't appear because. . . ." The reason would be stated, and we would then send a clerk to the residence or hospital. On one occasion a letter said the applicant was terminally ill and wanted to get married before he died. Instead of saying simply "terminally ill," the letter indicated that the man was terminally ill with AIDS.

No clerk wanted to go. These were the days when the disease was relatively new in the public's awareness, when one would enter the hospital room of an AIDS patient only while wearing a mask. I hadn't studied the disease, but I knew enough to know that the mask wasn't meant to protect the visitor, it was to protect the patient. So I went. This wasn't some heroic act. I simply knew that one couldn't get AIDS through the air and was willing to perform my duties with that knowledge. This man had a limited amount of time left and wanted to marry. I wasn't about to stand in his way.

After I made the first visit, the objections disappeared and on the rare occasions that AIDS patients applied for a marriage license, they were treated evenhandedly. I am proud to have had some small hand in that progress.

.   .   .

In January 1977, Percy Sutton announced his intention to run for the Democratic Party nomination for mayor of the city of New York. The notion was in many ways historic: this was the first time any black person had sought the city's highest office. Some of us, when confronted with the idea of a mayoral run, thought, *Well, that's never happened before, we can't get that done.* Percy, by his nature, was never deterred by the fact that something had not occurred before. He was a visionary. Born in San Antonio, Texas, he had stowed away on a train and arrived in New York City at age fifteen. Percy was a barnstorming stunt pilot who joined the Air Force and became one of the Tuskegee Airmen. The armed forces deemed his vision impaired just enough that he wasn't allowed to fly, so he became an intelligence officer. The way we tell the story, Percy was so smart that he got the other guys to fly for him.

Percy was prepared to become the first black mayor. That would be a triumph, a real racial milestone. I was proud that he would take on that challenge. Percy was vastly intelligent, dedicated, verbal, convincing, and capable of moving and shaking with the best of them.

He decided to announce his candidacy in Queens, which some thought was pretty clever and others considered not so smart. Queens was a populous borough, and most of its voters were white; in his first public appearance as a mayoral candidate, Percy was clearly attempting to send the message that, if elected, he not only would be Harlem's mayor but was intending to represent the entire city.

In 1973, when he was Manhattan borough president, Percy was viewed as the "dean" of the Board of Estimate. In those days, the board was the primary generator of city projects: if you wanted anything done, you had to get it past the board. The citywide elected officials on the board were the mayor, the president of the City Council, and the comptroller, all of whom had two votes. Each of the five borough presidents had one vote apiece. Through the force of his political acumen, supreme deal-making ability, and winning personality, Percy could move business through the board like no other. He assisted then-mayor Abe Beame in getting the mayor's agenda acted upon and actualized. In return, Percy told me, Beame promised to back him in the next mayoral election, in 1977.

But New York damn near went bankrupt under Abe Beame. In fact, Herman Badillo, a member of Congress from the South Bronx at the time, counseled for bankruptcy. The Municipal Assistance Corporation was formed to get New York City out of its fiscal difficulty. Bankruptcy papers were actually drafted to file in court. (I don't know where those papers are today, but they're probably in a frame on someone's wall.) Fortunately, that was avoided, but because Beame, the former city comptroller, had taken the brunt of the criticism for the city's financial straits, he apparently felt compelled to run for a second term to vindicate himself. He reneged on his promise to Percy not to run again and never offered his support.

The lineup of Democratic candidates for mayor in 1977 was formidable: incumbent mayor Abe Beame, Congressman Ed Koch, former congresswoman Bella Abzug, New York secretary of state Mario Cuomo, "civic watchdog" Joel Harnett, and Manhattan borough president Percy Sutton. Each came with expectations and constituencies, and each had his or her own relationship with the press. I remember vividly that Percy held a press conference in the Observation Tower of the Empire State Building to make the point that tourism in New York was big business. I thought the location was a clever choice. Unfortunately, because of the way the media treated Percy's candidacy, nobody showed up to cover the event, as I recall, except the *Amsterdam News*.

Nevertheless, Percy was doing well in the polls; none of the candidates had more than 22 or 23 percent, and there was a very real possibility that he might finish well enough to qualify for a runoff. In June, however, Congressman Badillo entered the race. Badillo was a very smart, self-made man, a lawyer and a CPA who was so gifted that he was sometimes accused of thinking himself the smartest man in the room. A former Bronx borough president who was born in Puerto Rico, Badillo was the first Puerto Rican to serve in the US House of Representatives and had a large Latino following. He lost the 1973 Democratic primary to Beame in a runoff and must have thought that by coming in late he could circumvent the field. He failed in that, though he did succeed in splitting the potential African American–Latino coalition vote sufficiently to undermine Percy's bid. Some say it was a maneuver that cost Badillo significantly in his future political life, particularly in regard to his subsequent inability to secure support from the African American community.

I was solidly behind Percy. I knew that if he was elected he would be an excellent mayor. When he told me he was running, it took me about thirty seconds to say, "What about borough president?" Manhattan borough president was not considered a "black" job, but it had been held by African Americans since Hulan Jack was elected to the position in 1953. "Oh," said Percy, "you should run for that."

I thought I had a pretty good shot at it. Percy was a friend and mentor, he was going to go all out to win his election, and he would turn out a large constituency that might vote for me as well.

What I did not know and did not understand was that Percy and some of his supporters really didn't want me to run. They felt that two black men on the Democratic ticket would be too much, that some white folks would look at the slate and not want to put political control of the city in so many black hands. They also feared that my presence on the ballot would give people who thought they were open-minded an out: they could withhold their vote from Percy and still tell themselves, "Well, I didn't vote for Sutton for mayor, but I'm not a bigot because I voted for Dinkins for borough president." I think Percy and his advisers were entirely wrong; if anything, two of us running would have increased the turnout, at least in Manhattan, and put both of us in a better position to win. But at that point I wasn't even politically savvy enough to be aware that I was being sandbagged. Percy told me to run, but I'm not sure that he didn't give the same advice to two or three others.

I was ready to be borough president. I was prepared to move the city forward, to tend to the neighborhoods, to work in the best interests of all the people of the city. I was in a tough primary race against State Assemblyman Andrew Stein, City Councilman Bobby Wagner, and Ronnie Eldridge, a very outspoken woman who was a good friend of the Kennedys, a good friend of John Lindsay, and a leader in founding the reform movement on the Upper West Side. Stein was well funded, but Wagner, who hadn't been able to bring himself to vote for me for city clerk, was the front-runner. Ronnie Eldridge and I were such good friends that we would share a car on our way from one club to the next for speaking engagements. On top of the recent debacle regarding the deputy mayorship and my taxes, I was largely frozen out of the Sutton campaign.

The highly effective and articulate community leader Lloyd Williams was having these "Harlem Day" events, and I thought it was perfectly logical that I, a former Carver Democratic Club captain and active community political presence, would be the centerpiece of one. That didn't happen. And though I was chairman of the Council of Black Elected Democrats, I would be shouted down at meetings when I tried to discuss my own candidacy; they were committed to Percy.

Only Charlie Rangel, Harlem's congressional representative, encouraged me. One day he found himself riding in a car with Jewell Jackson McCabe, who was former director of public affairs for the New York Urban coalition, former public relations officer at Special Services for Children, associate director for public information in the Women's Division of the New York State Office of the Governor, and a woman who had devoted a large portion of her life to advancing the cause of blacks and women. She proceeded to tell him she was supporting Bobby Wagner. That did it. He stopped the car and made her get out!

Andy Stein had a lot of family money and social connections but was not widely thought of as a considered or committed candidate. For much of the election the issue was "Are you for or against Andy Stein?" Wagner, Eldridge, and I split the "against Stein" vote. Stein won, and I came in third.

Percy lost as well, while Koch and Cuomo faced a runoff for the nomination. Contrary to popular opinion, African Americans did not vote in lockstep, and there was considerable jockeying for positions of power in the city among black politicians, particularly between Harlem and Brooklyn. In times of decision there is always opportunity, and Brooklyn's Vander L. Beatty, who had only recently lost his seat in the State Assembly, attempted to increase his political standing by putting an end run on Percy and what he described as the "Harlem leadership" by coming out for Cuomo. It is my assumption that Beatty thought that, if he came out early and Mario won, he would be in line for a quantitative leap in status. Percy's reaction was, "Fine, we're with Koch"—and by "we" I mean Percy Sutton, Basil Paterson, and the vast majority of black elected officials. It was certainly a calculated move. Koch, though he had a liberal past and was still perceived as a relative progressive at that time, ran a law-and-order/pro-death-penalty campaign to the right of the rest of the Democratic field and beat Cuomo for the nomination. Mario took 238 of the 250 votes cast in the Liberal Party primary and ran atop its ticket, but Koch defeated him and Republican Roy Goodman in the general election and became mayor. So began Ed Koch's twelve-year reign in New York. Among his first appointments was Basil Paterson as deputy mayor. And like all career politicians, Mario Cuomo did not forget who his friends were and who had not supported him.

.   .   .

One has a political life and at the same time one's personal life forges ahead. Often, if one's work is one's passion, they coalesce. Our daughter Donna attended Yale University and excelled, earning a degree in psychology in 1980. Of course she was politically active, as we knew she would be. At the time of her graduation a significant sexual harassment suit was pending at the university, and Donna, along with several women's and Third World student organizations, was considering not participating in the ceremonies. She told her mother, "I'm not going to march. At the very least, I will not wear a cap and gown." She and her fellow students felt that Yale's behavior demanded a statement from them and that by absenting themselves or showing disrespect for the traditions of the institution they would bring attention to the issue. Joyce saw things differently. "You will march," she told our daughter. She felt that in some way this degree was ours as well and that such disrespect extended not only to the educational institution but to others. Donna and her like-minded compadres did march, but wore armbands proudly displaying the universal sign for "woman."

Donna came home from Yale and announced that she had joined the Peace Corps. She did not ask, "What do you think?" or, "How about if I . . .?" She said, "I have joined the Peace Corps." I was her first call, I'm pleased to say, because I had always counseled our daughter to pursue what was important to her and she knew I would be supportive of her decision. Donna was also aware that her mother would be far more concerned. "Don't worry," I told her. "I'll take care of your mom. I'll tell her." Ultimately my bride agreed to her daughter's decision. Not that she or I had a say in the matter.

Donna earned an assignment to the Dominican Republic because she spoke Spanish, but turned it down because she wanted to go to Africa. When a placement in Liberia was offered, she took it.

Liberia was colonized by freed American slaves as part of the nineteenth-century Back-to-Africa movement, which held that ex-slaves would have greater freedom and equality in the land of their ancestry. The Republic of Liberia was founded as a democracy in 1847, and the colonists, known as Americo-Liberians, dominated the political and economic sectors of the country. Its government had a strong and healthy relationship with the United States and with the Peace Corps. Once your identity as a Peace Corps volunteer was established, Donna was informed, you were safe and secure. "That's one of the most stable governments in

Africa," she was told during training. "We've had Peace Corps volunteers there for years, and there's never been a problem." As with all Peace Corps assignments, there was a backup plan in which all personnel could be airlifted out in case of emergency.

Donna was stationed in a remote village, approximately one hundred miles up-country from Monrovia, in which individual homes not only had no telephone service but were not equipped with electricity. This was a time before the Internet and Skype and cell phones and the constant interactions of the modern world. Our only communication with our daughter was by mail, and letters would take two or three *weeks* to be delivered.

Donna arrived in Liberia in December 1979. In April 1980 the Liberian military staged a coup.

We heard about it on the morning news. Organized bands of indigenous soldiers led by Master Sergeant Samuel Doe had seized control of the country from the Americo-Liberian leadership class, brutally killing the president, his family, twenty-four members of his cabinet, and sixteen leading politicians. The threat to Liberians of American descent was palpable, and our American daughter was there in the middle of it.

We called the State Department and got a live person at the Peace Corps desk, not a machine. The man told us, "All American citizens are safe." I said, "No, you don't understand, this is our daughter here, you've got to tell me more than that."

"I'm sorry, sir, that's all the information I have."

I said, "Well, maybe Cy Vance could do better." I knew Secretary of State Cyrus Vance from our interaction at the New York City Bar Association. The Peace Corps representative said, "Well, you do what you think you have to."

My daughter was in danger, and of course I would use any and all contacts to secure her safety. Donald McHenry, whom I knew from his time as deputy to Andrew Young, the first African American U.S. ambassador to the United Nations, was by this time himself the UN ambassador. Carl McCall, whom I had known since he was a Harlem state senator and Percy Sutton's protégé, was McHenry's deputy. I reached them, and they moved mountains to communicate somehow, some way, with those out in the bush who could establish the health and whereabouts of our child. The wait was agonizing.

Fortunately, word came back that everyone was safe. The upheaval was in Monrovia. In the recesses of the backcountry, we were told, they barely knew the coup was going on.

Months went by, and we did not hear from the most important girl in our lives. Finally a letter arrived. Donna wrote home like a kid from college: "Send this" . . . "send that." On the second or third page, she said, "Oh, by the way, there was a coup." Daddy's angel, bless her heart.

When Donna finally returned to the United States, we learned that her experience had been a bit more harrowing. She and all the other volunteers had surrendered their passports to the local Peace Corps office so that in case of evacuation all would be simultaneously available. She had faced soldiers brandishing M-16s and became inured to the sight of people walking down the street carrying automatic weapons.

We were overjoyed when her Peace Corps service was finally ending and Donna was coming home. She had been away at college for four years and spent three years in Africa; Joyce and I as parents were looking forward to seeing our daughter again.

Donna had not been back a day before Joyce commented on the noticeable increase in maturity that had taken place during her time away. "It was like she grew up overnight," my bride remembers. "She was always interested in serving and helping people, but now she had real feeling and understanding for their problems, and she appreciated her own life." During college Donna had worked on various women's health issues. In Liberia she had worked as a maternal child health volunteer in a local clinic and taught science in the local school, as well as performing public health outreach activities. She had seen traditional birth attendants and many deliveries and came home passionate about midwifery; in choosing a career, she was now trying to decide between public health, nursing, and medicine. I thought she should aim high. "Why don't you think about med school?" I told her. She said, "Daddy, you don't have to be a doctor to help people!" For that response alone I am as proud of her as if she had won the Nobel Peace Prize.

. . .

I was a stronger candidate in my second race for borough president, in 1981, but Stein won a second term. He ran for Congress on Manhattan's Upper East Side in 1984 but lost to Republican Bill Green, and I think he was sufficiently concerned about my growing electoral power that in 1985 he chose not to attempt a third term but to run instead for City Council president.

The 1985 election was intricate. A group called the Coalition for a Just New York had formed sometime earlier to try to influence the selection of a schools chancellor, and when that effort ended the group had turned its attention to the city government as a whole. I, along with several prominent political leaders, was part of this group. There was an effort, spearheaded by Brooklyn state assemblyman Al Vann, who was chairman of the New York State Black & Puerto Rican Caucus, to build a citywide black-Latino coalition. Vann, a Bedford-Stuyvesant-born African American, was running for Brooklyn borough president; I was running to represent Manhattan; and Jose Serrano, born in Mayaguez, Puerto Rico, was running in the Bronx. Herman Badillo presented himself to the group, trying to win its endorsement for the Democratic nomination for mayor. He was a powerful presence and thought he would be the candidate. If we all won, the thinking went, we could control the city.

Some within the coalition organization thought they had the votes lined up to swing its endorsement to Badillo. A vote got canceled one week. We were a notable group, and the city was waiting for an announcement. At the last minute, Herman D. "Denny" Farrell Jr., an African American state assemblyman and New York Democratic Party county leader, made his move and approached the coalition for its endorsement. We had interviewed and heard from all the candidates; now we met with Denny, after which we were to make our decision.

There were fewer than thirty of us in the room, voting on whom to recommend for mayor. Basil Paterson, State Senator Leon Bogues, and Percy Sutton spoke. Charlie Rangel was present, and although I do not recall his actual words, knowing Charlie, I have to assume he spoke as well. At this particular meeting I didn't say a word; I just sat there and let it unfold as Herman Badillo's 1977 mayoral end run was prominently mentioned. I didn't feel we owed Herman anything, and there were many in the room who were strongly opposed to him.

Denny Farrell was awarded the coalition's endorsement.

Village Voice journalist Jack Newfield, who was very close to Badillo, wanted to be a kingmaker; he wanted to make the mayor, not report the news. Without actually having been in the room, he named Basil, Percy, Charlie, and me the "Gang of Four." His reference was to the Chinese Communist Party officials who came to prominence during the Chinese Cultural Revolution and were warned by Mao Tse-tung: "Do not try to begin a gang of four to accumulate power." Apparently, in this scenario, Jack was playing the part of Mao. We were clearly not plotting revolution, but the moniker stuck.

Unfortunately, the coalition's endorsement did not prove decisive. Ed Koch was reelected. Jose Serrano was narrowly defeated but went on to become a twenty-year congressman from the Bronx. Al Vann continued to represent Brooklyn in the State Assembly into the new millennium and became an active member of the New York City Council. Denny Farrell represented Harlem, Inwood, and Hudson Heights in the State Assembly and became a member of the Democratic National Committee.

In my third race for borough president, I ran against reform candidate Jerrold Nadler. The major issues were homelessness and affordable housing. Education and health care have always been Manhattan constants as well; it's hard to think of a time when those two issues were not vital to the well-being of New York.

Running for office is hard work. It is hard if you win, and it is even more difficult if you do not win. This is an inexact analogy, but if you play poker all night and you lose, you're in bad shape, you feel bone-weary, and you look like crap. If you win, you take a shower and go to work, and even though you're dog-tired you feel terrific. Running for office is grinding, and to survive intact you truly must love people and believe that your quest is of value. I was not looking forward to losing again. Fortunately, having run twice before, I was well known among the voters. I always believed—and it worked for us—that Manhattan was a collection of neighborhoods and that we had to find a way to pull them all together. I cared about all Manhattanites—not just the poor, not just people of color, but everyone from Wall Street to Washington Heights, from Irving Place to Inwood. I had an excellent campaign staff, a lot of really good, smart people, and we ran an intense campaign.

I am a great fan of tennis and I recall the wonderful player Vitas Gerulaitis. After he lost sixteen straight matches to Jimmy Connors, he finally beat him and then told the gathered media, "Let that be a lesson to you all. Nobody beats Vitas Gerulaitis seventeen times in a row!" Well, I defeated Jerry Nadler, and on my third try, in 1985, after ten years as city clerk, I was elected Manhattan borough president.

6

Borough President for Life

I loved the job of Manhattan borough president.

At the suggestion of Basil Paterson and City Councilwoman Ruth Messinger, I contacted Bill Lynch Jr. I had met Bill the previous year when I served as Manhattan coordinator of the Jesse Jackson for President campaign in the New York State Democratic primary and Bill was Jesse's chief of staff. In fact, I had been so impressed with Bill that I had asked him to run my borough president campaign, but he was a Badillo man who had been hurt by the turn of events that denied Herman the coalition's endorsement, and he said no. When I asked him to lead my transition team, however, he agreed.

Bill grew up on Long Island, the son of a potato farmer. He moved to Harlem in the 1960s and was a progressive force, active in the community. He was a highly acute political thinker with an intimate knowledge of the city and how it worked. His priority was always the working people of New York and how best to serve them. He had risen through the ranks and finally landed the job of director of legislation and political action for a small labor union that served day care and social service workers, District Council 1701 of the American Federation of State, County, and Municipal Employees (AFSCME). He had tried like hell to get that job; finally he had it, and he loved it. And now here I was. It had been quickly apparent to me, from his thoughts to his connections to his extremely direct way of putting his ideas across, that Bill was an extraordinary fellow; fortunately, when I asked him to become my chief of staff, he accepted.

Bill went to the president of the union, a little nervous about telling his boss that he was leaving. The man said, "Please go. I want you to go. You can be helpful to us over there!"

Bill came in and took over. He had deep roots in the progressive community, and he called many activists, most of them young and inexperienced in government but all of them extremely smart and committed—I cannot overstate how intelligent and devoted these young men and women were—and convinced them to join our team. We would be a voice for people who were not always at the top of everyone's list. He told them, "We're going to make our mark."

We began laying the groundwork immediately. Some who did not know me might have thought, *Oh, we've got an old-school Harlem politician: he's just going to run a typical borough president's office.* I had no intention of being typical. We brought in serious staff with background and interest in economic development projects and contracts as well as in community board, disability, youth, and land use issues. They were young—most of them were in their late twenties or early thirties—and of all races, colors, and backgrounds. We had Ivy League and City College graduates, street smarts and advanced degrees. Bill organized a retreat at which we all met and began the process of becoming a city-oriented team greater than the sum of its parts. They began as a diverse group of committed individuals; they ended up being my rock.

Maxine Griffith was deputy director of community development and housing policy for city planning when I hired her to be my policy analyst for development. "I was born in New York," she reminds me, "so I was born cynical. But I went in hopeful." She found herself surrounded by peers who also had what she describes as "that combination of cynicism and energy." "Those of us who worked in the agencies," she says, "thought that we were doing God's work. And we saw elected officials as impediments to that. Now, I've got to be frank, because David Dinkins was African American, I thought he was going to be different; I thought he was going to care."

One might wonder why she held those assumptions; clearly no one race has a monopoly on empathy or commitment, and the position had mostly been held by African Americans since 1953 (Andy Stein being the lone exception). Nevertheless, I was aware when I spoke to my new staff for the first time that I was looked upon as someone who had the potential to do good. These were largely outsiders who were being given an outsized opportunity. If they were adept at what they did, if they stood for something, if they had persuasive arguments, they could profoundly shape the borough and the city. They would be able to look out the window and see their impact.

I began by telling everyone assembled that in order for us to truly understand the significance of any issue, it was extremely important that we listen to the people who were immediately affected by it; their perspective on issues would probably be more informed and more passionate than that of others. Rather than governing from above, we would make a concerted effort to meet with constituents and determine their needs in order to satisfy them.

These meetings were organized, but information came to us in many ways. Early in my borough presidency, I invited various people to my office to participate in an advisory committee for our task force on disabilities. As we were riding in the Municipal Building elevator one of the committee members, who was confined to a wheelchair, pointed out that the emergency call buttons were positioned at the top of the floor selection panel. "This is common in most buildings," this committee person said. "The thinking is that if they were on the bottom, children would fool with them and create a nuisance. However, as you can see, someone in a wheelchair simply does not have access to these buttons, which can cause more than a nuisance, it can cause a disaster." We would never have thought of this if we had not been speaking with someone intimately involved with the issue. Curb cuts—the sloped ramps that allow people in wheelchairs to cross the street and glide back onto the sidewalk without having to jump the curb—had been rejected by the city as too expensive, but we found several hundred thousand dollars of discretionary money in the borough president's budget and moved it to the transportation department to install these necessary advances.

The borough president's office in the Municipal Building at 1 Centre Street was a visual stereotype. One walked down a long marble hallway with a series of musty, rickety oak doors on either side holding shatter-proof, dimpled, opaque glass with wire running through it. Exposed wires hung from the ceiling, the lighting from another age altogether. On one end was a bullpen that held almost my entire staff. There were smokers among them, and this was a smoke-filled room morning, noon, and night. Down at the other end of this corridor was an anteroom where my secretary sat, my office behind her. Maxine regularly performed what she called "walkmees," buttonholing me when I left my office as I hurried to a meeting. I would tell her, "Walk with me," and she would endeavor to convince me of the rightness of her proposals by the time the elevator reached the lobby.

Soon, because there was no conference room in which to hold meetings, the space itself was too small, and the place was decaying before our eyes, we were able to obtain funds from the folks who oversaw city government construction to move the borough president's office upstairs to more suitable accommodations on the nineteenth floor. Maxine, who held a degree in architecture, assisted in the design. At one end of the new space was an executive wing, including my office and those of Bill Lynch and Chief Deputy Sally Hernandez-Pinero and their support staff, while the rest of the borough president's staff was situated down a long hallway at the other end. The directors had offices, but everyone else was out in cubicles, not unlike the newsrooms one would see in old black-and-white movies. We encouraged synergies: you could not tell where the policy folks stopped and the communications or community out-reach or development people began. They always tried to work in groups, which I also encouraged.

Not all municipal offices are inspiring, but my young staff was full of energy and tried to be a departure from the norm. We invited community artists to enliven our drab institutional environment by hanging their work there. After examining the budget, we found that, if we shaved costs here and there, we could open up the conference room space to create something of a gallery and brighten our days by having light flooding everywhere. With walls to fill, we arranged exhibitions of New York City children's art and invited an ethnically diverse group of artists to join the process. This was just another way in which we could involve the people of Manhattan in their government.

Among the first items of business was to develop a list of programs we wanted in the city budget. Because most of my people were so young and so serious, so driven by mission, these meetings resembled a fight to the death. Homeless drop-in centers, after-school programs, decreasing class size in the city's school system, AIDS education—all had their champions who would jump up from their chairs and explain passionately why it was vital that funds be allocated to their issue. They wanted to change the world! And for the first time they were in a position to actually get things done. The competition within my new administration was fierce, and it grew even more intense when the time came for action. We were always looking for good ideas. Bill Lynch's management style was to hire good people and tell them, yes, go do it. Until something went wrong, he would leave them alone, and so would I.

.   .   .

The Board of Estimate controlled the allocation of funds for all New York City government projects. It was the body through which elected officials could put their agendas into practice. As is almost always the case in municipal government, funds were short, and during budget negotiations there was considerable jockeying among officials as to whose projects would be approved, and at what price.

As previously noted, the mayor, the City Council president, and the comptroller each had two votes on the board, while the presidents of each of the five boroughs held one apiece, which added up to eleven votes in toto; thus, a coalition of six would carry the day. Mayor Ed Koch more often than not could count on City Council president Andrew Stein, so he had four votes in hand entering most negotiations. He also generally could count on Staten Island, so he had five and was looking for one more. It took me entirely too long to realize that Comptroller Harrison "Jay" Goldin was playing politics from the moment he got up in the morning—shocking—and would never tell anyone how he was going to vote. So the borough presidents would speak earnestly with each other, with lobbyists, with whoever was necessary to bring our items to the fore, when someone would come over, tap us on the shoulder, and say, "It's over, they picked up Queens," and that would be the end of that. When the borough presidents held together, however, we could be formidable.

Board meetings were held in Andy Stein's office. One would think that, given the importance of such deliberations, this would have been a large and well-appointed room. One would be wrong. In both concept and reality, Board of Estimate meetings were held in a classic smoke-filled room. Seven of us were seated around a medium-sized conference table (Mayor Koch did not attend) and presented with the mayor's budget. The message was, "There is only so much that you fellows can contribute to the process." A dollar figure would be announced into which the cost for all the projects had to fit, and an aide to the board would keep a tally with an adding machine. Then each of us would pitch our proposals. The borough president of the Bronx, for example, would outline one of his projects, and we would ask, "Well, what'll that cost?" He would price it out in a grand approximation, and we would discuss the merits. Of course, this was a zero-sum negotiation: if any of us accepted another's proposal, there would be less money available for our own.

My assumption, since this was my first time in this rarefied world, was that a certain amount of horse trading had occurred in the past. The borough presidents arrived with slips of paper on which their plans were outlined, and the presentations themselves were stated and budgeted in broad generalities. I determined that I would not create city policy in this manner. I instructed my staff to research each of our projects intensively and be prepared to present and defend every aspect of them in great detail.

The hallway outside the conference room was almost always nearly empty when we arrived, with perhaps only the borough presidents' chiefs of staff in attendance. At my first meeting I brought perhaps a dozen of my staff. Maxine Griffith says, "We were like rabid dogs that had not been fed!" When it came time for me to present, I would turn to Maxine (policy analyst for development) or Nancy Wackstein (human services) or Barbara Turk (criminal justice) or Amina Abdur-Rahman (education) or Marcia Smith (housing) or Sharon King (health) or any one of my other excellent policy analysts—known around the borough president's office as "the Policy Gals," since each issue area was headed by a woman—and whichever policy analyst I asked to speak would stand and deliver. Other boroughs presented their plans in generalities, but ours were extremely specific. The issue leader would make our case and wait to rebut objections. I was proud and confident that ours was almost always the best proposal, the most advantageous position for the borough and the city, the best way to get things done.

We would also critique what came before us. "With all due respect," I might say, "your program will cost $5,000 a week, and my researchers tell me that it will take at least three months to gear up, in which case we can only allot nine months of funds"; money for a project of our own would thus become available.

The Board of Estimate met approximately every two weeks, and each of the Policy Gals had a portfolio. At an early meeting Maxine had been called upon, had presented successfully and in great depth, and had left the other boroughs in the dust. "Well, damn!" said Brooklyn borough president Howard Golden. "I didn't know you were gonna have thirty-five experts, each outstanding in their field!"

It was quickly apparent that we were annoying the other boroughs with the number of our analysts and the power of their presentations. I would not back off on either quality or quantity, but at Bill Lynch's suggestion, I did ask the Policy Gals to wait outside to be called. We had so many presenters that not all of them could fit comfortably even within the reception area. I would enter the meeting room, and my staff would sit or stand in the corridor, perhaps a dozen strong, waiting to be ushered in. Some remained back at headquarters in my office, waiting for the call. And it would come.

Sometimes it got wild out there in the hall. Carolyn Maloney (later a US congresswoman, then a member of the City Council) followed Bill Lynch into the men's room, where she tried to convince him of the benefits of a micro-loan program, in some cases as little as $500, for small entrepreneurs. My staff called this "Loans for Bodegas." Bill grabbed his sheaf of newspapers and tried to disappear, but Carolyn found a folding chair, set it up beside the door, and continued her presentation. When he came out, he said, "Max, talk to her, talk to her!" Carolyn made an impression: the program got presented to the board.

Nancy Wackstein was an advocate on child care issues when she was contacted to run the human services division of my administration. She was shocked to be offered the job; since human services issues disproportionately affect people of color, she had assumed we would want a person of color. She said, "You want a white Jewish woman for this?" Yes, we wanted her, and she performed extraordinarily well.

Barbara Turk was a generalist, a minister without a portfolio. Having grown up in Cleveland, Ohio, she arrived in the city in 1980 and worked at a health food store on Fifty-Seventh Street between Fifth and Sixth Avenues, then interned at the *Village Voice* for investigative journalists Wayne Barrett, Jack Newfield, and Joe Conason. Having grown interested in the characters on whom they were reporting, she went to work for City Council president Carol Bellamy, a job that she describes as being "like the poor woman's Kennedy School." Through Bellamy, Barbara met Ruth Messinger, who recommended her to Bill Lynch, who brought her to me. Barbara became very involved in the effort to fight AIDS.

Sally Hernandez-Pinero was my chief deputy and did very well. I lost Sally when Ed Koch appointed her finance administrator. For political reasons, I wanted to replace her, if possible, with another Puerto Rican. Dennis DeLeon interviewed and was impressive. He had been pre-screened and was entirely qualified, so I made an immediate decision. I said, "Well, you got it, man!" Dennis stood up to leave, and as he got to the door he turned back and said, "By the way, I'm HIV positive." I told him I was unconcerned. Dennis performed his job excellently and lived a lot longer than many people thought he would.

.　　.　　.

I arrived in the Manhattan borough president's office in 1986, just as AIDS was being recognized as an epidemic and developing into a major public health issue. People believed that AIDS was a gay disease, that Haitians got AIDS, that hemophiliacs got AIDS; these were not facts, but they were widely held perceptions. The notion of risky behavior was not a topic of discussion. The city's HIV prevention planning program, such as it was, consisted of a handful of people who spread the word via neighborhood barber shops and beauty salons. There were a few community-based organizations, each with a budget of no more than $100,000, that reached out to their constituencies: the Gay Men's Health Crisis dealt with gay men; the Minority Task Force on AIDS, which began as a project of the National Council on Churches, was most closely identified with the African American community; the Hispanic Gay Forum had a prevention contract from the city, as did the Haitian Centers Council; an organization called ADAPT worked with intravenous drug users. Mayor Koch had established an Office of Gay and Lesbian Health Concerns, led by Patricia Maher, whose job was to figure out what the lesbian health component was. There was a lack of such leadership, however, in the African American and Latino political communities.

People were dying, among them my good friend Jim Owles, a Manhattan political club leader and a gay white man. I spent a lot of time going to functions, and I met many New Yorkers who informed me of their problems. I met Michael Hirsch, head of the People With AIDS (PWA) Coalition, who was himself infected. I met with Suki Terada Ports of the Minority Task Force on AIDS. This was before officials started being bird-dogged, before regular citizens attending public events would stand up and say, "Look at me, I'm wasting away, what are you going to do for me?" I didn't have to be convinced that AIDS was an issue of great significance.

The African American community was slow to come to grips with what was happening to its people. The association of HIV with homosexuality was unsettling to a large portion of churchgoers. A minister would tell us, "I'm losing all my parishioners, all my congregation, to crack," but there was a will to ignore what was truly going on. I convened the first community conference on HIV and AIDS in northern Manhattan, held at City College, where my friend Richard James was vice chancellor. Boriken Neighborhood Health Center in East Harlem was involved, and folks at the City University of New York helped sponsor it. I spoke about the number of AIDS cases and the impact the disease was having. With people unwilling to face the facts of the disease, they were not acting in their own best interest and AIDS was tearing through the Lower East Side and through Harlem. It was important to me to awaken the communities of color to the danger they were in, as well as to involve women: no one was talking about the effect this disease was having on the entire female population.

I was on the first board of directors of the Black Leadership Commission on AIDS (BLACA). I worked closely with the Health Department to increase funding for AIDS prevention and collaborated with the Koch administration to open the city budget more fully to both individual community organizations and AIDS initiatives.

·   ·   ·

We tried to balance pragmatic politics with doing good things for people. One of our mottos was "Good government is good politics." Certainly there is nothing antithetical about the two ideas, and my staff and I enjoyed navigating the path between them. Some to the right or the left of me may have assumed that I was their guy, but they were often startled by the routes I decided to take.

One of our first priorities was to diversify the membership of the city's community boards. One thinks of New York City as a melting pot, but in fact it is a collection of neighborhoods: Manhattan is made up of Chinatown, Little Italy, Yorkville, the Upper West Side, the Upper East Side, the Theater District, the Lower East Side, Greenwich Village, Harlem, East Harlem, and many others. Community boards held great sway over the look and feel and economy of each neighborhood, influencing decisions regarding zoning matters, the municipal budget, and how the city provided services.

For instance, the placement of homeless shelters, a hugely important issue, was highly influenced by the community boards. Often the focus of problems involving crime, drugs, and civic unrest, shelters were routinely and overwhelmingly located in working-class neighborhoods instead of being distributed evenly throughout the borough, and the community boards played a major role in their placement. NIMBY— "Not In My Back Yard"—was an acronym whose time had come.

One way to address the NIMBY problem was to diversify board membership by enlisting representatives of all parts of each community. Yet access to the city's power structure was not widely distributed among the ethnicities. In fact, we found when we investigated that there was not one person of color on any community board in the entire borough of Manhattan. Not one! Boards were full of white people who had been on them for thirty years, who did not come to meetings, and for whom the position was a sinecure. Community boards had become the place to put local friends of City Council members or the borough president. We set about to change that. In a new application process, candidates had to write an essay and be interviewed. We began to professionalize the process.

We wanted gays on the boards, we wanted Latinos, African Americans, Asians. We developed a formula based on the population of the boards' neighborhoods, and we made it our goal to broaden the representation and therefore increase each community's actual control over itself. Half of the board members were appointed by the borough president and half by the City Council, so we had a lot of sway in determining the boards' makeup. The City Council, for its part, was not averse to our new and invigorated way of doing things.

Having just run a successful political campaign, we were aware of the people on the ground who we thought would make good board candidates, and we contacted them. Many of them either thought that they simply had no chance of success or did not understand the functions of the board. We recruited them, we educated them, and we placed them.

As my policy analyst, Maxine Griffith focused on economic development, which some would say is what New York is really all about. Often real estate developers would approach her with plans for a major project. "Forget that!" the left would tell her. "There are no stoops in that building! Besides, developers are just bad people in general and you've gotta be against that." The fringe on the other side would say, "Development is the engine that makes the city run. You can't have a New York City without us, we're the guys who meet in the basement and figure all the money out. We're the guys!"

Maxine recalls working on the One Worldwide Plaza project, the site of the original Madison Square Garden at Eighth Avenue and Fiftieth Street, with the Zeckendorf development organization. We gathered all the principals—including the local community board and the developers—in one suite of offices and worked hard to insert an affordable housing component into what was intended to be an extensive, mixed-use commercial-residential complex. The New York trend was higher building density, less public space, and more expensive real estate. We tried to be idealistically realistic and to look into urban design environments, not simply building form. We also were looking to craft a balance between the community interest in bringing back more of the green space that was rapidly disappearing from the city, the concern about providing housing that someone other than the very wealthy could afford, and the need for those investing in the growth of Manhattan to derive an acceptable profit.

Maxine spent her time running between these factions. Housing advocates told her, "We gotta have more affordable units." The developer responded, "You're killing me. I can't make any money!" "Well," she said, "we did a pro forma analysis, and of course we didn't have all the figures you have, but the cost of one unit is . . ."—she named a number—". . . and you're doing this many units . . ."—she quoted their figures. Our hallmark was our research; many on our team were only a few years out of Ivy League schools, and they expected high quality from one another. Apparently our work was far more sophisticated than had been encountered previously.

After some cajoling and some serious economic negotiation, the Zeckendorf representative said, "Well, okay, it's a *mitzvah* [Hebrew for a good deed]. We'll do it." They all laughed. Some buildings got lower, some less-expensive units were included, a little more open space was put into the plans, and the developers made money.

·　　·　　·

The Policy Gals talked to each other all the time. Maxine Griffith firmly believed that a city should not embark on development unless there was a concomitant increase in the number of schools and other infrastructure. Since she was not an expert in education policy, she would consult with education policy adviser Amina Abdur-Rahman and say, "We're thinking of putting in five hundred units of affordable housing. Would you just take a look at what the Board of Education has done in that area and what their projections are and tell me if it makes any sense? Should we try to encourage them to generate another school? Do we put money into the study?" She would ask community adviser Diane Morales, "Look, this is what the developer is floating. What's your sense?"

Or, "This guy from the community board is telling me one thing, but I'm getting the feeling that he doesn't really represent the community. Who appointed him? What's his story?" And Diane, whose expertise was in exactly that area, would say, "Oh, forget him! He came out of this club. . . . Let me tell you what happened in 1964. . . . Let me tell you who you've got to talk to. . . ." Their offices were all in one wing of the borough president's office, and there was a lot of staff intermingling.

Deep friendships were formed with staff at other borough presidents' offices. Board of Estimate meetings were long, and public hearings sometimes lasted all day. Many of our people would repair for dinner and other sustenance to TenBrooks, a bar and restaurant across Broadway from City Hall. Senior staffers would come back with dessert to eat at their desks, they celebrated birthdays together, and on holidays folks would bring in pictures of their kids. Bonds developed. Media strategist Laura Hart, director of scheduling Mark Benoit, and deputy chief speechwriter Nick Balamaci were hardworking characters who knew how to get the job done and still have a good time. As a result, it was not uncommon, during recess, for someone from my office to lean over to a staffer from another borough president's office and say, "You want to go over to TenBrooks and work this out?"

.   .   .

I felt that the voices of youth were very important to the city of New York. This was not a widely held position, but that did not deter me. Our Youth Advisory Board consisted of young people ages fourteen to twenty-one. We did not require that they live in Manhattan; board members only had to live, work, or attend school in the borough, and this diversity of experience served to expand our perspective. We recruited junior high, high school, and college-age kids from diverse backgrounds as well—all colors, from public schools and private; some from the inner city, and some from the Upper East Side; some who had been in trouble with the law, and some whose only contact with the police had been asking for directions. Together they engaged in leadership training, learned about the city, and reported back to the borough president's office each month with suggestions as to what would serve the needs of the city's youth. One of the board members and later its chairperson was Elie Tatum, daughter of *Amsterdam News* publisher Bill Tatum. She later succeeded him as publisher of the newspaper.

Herbert Block ran the Youth Advisory Board. I met Herbie—he's a grown man now with a wife and kids, but I still call him Herbie—when he was, as he described himself, "a nerdy twelve-year-old interested in politics." His father was a rabbi of note at the Brotherhood Synagogue in Gramercy Park who was on good terms with many elected officials owing to his work in the community, and he encouraged his son to get involved. Herbie's political awareness began around the time of Watergate and grew during the 1976 presidential campaign. Rabbi Block knew Percy Sutton, and in 1977 Herbie was, as he recalls, "probably the only white kid working on Percy Sutton's mayoral campaign, from a little table in Greenwich Village." He wanted to interview all the mayoral candidates for his elementary school newspaper, but they were difficult to contact, so instead he focused on those running for borough president. We were all speaking at a candidates' forum at Lenox Hill Hospital, and when he buttonholed each of us individually, he says, Andy Stein, Bob Wagner Jr., and Ronny Eldridge "gave me about thirty seconds."

Herbie was a little boy holding a big tape recorder when he approached me. I like kids, and I love to see them interested in politics, so when he began his query, I said, "Let's not stand here in the hallway, let's go sit down in the coffee shop. I'll buy you a soda, and we can talk." We spent about a half-hour together. He was clearly bright, very interested in increasing his knowledge, and quite determined. I gave him my phone number and encouraged him to call anytime. He did, and he also visited me several times in my city clerk's office. What a pleasure to have this little boy show up so full of faith and enthusiasm. By 1981 he was a junior in high school and a full-time paid volunteer in my second borough president's campaign (he insists he received around $25 a week) doing office and field work and outreach to the Jewish community. Herbie was fully involved in my successful 1985 campaign for borough president. And when the Youth Advisory Board came into being, he was the perfect person to place in charge.

The board met in the Municipal Building, which I think gave its members confidence that they actually had a voice in New York City government. I also met with the kids on a regular basis; I found it important not only to give them my time but to hear what they were saying. It is entirely necessary, in all areas, that kids feel that their concerns are being taken into account. In Manhattan I felt the experience would have a great impact on their relationship to the city for the rest of their lives.

Gangs and drugs were a large part of street life in some parts of Manhattan, and the Youth Advisory Board suggested the creation of "Safe Spaces"—designated areas with supervision and nurturing after school and in the evenings where kids could feel protected. Many young people didn't have these advantages in their homes, and the board felt that the city would be well served to give its children a safe haven. Green space—parks for young people—was another of their suggestions. Summer jobs was a primary issue: kids needed some way to earn money other than selling drugs, and rather than hanging on the corner, they needed somewhere to go each day and something worthwhile to do. Community centers, health care, teen pregnancy—there was high enthusiasm for coming to grips with the key issues that affected them and would affect kids coming up behind them.

We formed a youth lobby. Chaperoned by borough president office staff, four or five busloads of kids would journey each year to Albany, where they fanned out in teams and met with the city's representatives in the State Assembly and Senate to discuss issues of importance to their generation. The buses left the city at five in the morning, and by the time they returned at eight o'clock at night these kids were possessed of a new vision of the possibilities of government. More than anything we were engaging young men and women in the process of becoming better citizens of New York. Many of them are still involved in making the city a better place.

.　　.　　.

In 1986 I was approached by the pediatrician and public health activist Irwin Redlener and the singer-songwriter Paul Simon about improving the health of homeless children. They had just visited the Martinique, a notorious Manhattan welfare hotel. We met in my office, and the story they told was tremendously affecting. They spoke about homeless kids, children of homeless families living in city-run shelters or out on the street, some of whom were vision- or hearing-impaired but had never had their eyes examined or their ears tested. You could just picture the little rascals at school, sitting in the front row, wanting to learn but not responding to what was being taught and the teachers thinking they were stupid. They're not stupid, dammit, they can't hear, they can't see!

The borough president's office doesn't have a lot of money to support such projects, but I did allot Redlener and Simon in the neighborhood of $10,000 to pursue their good works. (Later, when Irwin would make his PowerPoint presentation about the New York Children's Health Project, he said, "And this is the list of elected officials who helped us." The screen was blank but for one name: "Manhattan Borough President David Dinkins.")

Karen Redlener, Irwin's wife whom he had met in Arkansas while they were both working as VISTA volunteers, had designed a big van, which I called a Clinic-on-Wheels. The van would park outside city shelters and offer free medical assistance to children who would otherwise receive none. Their program proved remarkably successful. Based on this initial project in New York City, the Redleners and Simon went on to found the Children's Health Fund, which replicated the model in twenty-one cities across the country. They were in New Orleans for many years before Hurricane Katrina, and they responded to that disaster by sending their vans to the Lower Ninth Ward. Since its inception, the program has provided care to over 200,000 medically underserved children in some of the most disadvantaged rural and urban communities in the nation, and I am proud to say not only that I helped them early in their existence but that I am now on the organization's board of directors.

.   .   .

Among the many people in my office on whom I came to rely heavily was my senior special assistant (and for a time, acting chief of staff), Barbara Fife. She was my sounding board who absorbed so much and responded only with the soundest of advice. Barbara had been a member of the Democratic State Committee since 1962, and as chair of the more liberal Democratic reform movement in 1966, she had reached out and made common cause with black leadership because of the many issues the two groups had in common. We found each other at some of the same functions in the peace movement during the 1960s. In 1969, as a party official working for Herman Badillo's mayoral campaign, she led a group of assemblymen and councilmen into my Board of Elections office before primary day to discuss arrangements to ensure that there was no bias at the polls and that the voting would be fair. I looked at her and said, "What are you doing? You come in loaded for bear?" She started to protest. "You don't have to do that," I told her. "It was going to be fair anyway."

I came to know Barbara better in the early 1970s when, as head of the Board of Elections, I certified her election as a delegate to the county judicial convention at which civil court judges were selected. She had received the highest number of votes of any delegate in the city, but for some reason, perhaps because they didn't want her to get a swelled head, the people on her district council—the First District, made up of Manhattan and the Bronx, the largest in the city—had neglected to inform her of this fact. When she presented herself at the convention, I said quite loudly, "Here comes the big vote-getter!" She looked around to see whom I was talking about. "Please, let the big vote-getter through!" Credit where credit is due. I believe she's had a soft spot in her heart for me ever since. She didn't support me the first two times I ran for borough president, but I forgave her.

As borough president, I was the highest-ranking elected African American official in New York City. Though I emphasized that my constituency consisted of every man, woman, and child in Manhattan, almost every time a black person was in the news—whether civic beneficence, criminal act, educational achievement, or social failure, but more often than not some inappropriate behavior—the press would call *me*. It didn't matter where the act occurred—it could have happened in another borough, but I would get the call. My staff would field it, either pass the question directly to me or issue a statement we had crafted (having anticipated that I'd get the call), hang up the phone, and say to one another, "Call the black guy! Why don't you call someone else? Why don't you call *everybody* else?! If something happens to a white guy, why don't you call the white guy?" On the one hand, I suppose it's understandable that a high-profile African American in a powerful public position would be called upon to explain the thinking of his race to those outside it. But often I would say to Barbara, "What am I? I have to be the representative of every African American in this country? Doesn't the press know anyone else to call?"

"No," she would tell me, "they obviously don't." New York at that time was filled with crime, and Barbara felt that if an elected official is constantly associated with inappropriate behavior by people he represents, he or she will sooner or later be called upon by the general population to take the blame for it. "You're going to take the hit for all of that anger," she said. "It's one of those things that happens and that the press fosters by not having a range of spokespeople." It was a problem that continued as my visibility began to rise. Barbara could not have been more prescient: when I became mayor, the situation in Crown Heights certainly brought it up again.

.   .   .

In addition to crime, the most difficult problem facing New York City in the mid-1980s was homelessness. The economy was weak, affordable housing was difficult to come by, the city itself was in financial need, and many individuals and families were finding themselves on the street when they lost a job or their circumstances changed. Revelations of squalid conditions in the city's mental institutions plus a legal ruling concerning the rights of the mentally ill served to empty New York's mental hospitals, and without social services or homes to turn to, those former patients also lived on the streets. In 1979 attorney Robert Hayes brought a class-action suit against the city and state, *Callahan v. Carey,* arguing for a person's state constitutional "right to shelter." Prior to that time, no such right was considered to exist. In August 1981, the city under the Koch administration and the state signed a consent decree agreeing to provide board and shelter to all qualifying homeless men, and by 1983 this right was extended to homeless women. The Coalition for the Homeless and the New York Legal Aid Society continued litigation, and the city was forced to shelter its citizens.

There was no Department of Homeless Services at that time, and no Administration for Children's Services, so the new responsibilities fell to the city's Human Resources Administration, which was overmatched for the task. This was the time when the subways were full of panhandlers, when the waiting rooms and corridors of Grand Central and Penn Station were overflowing with people with nowhere else to go, when at night the steps of churches around Manhattan and the rest of the city were filled with men and sometimes women wrapped in rags and sleeping in cardboard boxes. The Koch administration seemed to be offended by the homeless, whom some people stepped over on their way to work, who were regarded as unsightly, as if they were degenerates undeserving of the city's support, and whose presence on the streets of the city was bad for business.

Any graduate student in social welfare will know the long history, dating from feudal and Elizabethan England, of the conflicting views concerning the deserving and undeserving poor. Mayor Koch had become increasingly shrill and petty the longer he was in office, and the prevailing ideology in his administration was essentially, *These are drug addicts—these are people who have brought their circumstances upon themselves.* His view coincided with that of the Reagan administration, whose Omnibus Budget Reconciliation Act in 1981 repealed certain social benefits and left the responsibility for funding them to states and municipalities. The shelters created by the Koch administration demonstrated this view. Abandoned armories in working-class neighborhoods were pressed into service to create what were known as Tier 1 shelters: in barracks-style mass human warehouses that provided the bare minimum required under law, hundreds of men—unwashed, unstable, uncontrollable—slept side by side on a sea of cots on gym floors. And then Koch would say, in effect, *You can't make these shelters too nice, otherwise people will never leave.*

There was no need to worry about that; the Tier 1 shelters quickly became overcrowded, undersupervised, and quite simply dangerous places. Men feared for their safety and refused to enter even when rounded up off wintry streets by the NYPD. The *New York Times* reported, "When reporters suggested that some homeless people might have reason to fear city shelters, the mayor reacted with outrage, repeatedly shouting, 'baloney, baloney.'" He said that fear was generated by "ideologues." Koch persisted, calling anyone who resisted insane. "We believe that anyone who chooses to be out on the streets in the cold when we offer that person an opportunity to go to a shelter, that person is not competent," he said.

"It is a cruel posturing by the mayor to pretend that homeless people need to be rounded up to come inside," said Robert Hayes, who by this time was working for the Coalition for the Homeless. "The only effective outreach program for New York's homeless is to provide safe and decent shelter."

Richard Emery, a staff lawyer with the New York Civil Liberties Union, said he believed that the mayor was "subverting state law" that set standards for the involuntary treatment of the mentally ill.

Apparently, little thought was given to the placement of families in these shelters. They were originally intended only for single men, but as the housing stock ran out and the tide of homeless did not abate, the city rented apartments in fleabag hotels like the Martinique and the Hotel Carter, most of them in Manhattan's central business district, and began to cram entire families into one room. The Koch administration developed a plan to build twenty shelters, four in each borough, at the cost to the city of approximately $150 million.

Nancy Wackstein had been hired as a child welfare specialist by the advocacy group Citizens' Committee for Children of New York (Eleanor Roosevelt and Dr. Spock were among its founders and early leaders), and when it was reported to her that there were little children running around Herald Square at midnight, she and the organization produced a series of reports on the kids in these hotels. The Hotel Carter, as it happened, was across the street from the *New York Times* building in Times Square, and the *Times* highlighted the problem by covering the issue extensively. The paper's physical proximity didn't hurt; the Martinique and the Hotel Carter became notorious, and the *Times* ran editorial after editorial and moved homelessness to the forefront of New York political conversation.

I didn't have to be convinced that homelessness was an issue. The knowledge that kids were on the streets without schooling or supervision, in rooms that didn't have a refrigerator to hold a quart of milk so they could have cereal in the morning, was sufficient to move me. In fact, the largest segment of the homeless were children, half of whom were under the age of five. I said consistently that we should not blame the poor for their poverty; so many of us have been one paycheck away from being homeless.

For instance, in 1985 a woman known among the homeless in Grand Central Station as "Mama" froze to death on Christmas Eve when she was forcibly removed from the terminal. In response, George McDonald, who had known and fed this woman, founded and incorporated the Doe Fund, an organization whose goal was to "empower homeless men and women to achieve lives of self-sufficiency." You see them around the city these days in blue jumpsuits, the "Ready, Willing, and Able" folks providing civic improvement by picking up garbage. Through McDonald, I met a white, fortysomething man who spent his free time in school studying to become an accountant. He had worked as a bookkeeper, but after his wife took up with another man, the family discord caused him to start to drink; he lost his job, then his apartment, and then he was homeless.

Some of the homeless are mentally ill, and some are alcoholics, but people are homeless for all kinds of reasons, and our response should be to treat them as God's children. We can't just abandon them—they have to live somewhere.

We put together the Task Force for Housing for Homeless Families, chaired by New York City's first African American commissioner of human resources, New York Community Trust vice president James Dumpson; the task force also included New York City Partnership vice president Kathryn Wylde, Community Preservation Corporation president Michael Lappin, and representatives from service providers and mainstream and advocacy groups. It was staffed by my senior policy analysts Nancy Wackstein and Marcia Smith. This profoundly qualified task force was charged with investigating the shelter system and proposing new methods of dealing with a growing challenge.

The contrast between Mayor Koch's approach and mine could not have been more stark. My task force shifted from a view of the poor as undeserving to seeing them all as deserving. Yes, some homeless people had problems with mental illness, drug abuse, and welfare dependency, but they were not in the majority, and focusing primarily on them would prevent us from finding a solution to the city's true problems that contributed to homelessness: poverty, lack of economic opportunity, and a dire scarcity of affordable places to live. Koch planned to spend $150 million to build new shelters. We didn't need to spend $150 million to warehouse folks—we needed to find them apartments from which they could begin to emerge from helplessness. I didn't accuse the Koch administration of insensitivity or lack of caring, but I did accuse them of subscribing to the wrong philosophy. "Unless we do something to change their living conditions soon," I said, "we will have created an entire generation of disaffected and angry young people." Such a lost generation of children would feel they had no stake in society or in themselves.

In a 140-page report issued in March 1987, entitled "A Shelter Is Not a Home" and written by Smith and Wackstein, the task force acknowledged that the city was under court order to provide emergency shelter, but emphasized that no long-term plan was in place to solve the problems that contributed to homelessness, especially for families, the vast majority of whom were black or Hispanic. And it warned that we were seeing only the tip of the iceberg in the shelters: the total number of homeless was far higher than the count cited by city departments, which did not include those families who had doubled up with relatives.

The Koch administration's inattention to the city's poor was clear and made even worse by the growing trend among developers to focus on the construction of luxury apartments. The result was as much as an eighteen-year wait for those eligible for public housing. Our task force did not merely identify the problem but presented viable solutions—pointing, for instance, to nearly 60,000 vacant, city-owned apartments as the most readily available source of low-income housing.

Adequate housing must be accompanied, the report noted, by jobs that enable people to pay their rent. Koch's Transitional Housing Plan would be an enormous waste of city money: each one-room efficiency would cost up to $100,000 to build, and since the shelter units couldn't be converted into permanent apartments for families in the future, the plan would add nothing to the city's existing housing. His plan included 15 family shelters with tiny apartments and shared kitchens; ours included 2,500 more substantial family centers for those awaiting placement in permanent housing. Moreover, Koch's plan proposed that half the new or renovated apartments be allocated to the middle class; ours suggested that the largest share of apartments be designated for the homeless.

To that end, our report called for rehabilitating 8,000 city-owned apartments per year, twice the Koch administration's goal. Community opposition could be mitigated by involving each locale in decisions about the type and scale of the facilities in its area. Tax abatements would be offered to owners of existing low-income housing. Funding would be increased for tenant-organizing and anti-harassment activities. Buildings at risk of deterioration or abandonment would be identified early and targeted for preservation programs so that they did not fall into disrepair. An early warning system to identify families at risk of homelessness would be implemented quickly by the city's Human Resources Administration. Long-term stays of up to two years in transitional housing would be provided to families in need of intensive social services.

Social services to homeless and publicly assisted families would include preventive care, reduction of the ratio of caseworkers to families, child care assistance, life planning and job development, and an effort to reach out to the formerly homeless who had relocated to permanent housing. Administrative barriers would be overcome by including non-profits, encouraging small and minority-owned businesses to participate in building rehabilitation, consolidating city housing programs under one agency, eliminating overlapping agency responsibilities, and developing consistent and standard procedures and documents.

Taken in toto, the Task Force for Housing for Homeless Families plan would enable the city to provide permanent housing for the 4,700 families then housed in hotels and shelters, as well as the additional 7,000 families whom experts were predicting would become homeless each year. Here was a social and economic blueprint that would essentially end the problem of homelessness in New York in five years.

The Koch administration bridled, as we expected it would. Calling our proposal "a massive, open-ended commitment to housing for the homeless"—as if that were a negative commitment to make—Koch's spokesman said, "How would the task force members pay for these tremendously expensive programs? By raising taxes? So which taxes and by how much? By reducing city services? If so, which services?" New York Community Trust vice president James Dumpson responded, "I would hope the mayor would spend more time trying to find solutions, what is useful in the report, rather than rebutting it." As one can see, very little changes over decades in the public discourse.

I can't say that I was particularly cognizant of it at the time—though I can't speak for Bill Lynch—but this difference in our visions of the city put me and Mayor Koch in sharp contrast.

7

The Race for Mayor

Though it wasn't his intention to do so, Jesse Jackson played a significant role in New York City mayoral politics. I was the Manhattan coordinator of Jesse's historic candidacy for the Democratic nomination for president in 1984 and co-chaired his New York State presidential primary campaign in 1988 with labor leader Stanley Hill. Bill Lynch was Jesse's 1988 New York campaign manager, and though Jesse placed second statewide, he won New York City outright. For a black man to win the Democratic presidential primary in New York City was unheard of, and it started Bill, Stanley, and many other people in the progressive and labor communities thinking hard about the electoral possibilities of other African Americans in the city, myself included.

There was a precedent. When Basil Paterson considered running for mayor in 1985 against Ed Koch, he held a fund-raiser, attended and supported by Teddy Kennedy, where he raised more money in one evening than had any African American candidate in New York history. Unfortunately, and unbeknownst to almost everyone in the city, Basil had a heart condition. For that reason, after much soul-searching, he declined to run. He didn't reveal his reasons at the time. Twenty-five years later, he said, "I'm a lawyer. It's the way I make my living. Who's coming to a lawyer who has a heart problem?" He had bypass surgery in 1987. When Basil decided not to pursue the mayoralty, Lynch says, "it was like taking the air out of the balloon of the city." That is when Herman Badillo threw his hat in the ring, the black-Latino split occurred, and all hell broke loose.

In 1988 a group of labor and civic leaders were looking for a way to unseat Ed Koch. Many black leaders had supported him in 1977 over Mario Cuomo, but over the course of his three terms Mayor Koch had devolved. Historically, it has proven difficult for most of New York City's mayors to maintain their popularity through a third term in office. Even the beloved Fiorello LaGuardia was less popular by his third term, but Koch fell a great distance. In Greenwich Village in the 1950s and 1960s, he took on Tammany Hall machine boss Carmine DeSapio and was, in sequence, a very liberal, progressive member of the City Council; a very liberal, progressive member of Congress; and a relatively progressive first-term mayor of New York. He was anti–Vietnam War and pro–civil rights. But things went downhill for Koch after that first term as he supported the death penalty, presided over a wave of corruption scandals within his administration, hectored the poor, and exacerbated racial tensions. By the end of his third term, Mayor Koch's abrasive style and increasingly conservative crankiness had alienated large segments of the population of all races, creeds and colors. An NBC primary-day exit poll showed that 62 percent of city voters did not want him to run again. Mayor Koch was vulnerable.

In 1984 Jesse Jackson used the phrase "Hymietown" to describe New York City to a *Washington Post* reporter. When it turned into a great embarrassment and a major political issue, Jesse apologized and sought forgiveness before national Jewish leaders at a Manchester, New Hampshire, synagogue. But antipathy against Jesse remained. Four years later, Koch, who was vocal in supporting Tennessee senator Al Gore for the Democratic presidential nomination, tried to dredge up the issue and only a few weeks before the New York primary told Jews and supporters of Israel that "they got to be crazy" to vote for Jesse.

This appeared to have been a calculated political gesture by Koch, but instead of having their desired effect, his words demonstrated a miscalculation of considerable magnitude. Headlines ran playing up the controversy, and Bill Lynch seized on it, parading before the media one local Jackson supporter after another. "I'm Jewish. I'm for Israel. I'm for Jesse. And I'm not crazy," said Brooklyn state senator Marty Markowitz. Koch's own character was called into question. Barry Feinstein, president of Local 237 of the International Brotherhood of Teamsters, endorsed Jesse and said, "The mayor's rhetoric is inappropriate. It is divisive. It is wrong. The issue is not whether Ed Koch speaks for the Jews of this city. He does not." Charlie Rangel said, "How dare this man declare himself king of the Jews."

Gore distanced himself from the mayor, but it was too late. Jesse won 64 percent of the city vote and over 90 percent of the black vote statewide, while Gore did poorly and dropped out of the race soon thereafter. "While he was making hysteria, I was making history," Jackson said of the mayor.

A coalition of New Yorkers asked Basil Paterson to run, but he told them, "When they went in and did my heart, they took the political bug out. I'm not your guy." He suggested me. Without my knowledge, Lynch commissioned pollster Bill Johnson after Jesse's primary campaign to see whether there was a popular will to defeat Koch, and who could capitalize on that desire. This will did exist, the poll showed, and my name was on the list of those who could possibly perform the task at hand. Lynch and Johnson came to my house on Riverside Drive with the news. My wife Joyce was there, listening on the periphery but intimately involved and understanding, a presence. Bill said, "We've looked at the numbers. This is doable. We could go for a big piece of pie here!"

I was taken completely by surprise. I just didn't believe them. "Baloney. Get outta here. You guys cooked these books."

They showed me every angle. The voting population had shifted greatly in the past decade, they said. Jesse's run had brought in a large bloc of first-time voters, mostly Latinos and people of color, who had never participated in previous elections. Many others who were registered Democrats but had historically felt left out of the electoral process, their numbers showed, were now thinking about participating. "We've got a serious base to run off of," Bill told me. I had performed admirably, they added, as Manhattan borough president and could present a long and commendable list of achievements to the voting public. There was every good reason, they insisted, that I could and should be mayor. "We think you can do better than Jesse!"

I was still not convinced.

First, I was perfectly happy being borough president. The office was truly the goose that laid the golden egg for New York City, and in turn for the state. I was in the enviable position of being able to get things done, to advocate for change and see that advocacy through to fruition. I was following in some pretty big footsteps; from Percy Sutton to Constance Baker Motley, my predecessors were great people.

Then there was the possibility of failure. I had been so very close to a significant New York milestone when I was a day away from being named deputy mayor, and the fall had been personally punishing. I had gone from sugar to shit overnight, and it had taken me more than ten years to regain a place of respect in the city's hierarchy and in the public eye, but now I was back. I had run three times for borough president before winning, and from where I stood things were pretty sweet. I was happy with my position and had no desire to jeopardize it. I told the two Bills that I was not very interested.

Bill Lynch disregarded my response entirely. He had been involved in the 1981 mayoral campaign of Frank Barbaro, around whom a coalition of progressives and labor leaders had rallied, and he contacted them. Bill had seen the recent transformative elections of Harold Washington in Chicago, Wilson Goode in Philadelphia, Harvey Gantt in Charlotte, Kurt Schmoke in Baltimore—all Democrats and each the first African American mayor in his city—and he was convinced that New York could be on the cusp of making history as well. He showed his figures to Barry Feinstein of the Teamsters, Stanley Hill of the American Federation of

State, County, and Municipal Employees (AFSCME) District Council 37, Sandra Feldman of the United Federation of Teachers, Jay Mazur of the Union of Needletrades, Industrial, and Textile Employees (UNITE), and Jan Pierce of the Communications Workers of America (CWA), each of whom felt that they had not been treated well by Koch. They were all hopeful for a change in vision in city leadership and were convinced by what Bill showed them. I received phone calls from each saying, "Dave, we oughta do this."

Lynch performed subway diplomacy, traveling to Brooklyn to meet with people like US congressmen Major Owens and Ed Towns and state assemblyman Al Vann and showing them that if they could deliver the same vote in their borough that had come out for Jesse, "we had a real shot." His selling point was very direct. He told them, "We can win this!"

I wish I could say that when I was young I thought, *Gee, one day I'll be mayor of New York,* but unlike some, I was not born with that desire. Nor, truth be told, was I the absolutely perfect candidate. Lynch was selling this time in New York history as the moment when a black-Latino-labor coalition could win and take control; while labor had some experience with me, some in the Latino community resisted because of old grievances dating back to the Badillo campaign. Some objected to me personally, and others had no desire to cooperate with the black community that they felt had betrayed them. Latino elected officials were hedging their bets and looking elsewhere. Should they align themselves with Koch and attempt to negotiate with him for their support? Should they try to maximize their opportunity to build a white-Latino coalition and leave us out by throwing their numbers to Comptroller Jay Goldin or banker and former head of the Metropolitan Transit Authority Richard Ravitch?

Bill Lynch is a powerfully adept political strategist and thinker. He was convinced that I could win. To that end, he gathered the people to whom I had always turned—and would always turn—to seek political advice: Percy Sutton, Charlie Rangel, and Basil Paterson. Bill painted the picture for them. These men all had difficult histories with the city's establishment power structure, and they all grasped what was at stake. After I had received the telephone tree of labor encouragement, Percy, Charlie, and Basil got me in a room and voiced their support. They told me outright, "Dave, you've *got* to do this." I informed them that I was far from uninterested; I was concerned, however, that, if I lost, I would have given up a job of great importance and personal pleasure and that, having not practiced law for ten years, I would have no immediate way to make a living. Percy Sutton, who had become a wealthy man through his investments in media and real estate, assured me there was a job for me at his radio station WLIB in that eventuality. Percy also brought Jesse Jackson into the conversation, and Jesse gave me his personal encouragement to run. This Gang of Four had spoken. Bill Lynch arranged informal meetings with Basil, Charlie, and some others. Harry Belafonte insisted that I had to run. A plan began to take shape.

.   .   .

The futility of my candidacy was so taken for granted that in late 1988 an influential supporter of the Republican candidate, US Attorney Rudolph Giuliani, contacted Bill Lynch and asked him if, when Koch won the Democratic primary, he would come work for them. To win the top place on the Democratic ticket a candidate either needed to win more than 40 percent of the primary vote or, failing that, had to prevail in a runoff between the top two vote-getters. The Republicans assumed that, either directly or in a runoff, Koch or another Caucasian would win. A runoff would follow in which the Jewish community would unite behind whichever of the other candidates, each of whom was Jewish, opposed me, and the African American community would be so infuriated that it would be easy pickings for Giuliani. The Giuliani supporter assumed that Bill would want to be connected to a winner. They met twice at the World Trade Center. "Well, what do you think is gonna happen here?" Bill was asked. "We're thinking about running," he answered. The guy just shook his head.

It takes a sizable amount of money to run for elected office in New

York, and I certainly was not in possession of such wealth. My campaigns had been run on limited budgets that were nothing like what we would need to win the mayoralty. Bill organized a fund-raiser at Central Park's iconic Tavern on the Green, ostensibly for my next campaign for borough president but usable, if I so desired, for whichever race I decided to enter. When he totaled up the dollars, he came to me and told me the final tally was $1 million, a huge amount at the time. "Dave," he said, "we gotta do this!"

I listened.

Not everyone was in favor of my joining the race. Barbara Fife participated in a budget meeting with Koch's people at City Hall, where the accumulated wisdom was that, because of an economic downturn, city revenues were sliding substantially, tax revenues would decrease, and there would be fewer dollars available for social services and civil service—all the expenditures that kept New York going. We talked regularly in our offices, and she knew I was considering the race. One day she came in and said, "Dave, I think it is a bad time to run for mayor. The revenue picture is awful, and looking forward two, three years, it is getting worse. It is really bad. If you get elected, you are not going to have any funds to make changes and do the things you want. Half of the city will say, 'Ah, we got a black mayor and everything went down the tubes,' and the other half is going to be angry because they're not getting their need for resources addressed because you won't have the resources!"

Her reasons were sound, but I told her, "I see it differently than you."

"How?"

"If there is going to be such a reduction in resources, that's just where someone like me is needed—to direct them to the places where the need is greatest."

"You're not going to be able to deal with low-birth-weight babies and all your big issues here," she said.

"I don't agree with you."

When pressed, it became clear to me. I was running.

. . .

Ed Koch was the big bird we had to bring down in the Democratic primary. He had an outsized personality and after twelve years in office could crow about many achievements. He was the mayor who pulled the city out of a fiscal crisis, who stood up to the transit workers, and rallied New Yorkers over the Brooklyn Bridge in the midst of a transit strike, the one who signed a gay-and-lesbian rights bill. Koch had a substantial list of accomplishments and a national reputation. He strode around the city asking "How'm I doing?" and for a long time people told him he was doing very well.

However, this time his sheen was fading. There were deep problems with the disparity in hospital services in certain of the city's communities, including Harlem, and a sense that under Koch, and with his approval, there was a two-tiered administration of social services, one for the affluent, another for the working class. His rhetoric had turned sour and his persona more caustic; from a distance he looked like the same electoral juggernaut, but the nation did not realize how polarizing Ed Koch had become within his own city. His hammering Jesse on "Hymietown" had proved that he was heading in the wrong direction. Still, he had been mayor for twelve years—he was a New York fixture. Jay Goldin and Richard Ravitch, both of whom also joined the race, were in our sights, but Mayor Koch was the big prey.

The first thing I needed was a campaign manager. New York political campaigns are intricate affairs played by arcane rules, and it is important that the person in charge know all the angles. Each of the labor leaders was telling me, "You've gotta have somebody who's done this before." Since no black man or woman had ever managed a New York mayoralty campaign, that translated to me to mean, "You've gotta have somebody white." I insisted on Bill Lynch. He was an operator, a mechanic, he had functioned admirably as my chief of staff, he was very good at what he did . . . and he *cared*. There's a world of difference. There really was never any question.

Bill Lynch is as conversational a man as one will encounter. He carries his wealth of political, economic, strategic, and tactical wisdom with casual ease. He is experienced and intimately knowledgeable in the ways of New York City and has a unique ability to encourage the best in the people with whom he works while at the same time accepting no less. If I wanted to know how to get from one place to another—politically, intellectually— he was the man I would call. I consulted with him constantly and then left him alone to tend to the multitude of details necessary to run a citywide campaign. His management style was one that more managers should emulate: he found talented people, allowed them to pursue the issues about which they were passionate, and paid attention to the results. If a staff member was not a self-starter, he or she was unlikely to succeed under Bill, but once the way was found, he thoroughly empowered his people. His sartorial style featured disheveled clothing, untucked shirts, and a complete disregard for the way he looked. A burly man, he always held a sheaf of papers, often grasping them in great bunches to keep from dropping them in his wake. His speaking voice lay somewhere south of a growl. My chief of staff Ken Sunshine named him "the rumpled genius."

As Goldin and Ravitch were also in the running, I was up against formidable candidates with strong résumés and access to funds. But their campaigns focused more on Koch at the outset, and as a result, there was no strong opposition to my candidacy; few in the city's political corridors or the media took us very seriously. Even in the black community, as Lynch says, "people thought this was poppycock. 'He barely became borough president, how the hell is he thinking of running for mayor?'"

A man who was very instrumental in gathering our forces was Dennis Rivera, who had been recently elected president of Local 1199 of the Drug, Hospital, and Health Care Employees Union. Eleven-Ninety-Nine had a long history of supporting progressive causes. Dr. Martin Luther King Jr. called it "my favorite union," and it often organized with the energy of a popular movement. The union's grassroots leadership was not initially supportive of my candidacy; the people on the ground were not convinced I was sufficiently radical, progressive, or electable to lead their cause. Lynch, however, knew many of the activists personally; they had participated in the same demonstrations and walked the same picket lines, and he was trusted. In addition, Basil Paterson was 1199's lawyer.

In a true stroke of genius, Bill rented offices from 1199 and ran our campaign from there. I was in my borough president's office most days, doing my job, but the campaign had complete access to 1199. Bill could use their resources, rent their space, and print our material at rock-bottom prices. Eleven-Ninety-Nine not only provided us with matériel but delivered the troops—100,000 members, most of whom were poor black and Hispanic women. We had instant volunteers giving us any kind of help they could provide. Our enthusiasm was their enthusiasm. Bill energized the workers, and they spread the word in their communities. They leafleted, they spoke with their neighbors, they made their presence and mine known. Clearly there could and would be no direct quid pro quo arrangement, but Dennis Rivera was not unaware that if 1199 helped elect me as mayor, he could stand early in the line and say, "We made this happen!"

Just one among the scores of dedicated campaigners was our Bronx director and 1199 organizer Neva Shillingford. She was a single mother with two young children who seemed to eat, sleep, and drink the job. Neva was always at the helm, at her desk, putting up charts, running around the city, rallying troops, all the while spearheading a community campaign to rid her public housing development of drug dealers. The city was in the middle of a crack epidemic, teenagers were being killed in drive-by shootings, and Neva was being physically threatened and her automobile vandalized for her antidrug efforts. People were banging on her door at all hours, gunshots came through her window, drug dealers shot bullets into her apartment while her daughters were home, and still she arrived every morning and moved the campaign forward. This is the level of devotion our campaign received. The culture of New York political campaigns centers on visibility, and the organizing energy of 1199 helped ignite support for me in the rest of the city. And not incidentally, the union was used to monitoring its organizers, which brought a certain accountability and professionalism that other New York campaigns often lacked. As the Latino community began to move toward my candidacy, its elected officials could not help but take notice. They came "kicking and screaming," as Lynch says, yet slowly but surely they arrived.

As word spread that I was the "labor candidate," AFSCME, the CWA, the Teamsters, and the Service Employees International Union (SEIU) all supported me. Victor Gotbaum, who had only recently finished his twenty-two-year run as president of AFSCME District Council 37, was strongly supportive. Interestingly, because each of these unions had consistent and ongoing dealings with many industries, the union leaders whom Bill Lynch visited would often strongly suggest potential funders within the business community. Lynch found it stunning that labor leaders, who bargained hard and long to wring favorable contracts from management, could pick up the phone and get highly placed officers of Goldman Sachs on the line. One does not normally think of unions and investment firms being economic bedfellows. Union officials had significant relationships with the builders in town, as well as the developers, and these leads bore fruit. But just as often the labor connections reassured the business community, many of whom had not had significant ongoing contact with me, that I was not a wild-eyed, anticapitalist radical, that indeed I was aware of their interests and was not hostile to them. They too, we found, were tired of Koch.

Because of our strong union support, Lynch believed we were the only campaign in the primary with the capacity to turn out a huge vote; we needed not only a large percentage of African Americans, however, but a huge turnout all over the city. We established a "get out the vote" operation using political clubs and social organizations. We knew there were fifty thousand voters in Harlem, and we set out to win every one of them. We had an open-door policy: whomever we knew we brought into the campaign. If you want to campaign for us, we said, come on in!

Among the most efficacious endorsements we were hoping to receive was from Gus Bevona and Local 32BJ of the SEIU. Representing the doormen and maintenance people in the city's large apartment buildings,

the SEIU had been very successful, helping to make New York City janitors, handymen, and elevator operators the highest paid in the nation.
It was lost on no one that because they were inside so many buildings
they also had the capacity, if a candidate wanted flyers distributed, to use
their positions to reach a large portion of the voting public by morning.
Bevona was something of a recluse, and for a long time Bill was unable
to reach him. Finally, he was granted an audience. Bill rode a back elevator to a thirty-second-floor office and was surprised to find a big
spread of food awaiting him and waiters standing by to serve him. As
sophisticated a political operative as he was, Bill was quite astonished to
find such opulence in a labor leader's office. Bevona's extravagance and
extraordinary personal compensation would eventually catch up to him
when in 1999 the parent union forced him to resign. But I needed all the
help I could get: Local 32BJ endorsed us at that meeting.

Bill would visit the unions, listen to their suggestions, and then issue
marching orders—"I need money, I need troops"—and the organizations
would deliver. They did not ask for specific policies in return; they were
aware that we had a sympathetic outlook, and we found that their over-
arching goal was to end the tenure of Ed Koch.

· · ·

I also had to secure the black community, since none of the members
of the black-Latino-labor constituency could or should be taken for
granted. One reluctant convert was a young man named Patrick Gaspard.
The twenty-two-year-old New Yorker was, as he describes himself, "a
politics junkie." He had served as an advance man for Jesse Jackson's 1988
presidential primary campaign in Oregon and was with Jesse when the
campaign came to New York. Patrick grew up in a household where Malcolm X's picture was on the wall, not Dr. King's, and he wasn't altogether
certain I was the man for the job. The first time Patrick encountered me
was at a James Brown show at the Apollo Theater. He had been too young
to go by himself, so his older brother took him. "I was a huge James

Brown fan," Patrick recalls. "I loved him. I go to this show, and this funny-looking guy takes the stage and starts reading a proclamation."

Whereas: The King of Soul, James Brown, has left an indelible mark on the annals of contemporary music history, continuously refining and developing his compelling performances over the course of decades of stardom; and . . .

"I thought those proclamations were only issued in black-and-white movies!"

Whereas: Hits such as "I Feel Good," "Living in America," and "Say It Loud I'm Black and I'm Proud" continue to bring listening pleasure to loyal fans throughout this nation; and . . .

"Ad nauseam with these wherebys and whereases . . ."

Whereas: James Brown's dedication to musical excellence is matched only by his social activism and concern for those in need, whether unemployed workers or young people on the brink of adulthood; . . .

"Dude, we all came to hear James Brown!"

Now therefore, I, David N. Dinkins, President of the Borough of Manhattan, in honor of his enormous contributions to the world of music and entertainment, do hereby proclaim Saturday, October 17, 1987, in the Borough of Manhattan, as "James Brown Day." In witness whereof I have hereunto set my hand and caused the seal of the Borough of Manhattan to be affixed.

Patrick may not recall this scene entirely correctly. I am a politician, and I learned long ago that you do not go to the Golden Gloves under any circumstances because, I don't care who you are, the crowd will boo you mercilessly. Likewise, you don't go to the Apollo Theater and read a lot of "whereby whereas" mumbo jumbo. I'm sure I was wise enough to read only the concluding clause. Maybe that's what Patrick remembers. Nevertheless, he had all but dismissed me as a potential leader of the black community because of the way I spoke. "This guy was weird and quirky, and even when he wasn't reading from the proclamation, he spoke in that same sort of tone. This guy ain't going nowhere."

I realize that it is often expected, even by members of their own community, that African American public speakers will declaim with a gospel cadence. Jesse Jackson uses this cadence to perfection. He will introduce the phrase "a rising tide lifts all boats," for instance, offer an example, and then refer to it simply as "rising tide." Three repetitions, and it becomes a remarkable and effective song. He will talk about how hardworking people have to get up before dawn to catch the early bus, and then he'll come back to the concept needing only to refer to it as "early bus." People know what he means. I admire the ability to move a crowd with a gospel cadence, and there are many people who deliver great speeches using this technique. Barack Obama delivers a great speech, and so does Bill Clinton; each brought his career to the forefront by speaking eloquently at the Democratic convention. But I don't want to sound like Jesse, and I don't want to sound like Charlie Rangel or Obama or Clinton. I'm not criticizing them, I'm not saying they're not effective or good at what they do. I have a different style, a different language. I grew up listening to Winston Churchill, Franklin D. Roosevelt, Douglas MacArthur. These were the speakers whom I admired. It matters to me that my grammar be correct. The first time I heard Harry Truman speak I blanched!

I am aware that in large parts of the African American community the use of proper diction and elocution is derided as "speaking white" and somehow defines those who use the language with such precision as lacking in cultural pride, if not worse. I find this unfortunate. I am not a supporter of "Ebonics." I was raised in an age when language distinguished a person who was going places from one who wasn't. Integration was a goal, not a certainty, and all variety of excuses were used to deny rights and privileges to people of color who deserved them; language and appearance were high up on the list of disqualifiers. Keeping in mind the education I was given by my English teacher, Alice Jackson Houston, I was determined never to be thus disqualified. I want to be heard as a man, not as a black man.

There was a question as to whether the African American community would support me fully. There is a wariness, after generations of disappointment, that imbues the possibility of great triumph with the fear of great failure; it appears just as success seems right over the horizon. My candidacy occasioned some of that wariness. Who could believe New York would elect a black mayor? I started to make the rounds, to talk to groups of people who might have been experiencing some hesitation. Some thought the system was rigged against them, and some thought that even to consider participating in an election was an exercise in futility. This is the story I told them:

When I was first married, my bride and I were very poor. I was going to law school full-time during the day and had a job at a liquor store in Harlem at night. I would get off work at midnight, drive home, get into bed, rise early the next morning, get on the subway, carry my heavy books all the way to Brooklyn, sit in class all day, ride the subway back to Manhattan, have dinner, drive to work, and prepare to start all over again. When I came home, my wife would tell me about the bills that had arrived in the daily mail and the debts that were piling up and which creditor had sent a second notice and who had called demanding payment. She asked me, "What shall I tell them?"

"Honey," I'd say, "I'm really tired."

"Well, I have to tell them something."

"Okay then." And I devised this plan. "You tell them I'm gonna take all the bills at the first of the month, and I'm gonna put them in a hat. Then I'm gonna draw out three bills from this hat, and I'm gonna pay those three. Now tell them, if they keep annoying me, *they won't get in the hat!*"

That's why it's important to register to vote, I told these folks, because if you're not registered then you can't vote. And if you can't vote, *you are not in the hat!*

It was only when we raised enough money to purchase television advertising time, when my face and ideas began to be viewed with regularity by people in their homes and neighborhood places of business, that the community began to throw off the wariness and embrace my candidacy. When people saw that this was for real, that there was a true possibility that this milestone might occur, they came together with great strength and solidarity. The election would focus on ideas and programs, but it would depend for its life on getting people excited about the possibility of change and getting those excited people to the polls. The black-Latino-labor coalition began to coalesce.

Patrick Gaspard was brought into the borough president's office as an intern by Lynch, was promoted to a staff position, and eventually came to work on my campaign, though, as he tells it, "David Dinkins wasn't exactly, in my mind, a great leap forward." Patrick had the ability to be an effective leader among his peers, but he was extremely shy. He was functioning one morning as my advance man for an event to be held at the beautiful Cathedral of St. John the Divine near Columbia University, and despite his experience with Jesse, he appeared awkward and perhaps a little overwhelmed in the company of a man running for mayor. I saw promise in the young man and began to talk to him about appearances, about how when I was his age and preparing to appear in public, whether to call on an insurance client, or speak before the assembly of my school, or address a jury in court, I would always check that my fingernails were clean and my hair was tidy; I told him that I found such small details important in presenting the proper appearance, and that I still maintained that habit. I was speaking to Patrick about grooming, but he understood the underlying lesson about making one's ideas acceptable by presenting one's self as acceptable. (My father had taught me this lesson in deed. A working man, Pop had founded and been president of the Tuxedo Club of Trenton.) Patrick recalls the conversation. I take pride in, but no credit for, his ascension to the Obama White House and the position of executive director of the Democratic National Committee.

·   ·   ·   ·

As the primary unfolded, my fellow candidates were relatively gentle on the issue of race, on the assumption that I was not likely to succeed and attacking me might alienate the black voters whom they would need if they were to win the nomination. As Bill Lynch said, "We didn't get a lot of incoming fire from them."

But New York was not a black-majority city, and I could not get elected mayor in 1989 simply by being the black candidate. Just as I had not accepted the role of Deputy Mayor for Black People, I was running to represent the interests of all New Yorkers. Fund-raisers were organized in all parts of the city by people of all walks and colors: businesspeople held cocktail parties in the penthouses, while less affluent folks held house parties in the projects. Bill Lynch got more free television time than we could have paid for when local and national news networks began covering these house parties as signifiers of a growing movement. The liberal constituency, which had been Koch's for many years, started to look my way. Progressives began to believe they might have someone in the mayor's office to whom they could relate.

What was I running on? I addressed a fund-raiser in June and told them, "First of all, thank you for sharing my determination to take New York City back from the fixers and the corrupters, from the pushers and the muggers—and most of all, from the indifference and the cynicism that have sold out the ideals and the soul of this city. With your help, I intend to be a mayor who appeals to what is best in our people, not one who exploits divisions and apprehensions for a momentary political advantage.

"With your help, I intend to be a mayor who stands for the rule of law—from the offices of City Hall to the streets of every neighborhood and the jogging paths of every park.

"With your help, I intend to be a mayor who says that this city is *not for sale*—and who knows that a mayor has a higher duty than pleading that he didn't happen to notice the dirty dealing all around him.

"With your help, I intend to be a mayor who pursues basic principles of justice, opportunity, and caring—a mayor who attacks the problems and not the victims."

There were many issues in this election, many separate concerns, but through all of them ran a common thread. My campaign—our cause—was about change. Not for its own sake, not simply as a matter of reaction or dissatisfaction, but change for a purpose, change nourished and guided by the fundamental democratic values, the progressive values that are the best heritage and hope of New York City.

"We cannot be content with a mayor who has forgotten those values," I said, "or with a candidate who doesn't share them. I believe that the next mayor has to be committed both to integrity *and* to social justice."

My platform centered on the following issues: crime, with an emphasis on community policing and an increase in the size of the NYPD; antidrug efforts, including a comprehensive program that would advocate the testing of criminals on probation or parole, the creation of drug-free school zones, drug education in every school in every grade, stronger forfeiture laws to take the profits out of the trade, and an update of the "Bawdy House" laws to enable community groups to shut down crack houses; affordable housing; economic development; the environment; infrastructure; cessation of government corruption; and care for the young.

"I've actually been criticized for having the support of the trade union movement," I said. "I welcome that criticism because I welcome that support. I'm proud to have their backing, for they are all of us. They're neighbors, customers, friends. They send their kids to public schools. They are the people we see on the subway every day." On a national level I supported a woman's right to choose. On the most local of levels, I told the people who had gathered, "if everyone says, 'I don't give a damn,' then we are all damned."

I unveiled my "Marshall Plan" for education. New York City's schools were failing their students. In the twelve years since that year's high school graduating class entered first grade—the same twelve years Ed Koch had been in office—more than one out of three students had failed to graduate, including over 50 percent of African Americans and 60 percent of Latinos. What would happen to these children in a city where 90 percent of all new jobs demanded at least a high school education? We were leaving them without prospects, and sooner rather than later this absence of opportunity would cripple New York's economic and social institutions. There were some who were awfully loud in denouncing the failings of the school system, but silent when it came time to actually do something about it. Others turned to gimmicks such as tuition tax credits, which would misuse public money to finance private schools and would be the death knell of public education. "The day this city gives up on public education," I said, "is the day that it loses its future and its soul."

First, we would set up School Improvement Action Teams to intervene in crisis schools. If we could send law enforcement teams into drug-infested neighborhoods, why not deploy educational "SWAT teams" to take hold of failing schools and turn them around?

Second, we would redesign the worst-performing elementary and middle schools in each borough into year-round Community Schools, bringing teachers, students, parents, and the local business community together in a moral covenant for neighborhoods in need. These schools would become centers for adults as well as the young, for senior citizens seeking companionship, for local organizations working to improve community safety, for pregnant women in need of prenatal care. The more people we involved, the greater the stake everyone would have in the state of our schools. The more public they were, the better our public schools would be.

Third, we would help our teachers and treat teaching as a profession, not just a job. We would eliminate clerical and lunchroom duties and allow teachers time to think and plan and share ideas with one another, and we would increase their expertise by obligating them to keep their own education up to date.

We would make schools drug-free zones and form an alliance with police and community leaders to draw a line at the door. "What happens in the classroom between teacher and student is sacred," I said. "The classroom must be a sanctuary from the problems of the outside world."

How to pay for this? It cost the city approximately $4,500 a year to educate each student. It cost $80,000 a year for each juvenile offender to serve time in a secure facility. And when students failed or left school, the city lost millions in potential productivity and talent. I noted another element that is often overlooked when estimating the cost of social policy: if we widened our scope and made more than a purely economic valuation of our young, we would see that by shortchanging our children's education we were facing a devastating human and moral cost in dispirited lives and destroyed dreams over the course of a lifetime.

I find it significant that these battles are still being fought today.

. . .

Every poll and every reporter verified that the largest issue I faced was the question of whether I was soft on crime, soft on criminals, and particularly whether I was soft on black criminals. Every community in every part of the city struggled with its own crime and drug problems. However, just because crime was the biggest issue did not mean we had to try to win the election on that issue alone. I would never be perceived as a super-crime-fighter like Rudolph Giuliani, nor as the embodiment of the people's outrage over the most heinous violent crimes like Ed Koch. Our goal was to be perceived by all as having an "acceptable" rating on crime and antidrug initiatives, after which I could emphasize that my standing on other issues—city services, integrity in government, moral leadership—was clearly superior. I needed to be perceived as credibly concerned, sensible, and tough on crime and drugs by those voters who saw those as the major campaign issues.

The problem was that I had quite a distance to go before this was the case. I had never been associated in the public's mind with those issues,

I had not yet addressed them in the campaign, and my personal style of building consensus contrasted sharply with the aggressively visceral style that New Yorkers had come to expect in tough-on-crime politicians. Furthermore, because of the racial dynamics of the city, I had a special burden to meet in the white community. Our focus groups showed quite clearly that many people associated crime with young black men wearing sneakers, and we had to recognize that some would be wary of me because of those fears.

Nevertheless, we had three very distinct advantages over Ed Koch on the issues of crime and drugs:

First, Ed Koch had been mayor for twelve years, and he could not credibly advocate any new solutions to the crime problem—including the death penalty, which he was touting loudly—without facing the question of why he had failed to do anything about it during his three administrations, when he had had every opportunity.

Second, Koch was viewed by many in New York as increasingly isolated during his years as mayor; he no longer dealt with the concerns about crime that real people faced every day. In contrast, I lived with my family in the community and could speak credibly about understanding firsthand the true impact of the fear of crime. He could not get away with participating in a tenants' anticrime organization, but I could put on a windbreaker, carry a walkie-talkie, and take a turn on a community crime watch patrol.

And third, since Koch had spent the previous twelve years appealing to people's fears instead of their hopes, he could not speak of restoring respect for the law and other positive values that our studies showed people believed had been lost. In contrast to Koch's embittered denunciations of crime, I offered a more optimistic, inclusive leadership that advocated respect and discipline. I was determined to return to fundamental values, and I referred to the multitude of scandals on his watch when I endeavored to include in each speech an appeal to respect the law "from the highest offices in City Hall to every street and park in this city."

To raise my standing on the crime and drug issues I had to discuss them at every opportunity, be aggressive in proposing legitimate solutions, and make people understand that I was ready to do *anything that worked* to combat the problem. Under the leadership of Bill Lynch, policy analyst for criminal affairs Barbara Turk, and director and deputy campaign manager John Siegal, we developed a twenty-point plan that would improve the quality of New York City life considerably; to this day I think this plan would serve any modern mayor. It included doubling the number of community patrol cops on the street; administering more meaningful punishment for first-time offenders; providing funding for the court system; putting a cop on every subway train at night; providing drug treatment for inmates, boot camp for drug offenders, and random drug testing for parolees; closing the crack houses; seizing drug profits; staunching the flow of illegal guns and banning assault weapons; establishing harsher sentencing for dealing drugs on school property; mandating life without parole for cop killers; redirecting non-life-threatening 911 calls to the precincts; funding and organizing community anticrime groups; creating a deputy mayor position as the "crime czar"; passing an "anti-wilding" law to increase penalties for crimes committed by large groups; improving crime victims' services; nurturing an "adopt-a-school" program; and rooting out and punishing corruption at the highest levels of city government.

Where would I deliver the speech introducing these ideas? The most expedient political move would have been to go to Sheepshead Bay, a largely white neighborhood in Brooklyn where there was a palpable anger at the rising rate of crime in the city and where I would have been well received for identifying the problem precisely and promising to give that segment what it wanted: more law enforcement, less leniency, more vigilance. I might have won over some voters who had not heard my anger and might have assumed that I was unaware of or untroubled by their concerns or that I was reflexively supportive of the black community, whom they might have blamed for the troubles. That might have been the conventional political wisdom. Instead, Bill Lynch decided, and I concurred, that I would deliver the speech in Harlem. "You go to the black community, and you give this speech to show the city that crime is not a black issue or a white issue, crime is affecting everyone, and that the black community is as responsible as any other and wants safety and justice just like all the others." Not because I was a black man admonishing my own community not to commit crime, but because I was of that community and could share with them the knowledge that they, in their humanity, were just as concerned about crime as everyone else in New York.

First Bill suggested speaking at the Abyssinian Baptist Church, Adam Clayton Powell's old church, the best-known and most politically connected religious institution in Harlem. As we were about to finalize arrangements Bill said, "I've made a mistake. You don't go to the bourgeois church on the hill. You go to a church in the projects and lay this out."

There was never any question of what I would say. I made a firm and absolute commitment to say the same thing to every community I visited in the city. That commitment was inviolable both as tactic and as principle: I would not be one of those politicians who cuts his message to the shape of his audience. In fact, on those days when I was to give a speech to a Jewish group about the historic connection between blacks and Jews, we would schedule a stop at a black church, where I would deliver the same speech.

I spoke at the Upper Madison Avenue United Methodist Church, and Bill was exactly right. Of course the black community was equally concerned about crime, equally concerned about the safety of its neighborhood and the future of its people. I told them, "There are many who misread the character of this city, who believe that the people in the neighborhoods are ready to give up, that we can no longer come together, that leadership has to be cynical and divisive, and that the politics of fear and intolerance is too powerful to overcome." I told them, "The only thing sadder than the broken-down crackheads lurking in the shadows of our neighborhoods are the sleazy glamour-boys downtown, those who take bribes and trade on inside information, loading up on cocaine while shaking down the hopes and dreams of the rest of us who insist on playing by the rules."

I had the opportunity to take a shot at US Attorney Rudy Giuliani, a prosecutor who was portraying himself as a caped crusader, and Ed

Koch, who for some time had been making light of people's misfortune. In the first draft of this speech, John Siegal, a wonderful speechwriter, had come up with a line that he and I both knew would garner a lot of attention and put my challengers' behavior in stark relief. First he had established the fact that the city was under siege, that crime and drugs and cynicism and indifference were ruining New York. One must define a problem before curing it. Then John had written, "I have my own program for fighting crime. I'm not Rudy Giuliani, I'm not Ed Koch. Rudy thinks he's Batman, and Koch, he's the Joker." It was a great tabloid line and would have been the talk of the city. "No," I told him, "I'm not going to do that." That sort of direct attack did not sit well with me; it was too explicit, it seemed crass. "That's not how you do it. You say it without using names. Everyone will know what you're talking about, and it will be much more effective."

I ultimately told the congregation, and by extension the city, "Now some will tell you that the only thing that can save this city is some sort of crime-fighting superhero." The crowd murmured. Of course they got it. "They want us to believe that we can only be rescued by placing our faith in a tough guy who will root out the villains and restore law and order to this town." Again, the murmur.

"But I'm here to tell you that no stranger in a dark suit can swoop down and save us from this epidemic of crime and drugs. For Batman is just a character in a movie, and"—I simply could not call Ed Koch the Joker—"we're not living in the land of make-believe." I believe, from the reaction of the people in the pews, that I was understood.

Which is not to say I spared the mayor altogether. In my summation, I said, "Victory . . . will only be the beginning of the journey. We won't finish it overnight, but we will end the long twilight of principle in City Hall.

"We will replace wisecracks with wisdom.

"We will be activist and strong and hopeful.

"We will make this city work. We will make it safe. And we will bring New York together."

.   .   .

The primary race really was between me and Mayor Ed Koch, for neither Jay Goldin's nor Dick Ravitch's campaigns caught fire. We were working with the political consultants David Doak and Bob Shrum, who, along with Bill Lynch, had put together a devastating series of negative advertisements concerning the mayor and the commissioners, appointees, and political allies who had engaged in corrupt activities, including graft, extortion, and bribery, during his administration. "We had the goods on Koch" is how Lynch describes it. They, along with Andrew Cuomo, met with me at the Sheraton Hotel and screened the footage that had been amassed of the rogues' gallery of municipal miscreants, including Donald Manes, Stanley Friedman, and Meade Esposito. The negative ads were powerful and ready to go. "We had it in the can," Lynch says. The polls showed that the race was tight, and they were convinced that making the mayor shoulder the responsibility in such a visceral way would clinch it for us. I told them, "Let's not do this." They were disappointed by my decision, but I did not feel it was proper to engage in that sort of attack, as factually correct as it was.

Which is not to say I refused to hold the mayor responsible for his actions on behalf of the city. At the televised mayoral debate, I addressed him directly. Ed Koch has always been quick on his feet, and he is known for his feisty repartee; for much of the evening he had succeeded in presenting himself as he wanted to be viewed. But there's an old debater's trick: you wait until the closing and then you hammer your opponent. With my final words, I took this opportunity.

"First of all, let me say to Mr. Koch that for most people who live here, for those who fear to ride the subway at night and who've seen crack and drugs explode like a bomb; for the middle class who struggle to make ends meet and for all who fear to send their kids to school each morning, what's happened to this city in the last four years isn't very funny."

The mayor was widely regarded as increasingly flippant, his arrogance seeming to come from him unavoidably. "I don't think anyone, even the mayor himself," I said, "believes most of what he's been saying in the campaign.

"Ed, are you really satisfied with your record on law enforcement, or with a city that ranks second in violent crime and has the highest murder rate in its entire history? One thousand eight hundred and ninety-six murders in a year, Ed. That's no laughing matter.

"And, Ed, do you really believe that the corruption all around you isn't your fault? That it's all right to have 184 members of your administration convicted in the past four years?

"The truth is, you can't get away with running as the protest candidate when you've already been in office for twelve long years."

I wanted to make undeniably clear the wide gulf between Mayor Koch and myself. "The greatest difference I have with the mayor," I concluded, "is that he wants to keep the job without meeting the challenges. He tells us it's tough—and it is—but it's time for someone to start doing it. It's time to put aside the wisecracks and look for some wisdom. It's time to stop tearing this city apart and to begin the difficult, fundamental task of bringing it together. It's time to be strong without being loud. It's time for a change."

.　　.　　.

On August 23, 1989, a sixteen-year-old black boy named Yusef Hawkins was attacked by a group of ten to thirty white teenagers and shot to death in Bensonhurst, Brooklyn, where he had gone to look into buying a 1983 Pontiac. The gang thought he was dating a white girl from the neighborhood. They lay in wait for him and killed the young man in cold blood. Alice T. McGillion, deputy police commissioner for public information, said, "Prior to the shooting, witnesses overheard, 'Let's club the [expletive] nigger.'" Followed by: "No, let's not club, let's shoot one." This was the third killing of a young black man by a white mob in New York City during the 1980s, and it occasioned strong protests. Al Sharpton led several multiracial marches in the area that "were greeted," the

New York Times reported, "with a barrage of racial epithets and obscenities, yelled out from among several hundred white onlookers, some of whom taunted the protesters with watermelons and signs saying 'Go home.'" Sharpton remembers there being bricks. Mayor Koch criticized the marchers, saying that they were wrong to hold demonstrations in Bensonhurst and they should have stayed home. "The question is," Koch said, "do you want to be helpful to reduce the tensions or do you want to escalate the tensions? . . . You're not quieting the passions by marching into Bensonhurst."

Mayor Koch opposed the demonstrations, saying that they could be interpreted as a condemnation of the whole Bensonhurst community rather than of the individuals who committed the crime. "This is a case involving bias," he said, "but it's more than that. It's a spurned lover." Missing was his trademark outrage, absent was the cry for justice. Instead, he appeared to absolve the community in which the killing occurred. Even in reprimanding the crowd that taunted the black protesters, he was restrained. "The relative handful of jeering bystanders brought shame to those who remained silent and let an ignorant few add outrage to tragedy," he said later in a written statement.

Defying the civil rights tradition, Koch said, "It's just as wrong to march into Bensonhurst as it would be to march into Harlem after that young woman in the jogging case," a reference to the 1989 "wilding" attack on Trisha Meili, allegedly by a gang of thirty black youths. The five young men convicted of the attack were exonerated in 2002.

Jay Goldin denounced Koch, saying, "New Yorkers deserve better than a yahoo mayor."

I defended the marches—"To suggest that peaceful demonstrations, led by members of the clergy, had no right to be there, that somehow [they] would exacerbate tension is a position from which I dissent"— and called upon the good people of Bensonhurst to speak out against the racial hostility in their community that had led to this crime and these outbursts of bigotry. I was disappointed that Yusef Hawkins's death had not prompted greater outrage from the general New York community, not just the African American community. There were an awful lot of good people who remained silent, while others behaved less than admirably.

Clearly a tide turned in the face of this tragedy. The tone and climate of the city is set at City Hall. Koch's belligerence was on full display, while my handling of the situation largely met with approval by the media and the people. There were only three weeks until the primary.

.   .   .

I met over breakfast with the editorial board of the *Wall Street Journal*. The newspaper had a long-standing tradition of refraining from endorsing candidates for mayor, but it did cover the election, and we felt it was extremely important that the editors understand the ideas informing my positions. Policy analyst Barbara Turk accompanied me. She recalls a beautifully appointed wood-paneled room and orange juice served in glass stemware; she had never before seen this level of breakfast opulence. The *Journal* was represented by approximately thirty people, all but one white, all but one a man. Barbara was seated next to the woman. The board asked many questions concerning my approach to managing the economics of the city. The stock market had dropped precipitously in October 1987; now, in the summer of 1989, the economy remained weak. The extravagant corporate bonuses to which Wall Street had become accustomed had been severely curtailed, and the associated taxes and revenue derived by the city treasury from the spending of that income were being savagely decreased. The outlook was quite bleak, and the *Journal*'s board wanted to discuss how I would handle this state of affairs if I became mayor.

I spoke to them about the homeless. I told them I thought it was important to note the value of New York's poor and working class to the city's economy. If we decreased the number of foster-care placements, I said, and if we solved the problems causing homelessness, we would save the city many more millions of dollars in the costs of housing, health care, and social services than the investment in the government programs required for these solutions. These savings, I explained, would compound, and the funds could then be put to strong use in building a more dynamic and prosperous New York. I said I believed they ought to join me in this argument.

.   .   .

The *New York Times* and the *New York Post,* "with genuine enthusiasm—and without hesitation," endorsed Mayor Ed Koch for reelection. On the Sunday before the Tuesday primary, the *Daily News* ran a large front-page photo of me in tennis whites, with the headline "He's Ready to Serve." Inside was an article discussing my game, under the headline "Dinkins Wields a Racket—Koch Just Makes One." *Daily News* editor F. Gilman Spencer had strongly opposed publisher James Hoge's desire to endorse Koch. In a compromise, the paper endorsed Dick Ravitch. The next day Spencer resigned. We had begun with a sizable lead, but as election day neared the polls showed the race to be close.

Among the rules governing this primary election was that if no individual candidate received more than 40 percent of the popular vote, a runoff would be conducted between the top two vote-getters to decide who received the nomination. This spelled real trouble for us because we were running out of funds. Despite our best efforts, we were very close to the bone. In fact, we were not prepared for a runoff; if we did not win the election outright, we would not be able to continue.

Barbara Fife reminds me that New York City primary runoffs have a history of being extremely destructive. Race becomes an even more decisive issue. It figured in the Herman Badillo–Abe Beame runoff in 1973 and was a large element when various factions were choosing between Koch and Mario Cuomo in 1977. We were not looking forward to such a contest. Nevertheless, it was expected that Ed Koch and I would be facing each other once again, and in that event not only would we be financially dead in the water, but we believed that the Jewish voters who had split their votes among the three Jewish candidates would largely coalesce behind Koch and make our primary victory that much more difficult.

We would need everyone. The *Amsterdam News* had been running a front-page "Koch Must Go" drumbeat for 190 consecutive weeks, since soon after his election to a third term, and under the headline "Experts Predict Dinkins Can Win Mayor's Election" said, "Leaders urge Blacks vote on Primary Day." Lynch rolled out his army of labor volunteers. Young Turks in the neighborhood wanted to get involved. Bill worked with Democratic county organizations in Manhattan and the Bronx and with many Democratic clubs in the African American neighborhoods of Brooklyn and Queens, and he had storefronts loaded with people on election day in what he describes as "the mother of all field operations"— people knocking on doors, bringing elderly voters to the polls, and leafleting at subway entrances. Barbara Turk recalls sitting side by side at a field office with Paul Robeson, Jr. "African American men and women of a certain age were making calls," she remembers. "For them this was the civil rights movement."

The United Federation of Teachers, which rarely endorsed a candidate in a mayoral primary, had come with me and was a significant ally. Dennis Rivera of Local 1199 put sound trucks in the streets that rolled through the neighborhoods encouraging everyone to exercise his or her constitutional right to cast a ballot for mayor of the city of New York. Lynch would argue that our effort was better organized than Jesse's, that the optimism and collective sense of power was greater in this mayoral race than in the presidential primary. As the day progressed he had an inkling that we might not need a runoff, that we could win this thing outright.

When the polls closed, I had received 96 percent of the African American turnout, but blacks comprised only 25 percent of New York's 2.3 million Democratic voters. In fact, blacks came out in fewer numbers (26 percent of the voters) than they had for Jesse's 1988 primary run, which garnered 31 percent. I also received 50 percent of the Hispanic vote, 30 percent of the non-Hispanic Catholic vote, and about 27 percent of the Jewish vote. Many had thought that the polarizing effect of the Yusef Hawkins killing and Koch's handling of it would lead as much as 90 percent of the white electorate to vote for the mayor. Perhaps it was the calming effect of my words or the unsettling effect of his, but 34 percent of New York's white Democratic voters chose me, about twice as many as had voted for Jesse. Not only did I surpass the 40 percent threshold, I won with 51 percent and eliminated a runoff completely. Bill Lynch and the black-Latino-labor coalition had prevailed.

.　　.　　.

Ed Koch, Jay Goldin, and Dick Ravitch all called to graciously concede. The next day the mayor invited me to visit to discuss the general election. He welcomed me and Barbara Fife to his office, where he said he would support me and do everything in his power to see that I succeeded him. As mayor, he controlled the steps of City Hall and held a large unifying rally there, surrounded by Democrats.

Ed Koch was an imperfect human being, as each of us is. When he died in 2013, he was well eulogized as an outspoken New York character. It should be remembered as part of his legacy that, following the fiscal crisis of the mid-1970s, Mayor Koch helped pay off the city's debt in three years instead of four, and that he did some good work in the production of housing, which we were pleased to continue in our administration. While he was not served well by some with whom he had an association, like Queens Borough President Donald Manes and Deputy Mayor Stanley Friedman, there were many who did serve him admirably. I think of Diane Coffey and John LoCicero, in particular.

Fund-raising improved immediately. Aside from John Lindsay, a charismatic politician I used to call "Big John" who was so separate from the Republican Party that he had left it in 1969 and won a second term on the Democrat/Liberal ticket that I supported, we had seen a succession of Democratic mayors ever since 1945 and Fiorello LaGuardia. There were only two months between the primary and the general election, I had decisively defeated the incumbent mayor, and New York Democrats outnumbered Republicans five to one; this race was supposed to be over before it began.

Of course, it wasn't. Early polls showed that we started the general election with a substantial lead, as much as thirty points, but quickly revealed that 22 percent of Mayor Koch's white Democratic vote said they would now vote Republican, and 54 percent said New York wasn't ready for a black mayor. Perhaps I should not have been surprised by these numbers—many people of color hold certain assumptions that others do not—but this news told me something about New York City that I did not wish to believe.

The Giuliani campaign must have been doing its own polling and arriving at the same conclusion. I was prepared to run on my platform of ideas, but Roger Ailes was running the Giuliani campaign. Ailes had advised Richard Nixon and written the "revolving door" ad that was so effective in undermining Michael Dukakis and electing George H. W. Bush in 1988. We were expecting a lot of mud-slinging. Rudy Giuliani was a prosecutor, and he played his role to the hilt. He was known for arresting Wall Street white-collar criminal suspects at their places of business and perp-walking them out of their offices in handcuffs. Though not yet indicted, these guys were dragged out in the middle of the day in full view of their peers and the press. Rudy was a cold, unkind person, but it was an effective image in a city where the crime rate had been escalating for more than twenty-five years. The major planks in his platform were anticrime and anticorruption. While he appeared to recognize that his image was that of a hard man and he tried to portray himself as a unity candidate—"It's time for the city to come together," he would say, and also, "I'm running a fusion candidacy which crosses all political lines"—his inner circle was quite homogeneous and his vision unenlightened. Bill Lynch and I believed that Giuliani and his advisers were taken by surprise when I defeated Mayor Koch and avoided a runoff. Without a dedicated coalition comparable to my own, Giuliani would have to find another way to win. He and his campaign turned to portraying my campaign as financially negligent and me as personally corrupt. And the issue of race was never very far from view.

First they suggested that my policies regarding the homeless were robbing the middle class. According to the Republicans, I was going to give the city away; all resources would go to the poorer population, leaving the hardworking people in the boroughs out in the cold. Crime was rising, in the city and nationwide, and I was supposedly soft on crime. There was a strong subtext to the Giuliani campaign's message. In New York, when one spoke of the poor, the picture that came to mind was the black poor, and in the public mind the face of crime was black.

On a personal level, they suggested there had been malfeasance in my transfer of stock in Percy Sutton's Inner City Broadcasting Corporation to my son without reporting it as a gift on my tax returns. Although an independent city investigator, after going so far as to analyze the paper quality of the letter my son wrote me concerning the terms—the so-called "Dear Dad" letter—declined to find criminal wrongdoing, the tempest around the inquiry grabbed extensive headlines and distracted the voting public from the important city issues at hand.

Then there was the matter of Sonny Carson. Bill Lynch had paid a total of $9,500 to Carson for field work, particularly in the projects because, as Bill says, "nobody would go in there except Sonny." Giuliani's consultant David Garth didn't believe in field work; his focus was on television advertising and the media, and his media contacts were far deeper and more extensive than Bill's. The *New York Times* and other media outlets, steered to investigate these allegations, we assumed, by the Giuliani campaign, accused us of failing to provide adequate documentation for those and other expenses. There had been no hanky-panky—Carson had been paid on the books—but local news stations picked up the story and converged on our offices, demanding that Lynch show them the canceled checks. He displayed them, as well as the applicable receipts, but meanwhile, instead of talking about issues, the headlines trumpeted "Unexplained Payments by Dinkins Campaign." The story went on for weeks, and we lost momentum and were put on the defensive by the barrage of accusations. The Giuliani campaign accused me of "sloppy bookkeeping," a code phrase meant to trigger discomfort with having a black man in charge of the city's finances, and said it fit into a "pattern of negligence"; Giuliani then dredged up the old and painful charges concerning the tax situation that had led to my being rejected as deputy mayor under Abe Beame sixteen years earlier. He prosecuted those old charges with a vengeance. He accused me of "a complete cover-up" for filing incomplete campaign finance reports. "Once again, David Dinkins demonstrates his blatant disregard for the law," he said. This wasn't campaign hyperbole, this was utter trash.

The issue of my taxes played into long-standing white discomfort with the idea of African Americans possessing the intellectual capacity and moral responsibility necessary for financial reliability. We have long been viewed as simple folks with little background and less ability in these matters. "You know they can't handle money." Given the polls indicating that a significant number of voters did not think New York was ready for a black mayor, Giuliani made his move. Issues of trustworthiness and competence are key in the selection of an elected official, and the Giuliani campaign exploited them for all they were worth. Giuliani had no polish, and he had not been in the public eye for any length of time; he was the kind of man who went for the jugular, and the campaign became exceedingly vicious. His underlying message was clear for all to see: *The city is in terrible financial straits. Do you really want a black man presiding over it in this time of trouble?*

To top it off, Sonny Carson had made anti-Semitic remarks twenty years earlier, charges that were extremely fraught in New York, and we were being castigated for having such a person in any way connected to our organization. I had had dealings with Carson for years and knew he was a radical rabble-rouser who had spent time in prison and was a difficult man, but clearly, if I'd known he was a bigot, I would have had nothing to do with him. We decided immediately that he would have nothing more to do with the campaign. Nevertheless, Giuliani called the contact "shocking" and then, in a classic case of overreaching, charged that we had given money to one of Carson's organizations to stop it from marching in protest of the Yusef Hawkins killing. All of this was utter nonsense, but the strategy was clear. Scaring an electorate works. Were they looking for another Willie Horton, the furloughed convicted felon who became a symbol of liberal leniency in the 1988 presidential campaign?

For his part, Carson played right into their hands. He held a press conference and told the assembled what he thought of the charges of anti-Semitism. "That's absolutely absurd, 'anti-Semitic.' I'm anti-white! Don't limit my 'antis' to just one group of people." That certainly didn't help the campaign.

For several days we could muster no pushback. With two weeks to go, they began hammering us relentlessly, using guilt-by-association to link me to racism and anti-Semitism. In an ad with the tag line "Let the People of New York Choose Their Own Destiny," placed in the city's largest-circulation Yiddish newspaper, pictures of Giuliani with President George H. W. Bush were juxtaposed with pictures of me with Jesse Jackson. Ken Caruso, Giuliani's deputy campaign manager, said there was "nothing objectionable" about the ad because it "has to do with the fundamental question of who are the political supporters of each candidate. Rudy and Bush are strong for Israel. Dinkins and Jackson are not. Jesse Jackson wants a separate Palestinian state; so does David Dinkins. He wants to let Yasser Arafat, a terrorist, into the country; so does David Dinkins. . . . Obviously he's going to be advising David Dinkins if Dinkins becomes mayor, and that's something that people are entitled to know."

For the record, my support of Israel had been extensive, public, long-term, and unwavering. I differed with Jesse in that I supported a Palestinian state only if Israel and Palestine negotiated a mutually acceptable agreement. I believed that international law, not the mayor of New York, should govern whether Arafat could enter the United States and speak at the United Nations. David Fishlow, my spokesman, said quite accurately, "Mr. Giuliani is obviously trying to equate respect for that law with an endorsement of terrorism, which is such a bizarre distortion as to defy comprehension." Rudy was revealing his true self.

Some progressive Jewish leaders responded that in a racially polarized city Giuliani was openly seeking to play on Jewish fears. Nevertheless, the overall effect was devastating. The idea that somehow, after all my history of standing with the Jewish community, I was on the side of bigots seemed to be taking hold. Jesse Jackson's reference to New York as "Hymietown" was being introduced yet again into the political conversation. Our poll numbers were dropping precipitately.

Our standing in the media fell as well. During the primary, there had been an element of romanticism surrounding the possibility of a black man being elected mayor of New York City. As Lynch says, the press loved us when we took out Koch. But as possibility appeared to be growing into reality there was a palpable change in the air. *Are we sure we want these guys to run the city?* Giuliani's air attack was working.

Bill came into my office and said, "If you want me to resign, I'll resign." He says now, "I thought we had come this far and I had done screwed it up and blew it." I stood up and told him, "You're not going anywhere!"

Barbara Fife, whom I had elevated to chief of staff when Bill left to run the campaign, may actually have paid for at least one vote. I'll let her tell the story: "I was on the subway, and a homeless woman was coming through the car panhandling, with the sixteen scarves and clothes and bags she was carrying. It was known publicly that Dave had been sympathetic to the homeless, and she was wearing a big DINKINS button, and I'm sitting there thinking, 'She is walking down this subway and she is losing votes for us every step she takes! I can't believe it. What am I going to do?' *She was wearing a big DINKINS button!* When she got to where I was sitting, I looked at her and said, 'I'll give you three dollars for the bus.' She said, 'Fine.' It was the only thing I could think of."

.   .   .

I campaigned in every borough, in every community. Of course, like any good politician, I went where the votes were, so I spent considerable time with the African American community, encouraging them to come out in substantial numbers. It was one thing to be the first black major-party nominee for mayor—it was quite another to be the first black mayor, and I needed full electoral participation from a population that had in the past been known for apathy or even disinterest when it came to actually going to the polls. A lack of enthusiasm among African Americans would have had an inhibiting effect on the participation of other voting blocs as well; all other blocs might have said, "Well, where are your own people? If you can't mobilize your own community, how can you expect to mobilize ours?" So we energized our base, as they say. Bill conducted the city as if it were an electoral orchestra, calling on one section after another to work in unison and harmony, adding to the building crescendo. With blacks giving every indication that they would come to the polls in record numbers, he was able to craft Latinos, Asians, Greeks, Jews, the Irish, gays, straights, senior citizens, the young, and so much of the city into a powerful gathering of positive voters who represented the city at its best. I was pleased to hear of groups calling themselves Irish Americans for Dinkins, Greek Americans for Dinkins, Japanese Americans for Dinkins.

For many years New York City had been referred to as a melting pot, the place where immigrants arrived and began their assimilation into America. New York was the center of the American way of life, and there was every opportunity for its new residents to learn the language, absorb the attitudes, and mind the mores of the dominant American culture. The concept was that each ethnic or racial or religious group would add its individual spice and flavor to the stew or casserole or gumbo or fricassee that was always on the city's burner, and the country's burner, and in the process lose its otherness and find a common identity as Americans.

There had been much discussion about whether that moniker, the "melting pot," was accurate or positive. Did an immigrant really need to lose his or her identity in order to become a true American? Could not one maintain a sense of ethnic pride while still contributing to the fullness of the country in his or her own special way? Did America demand such a diffusion, or did not its power and glory spring from its ability to blend individuals into a whole that was at once transformative in its commonality and respectful of each individual's contribution?

New York is not a melting pot, but a gorgeous mosaic. We have almost as many separate ethnic identities in the city as the United Nations has member nations. Our religious and cultural institutions are multitudinous. I did not feel the need to scrub the unique qualities from each. I celebrated the beautiful work of economic, political, and social art, created by the millions of daily interactions, that came to define the look, feel, taste, and sense of the city.

. . .

But these views were drowned out by the howling of Giuliani's campaign. For decades, the city had been a beacon of hope and belief for those of us who aspired to make America a more decent and just democracy. From civil rights to women's rights, from public housing to public schools, New York had always stood in the forefront, unwavering in its commitment to the progressive, Democratic values that are the best heritage and hope of the city and the nation. I felt that those who entered government should be moved by an ethic of public service, not self-service, and that people who joined our administration would hold fundamental convictions about social welfare, environmental protection, public safety, and economic justice.

Giuliani apparently had a different view. As I prosecuted an agenda for justice and opportunity, Giuliani desperately tried a case of accusation and innuendo. His was the politics of boundless ambition without the guidance of a set of core beliefs or the humility and restraint of experience. Giuliani seemed to assume that in politics, as in prosecution, what counted was the number of convictions one got, but his own convictions were many and contradictory. History shows that he had been a man of flexible positions. He started out as a McGovern Democrat, became a Reagan Republican, sought the Conservative Party nomination, and then cut a deal to get on the Liberal line. First he said he opposed *Roe v. Wade,* then he said he didn't, then he said that reproductive freedom was a "silly and irrelevant" issue. He said he favored a ban on cop-killer bullets, but he testified in Congress against the ban. He said he believed in human rights, then locked up Haitian refugees and Irish patriot Joe Doherty and accepted as a legal client Panama's dictator Manuel Noriega. He said he was tough on crime, but he dressed up like a goofball on a drug bust ride-along, looking to make a photo, not an arrest. And he was smug in his denials of such obvious emptiness.

As to his tactics, we believed the Giuliani campaign started spying on us. Although they denied it, we could find no other reason for someone to consistently tail Bill Lynch as he left campaign headquarters and made his way home. At the end of long campaign days, sometimes as late as 3:00 in the morning, Bill, labor leader Jim Bell, and Ken Sunshine, known to each other as "the Mod Squad," made a regular habit of driving from headquarters to the Gray's Papaya stand on the corner of Amsterdam Avenue and Seventy-Second Street to grab a couple of hot dogs, after which they would drop off Sunshine and Bell would drive Bill uptown. Bill says, "There was a guy who used to follow us. One time Jim, who was a really tough guy, jumped out of the car at 110th Street and said, 'I'm gonna confront this guy.' When the driver in the tail car saw Bell coming, he cut down the next street and disappeared."

A month before election day, comedian Jackie Mason was quoted in *Newsweek* as having called me a "fancy *schvartze* with a mustache." I was not unfamiliar with that derogatory term. According to *The Joys of Yiddish* by Leo Rosten, "*shvartzer* and *shvartzeh,* to mean Negro man and woman, became 'inside' words among Jews—cryptonyms for Negro servants or employees." So Jackie Mason was essentially calling me a nigger. Giuliani attended the *Newsweek* luncheon where the remark was made and, according to the magazine, "joined in the nervous laughter, making no attempt to rebuke Mason." Giuliani denied hearing the slur. I don't know whether he heard it or not, but there were only six or eight people in the room having lunch.

Apparently that was not sufficient grounds for Giuliani to distance himself from Mason. They parted ways a month later, and only after the comedian told the *Village Voice* that Jewish support for me was based on guilt and that Jews were "sick with complexes." That same week Giuliani stepped up his attacks on me and my relationship with Jesse Jackson.

My campaign's response was to run an advertisement reminding the city that in 1985, when Black Muslim minister Louis Farrakhan was scheduled to speak at Madison Square Garden, I held a press conference and repudiated him for having called Judaism a "dirty religion" and Adolf Hitler a "great man." I received police protection when Farrakhan, that same day, issued what the NYPD considered a possible threat on my life. Not everyone thought this ad was a good idea. Percy Sutton called Bill Lynch and upbraided him. Percy felt that the ad would hurt my standing in the black community, that it would appear as though I were pandering to whites. Bill and I disagreed. I would not allow Giuliani to portray me in any way but as a friend to the Jews of New York, and we felt it would resonate politically with the Jewish community, which we needed in order to succeed.

I addressed a Jewish leadership breakfast and said, "There is something I want to say at the outset, as candidly and plainly as I can. All my life I have believed in principles of tolerance and mutual respect. As mayor, I will set those principles at the center of all my endeavors. I hate bigotry and intolerance. There is no room in my campaign, and there will never be room in my administration, for any form of anti-Semitism or anti-Catholicism or racism, or any prejudice based on national origin.

"Now let me say something about the events of recent months in this city. We have had hard moments, moments of tension and testing. But so far we have come through stronger than ever. In truth, I believe that this campaign has given new life to the old faith that we can stand together in the cause of progress and justice, that we can see beyond differences of skin color to the mighty ideals of the spirit that should be our guiding stars.

"In that spirit, let me speak frankly now about race and religion and ethnicity, for they are part of the defining identity of our city.

"The people do not want a city divided against itself, the people do not want a campaign that descends into a bitter, negative struggle, playing upon fear or pitting New Yorkers against one another. It is a time for hope in New York, not for mutual suspicion and recrimination. It is a time to say no to the politics of slam and slash and anger. It is time to send forth the word to all who seek to lead this city that no one can succeed by turning neighbor against neighbor or group against group. . . . I ask that nobody vote for me because I am an African American, but I ask as well that nobody vote against me because I am an African American. Quite simply, we have a choice: we can bring this city together to attack our common problems, or we can allow ourselves to drift apart, to turn on our fellow citizens instead of turning on our real enemies.

"Our two communities, Jewish and African American, each have a history that has taught us in the most profound and painful ways the evils of group hate. And we have a common heritage of witnessing and working for the human rights of all, often against the longest of odds. Ours is an historic alliance. . . . These are my fundamental convictions, and I express them everywhere I go."

I delivered the same message that Sunday at the Bridge Street Church in Bedford-Stuyvesant.

"And there is something else that needs to be said, now and then," I told each gathering. "I believe there are more important issues in this election than race and religion. Because let's face it: there's no black way to fight crime, and there's no Jewish way to fight crime. I offer a New York way!"

But all did not go smoothly. About two weeks later, at a Queens forum I attended with Jewish civic and religious leaders, a flier was passed out among the audience that read, "If David Dinkins is such a healer, why does he surround himself with hate-mongers?" and two rabbis attacked me for my relationship with Jesse Jackson. I had no way of knowing the origin of that flier, but it was of a piece with the tenor of the Giuliani campaign. "So what are we really talking about?" I said. "You want me to denounce Jesse Jackson. I'm not going to do it. I do not believe Jesse Jackson to be anti-Semitic. If I did, I would not support him. It's that simple."

Several people in the crowd shouted out "Hymietown! Hymietown!"

"When he said 'Hymietown,' I condemned him. Publicly, loudly, and among the first."

Rabbi Fabian Schonfeld stated his concern at the presence of Jesse at the celebration on the night of my primary victory and asked why there was "so much anti-Jewish hatred in the black community." I tried to explain that Jesse Jackson was not running for mayor, I was.

I was accompanied by several Jewish politicians, including Queens borough president Claire Shulman and New York attorney general Bob Abrams, who had noted to the crowd my history of support for Israel, my condemnation of Louis Farrakhan, and several instances of my support for the Jewish community. I did not do those things to court the Jewish vote, I told the crowd, but because they were right. "What about me and the Jewish community?" I asked. "And I say to you with the deepest respect, if I'm not all right, who is?" This did not mollify the people gathered. The tone was nasty.

"You speak of Jesse Jackson and your concern that he might come to town," I said. "I wonder if you think he'll come less if I'm not mayor. I wonder if one believes that having an African American as mayor might not assist in bringing things together." I told the crowd that if they chose not to vote for me because "you think I have insufficient experience, because you think I'm not bright enough or tall enough, I don't wear the right ties—that's okay. But if your difficulty with me is that you feel that somehow or other I'm not right with the Jewish community . . . if you assign some other reason, such as 'I didn't like his vote on this or that' . . . you and God will know whether or not that's your real reason. And if your real reason is somehow or other you feel I'm not right with the Jewish community, I ask you to reexamine the judgment and yourself."

·　　·　　·

Despite Giuliani's concentrated advertising attacks, polls taken the day before the election indicated that I had rebounded. My lead in the *Daily News*/ABC-TV poll was fourteen points. The *New York Observer* had me ahead by eighteen.

I earned the endorsements of the *Times*, the *Daily News*, and *Newsday*. Rupert Murdoch's *New York Post* endorsed Giuliani. Bill mobilized his forces, and the same army of volunteers that produced so spectacularly on primary day hit the streets. Entry polls looked promising. *Newsweek's* Gallup poll had me up 51–36 among those who had made a choice, and they split the remaining undecideds equally. "We would have had a dead-perfect number if we'd given all the undecideds to Giuliani," said their representative. "But that's not what our analysis told us was the right way to do it; there was no evidence that that was correct."

"In every black-white race that I have ever seen," said Democratic pollster Paul Maslin, "you can absolutely place the white undecided voters into the white candidate's column in the last poll before election day."

I won by 2 percent, a margin of 47,080 votes. What accounted for the large defection? I think it was just racism, pure and simple.

Patrick Gaspard recalls election eve: "We were at the Sheraton Hotel, getting exit polls from around town. One moment we're up, one moment it's too close to call. There was a guy named Jack Kelly who was managing the data and tracking the numbers for Bill Lynch as we got results from all the precincts around the city. He's the one who first told me we have this, that it's a done deal.

"I remember being in the room with all the numbers coming in and getting the verdict and just bursting and running out of there, through the halls of the Sheraton, and grabbing all the other young kids and shouting the news to them, and jumping up and down, hugging everybody. It was like victory over Japan. We had to kiss everybody in Times Square that night!

"I come from a family of six kids, and all my siblings were out volunteering for the campaign. That night all of us were in my hotel room, and I remember never falling asleep. The next morning my siblings went out and bought every newspaper in New York, and they spread them all around my bed, and I knew that it actually happened and I hadn't just dreamed it. There were screaming headlines. It was like waking up and finding a million dollars in your bed. It was the best feeling ever!"

I felt elation and relief. I was relieved because if I had lost I had no job and no way to pursue my vision for the city. I was elated for myself, of course, and for the people around me, who had run such a fine campaign. I was surrounded by people at the top of their emotions, and I was at the pinnacle of mine. We had come a long way from the streets of Trenton, the sidewalks of Harlem, the liquor store, the Carver club, the plummet from sugar to shit. This was resurrection for me, and I planned a revival for New York. I felt the responsibility for bringing the city I loved back to balance. There would be no blaming of victims or coddling of criminals. New Yorkers would be helped, not harangued. Good government would mean good politics. We would represent all the people, including many who had never felt the warmth of representation before. The business community would be served, each local community serviced. With my bride by my side and wonderful people on all sides of me, I raised my arms in triumph.

8

―――――

Attacking the Problems,
Not the Victims

I was sworn in as the 106th mayor of New York City directly after midnight as the year 1990 commenced. The ceremony took place in the Bronx apartment of my old law partner Fritz Alexander, who was a Court of Appeals judge at the time. Of course, Joyce, David Jr., and Donna were there to witness the occasion. Deputy mayors Norman Steisel, Barbara Fife, Sally Hernandez-Pinero, and Bill Lynch, as well as corporation counsel Victor Kovner and police commissioner Lee Brown, were sworn in after my induction. Charlie Rangel, Percy Sutton, Basil Paterson, and Jesse Jackson, along with a loyal crowd of approximately one hundred supporters, squeezed into Fritz's apartment. I held together quite well through the oath itself, but when I kissed my family and the room filled with applause, I swelled with emotion.

It was pouring outside, a dreadfully inclement evening, rain coming down in buckets, but there were parties around the city to attend and a new day on its way to dawning. As Barbara Fife and her husband Martin were driving downtown to celebrate, their car hit a giant pothole, a divot in the pavement so deep they had some difficulty driving out. Barbara looked at Marty, wipers slapping the windshield, rain drumming on the roof, and said, "Oh my God, it is our fault now!" Our days of advocacy were over—from that point forward we had to get things done.

I was inaugurated at midday on the steps of City Hall. My mother had passed away, but my father and stepmother were present for the event. I was sorry my mother was not there to see this; she had thought it was a great day when I finished high school. The crowd was estimated to be three times the size of those at previous mayoral ceremonies, as clearly this was an occasion of some moment. I was joined by former New York mayors Koch, Lindsay, Beame, and Wagner, and African American mayors Wilson Goode of Philadelphia, Sharpe James of Newark, and Marion Barry of Washington, as well as Governor Mario Cuomo. Harry Belafonte presided over the ceremonies, and South Africa's Archbishop Desmond Tutu delivered remarks. Finally it was my turn to speak.

"Today," I told the invited guests and members of the public, "we mark more than a transfer of power. Today we travel another mile on freedom's road. . . . I stand before you today as the elected leader of the greatest city of a great nation, to which my ancestors were brought, chained and whipped in the hold of a slave ship. We have not finished the journey toward liberty and justice, but surely we have come a long way.

"I see New York as a gorgeous mosaic of race and religious faith, of national origin and sexual orientation—of individuals whose families arrived yesterday and generations ago, coming through Ellis Island, or Kennedy Airport, or on Greyhound buses bound for the Port Authority. In that spirit, I offer this fundamental pledge: I intend to be the mayor of all the people of New York."

And so I was mayor.

·   ·   ·

Mario Cuomo said that one campaigns in poetry and governs in prose. I began writing my mayoralty.

I had asked Nat Leventhal to chair my transition team, assisted by Barbara Fife, who was herself assisted by Marcia Smith. Leventhal had been deputy mayor for operations under Koch and knew how the government operated and many of the people who were adept at operating it. They had separated the policy and personnel sides of the equation.

I wanted to change the way decisions were made in city administration and the manner in which the person who was mayor was perceived. Mayor Koch had been a bully in the bully pulpit. I didn't want to be that man. That pulpit is easy to abuse, and having it can make one not only arrogant but a target for abuse. It was my intention to be a leader who found common ground and then moved the city in a direction I deemed valuable. I wanted smart, acknowledged leaders from a variety of the city's many sectors who would have the stature to announce, "This is what our city should be doing," and be recognized. I wanted multiple involvements. That would be my management style.

I had seen mayors buffeted by criticism of their point of view, by the sharp oversimplification of the press, and by the time it took to cut through that fog to have the public understand actual policy. I had no intention of being combative or reactive. I would overcome personal criticism by conducting a chorus, an orchestra of municipal virtuosos. My advisers and I would generate ideas, I would encourage consensus, and my highly accomplished staff would flesh out these concepts and create the momentum necessary to see them through.

Consensus, while preferable, was not always necessary. Abe Lincoln, the story goes, would convene his cabinet and after discussion put an issue to a vote. The question would go around the table, and these esteemed gentlemen would say, "Nay," "Nay," "Nay," "Nay," and on occasion Lincoln would say, "The ayes have it." I would get all the information and tell my staff, "I'll do what you all want 95 percent of the time, but the Lincoln Rule obtains."

Presented in this way, our ideas to move New York forward would be perceived properly: "These are the views of accepted business leaders. It's not some yahoo over here to whom the mayor is responding, or someone with an insider's influence who is putting on the squeeze to move in a given direction." I was not the type to say, "That is a stupid idea," or, "That's ridiculous," as had my predecessor. I would orchestrate a more robust and fulsome discussion of the issues and mobilize support.

The central concept I wanted to reintroduce to municipal government was that of community. It had been missing for years, this sense that everyone in the city was connected, that there was a greater good to be considered than simply the selfish, and that we were all tied to it. It was important to me that this sense of community permeate the government because one cannot manage a government like New York City's without it.

The essential conversation concerned the people I would select to surround me. Would I reinvent government with the lifetime outsiders whom Bill Lynch and I had introduced into my borough president's administration, while sweeping out all traces of the Koch mayoralty, or would I search out the experienced insiders in what is known as the permanent government and attempt to work from within? There was some pressure from the Democratic Party leadership to maintain continuity, Ed Koch having been a Democrat and much of his staff having risen through those ranks. There was equal pressure from those who represented the constituency that felt it had been fundamentally ignored for the previous twelve years of the Koch administration, if not significantly longer. I could feel the weight of these expectations from each side; the former's was intellectual and political, the latter's was palpable.

Norman Steisel had started government service in the Lindsay administration and then entered the private sector. In the mid- to late 1970s, when there was public discussion of New York City declaring bankruptcy, a new financial team was assembled, and he reentered city government as first deputy budget director. This was around the time the *Daily News* ran the headline, "Ford to City: Drop Dead." The national, state, and city economies were in trouble, income was dropping, and as a result so were the tax revenues on which the city depended. Deep budget cuts were necessary in an environment of constantly declining resources, and the city was not handling the crisis effectively. In 1975 the state legislature created the New York State Financial Control Board to oversee the financial management of the city and various related public authorities. Under its mandate, all financial plans and certain contracts were subject to its approval.

Steisel's responsibilities at that time dealt mainly with the expenditure side of the budget. He was centrally involved in the large cutbacks that took place: the significant layoffs; the breach of contracts with major vendors; the negotiations with the unions, whose members were being asked to give up their jobs but whose pension funds were at the same time being asked to buy the city's municipal bonds. He had been involved in some difficult negotiations.

To re-secure federal loan guarantees, as well as meet certain requirements that had been imposed on the city by the Financial Control Board, the city was required in 1977, when Ed Koch was first elected, to submit a revised financial plan in the first twenty days of his term. Even though Koch began work on this plan almost immediately following his election, which gave him perhaps two months in toto, it was a tall order to submit a revised plan in such a short amount of time. Even as he needed to create this plan, the mayor was focusing on creating his own administration and bringing in his own people to replace or augment Abe Beame's staff of eight years. It was a time of high stress.

Steisel considered himself a bureaucrat and belonged to no political club. He was asked to stay on by Koch as his budget director, and he saw Koch's first budget through the Board of Estimate. He served eight years as the New York City sanitation commissioner, becoming at the time that department's longest-serving commissioner in the twentieth century. Steisel became highly involved in waste-to-energy conservation and especially favored the use of incinerators. He was an advocate for the rehabilitation of the Brooklyn Navy Yard, which had fallen into disrepair after a decade of disuse, and was active nationally in promoting technology. Steisel started the city's first curbside collection of recycled materials and, most significantly, reduced the Sanitation Department truck crew size from three to two by introducing performance- and productivity-based incentive payments to workers. The resulting 25 percent reduction of the workforce is still considered by many municipal experts and observers the signal productivity gain in New York City government operations in the past three or four decades.

During Koch's third term, Steisel left government to work at Lazard Freres. While at the firm, he became the chairman of the School Construction Authority, which had been mandated by the State Legislature to manage the design, construction, and renovation of capital projects in New York City's more than 1,200 public school buildings, half of which had been constructed prior to 1949. This is where Steisel and I first came to really know one another while I was Manhattan borough president. It didn't hurt that we were both tennis players; I knew how he carried himself on the court, which I believe helps considerably in estimating a person's character.

Norman is also a cigar chomper. He looks like a man who would be at home in the inner workings of city government, and he was. His knowledge of city government was encyclopedic. I felt I needed a person in a position of high responsibility who knew how to get things done. The business community felt I needed someone with Norman's know-how. I offered him the job of first deputy mayor, and he accepted.

I named Bill Lynch deputy mayor for intergovernmental relations, Barbara Fife deputy mayor for planning and development, and Sally Hernandez-Pinero deputy mayor for finance and economic development. I now had an excellent inner circle.

. . .

As with my predecessors, the first two orders of business were staffing the government and creating the budget. Good government begins with good commissioners, and our elaborate process began with search committees to find not only suitable but excellent candidates. I decided that one did not sweep out an entire functioning government upon winning an election; one assessed the available talent and availed oneself of the best while letting the others pursue their private paths.

Imagine stepping into a business and having only seven weeks to identify, interview, and hire twenty-five high-level executives. Among the possibilities were Koch holdovers with substantial experience who wanted to keep their positions; staff members in my borough president's office in whom I had great trust and who wanted to step up in responsibility; individuals heretofore unknown to us who wanted to be heard; and highly visible people who were known quantities to whom we felt obliged to listen. The process was time-consuming and filled with pressure. The city's newspapers, which often concentrate on the horse race instead of the horses, soon began making comparisons between our timetable and those of my predecessors. *By January first, Mayor Beame had X number of commissioners in place; Mayor Koch had Y, Mayor Dinkins has. . . .* A month later they would run the next score-card.

My choice of Steisel for first deputy mayor was not greeted entirely with open arms. Many of the outsiders-turned-insiders who were working in my borough president's office went to be interviewed by Norman's chief of staff, Ellen Baer, and came away miffed that the quality and importance of their work were not recognized. Activism, it appeared, was valued less highly than experience. There was a sense among some that these were tough, cold, nasty Koch people who didn't understand a thing about what had gone on and what my election meant. There was initial consternation, but although the transition was hectic and difficult, ultimately people were placed in the jobs at which they were competent and the ones they deserved. Several of the policy analysts in my borough president's office were assigned as program or policy office heads under Barbara Fife (environment, culture, land use) or Norman Steisel (health, education, homelessness, criminal justice, transportation), consistent with the portfolio of agencies reporting to each. My deputy, Dennis deLeon, was appointed chair of the Human Rights Commission, and several of the folks in constituent relations were assigned by Bill Lynch to head offices involving African American, Latino, Jewish, gay and lesbian, and veterans affairs. When asked, Milt Mollen, the presiding justice of the Appellate Division, Second Department, resigned his post to become deputy mayor for public safety. Two years later, in a remarkable display of civic-mindedness, Fritz Alexander stepped down from the Court of Appeals to succeed him.

Basil Paterson said, "I've got just the guy for your counsel."

"Who?" I asked.

"George Daniels."

"Who's he?"

"He's a Criminal Court judge, appointed by Koch."

"He's not going to give that up."

"Oh yes he will."

Basil, of course, knew what he was talking about. Daniels resigned as a Criminal Court judge. Three judges stepped down to join me. I tell people that the three of them, George and Milt and Fritz, needed a psychiatrist and I could probably get a fleet rate because they were all crazy for doing so. George served ably, with great insight and subtle skill. Four years later, before I left office, I appointed him back to the Criminal Court. He was then elected to the New York Supreme Court, and President Bill Clinton nominated him to be a judge in the US District Court, Southern District of New York, where he presides today. George has ascended to the position of "the Heavy Judge."

The transition was not without its disappointments. Grassroots people thought, *I used to hate dealing with that deputy commissioner, I was hoping he was going to be out, but he's not.* There were new lines of communication and authority, much of it through Steisel, and many people who had had casual access to me as borough president now were more restricted in their contact with me as mayor. There is always a highly pressing matter in the life of a mayor, there are more issues to be decided, and there are more decisions to be made and reviewed. Before problems or solutions were placed on my desk, Norman was at the top of this chain of command. Norman is a droll human being with a gruff way about him. I used to tell people, "Norman's all right, he just doesn't smile a lot."

So much of the way New York City does its business is driven through the budget process. Policymaking equals resource allocation. If you don't have the money, you cannot do what you want to do; it's as simple as that. When we began to examine the actual city budget left to us by the Koch administration, we found a disturbing surprise. What we had been led to believe was a deficit of approximately $175 million on a going-forward basis—which is to say, the money needed to finance the remaining six months of the city's fiscal year—was in actual fact closer to $750 million. As we began working on the next year's budget and forecast those figures, we were close to a billion dollars in the hole! The city and country were already in a revenue free-fall. Where were we supposed to come up with this money?

Under the Financial Control Board agreement, the city was obligated to balance its budget. (The board consists of the governor, who is its chairman; the state comptroller; the mayor; the city comptroller; and three members who are appointed by the governor, with the advice and consent of the State Senate, and who serve at the governor's pleasure. The public members are hardly shy and retiring types and will say and do what they want, but since they are appointees and can be influenced by the governor, the board is essentially under his control.) Unless the city ended its fiscal year and presented its audited final budget out of balance by less than $100 million, New York would go into receivership and the board would take over management of the city's finances.

One hundred million dollars sounds like a lot of money. At the time, however, the budget was approximately $30 billion; $100 million is 0.0033 percent of that amount. In layman's terms, for an individual making $50,000 a year, a takeover would occur if he or she exceeded expenses by $165 a year! Obviously, we were on a very tight leash.

Everyone in my administration felt passionately that we could not allow this to happen. I did not want to be elected mayor and immediately lose control of the city to the Financial Control Board and the governor. To be mayor but not be mayor—that would be unfathomable.

I recognize that there was significant skepticism about my ability to handle this crisis. I was elected in some part because New Yorkers were fed up with Ed Koch's belligerent attitude in dealing with many issues and communities, minority groups in particular. My style and his were substantially different. I was perceived as more civil and less confrontational, more considered and less likely to fly off the handle. I was supposed to bring a different tone, a different level of discussion to the table, and to possess the ability to get people to work together and behave more harmoniously. However, my measured manner and precise diction seemed to some to be lacking in the fire or urgency New Yorkers had come to identify as mayoral prerequisites. Wall Street and the media in particular doubted my abilities. Opinion makers and people on editorial boards asked my senior staff, in so many words, *Can the black guy count?* My degree in mathematics from Howard apparently did not calm their fears that I needed to take off my shoes to count to twenty.

When told that the upcoming deficit might hit $1 billion, Mayor Koch denied responsibility. (In fact, when the time came, the deficit hit $1.8 billion.) He had earned credibility with the Financial Control Board by presenting quarterly reviews, and although at times when the city was not doing well the board would make its displeasure known, those displays would be subtle, not cataclysmic. "If I were here," Koch told the *New York Times* after my election, "I'd take action to eliminate the deficit. It's not hard; you have to have intestinal fortitude to increase taxes and reduce services." Why, during the many years in which this deficit was mushrooming and he was in office, the mayor did not take these actions remains a mystery.

Mayor Beame had a more nuanced response to the problems facing New York City as I took office. "In my memory," he said, "no mayor has ever inherited a more serious and overwhelming condition in both financial and social problems." Crack, AIDS, and homelessness were cresting.

Governor Mario Cuomo was, of course, connected to the New York business community, and he heard this noise. When I came into office, the spotlights seemed to be trained a little more brightly on our perform-ance. The huge deficit altered the dynamics of my mayoralty from the beginning. I had an economic and social agenda when I entered the mayor's office. I ran on a platform of specific change and was determined to move the city forward. But could I get it done? It became immediately clear that if I closed the $1.8 billion deficit and avoided receivership, the answer would be no.

This was a blow not only to me but to the entire city that elected me. Some of the grassroots constituents' representatives who had worked so hard to see me elected, including many who had joined me in the bor-ough president's office, were particularly upset. They were the outsiders; they had spent years pounding against the Koch administration, and finally, they felt as they came to the table, they were going to be in charge. Ignored by a particularly insensitive mayor, they had replaced him with a man who had their best interests at heart, and they were ready to put the city's residents on a different path. They had committed themselves and fought for years. They truly believed in the issues they had worked on and the people for whom they worked. Now they were being told, "Well, you can't do this, we have no money. Not only can we not expand city services to fill all the gaps in the unmet needs, as legitimate and important as they are, but we must cut back and cut back even more."

Norman Steisel, whose Koch credentials made him a classic repre-sentative of the permanent government, was the bearer of this bad news. In his gruff way he let it be known: if the mayor has to succeed first by being tough and bottom-line-oriented and postponing some of his com-mitments and promises, then that was what he had to do so he could fight another day.

This setback was very difficult for people to accept. First, the transi-tion from outsider to insider was not easy to accomplish. Many in my new administration had spent their professional careers as advocates and had to learn the consequences of their new responsibilities. Outside, they had found it easy to write reports and issue directives concerning what agencies should be doing, but once they were inside and had learned the finite nature of government funds and the intricate parceling necessary to satisfy all constituents, not simply theirs, they soon became aware of the true difficulty of governing. Given who I was and the platform on which I had been elected, the expectations for progress on many fronts were profound.

.   .   .

Nancy Wackstein was encouraged by her friends and former coworkers in the social services field to take the job offered her as director of the Mayor's Office on Homelessness. "We need you there," they told her. Within ninety days, they were beating the hell out of her because we hadn't shut down all the welfare hotels yet. "Ninety days!" she says. "We couldn't even find the toilets!"

Addressing poverty and homelessness is never a winning strategy for a mayor. The issue has a very small constituency—far less powerful and well funded than, for example, the real estate or business communities— and the problems are so deeply entrenched and intractable that the best one can accomplish is to make headway, not truly solve these massive societal difficulties in one or two terms in office. Nevertheless, I felt it was important to focus on the issue of homelessness early in my administration. I had been elected on a platform that placed it front and center, and I could speak to the issues directly from the heart.

First, I wanted to empty the Manhattan welfare hotels of homeless families. The hotels were a blight, and they were not providing safety or comfort to the people whom they were housing. Children in particular were being damaged by the arrangement. It was inhumane and expensive, and two of the major offenders—the Hotel Carter and the Martinique— were in Times Square and Herald Square, respectively, crossroads of cultural and mercantile activity, which made them highly visible. Those hotels and dozens like them were costing the city millions of dollars and giving it a black eye. The Hotel Carter was only a few blocks from the offices of the *New York Times,* which almost guaranteed a continuing flow of negative press coverage. We began the relocation effort. Where could we house the residents? Our first choice was to place folks in hospitable shelters, most of which we would have to create, as few were immediately available. We had developed an aggressive program to develop alternatives to these hotels that we called Tier 2 shelters. Our plan was to use city-owned, tax-foreclosed *in rem* housing stock, rehabilitate it into private apartments with private kitchens and baths, and have these buildings run by social service agencies, not private landlords. We accelerated the production schedule at the New York City Department of Housing Preservation and Development (HPD) to achieve this goal. At the same time, we put immediate pressure on the NYC Housing Authority to find suitable quarters for what was to be an extremely large group of relocated families.

Mayor Koch's approach to the homeless had been punitive. He had created Tier 1 shelters, those huge Quonset hut–style armory structures, in places like Roberto Clemente State Park, where as many as a thousand men were housed in row after row of beds on an open drill floor with an absolute lack of privacy. His concept boiled down to: *Don't make shelters too nice because it will coddle people and they'll stay there too long.* I was of another belief altogether. I felt it was society's duty to help the less fortunate among us live acceptably comfortable lives. We wanted these places to be pleasant. We also wanted them to offer social services so residents could not only live with some element of dignity but also begin the transition to better lives.

None of this came without a fight. The shelter system was administered by the NYC Human Resources Administration (HRA), whose commissioner, Barbara Sabol, was determined to fix the child welfare system; some of those trying to resolve the homeless situation found her disinterested in their cause. Some found HPD commissioner Felice Michetti overtly hostile to the notion of moving homeless families into newly renovated housing units, fearing damage to the equity, and Michetti battled with Nancy Wackstein over the order in which and to whom these units became available. Wackstein had leaned heavily on the Housing Authority to open some of the vacant units in city-seized abandoned properties and take in a larger number of homeless families by giving them priority of placement, and then she was castigated—shrieked at—by housing advocates for "ruining" public housing by putting so many homeless families in these units!

This was a complicated issue. Who gets first dibs on government housing—a hardworking secretary with a family who earns $23,000 a year, or a homeless family living in terrible conditions in a welfare hotel costing the city $3,000 a month?

I have an HPD secretary here who comes to work every day—why doesn't she have priority for those apartments?!

I have a family of six living in one room with a hot plate for a stove—why don't they have priority?!

The wait for subsidized housing was eternal. Who would get it? People who had followed all the rules and done the right thing or people who had nothing at all? There was no right answer because there were too many New Yorkers in need and not enough government services to help all of them. (Modern conservative thought would have them all out on the street, unserved by government whatsoever. I find that appalling.) Nancy Wackstein was berated by a *New York Times* editorial writer who told her, "You are ruining the New York City Public Housing Authority, which has been the jewel in the crown of municipal government, because you are, in effect, allowing people to jump the line!" Norman Steisel initially felt that this was an alarmist argument, that the number of people being relocated was sufficiently small that the effect on the Housing Authority properties was negligible, and besides, their need was great. Bill Lynch was initially supportive of the move as well because he had spent sizable resources and a significant amount of time in city housing getting out the vote and he found it a large and dependable political constituency whose increase in size could only help us.

Were people with substandard housing trying to abuse the system, declaring themselves homeless and knowing they could therefore jump

the line for subsidized housing, or were they legitimate potential recipients of government assistance? Certainly some people were trying to
scam the system, and the public at large does fix on anecdotes. (Ronald
Reagan's bogus "welfare queens" story comes immediately to mind.) But
just as our system of jurisprudence says it is far better to let nine guilty
people go free than to convict an innocent person, one does not formu-
late policy based upon outliers; one creates policy based on the majority,
and this policy response was entirely appropriate to the needs shared by
most of the homeless. I do not believe anyone in my administration ever
imagined he or she was doing harm; we were only dividing precious
resources in the best way possible.

Our initial efforts were enormously successful. Under my mandate,
Steisel and Wackstein would knock heads every week with representatives of the Human Resources Administration, the Department of Housing Preservation and Development, and the Housing Authority. "Where
are we? What are the numbers? How many units are coming on line?
How are we moving the move-ins?" Within a year we had relocated
almost all of the hotels' homeless families; the residential population fell
from 3,300 families to 150. Funding was divided 50 percent federal, 25
percent state, and 25 percent city; the New York State Department of
Social Services had oversight of the shelter system, however, and it supported our Tier 2 concept. We had to demonstrate that we were meeting
the state's considerable regulations, and when we gained their approval
they turned on the money.

Then came a surge.

When it became clear that the homeless were indeed receiving priority and that the supply of higher-quality housing was increasing, the
number of people entering the shelter system began to rise dramatically.
Those who had been concerned about such an eventuality were proved
correct. Were there people on the edge who decided to become homeless
in order to gain a better deal? Did an increased availability of housing
stock, the belief that one could obtain this housing by declaring homelessness, and a national economic downturn that threw people out of

their jobs and homes all conspire to create a homeless epidemic? It is entirely possible.

We had eliminated Koch's Tier 1 shelters. I felt this to be a major accomplishment; they had come to symbolize all that was wrong with the shelter system. We were building Tier 2s as fast as we could but were forced by the circumstance of overwhelming demand to become reliant on hotels again. Outer-borough "hot sheet" motels could make more money renting to the city than letting out rooms by the hour, and we found some acceptable lodging there. But even they began to decrease in supply.

In 1979 attorney Robert Hayes had found a passage in the New York State Constitution that mandated "the aid, care, and support of the needy," and he had sued New York City in an effort to help the city's panhandlers, presumably all single people. Soon thereafter, Legal Aid sued on behalf of homeless families. Hayes found a receptive ear with Supreme Court judge Richard Wallach, and an agreement was reached. Hayes wanted small shelters and housing, but Mayor Koch disagreed. "I believe there are minimums below which nobody should be permitted to fall," Koch said later, "but after that, this country is so big, so wonderful and filled with opportunities, after that you have to earn it."

After much negotiation, the city and Hayes signed a consent decree that made New York the first municipality in the United States to guarantee each homeless person, as the *New York Times* put it, "the bare necessities of shelter: a mattress, a pillow, clean sheets, soap, a roof over his head." The regulations included the proviso that anyone who applied to the city for shelter before 11:00 PM had to be placed by 8:00 the next morning. In an unpredictable twist, the New York State Social Services commissioner who approved that regulation had been Cesar Perales, who became my deputy mayor for health and human services. "My anger at the time I approved those regulations," he says, "had been motivated by local upstate conservative communities who felt that if their homeless sat there long enough, they would just go to a relative or somewhere else, and the taxpayers of, say, Allegheny County would not have to put them up in a hotel.

"In New York City," he continues, "there was a giant Human Resources

Administration, but in most small counties there was only a small Department of Social Services. We got federal money, which was matched by the cities and localities, but we were in charge of the rules, one of which I thought was perfectly logical: if someone showed up at the Department of Social Services and said, 'I'm homeless,' filled out all the forms, and indicated they had no place to go, they had forty-eight hours to put them somewhere. You couldn't just let them sit around your office, which was what was happening in most places upstate."

In New York City there was also the issue of admission. The screening process itself was suspect. People would appear at the intake centers and say, "I'm homeless." They would be asked, in effect, "Where did you stay last night?"

"Well, I was with my brother-in-law, but his wife won't let me stay there anymore."

"Go back." The examiner would assess the situation and determine that the person had an acceptable lodging and was therefore ineligible. Representatives from the Coalition for the Homeless and the Legal Aid Society opined that while this might be true in X number of cases, in Y number the person really had no place to go, yet all were being put out. What were they supposed to do? So you have to envision a mother with two or three little kids and no roof over their heads for the night out in the damn street. It didn't stop there. Once applicants were ruled ineligible, they were not entitled to reapply for a specific amount of time, so they were out in the street for the duration.

The need was never-ending. The harder the Office on Homelessness worked, the more successful it was in shutting down these unspeakable hotels, the more people poured into the streets and the demand for affordable housing skyrocketed. The Office of Management and Budget would constantly ask, "How do you close the front door?" The answer was, until there is work available sufficient to enable families and individuals to pay acceptable rent, you don't.

.   .   .

One of the ideas we brought to fruition was the "New York/New York Agreement," a housing initiative jointly supported between New York City and the state. A number of recent legal decisions had made it more difficult to commit people to mental institutions against their will, and as a result, from 1963 to 1976, the national census of public mental hospital patients fell from 504,000 to 16,000. In the 1980s, managed care systems created financial incentives to admit fewer people to mental hospitals and to discharge them more quickly. The phrase "mental hospitals emptied" was not uncommon among policymakers and the media in New York at that time, and the streets and subways seemed inundated with people with mental difficulties who had nowhere to go. The city and state agreement assisted homeless people with mental illness or substance abuse problems by providing housing accompanied by a wide variety of social services located within the shelters. While that was an important breakthrough, because these residents were particularly troubled, their potential presence contributed to the Not In My Backyard (NIMBY) problems and made finding locations for the new Tier 2 facilities even more difficult; we had to reach out to the City Council for assistance. We needed local goodwill and ultimately acceptance to place facilities in individual neighborhoods, and while the Human Resources Administration had strong experience in working with advocacy groups on general issues, it was less experienced in working with community boards on a block-by-block basis on neighborhood issues.

The shelter system's intake centers, called Emergency Assistance Units (EAUs) and run by the Human Resources Administration, were swamped. These were the offices established to interview and evaluate housing applicants as to whether they were in fact eligible, and if so, where they could be placed. The intake centers were the valve into the system. But as the demand surged we were faced with an overflow of applicants whom we could not get through the pipeline; there was no place on the back end to put them. Housing Authority stock was full, hotels were all taken, and Tier 2s were not yet built with capacity to meet the demand. As a result, the entire shelter system was overwhelmed. And so we were faced with the unsettling and entirely unacceptable picture of families camping out at intake centers, people sleeping on plastic chairs, babies diapered on desks, pregnant women and people with mental illnesses spending the night without food in office lobbies. The situation deteriorated so much that Judge Helen E. Freedman of the State Supreme Court found New York City in contempt of court and ordered four members of my administration to spend a night in the intake centers themselves. Norman Steisel and Barbara Sabol did not get along, and Nancy Wackstein, who worked with both, was keen on the idea of their sharing a jail cell. (Shortly thereafter, burned out from the battles, Nancy left government to direct the Lenox Hill Neighborhood House and, later, the United Neighborhood Houses of New York. She has been a tireless advocate ever since.) The contempt-of-court citations were later overturned by the Court of Appeals. The Legal Aid suit was finally settled with the Bloomberg administration in 2011.

Meanwhile, resistance from the Housing Authority increased. With the new families came heightened property damage and community destabilization. The formerly homeless were not entirely welcomed and did not always behave well, creating a physical, cultural, and political upheaval in the housing projects. Both Lynch and Steisel recognized the damage being done in their areas and were pursuing solutions.

The federal government ran a subsidy program called Section 8 that included a housing voucher for low-income people, but there was no possibility of its being used on New York City's behalf. Mayors and governors habitually say that the federal government "walked away," but this was the end of the Reagan era, when his administration had almost completely disinvested the federal Department of Housing and Urban Development; none of the Reagan people displayed any interest in putting money into affordable housing in New York or anywhere else. They didn't so much walk away as hightail it.

Advocates for the homeless proposed that New York City create a Section 8 of its own. They suggested increasing the amount of money given to welfare recipients for rent supplements, on the theory that if you gave them another $20 a month they would be able to rent more commodious apartments in the community. We studied the idea and found that $20 would make no difference whatsoever: landlords would simply increase their rents without raising the quality of the housing. We found that raising benefits by $100 a month was more like it. In concept this made sense. Unfortunately, in New York City at a time of severe financial setback, the idea was a budget buster. The Office of Management and Budget ran the numbers and Deputy Director Beverly Donohue came running into Nancy Wackstein's office saying, "We can't do this, it will bankrupt the city!"

.   .   .

A pitched battle was erupting between the advocates, on the one hand, and what Norman Steisel calls the "naysayer ideologues," on the other. We needed to broaden the discussion. We established the New York City Commission on the Homeless, headed by Andrew Cuomo, which, after some time, came back with a series of policy initiatives. One was the creation of the Department of Homeless Services, which would focus exclusively on this problem that was clearly going to be an urban issue for at least a generation.

I named Charles "Chip" Raymond that department's first commissioner. I felt that we had sufficient advisers with advocacy backgrounds on our team and that we needed a person with strong managerial skills and experience. Raymond had distinguished himself while improving the conditions at the Willowbrook State School for mentally disabled children after WABC-TV reporter Geraldo Rivera's startling revelations of its horrible conditions in 1972. The work Raymond did at Willowbrook not only made life better for the six thousand children exposed to these conditions, but set the groundwork for ultimately closing that institution in 1987 and putting people into community-based supportive settings. The state had hired a team of people led by Norman Steisel, who was a consultant at the time, to get that job done, and Chip Raymond had performed admirably. The fact that Chip and Norman had already worked together was an added benefit when we established the Department of Homeless Services and put Chip in charge.

The shelters would be taken out of the hands of the Human Resources Administration, and the city would hire nonprofit groups to provide drug treatment, job training, and other services for the homeless. Not-for-profit organizations were linked to the communities they served, while the city was viewed as an outside force; they could provide social services while capitalizing on and leveraging other available social service funds. Among the homeless commission's suggestions was that families tie their eligibility for housing to their willingness to accept treatment or services for problems like drug abuse, alcoholism, and mental illness, which had been found to be rampant in the homeless population. Also offered would be stabilizing services such as parenting classes, so that once families had moved into Housing Authority and other facilities they had the knowledge and skills to maintain them properly. Without those skills, the homeless were feared to be destabilizing groups of people who just couldn't take care of themselves. *You give them new housing and they'll just wreck it. Kids will get mugged.* And so on. Participation in those programs became a ticket into permanent housing; in order to earn placement one had to successfully complete these initiatives. There was no such thing as a free ticket.

The New York City Commission on the Homeless reinforced the many proposals made by my administration and by advocacy groups, including expanding investment in housing for the mentally ill and affordable rentals for homeless families; eliminating the warehouse-style armory shelters; and expanding supportive services to the homeless living on the streets.

Andrew Cuomo chaired that commission until 1993, when he moved into President Bill Clinton's administration as assistant secretary responsible for community and economic development at the US Department of Housing and Urban Development.

Our approach was successful. According to Department of Homeless Services and Human Resources Administration figures, during the Koch years the homeless population rose to 28,000. During my administration, the figure was reduced to between 17,000 and 24,000. It remained steady during the Giuliani years, but has skyrocketed to between 35,000 and 40,000 under Mayor Michael Bloomberg.

.   •   .

It was apparent to me that New York City's public health care system, if not entirely broken, needed intensive strengthening.

Think of Medicaid as insurance for the very poor. Under insurance plans, you visit a doctor, the doctor treats you, and then the doctor is paid a proscribed fee from the insurance company plus your individual copayment. The problem for poor folks was that the fee the doctor received from the government for his or her services was extremely minimal and that rate never increased. This payment had not been sufficient when the program commenced in 1965, and in 1991 it was no longer anywhere near realistic. As a result, most private practitioners were no longer accepting Medicaid patients. People who knew what was happening in the ghetto, in poor communities, understood that whatever health care existed was found in Medicaid mills, often run-down filthy offices in which a doctor would be set up to see one person every seven minutes to make even sixty bucks in an hour. Medical care was brief and perfunctory at best, and often shoddy. Sometimes the doctor would bill the government for serving the whole family when he had seen only one individual, because that was the only way these guys could make it. Not that they were nice guys to begin with.

The other alternative for care was in hospital clinics, where tradition held that everyone who entered was seen. Clinics were aligned with teaching hospitals. There were no appointments; one would arrive at 9:00 AM and by 10:00, when the doctor and student showed up, there would be another hundred patients waiting to be examined. Then they'd let 'em loose out of the corral, like they were cattle. This is the way doctors were being taught to practice medicine. Poor people, with little access to doctors and no money to pay them, had also for some time been using the city's public hospital emergency rooms for primary care, going there to have all manner of medical circumstance treated instead of only emergencies. This was not only driving up hospital costs at taxpayer expense, but creating a logjam that underserved the working class and prevented those in desperate medical need from being tended to in a timely manner. I created the position of deputy mayor for health and human services to create a system to cure these ills.

We recruited Cesar A. Perales, who for the previous nine years had been commissioner of the New York State Department of Social Services under Gov. Mario Cuomo, and before that had been assistant secretary for human services in the newly created Department of Health and Human Services in the Jimmy Carter White House. We had heard that he was tired of living in Albany and was excited about the possibility of returning to the city, where he had been raised, earned a bachelor's degree from City College, and graduated from Fordham Law School. Perales had represented the Young Lords, an activist Puerto Rican community organization, after they took control of a church to provide social services to the poor in El Barrio, and he had negotiated the early-morning nonviolent arrest of over a hundred members who refused to obey a police demand to leave. "The Young Lords were seen as a radical young Puerto Rican group that, actually in that situation had taken over that church and were offering breakfast to the kids," he says. "These young people had a right to have a lawyer. I was doing my job as a lawyer for a group that I thought was doing good things."

During the interview process, Perales was introduced to the variety of styles and people in my administration. His initial meeting was with Bill Lynch, whom he had previously met casually. Lynch wanted to know how Perales thought, how he related to people, whom he knew in the community. Though this is not standard procedure for deputy mayoral interviews, they talked politics. Lynch tried to draw him out: What were his interests? What kind of person was he? "He wasn't going to quiz me on what I knew about the latest changes in the welfare law, or in Medicaid or anything else," Cesar recalls. "I don't even know whether Bill knew anything about it." Perales came away with the distinct impression that Lynch was interested in what he was about as a person, not simply as a government functionary. "You'll hear from somebody," Lynch told him when they concluded. "And a couple of days later a guy named Norman Steisel calls me," Perales recalls now.

Rather than meet at someone's home, Steisel suggested a more formal breakfast at a restaurant in the World Trade Center. "Norman was interested in what I knew," Perales recalls. "What I wanted to do in the government, what I had heard about what was going on in the Dinkins administration. He was a tough interviewer. Pure business."

Bill and Norman both reported back to me, each from his individual perspective. "I would hope that Lynch would say, 'This is a solid guy,' and that Norman would say, 'This guy knows his business,'" Perales says. "I, like so many other people, had read in the newspapers that there was a war going on between the Lynches and the Steisels, and that it just wasn't working. I could understand how somebody would say, 'These guys have got to stab each other in the back every day of the week,' because they were so totally different and approached people so differently. I mean, Norman was not a warm and cuddly guy. But I clearly got a very different impression, that while they were two very different people, they both were very serious about government. Both of them were extremely loyal to the mayor and were interested in giving him the best advice they could give him, but from two totally different perspectives."

After Perales survived both Lynch and Steisel, he met with me. My question was: What do you want to do for the people of New York? Prepared to persuade me of his great talents, he gave me an insight into his many years in government: "The one thing I've learned is, we're all short-timers. And that we have to decide what it is we want to do, and then narrow that down to what we think we can do within a period of time, and then decide that that's what we want to do. And every morning when you get up and go to work, that's what you're about, and that's what you're going to tell the people who work for you."

"Well," I asked, "what do you want to do?"

Perales laid out the problem. Medicaid did not in any real sense give poor people access to care; most competent doctors would not see them because the program paid so little, which left a substantial portion of the city's population to the mercies of Medicaid mills and emergency rooms. Neither was acceptable.

What was becoming increasingly clear to those conversant in public health was that unless a patient had a doctor whom he or she had seen before, that patient was at a serious disadvantage. A doctor treating a patient for the first time would have no medical history, would be unaware of the medicines being taken or previous reactions, and would have to start running tests in order to document symptoms, though usually the doctor wouldn't even bother. What was needed—and the phrase became dogma among physicians who were concerned about primary care—was "continuity of care." This was essential. Also, because of its progressive traditions, New York City maintained that people ought not to be forced to see a particular doctor; the concept of freedom of choice in selection of a physician was another accepted doctrine. Many members of my team believed in that freedom. Nevertheless, Perales suggested Medicaid Managed Care.

Until that moment, New York City had resisted the concept, and my predecessor was vilified for even mentioning it. Ed Koch had taken some heat on the issue, and during my first two years in office I had stayed away from it. But Perales was a smart and progressive man whom I trusted to give me an honest appraisal, and as I listened he made a lot of sense. I could take the heat if it meant improving the health of the city community.

There was an additional incentive to create such a system. At between 11 and 12 percent, the cost of Medicaid was the most rapidly rising expenditure in the city budget; citywide, other expenditures were increasing by between only 1 and 3 percent. If we could effectively control the growth of these health costs, we could save the city approximately $2 billion. The issue was a winner in the business community and with the public at large.

We decided to present Medicaid Managed Care as an experiment, but we were really just getting the ball rolling. Under our Medicaid plan, doctors would receive a monthly fee of $75 for every patient seen, but each patient would have unlimited access to the physician and could show up at the doctor's office as many times as he or she desired. If the patient chose not to avail himself or herself of those services, the doctor would still receive the $75. The concept was that, unlike the Medicaid mill, where a doctor had incentive to say, "Come back tomorrow" in order to pick up another payday, physicians would act like real doctors and attempt to cure their patients as quickly and humanely as possible. In fact, it was in the doctor's best interest to treat patients successfully from the start; any patient who got sick was going to come back and see that doctor three times that month, taking time and space away from other potential clients.

There were many in the health care field who said we ought not to change Medicaid and require people to join managed care, but Perales believed that if we had facilities and could put together decent plans, we had a true opportunity to improve the health care of a large number of New York City residents. Health care plans had been criticized for limiting the number of doctors available to each of their participants. Health care was a right, these critics held, and if the state put people in health maintenance organizations, it was abridging those rights. In concept this was fine, but in the real world the argument lost much of its luster; it was unacceptable to me to have people using emergency rooms as their primary care source and so getting no care. This wasn't about denying people the freedom of choice. The choices available to them were so terrible that it was a meaningless argument!

For those who felt strongly about the importance of continuity of care, Perales had another plan.

Again I asked, "What do you want to do?"

"Well, we've got hospitals up the kazoo," Perales told me. "We've got the Department of Health on the other side with all sorts of clinics. We ought to put them together and focus on providing people with family doctors right in their neighborhood."

My mother, Sally Dinkins, as a young woman.

My father, Bill Dinkins Jr. (center), with Les Hayling.

LEFT: Trenton Central High School, 1944.

RIGHT: I fought my way into the Marine Corps just before the end of World War II.

My bride, Joyce Burrows, on our wedding day, August 30, 1953.

"The Three Musketeers":
Fred Schenck, Hilmar Ludwig "Junky Joe"
Jensen Jr., and me.

Several years later:
Dr. Les Hayling, Fred Schenck,
Junky Joe, and me.

An early campaign headquarters.

Bill Lynch was "the rumpled genius." There
is no better political strategist in New York,
Period.

Campaigning at Broadway and Canal Street, 1989.

CREDIT: NEAL BOENZI/NEW YORK TIMES

Jesse Jackson, me, and Bill Lynch. Jesse's success in the 1988 New York Democratic presidential primary helped lay the foundation for my victory in 1989.

With Joyce by my side and Court of Appeals Judge Fritz Alexander swearing me in on inauguration day, January 1, 1990, I became New York City's first African American mayor. CREDIT: JOAN VITALE STRONG

When the World Trade Center was bombed in 1993, I was in Japan. First Deputy Mayor Norman Steisel and Police Commissioner Ray Kelly (not pictured) performed exquisitely. Upon my return I found the city in good hands.

CREDIT: JOAN VITALE STRONG

There are a few perquisites that come with being mayor, but very little time to enjoy them.

CREDIT: © CHESTER HIGGINS, JR./
CHESTERHIGGINS.COM

Sharing my favorite city with my personal hero, "Madiba"—Nelson Mandela.

CREDIT: CHESTER HIGGINS, JR./
NEW YORK TIMES

We had our trials during my mayoralty,
and we developed ideas and initiatives to deal with them.

President Bill Clinton and NYPD Commissioner Ray Kelly.
With rates surging nationwide, we drove down crime faster
than any prior administration in New York City.

Assemblywoman Geraldine Daniels (smiling), J. Raymond Jones (seated), Charlie Rangel, and me at City Hall. Long retired, "the Fox" was visiting from the West Indies and checking on his protégés.

The Gang of 4—me, Basil Paterson, Percy Sutton, and Charlie Rangel—through the ages.

President Obama and I faced and overcame similar obstacles.

CREDIT: MANDEL NGAN/GETTY IMAGES

Big forehand—wish I had a backhand to match.

I am so proud of my wonderful family: (with me, from left) Jamal, Joyce, Dave Jr., Donna, and Kalila. CREDIT: ALLEN MORGEN

Kalila ("Granddaddy's Little Cupcake") graduated from Columbia University and Jamal ("Daddy's Little Tiger") from University of Massachusetts at Amherst.

With Nelson Mandela (holding my granddaughter Kalila), my daughter Donna, son Dave Jr., and Joyce at Gracie Mansion. CREDIT: JOAN VITALE STRONG

I see New York as a gorgeous mosaic of race and religious faith, of national origin and sexual orientation. We have made history. Mayors come and mayors go, but the city must endure. CREDIT: © RICK MAIMAN/SYGMA/CORBIS

"How would we do that?"

"The first, the most important thing," he told me, "is to lay out a plan. Once you've got a plan in place, it'll happen. The most difficult element will be to get people to focus on how you get parts of the hospital system to work with the Department of Health clinics and all of the other facilities that might be available to do this. This takes planning, because not everything is going to fit."

"How long do you think it would take you to do something like that?"

"I bet I could do it in about three months."

"Are you sure?"

"Yeah, I could do that in about three months."

I hired him.

On Cesar Perales's first day on the job, I delivered the State of the City Address. He was seated prominently near the front. "I was thinking, *Wow! with the City Council sitting behind me, I feel very important,*" he remembers. I announced his appointment with great pride and seriousness, and then told the gathered dignitaries and press, "In one hundred days we will have a plan for Communi-care. Primary care facilities in the communities. One hundred days." I gave him an extra ten!

The press surrounded Cesar afterwards. How could he possibly succeed?

Every twenty days, print and broadcast reporters would call Perales's office to see if he was getting anywhere. Our entire operation was working hard, but there was a palpable sense that the media wanted us to fail. Success would mean an improvement in the health and welfare of hundreds of thousands of New Yorkers, but failure would mean a better story of broken government promises—always a winner.

Bureaucracy is notoriously slow to budge, and it is a Sisyphean effort to move the municipal rock. This had been Perales's experience of federal and state bureaucracy, which was why he had come to the conclusion that all one could reasonably expect was to pick a small piece and try one's best to dislodge it. However, Cesar was pleased to find that, working with tough and ruthless operatives such as Director of Operations Harvey

Robins and Deputy Director of the Office of Management and Budget Barbara Turk, they got the bureaucracy moving.

One fight encapsulated the larger struggle. The doctors at the Department of Health worked nine-to-five. This was the expected routine: one passed the Civil Service exam or its medical equivalent, one became a government doctor, one worked at the clinic, and one left at five o'clock sharp. Well, that wasn't going to work if we were going to have family doctors in the community. People—patients!—worked from nine to five, Monday to Friday, and often Saturday, and many were not in a position to take time off to visit their doctor. Our physicians would have to take turns being on call. This was the deal or else the whole concept would die.

So, believe it or not, there was a negotiation, a Civil Service negotiation, as to how much more we would have to pay doctors in the Health Department to change their title and create a class of physician, and a class of assistants and nurses and others, who would be available after hours a certain number of days each week to serve the community. All of this had to be negotiated. People outside of government cannot imagine that something like that would literally take weeks. And Cesar had the deadline of one hundred days looming.

How did this get done? Perales had a lot of help from his staff, people who would muscle everybody. "I mean, they were pushing people around," he says. Dr. Margaret "Peggy" Hamburg's preferred expression was a smile, so she smiled her way through while Barbara Turk applied the muscle. They found office space in which to situate community health care centers. They organized doctors, nurses, and aides to staff these offices, and they found supplies to make them whole. They created a network of community health care centers—Communi-care—and they succeeded. They came back to Cesar one day and said, "It's done." Peggy rose to the position of commissioner of the New York City Department of Health in my administration and later became the commissioner of the Food and Drug Administration in the Obama administration.

Cesar delivered Communi-care to Gracie Mansion on the ninety-ninth day, at about 5:00 PM. The plan changed the very nature of health care in New York City by opening thirteen community family health centers in underserved areas; in these centers, individuals would have their own doctors and access to care twenty-four hours a day. With this level of access to primary and preventive care within the community, in warm, attractive settings, poor New Yorkers no longer were forced to resort to emergency rooms to serve as their family doctors. For the ten centers for which statistics were available, 637,493 visits were recorded from September 1992 to August 1993.

Our Medicaid Managed Care program was the largest privatization effort ever undertaken in municipal government. It replaced the problematic, cumbersome "fee-for-service" system with coordinated health networks offering comprehensive, preventive, and primary care for Medicaid recipients. The streamlined system gave doctors greater incentives to serve Medicaid clients and made a wide range of commercial health care plans available to Medicaid recipients. From 1990 to December 1993, the number of health care plans participating in our Medicaid Managed Care program grew from six to sixteen. Under this initiative, 162,000 Medicaid recipients joined managed care plans, greater even than our goal of 100,000, and more than tripling the number of those who had joined the small, voluntary plans that had been available over the previous twenty years, like Group Health Incorporated (GHI) and Health Plan of New York (HIP) (which had their own problems and needed a shot in the arm). Our plan was to sign up approximately a half-million recipients over a four-year period.

Our health programs were so successful that my successor, Rudy Giuliani, in one of his rare efforts to maintain a program from my administration, tried to expand them. His commissioners were instructed to really step on the gas and try to enroll 800,000 eligible New Yorkers almost immediately. Medicaid Managed Care was dependent on matching patients with provider networks, and whereas we worked diligently within reachable timelines and guidelines, Giuliani could not put these networks in place to match their increased enrollment. Insurers did not have the administrative capabilities to properly meet the medical needs of all those who were eligible. Giuliani's effort failed miserably and collapsed for several years until it was reinstated on a more reasonable growth trajectory. What could have been a legacy of significantly improved health throughout the city died owing to overreaching. It was a shame. We were ahead of the curve.

Recently programs similar to ours have begun to be legislated in several states, most notably Florida, in response to or as an enhancement of the Affordable Care Act, or what is being called "Obamacare."

We also created the innovative Primary Care Development Corporation to leverage funds and provide seed money and incentives for nonprofit organizations to open health centers in their neighborhoods; this program offered access to financing, allowed for primary care expansion, and further enhanced accessibility to health care for New Yorkers. We placed $17 million in a revolving fund for planning and development of these centers, and under this program $250 million in long-term, low-interest, tax-exempt bonds became available for construction costs. The program represented the single largest infusion of primary care capacity since the original federal community health center program of the 1960s and provided care for an additional 300,000 New Yorkers.

.   .   .

In December 1992, a nor'easter tore through New York, damaging and isolating a huge stretch from Staten Island through the Bronx. From a distance New York may appear to be a gruff city, but that's a bad rap; New Yorkers have a tradition of pulling together during times of emergency. However, its service agencies sometimes do not get the message. This storm required a coordinated effort among the Sanitation, Transportation, Parks, and Fire Departments. Each had individual expertise and separate equipment, and each was historically protective of its turf. Instead of having each agency work in its own silo, we told them, "Forget about what badge you're wearing, we're all one city." This was my vision of the true New York community—a unity of neighborhoods, a gorgeous mosaic, put to the test—and I am very proud to say we responded generously. We brought the talent and resources of the city to the stoops of people in every borough along the border. For a city of more than seven million people, we went so far as to do boutique scheduling. If an elderly woman's basement in Queens had filled with water and she said, "Well, my son-in-law is coming Saturday at two o'clock," we had the first available department there to help her when he arrived. If a tree had fallen on someone's home in the Bronx, the Fire Department company most available would get out its saws and solve the problem. It didn't matter which neighborhood was in need. Regardless of neighborhood, people in crisis, whether an AIDS patient or a homeless person or one of the elderly, had the talent and expertise of all city agencies at their disposal. As Harvey Robins said, "Everybody got whacked, everybody got help."

Infrastructure was vital to my vision of the city. New York is filled with aging bridges whose importance to city commerce and personal traffic is paramount. We were fighting for each dollar, yet I told the staff, "We cannot *not* have our bridges inspected." They could not be allowed to fall into disrepair. Politicians generally don't think about maintenance; there's no photo-op to painting a bridge, and one cannot hold a child's hand and walk him across six lanes of truck traffic to demonstrate such a thing the way one can escort a schoolboy into an after-school program at a library. But let the damn thing fall down and there's hell to pay. (If one erects a new bridge, one can stand there and take bows, but we did not have that kind of money.)

The *Daily News* published a photo op-ed of a place beside one of the highways in the Bronx where people were dumping garbage. The image didn't need a whole lot of words. The headline said approximately, "Why isn't the Mayor taking on these dumping grounds?" Although I didn't like the heat, I was glad the situation had been brought to our attention. We called in the sanitation commissioner and developed a vacant lot cleaning program. As a result, the number of vacant lots cleaned by the city that year doubled.

Not satisfied with a simple cleanup, we pursued a larger community effect. What was in short supply? Ball fields. We converted rubble-strewn lots that were of sufficient size into playing fields. New York was filled with vacant lots, and our program was highly successful. Didn't mean they were going to be there forever; if the footprint was big enough, the land would probably, ultimately, be used for housing development. Still, we were straightforward with the communities, which were thrilled to have these dangerous eyesores rehabilitated. We leveled with them: "This is not for life. You can have it—until." Housing did claim some of these renovated fields, but a number are still in place and being used by kids and adults to this day.

Harvey Robins was struck by the fact that abandoned vehicles routinely littered the poorest parts of the city but none whatsoever could be found in our wealthier neighborhoods. He put together a small task force of sanitation, transportation, and parks administrators. "Look, I don't know how to get there, but this is what I want," he told them. "I want, within three days, if there's a vehicle in a neighborhood, if it's in a park or it's on a street—I want it gone."

"Why is this such an important priority?" he was asked. "You know we don't have money. We're getting our budgets cut. Times are tight."

Harvey said, "An eyesore in a neighborhood tells people that government doesn't care." And often an eyesore became a more serious problem: abandoned vehicles became filled with trash, then fires started and even more danger accrued. This is not unlike the James Wilson and George Kelling "broken windows" theory of criminology that Bill Bratton used so successfully when he became police commissioner. "I know you guys care," Harvey told them, "so let's get on with it." The administrators said, "Feed us and get out of the room, we'll figure it out."

Meals were brought in for several days while the men and women conferred. When they finally emerged, they had created what they called a public-private partnership. In the past the three agencies had hated this work. It had involved picking up the abandoned vehicles, then towing them to a distant junk lot in Brooklyn, after which they had no use for them. All that changed.

First, the administrators developed a tracking system whereby, rather than reporting an abandoned vehicle to their agency, transportation or sanitation agents would simply tag the junker, note the cross street, and contact a scrap dealer, who would call in his own truck, take the wreck to his own shop, and turn it into a profit. If the first scrap dealer did not pick it up within three days, the agents went down the alphabet to find another.

The program was magical. Overnight what had been an urban blight became a job-creating economic opportunity. The administrators said, "This is great! All we have to do is phone it in, put it on a computer, and some guy comes and takes it away!" For our part, we could properly and accurately tell people in the city's poorest neighborhoods, "We care."

Our abandoned vehicle initiative has now become a national program.

.   .   .

I recruited a number of passionate, progressive advocates who, after twelve years of being on the outside during the Koch administration, were eager to make real change from within when they came to work for me. They felt their moment had arrived. But without any money, we were often reduced to maintaining the status quo, and even that was sometimes considered a win. Not only did this pain me, but it was hard to explain clearly to those on the outside whose needs were legitimate and continued to be unmet.

The Financial Control Board was a constant presence. It could not determine policy, and it could not recommend one course of action over another. Put simply, they couldn't tell you how many eggs to buy—you could buy all eggs and no bread if that was the way you wanted to spend your grocery money—but they could tell you *how much* you could spend on eggs and bread. The need to cut spending rather than put government money to good use was an issue that invaded every aspect of my mayoralty. To that end, we monitored the agencies to keep the expenses consistent with the falling revenues. Belts were tightened all around.

Norman Steisel was a key strategist, as was Director of Operations Harvey Robins. We went over the city budget line by line. Do we need an annual report in color? Do we need another driver? Do we need to take so many trips? Harvey was particularly expert in this regard, and among the areas on which he concentrated was the reduction of overtime. In the police, fire, and sanitation departments, overtime is what commissioners use as goodies. Civil service pension rates are based on the final three years of one's government employment, and if one has earned significant amounts of time-and-a-half or double-time overtime during this period, the added benefit can last a lifetime. This behavior had been institutionalized, and we found that commissioners were less than willing to alter the awarding of these perquisites, which would of course have decreased their individual power and ability to bargain. However, in a difficult fiscal climate the last thing New York City needed was a rising debt burden.

What leverage did we have to encourage the commissioners to control their spending? Harvey felt that he could not get this done quietly, that the Office of Operations simply did not have the clout. What he did have was access to the press. Twice a year Harvey provided the media with reports on the pension benefits the city was paying to the recently retired. You may have seen these stories: illustrated by bar graphs and pictures, they list former city employees, their jobs, their salaries, the overtime they accrued in their final years, and the total. They are newspaper classics—for the rest of his or her life, a former commissioner will be making more each year than the mayor—and an embarrassment to the people in charge of signing off on these arrangements. Harvey named names.

Our biggest nut to crack was the Police Department. Commissioner Ray Kelly was not particularly pleased with Harvey, but he did authorize less overtime, and we were able to drive several million dollars out of the NYPD budget. This effort continued into the next administration. Commissioner Kelly was succeeded by Bill Bratton, whose first deputy, John Timoney, called Harvey and told him, "I'm gonna beat you. You're out of office, but I'm gonna beat you anyway. We don't need the Office of Operations to tell us how to reduce overtime, that's an operations decision within the Police Department!" He then proceeded to drive overtime in his department down from approximately $300 million to around $80 million. I am pleased to have helped New York City save millions even when I was no longer mayor.

The concept of prevention had some currency. New York City could not print money, but if we invested what funds we did have in preventive services, we could see substantial future returns. If we taught and encouraged parents to care for and not abandon their children, the city not only would benefit from the solidity of the family unit but would save money for decades by avoiding expensive foster-care placement. If we offered resources and services in the community, we could prevent people from becoming homeless and therefore alleviate a huge drain on the city's finances. If we put money into after-school programs, we could prevent the social disruption and significant expense of juvenile justice placement. For some people the sociocultural advantages are the deciding factor in the creation and nourishment of such programs; for others it is the dollar savings. What was important to me was that the city move forward on all levels. These arguments are being made on the local and national levels to this day, with varying degrees of success.

One possible solution was to cut the budget across the board. From a distance this sounds like a fair and sound policy—share the pain equally—but it was not a course I chose. In practice it is not fair or sound at all. The loss of, let us say, 5 percent of one agency's budget might make it unable to hire staff who would do their jobs more effectively; a 5 percent cut at another agency could mean that a thousand people didn't get breakfast anymore! I felt it would be negligent to engage in such blind cutting.

Wall Street was also involved in the financial underpinnings of New York City, and these financial interests were under no governmental stipulations as to how they might influence the budget. It appeared to us that the banks, the institutions that purchased the New York City municipal bonds upon which we relied for funds, also had some trepidation concerning my personal and my administration's financial acumen. They were not comfortable at all with us, and they made these feelings known. Wall Street firms were cutting back on the size of their workforces, and they suggested that the city ought to downsize as well. "We think you guys should reduce the size of your head count," we were told, "and there should be a '2' in front of it." In other words, they were looking for a reduction in the size of New York City's workforce of at least 20,000 people.

Surprisingly, this was within reach. As vacancies appeared in each agency, a threshold decision had to be made: Will we backfill this position or shall we let it go vacant? If we replace one worker with another, will we fill the replacement's position? This was planned shrinkage, and working with Comptroller Elizabeth Holtzman, we pursued it thoroughly. Early retirement packages were offered in order to create more vacancies. It was a laborious process, but in the end we were able to weather the crisis with limited layoffs. This wasn't 1975, when the city was forced to let large numbers of cops and firefighters go. Now, even though I had been a math major, there was no calculus called for, no fancy division or multiplication. I was more often called upon to subtract than to add.

The economy was severely damaged, national unemployment had risen by 18 percent in 1990, and tax revenues had been savaged by it. In that atmosphere, we still had to get things done. I was not elected mayor to ignore the promises on which I had campaigned. I needed to achieve my goals within these trying parameters. Despite these challenges, I believe I held true to one of the tenets I put forth while campaigning: "With your help, I intend to be a mayor who pursues basic principles of justice, opportunity, and caring—a mayor who attacks the problems and not the victims."

9

<hr>

Safe Streets, Safe City

Crime was New York City's number-one problem when I was elected mayor. The size of the Police Department had dwindled under my predecessor, Ed Koch, and crime had risen. In fact, when I entered office, crime in New York City had been on an almost uninterrupted climb for fifteen years. Despite the NYPD's best efforts, there had been 2,246 homicides in 1989, 211,130 burglaries, and 91,571 aggravated assaults. Crack cocaine had been introduced to the city's streets and quickly metastasized into a plague. In the first year of my mayoralty, those numbers continued to increase. Developing and implementing a successful anticrime plan takes time, but I hadn't been in office nine months when the *New York Post* ran a headline that screamed, "Dave, Do Something!" One would have gotten the impression that on December 31, 1989, there was no crime, and the next day, when I took office, the homicide rate was over 2,000 a year, as though it had occurred overnight.

I recognize that the accepted wisdom is that crime ran amok under my administration; it is an image that was hammered into the public mind by my opponent, Rudolph Giuliani, in his political campaigns. He and his brain trust needed an avenue of attack that was at once potent and visceral. They chose to tell New Yorkers—relentlessly and untruthfully—that our citizens were under assault, when in fact New York's population was being defended as never before. The truth is in the details. From its peak in 1991, crime decreased more dramatically and more rapidly, both in terms of actual numbers and percentage, than at any time in modern New York City history. I drove down crime faster than any New York City mayor who came before me. Despite the budget deficit, my administration hired more new police officers than any other mayoral administration in the twentieth century. These were the same cops who were used to such advantage by Police Commissioner Bill Bratton and Mayor Giuliani in their highly trumpeted turnaround of New York. Putting our community policing theory into practice, we took these new cops out of patrol cars and put them on the street and in the city's neighborhoods, creating a new kind of law enforcement that affected all levels of society. I hired Ray Kelly, whose reputation has grown so exponentially under Mayor Michael Bloomberg. The result was the successful turnaround of New York City's crime rate, and it was conceived, initiated, and put into practice by my administration.

We implemented these changes within the bounds of an inherited budget that had been decimated by the struggling national economy in the middle of a massive recession. Before I took office, we had been told that the municipal budget was running at a deficit of $175 million; upon our arrival, my administration opened the books and found to our horror that the deficit was in fact $750 million. Rather than expanding the scope of city government to meet the needs of all New Yorkers, as we had envisioned, we were obliged to cut programs that would have served the community. (President Barack Obama faced much the same circumstance upon his election in 2008.)

I was not unaware that some portion of the electorate felt that now, with a black man elected mayor, crime would run rampant. Yet who were the victims of the majority of these crimes? We found that they were largely people from the city's poor black and Hispanic neighborhoods.

Many of these folks had put me in office, and while I was determined to be mayor of all New Yorkers, I would not forget the constituents who most solidly supported me. According to some, the victim was the entire concept of civil order, as if New Yorkers were being forced to cower before barbarians. The implication, which I found racist in the extreme, was that the criminal element was of color and their victims were civil society itself and the good citizens within. For example, the "squeegee men"—the homeless and mostly black men who congregated at off-ramps and highly trafficked crosstown corners to panhandle and harass motorists—were an intimidating symbol of civil disorder. Giuliani and others did their best to link me to them, as if I personified this disorder, which connected me to crime. The fact that in a city of eight million residents there were only approximately seventy-five of these men did not seem to matter. Nor did the fact that I had been a law-and-order candidate and had vowed to be, as I said in my inauguration speech, "the toughest mayor on crime the city has ever seen."

How does one control crime? Well, that's why every city has a police department. Where were the cops needed? When we asked, we found that the NYPD had not conducted an analytic study of the allocation of police officers throughout the city and precincts in about twenty-five years. Lee Brown was my police commissioner, with Ray Kelly his first deputy, and I asked that the department move quickly to give me the information I needed.

There was some talk about putting on an extra thousand officers. One thousand was a nice round number and would look good in the newspapers—as First Deputy Mayor Norman Steisel said, "It's kind of a sniff test. How can anybody argue with a thousand cops?"—but that was just a guess. We didn't need to guess at what was necessary to make New York safe: we required specific information that would yield effective results. Brown and Kelly gathered the brass and set about the task of gathering that information.

My vision of solving the crime problem extended beyond simply fanning out cops. The problems that afflicted New York were social and economic as well as criminal, and they involved the city's children. You have heard the phrase "No chain is stronger than its weakest link." This was particularly true of the criminal justice system. If we put more cops on the street, more arrests would inevitably follow. We would then need more assistant district attorneys to file the complaints, more court personnel to handle the increased number of cases, and an expanded probation department to help the judges decide the proper punishment in each case. The Corrections Department would need to be addressed, because if we were going to have more effective police protection and a greater number of arrests, we would need facilities in which to house the large influx of suspects and criminals. We would need an expanded parole system to handle people coming out of jail after serving their sentences. We needed a comprehensive plan to attack New York City's crime in a way that would last a lifetime, and we needed the municipal funds to implement it.

From the outset I required a smart, experienced, highly respected person to head the Criminal Justice Department. My first choice was Judge Milton Mollen, the presiding justice of the Appellate Division of the New York State Supreme Court, Second Department. I was playing tennis with his son Scott one day and said, "I've got a great job for Milt, but he'll never take it." I explained what I had in mind. Scott said, "Why don't you ask him?"

I invited Judge Mollen to breakfast with deputy mayors Bill Lynch and Norman Steisel at Gracie Mansion on a Saturday and told him I had an important job that needed doing desperately—criminal justice coordinator. He turned it down. I did not know that in his capacities as presiding justice he had been a member of the Criminal Justice Coordinating Council and had seen a succession of criminal justice coordinators, most of them very capable people, come and go. "None of them have been the least bit productive," he told me. The city's five district attorneys were all elected, each had a constituency to whom to answer, and none cared what the coordinator wanted; they paid him no attention. Milt told me, "Criminal justice coordinators are totally useless. They don't accomplish anything. If you want to serve the public interest, you do one of two things: you either abolish the job in its present form and forget about it, and save the taxpayers money"—the office was fully staffed—"or make it meaningful. 'Cause it's not meaningful now. You've gotta make it a meaningful position."

"What do you mean 'a meaningful position'?"

"You've gotta give the person who holds that position deputy mayor status, so when he speaks, he speaks as a representative of the mayor, he's not just another bureaucrat. The status will generate respect and cooperation. A person who can implement that and use that status to the public's advantage, and the mayor's, there's a chance, if he's a strong enough personality, that he can truly be meaningful in the position and accomplish things on your and the city's behalf."

The meeting lasted about an hour and a half. I spent a good part of the weekend considering the judge's advice. Monday morning I started tongues wagging by visiting him at his courthouse. "I've thought about it," I told him, "and I want to do it your way. Give it any title you want—deputy mayor for public safety, deputy mayor for criminal justice—but with deputy mayor status."

He said he would make his decision within forty-eight hours.

Milt Mollen was born and raised in New York City, went to college and law school here, and after serving in World War II came back to the city to live and work. New York was in his bones—he understood and knew it intimately. He had earned many significant jobs in government. When the *New York World-Telegram and Sun*, one of the city's many newspapers in existence at that time, called him the new "housing czar" of the Robert Wagner administration, his friends called him Czar Milton the First. It was by no means his last position of importance.

When we spoke of his joining my administration, Milt had been a judge for twenty-four years, serving at the Appellate Division fourteen years, almost thirteen of those as the presiding justice, which within the world of the law and the court system was a very prestigious position. His was the busiest appellate court in the United States. Five judges would listen to the arguments, and they essentially established the law for the State of New York. The court had become known as the Mollen Court, and he loved that life.

I did not know this at the time, but one of the reasons Judge Mollen was ultimately receptive to my entreaty was that he was about to embark on his final year as presiding justice. He had served longer at that position than anyone in New York State history, but New York law mandated that he step down as presiding justice at age seventy. Although he was permitted to remain as a justice on the court until age seventy-six, he had made the decision to retire. His successor would be one of three colleagues who were vying for the position. They were a closely knit court, and he knew that some of those who were not chosen to preside would be looking to him for leadership and guidance. They had been looking to him for these qualities for the thirteen years he had served as a strong and effective presiding justice, and he knew they would continue to do so even after he stepped down. This would create problems for his successor, however, so he pledged his colleagues to secrecy and decided to clear out. In December 1989, two months before he and I had our discussion, Judge Mollen had told his colleagues that at the end of the following year he would be leaving the court. He didn't tell them why. He had received partnership offers from large law firms and was considering them. He had been planning to wait until the end of the year before leaving, but my offer moved him along.

I told him the job was to help make the law enforcement aspects of public safety more effective. With that mandate, Judge Mollen called and accepted the job of deputy mayor for public safety. Some people ultimately referred to the position as deputy mayor for public safety and criminal justice. He said he would work with us for two years, which gave us enough time to get this right.

Dr. Lee Patrick Brown was police commissioner. An excellent staff was assembled to gather and analyze information and prepare a plan to fulfill this mandate, consisting of NYPD first deputy commissioner Ray Kelly, Office of Management deputy budget director Mike Jacobson,

Office of Operations deputy director Regina Morris, and Judge Mollen's chief of staff, Katie Lapp. They would report to Judge Mollen regarding general and law enforcement policy and to Norman Steisel concerning finances. By October 1990, we received the report. The 536-page document laid out in significant detail exactly what was needed to bring the department to its fullest working capacity. Some units would be consolidated, some restructured, others eliminated. Uniformed personnel on the entire force would increase by 25 percent, from 25,465 to 31,944. Uniformed personnel at the precinct level would increase 54 percent, and the number of investigators assigned to precinct detective squads would rise by 67 percent. There would be an increase in enforcement strength of 50 percent, dispatch time for crimes in progress would not exceed a minute and a half, and the 911 emergency system would continue to field approximately 4.2 million calls a year. Most significantly, the number of police officers on patrol every day would increase from 6,640 to 10,238, a gain of 54 percent.

In addition to personnel requirements, the report included a plan for substantially restructuring the organization of the department in order to implement the policy of community policing. The Community Patrol Officer Program (CPOP) would increase its size by 523 percent. Along with the extensive addition of uniformed personnel, a commitment was made to increase civilian personnel serving in a host of law enforcement functions to support the activities of the larger police presence— lawyers in the five district attorneys' offices and Legal Aid, police crime lab technicians, food preparation workers in the jails, administrative clerks throughout the criminal justice system, social workers in the various Board of Education youth programs, librarians—which ultimately rose 41 percent, from 7,237 to 10,198.

We called our program Safe Streets, Safe City, with the subtitle Cops and Kids. In conjunction with increased spending and staffing for the NYPD, we developed a plan to create a series of newly conceived community centers. Our Department of Youth and Community Development commissioner Richard Murphy was very adept at devising ways and means to get things done without spending a lot of money, and he created this program. The idea was this: New York City public schools routinely closed after three o'clock in the afternoon, but since this was public space, why not use these buildings beyond the hours of instruction? Richard's vision was that families should have a place they could go to for a period of time equal to the number of hours children were in school. He suggested that the city use these edifices during the nine hours from three until midnight by filling them with programs determined by the communities in which they were located. New York has recreational, vocational, and rehabilitative needs that change within a matter of blocks. Sports, art, drama—the possibilities were extensive. In Flushing there would be large numbers of immigrants who might need instruction in English as a second language; in five different sections of Brooklyn the population would be completely different, as would the programs. After school, at night, on weekends—why not use the resources available to us, fund them properly, and focus on an area not being well served by city government: the family? The communities would design the programs themselves. They would tell us, "You provide safe, secure, clean space and then leave and let us decide what to do with it."

It is easy to laugh at the concept of basketball-after-dark as a justifiable use of precious city funds, and there was some derision from more than one municipal yahoo, but if at night young men and women are on the court learning teamwork and body control instead of on the corner looking for cheap thrills or a quick score, I feel that we as a government have done our job well. This amount of trust in and respect for the people of New York was startlingly unique.

We called them Beacon schools. They would be sources of light and inspiration.

Of course there were obstacles to overcome. The mayor's office did not control these buildings; union contracts had left them largely under the purview of the janitors' union, with whom we had to negotiate.

As we developed a comprehensive plan, our major question was always, where does the money come from? The program as conceived—

hiring more cops and staffing the schools after hours—was costly, but we thought it was essential for the city and for the people to implement it. Budget director Phil Michaels, a conscientious guy trying to do his job, made it clear that the city did not have the funds, and he was not enamored of the restrictions on his discretionary spending that such a program would entail. Budget directors want complete flexibility concerning what they can do with money, so they can plug a hole here, fix a leak there. With the city unable to provide financing for such a project, we had to go to the state. The only way to come up with the needed funds was through a surcharge on the state personal income tax. This was no small problem.

Before we could approach the State Legislature, however, we needed to gain the support of the City Council. A mayor cannot personally request an increase in his city's tax rate; it is required under the state constitution that the city itself present a local home rule message, a request from the City Council to the State Legislature for such a surcharge. Of course the City Council needed to put its fingerprint on the program.

When I first broached the idea of this plan, I focused entirely on funding for law enforcement, primarily police, district attorneys, corrections, probation, and courts. City Council speaker Peter Vallone of Queens, apparently fearful of a political backlash, argued that the program should be funded through the state lottery rather than with income tax surcharges or property tax increases. Our soundings from Albany indicated that the legislature would not change the law concerning the lottery, whose sole purpose was to fund education and related programs; it could not be used without amendment to cover any other public expenditure, no matter how laudable the criminal justice programs seemed. The legislative leadership feared that using the lottery to finance Safe Streets would reduce the revenue going to school systems around the state, thereby either forcing the state to find other sources to make up the difference or putting the burden on cities, counties, and school districts. The idea was dead on arrival.

Moreover, they felt that the City Council, which was in the forefront of demanding increased police services, needed to put skin in the game and agree to increase local taxes. At the same time, we were hearing from our constituents that more needed to be done than simply hiring more cops to prevent young people from engaging in criminal activity. Judge Mollen and Norman Steisel realized that we could support such initiatives, and use the lottery for those undertakings, if they had an educational component. It was at this point that the program was expanded to include Beacon schools and other after-school mentoring initiatives. Speaker Vallone, not enamored of those parts of the plan, was nevertheless boxed in by his early advocacy of the lottery and did not want to oppose my social-minded advocacy organizations; he was also already committed to raising taxes for the police portion of the program we all desperately wanted to implement.

At my insistence, the planners were given a month to develop a comprehensive, thoughtful plan, a time frame that was roundly criticized by many who said it demonstrated my indecisiveness. Rather than wasting time, they argued, we should merely hire a thousand cops and be done with it. Although we were badgered by critics and opinion makers, by biding our time we were able to tease out the political positions of those whom we needed to win over and to modify the plan before it was actually announced. We accomplished our goals, and the benefits continue to accrue to the city to this day.

·   ·   ·

Judge Mollen was our chief negotiator with Albany. His position— and he fought like hell for it in our meetings preceding his lobbying efforts—was that in order to be realistic and not engender political flak, the legislation had to be targeted. He said, "If we're going to get this legislation through, it must have a section stating that the increase in personal income tax will be provided solely for the funding of Safe Streets, Safe City; it will be segregated, it will not go into the general treasury, and it will be used for no other budgetary purposes; otherwise, they won't give us the increase."

Why? Because upstate legislators don't trust the city of New York. And they don't trust the mayor. They don't care who the mayor is—they don't trust him. They didn't trust Ed Koch, they didn't trust me, and they didn't trust Rudy Giuliani or Michael Bloomberg. Their position is that the mayor of New York always tries to get money and then doesn't stick to the original plans for which the funds were conceived; the legislators feel that New York City mayors use state funds for budgetary purposes other than those originally stated, and often the legislators don't agree with these purposes. Upstaters think that social programs do not mean anything in the city.

Judge Mollen's staff included budget director Phil Michaels, the very bright and cooperative deputy budget director Mike Jacobson, chief of staff and special counsel Katie Lapp, and City Council special advisor Linda Gibbs. All but Michaels headed for Albany during a special session called by Gov. Mario Cuomo in early December 1990 with the specific intention of getting our legislation passed immediately, because we were truly in an emergency situation. We were concerned about crime and its impact on New Yorkers, and we were concerned about our kids.

In a corridor, Judge Mollen passed Democratic assemblyman from Staten Island Eric N. Vitaliano. "Eric," he said, "I assume we have your vote on Safe Streets, Safe City." The assemblyman responded, "Judge, I can't support it. My people, they want cops. They don't care about kids, they want cops. They don't want to pay increased taxes. If you take the cost for the kids' program out, I can be for it." Mollen told him, "The kids are staying in there. Along with cops, kids are nearest and dearest to the mayor's heart. It's the right thing to do. I can't believe you're going to hesitate voting for it. Do whatever your conscience tells you to do, but I cannot believe you are going to vote against this because we included programs for kids along with the cops. The criminals on Staten Island, at one time they were kids and they became criminals because we didn't have the right types of programs for them." Ultimately we got this assemblyman's vote.

The key players were the governor, the State Senate, and the State

Assembly. Governor Cuomo wasn't a problem; he understood the urgency of our situation and when approached supported our efforts. Judge Mollen then started down the list. The Senate was under Republican control, and he turned his attention to Majority Leader Ralph Marino, of Nassau County on Long Island. The judge paid his respects and then said, "We'd like your support." Judge Mollen felt like Santa Claus handing out goodies—how could anybody oppose more cops and more help for kids? Our plan was sound, we were offering expanded services after a long period of having received none, and we were not being profligate in attempting to handle our need. People accepted the fact that you had to pay to get more cops and that government attention to the facilities for the kids would make them useful, worthy, and productive.

Republicans held about a four-vote majority in the Senate, and Majority Leader Marino was a straight shooter. Judge Mollen didn't like what he had to say, but at least it was honest. Marino told him, "We have six Republican senators from New York City. If they favor this, I'll let it go to the floor of the Senate. Otherwise, it doesn't get there." Without the support of these six men, our bill would not come to a vote. Judge Mollen went to work. Manhattan senator Roy Goodman, who had run for mayor against Ed Koch in 1977, was entirely supportive. Guy Velella of the Bronx was similarly agreeable. John Marchi, a sweetheart from Staten Island who had beaten John Lindsay in the 1969 Republican mayoral primary but lost to him in the general election and lost again to Abe Beame in 1973, was also on board. Unfortunately, two senators from Queens were not so cooperative: Frank Padavan and Serphin Maltese. Mollen went to see Maltese. "Judge," the senator told him, "I understand what you want to do. We do need the cops, we need this. But I am historically always opposed to increased taxes. I cannot support the tax." Judge Mollen was preparing a reply when Senator Maltese said, "But I'll tell you what I'll do. I won't put my thumb on it." Meaning, he would tell Majority Leader Marino that he did not oppose the bill going to the floor. Maltese said, "You don't need my vote. Everybody else is going to vote for it. I'm going to vote against it so I'm consistent with my principles, but I'm not going to stop it from getting to the floor." The judge appreciated the gesture, which went a long way toward sealing our victory.

Senator Padavan had his own concerns. He asked Mollen, "Who's gonna decide where the additional police go?"

"The police commissioner," the judge replied. A significant portion of the NYPD's report on resource allocation was focused on a breakout of exactly how many cops were required in specific locations. "That's his responsibility, that's his job. He knows where they're needed most."

"I don't trust them," Padavan said. "I want to have a say in how many police come to my precinct."

"The mayor doesn't interfere with the police commissioner. The commissioner decides on the basis of need where the police are allocated; he puts them where the murders take place, and the robberies."

Padavan should have known better. He had been in city government as deputy commissioner of buildings under Mayor Lindsay. Yet he was unmoved. He refused out of hand to agree to this legislation without a deal. Judge Mollen said, "Senator, forget it. It isn't going to happen. I'll call the mayor. You want me to do that? I'll call the mayor." Mollen put me on the phone. "Mr. Mayor, Padavan wants to decide how many cops his precincts are going to get. You talk to him."

"Senator Padavan."

"Mr. Mayor."

"You know we need these cops. Times are bad, as of course you are aware. Our forces are depleted. People are dying in the streets of Harlem."

Senator Padavan told me, "My constituency is concerned with auto theft and graffiti."

I about hit the roof. Such remarkable selfishness. I believe I cursed him up and down, and he deserved it.

Judge Mollen saved the day. "I'll tell you what I'll do," he said to the senator once I had put down the phone. "When the police commissioner makes his allocations, if you want, I will arrange for you to ask him, and he will tell you the breakdown of where all the cops are going." The judge made the offer sound like a concession, but this information was actually a matter of public record to which the average citizen is entitled. Padavan took what he must have considered a victory and finally agreed to support the bill. Now we had all six. Judge Mollen reported back to Marino, "You can go to the floor with this."

That was only the beginning of the process, however. Now that he was committed to bringing the bill to a vote, Marino assigned Republican aide Abe Blackman to work with us on the details of the legislation. The hours they devoted to this work were extensive, and it was necessary to abide by the legislature's culture. When members of the Assembly heard we were meeting with Senate people, they got suspicious. So we had to meet with the Assembly people. When the senators heard we had met with the Assembly people, they wanted more time. It was that kind of madhouse up there. Still, one by one we eliminated all of the problems.

One night near the end of our negotiations, around one o'clock in the morning, as we were trying to win the approval and support of both parties on a nonpartisan basis, trying to make everybody happy, one of the Senate Republicans brought in a document he thought all involved ought to see. "Judge," he said, "we just got this message from the fire department saying you are going to close a dozen firehouses."

There it was on Fire Department stationery. Judge Mollen called and woke up Norman Steisel. "Do you know anything about this supposed letter from the fire commissioner?" He did not. The judge woke up several other members of our inner circle. No one knew anything about it.

In fact, it was a lie. The document was a forgery, a counterfeit letter supposedly from the fire commissioner saying I had authorized that the fire department be included in the Safe Streets program, adding to its expense; otherwise, there would be closings. We tried to piece this together. The answer we ultimately arrived at was that the fire unions always worked on the principle "Anything the police get, we want to get," and since Safe Streets, Safe City was going to increase the size of the Police Department by 40 percent, they were going to use this increased police budget to get their share of the goodies and wanted to stop the process until they could work out a deal. For this reason, someone created this phony letter and sent it up to Albany. Discovered to be a forgery, the document was discounted and the work moved forward.

Judge Mollen, his group, Blackman, and the Senate staff had an agreement in principle but were working on the technical details. By this time it was very late, and they were still working on the provisions. Time was of the essence; we wanted to get the bill passed later that same day. Someone whom the judge did not recognize entered the room, walked over to Blackman, whispered in his ear, and then departed. Blackman looked at Mollen. "Judge," he said, "I have bad news for you." Mollen looked back. It was three o'clock in the morning. "They just voted to adjourn." The special session was over.

Often in the newspapers Judge Mollen is referred to as a soft-spoken gentleman. Not this time. He took out a book and threw it on the table. "I'm getting out of this nest of vipers!" He quickly gathered his papers and headed out the door. To his credit, Blackman ran and stopped him just outside the door.

"Judge," Blackman said, "relax. I know how upset you are, and I appreciate that. You'll get your bill the first thing when we come back in January. You're going to get your bill." He said, "I can't do anything about the recess. If they're adjourned, I can't stop that. But I promise you, you'll get it early in the session. You're not going to have to wait long."

Judge Mollen was not happy to be on the 5:00 AM train back to the city.

But the Republicans did keep their word. The legislature reconvened in January 1991 and by the end of the first month the legislation was passed. Governor Cuomo signed it on Lincoln's birthday, February 12. But there was still one last piece of flesh they had to get out of us!

Because the senators still didn't trust us about the money, because they were concerned that we would use the allocated funds to satisfy other New York City needs, the legislature demanded a memorandum of understanding, signed by me and Judge Mollen on behalf of the city, and also by the governor's office, the Senate, and the Assembly, stating that the money would be used only for the purposes of Safe Streets, Safe

City. If any money was diverted from that program, New York City would lose that amount from the taxes we collected. After another round of negotiation, we worked out the terms of the memorandum of understanding and signed it. The bill passed. Safe Streets, Safe City: Cops and Kids was on its way.

.　　　.　　　.

We kept our word and never abused the sanctity of the funds. The money was used in accordance with the memorandum of understanding, and it turned the tide.

A popular conception is that crime in New York City ran rampant during my administration. This is simply not true. Crime, which had been rising steadily for almost fifteen years, crested during my time in office and began to fall. In the last two years of my term, 1992 and 1993, for the first time in history, all seven major crime categories—murder, rape, assault, robbery, burglary, grand larceny, and arson—declined. These are not New York Police Department statistics, these are FBI statistics.

In fact, the decrease could have begun earlier, and there are some who believe that I did myself a political disservice by planning for these cops to be hired over the course of several years. NYPD commissioner Bill Bratton in his autobiography *Turnaround* (written with my co-author, Peter Knobler) noted:

> If [Dinkins] had hired 2,000 cops in January 1993 they would have been through the academy and on the streets that summer, just in time to be a positive issue in the campaign. The streets would have been swimming with cops. To all those who felt Dinkins was soft on crime, he could have shown pictures of himself and 2,000 cops being sworn in at Madison Square Garden. . . . Dinkins got no credit; most of the cops for whom he won funding didn't come on the job until after the election. In the first six months of Giuliani's term, the new mayor attended two gradua-

tion ceremonies and implicitly took credit for 4,200 additional
police officers.

The idea did occur to me.

The original Safe Streets, Safe City document mandated that the hiring be done over a two-year period. However, in an attempt to limit
annual taxes, when the legislature approved the plan the expansion of
the police force was spread over three years. Because this was funded by
a surcharge to existing taxes, the city and state agreed in a memorandum
of understanding that we could delay hiring up to 25 percent of any
police recruitment class in a given year if we promised to make it up by
the end of the plan, sometime in the coming three years. In this way, at
my discretion, we could take a temporary budget saving if necessary.
There was also a fallback plan in the eventuality of an even deeper financial emergency: New York City could skip a full year's worth of hiring if
we could justify doing so in writing to the legislature and convince them
of our terrible state of affairs, on the condition that we would hire a full
complement of officers the following year.

Because of the continuing recession throughout the United States,
New York City's general tax collections were declining and our budget
projections were not realized. What we thought we had enough money
to pay for, we didn't. As a result, we exercised that 25 percent rule more
than once and cut back on the number of hirings. By the time we got
into the last year, we were constantly under pressure from the governor
and the Financial Control Board to do a better job of managing the
budget. The question became: should we stick with our budget plan? We
had demonstrated the efficacy of our policing initiative with two years'
worth of police hiring: for the first time in years, crime in New York City
was beginning to come down. A debate arose among my deputy mayors
and advisers: do we hire more cops now, or do we keep the budget tighter
by rolling the hires forward?

Some argued that we were under legislative mandate and our course
of action was cast in iron. We had implemented two years of Safe Streets,

Safe City; did we now want to admit that, under heavy pressure from Governor Cuomo and the Financial Control Board, and for political purposes—to manage the budget—we were abandoning that commitment? Their feeling was that we had made a commitment to the legislature, we had a plan, we had implemented half of it, and we needed to stay on course.

Others argued that this course would cost us somewhere in the neighborhood of $50 million at a time when we could ill afford it. If we rolled the hires forward, it would achieve the equivalent savings of firing or losing by attrition, somewhere else in the system, five thousand city workers without five thousand workers actually losing their jobs.

Adding to their argument was the fact that when I had instructed Commissioner Brown to investigate the needs of the Police Department, I had simultaneously asked for specific proposals to reorganize the agency and improve productivity. Commissioner Brown had responded with substantial recommendations; he suggested internal redeployments, improved reassignments, and elimination of certain staff functions. Those who argued for delaying the hiring insisted that even if we slowed the introduction of more police officers onto the force, the number of police on patrol, on the street, and available to fight crime had actually already risen, and that growth had already contributed to a drop in crime. We would get double duty: greater productivity and low cost. We would protect and serve the citizens of New York with increased effectiveness, and we would have a better story to tell come election time, including a story of more effective budget management: there were more cops on the force, as we had promised, though it was going to take a little longer before they had all arrived on the job; there were already more cops on the street; and lo and behold, there was less crime across the board in New York City for the first time since the 1950s.

We went where the money was. We made the decision not to hire the extra cops that year. The city was still in grave financial difficulty, and I felt it was necessary to postpone what might have been a political bonanza as well as a civic benefit. Then, of course, we lost the election and looked like jerks. We really did not see that coming. As Commissioner Bratton indicated, the decrease in crime that was so instrumental in New York City's 1990s renaissance, and for which my successor took credit, was conceived and begun on my watch.

10

———

From "Dave, Do Something!"
to "Mayor Cool"

We had several trials, beyond abject lack of funds, that befell the city while I was mayor. Homelessness, poverty, crime, lack of opportunity—these are all undercurrents that run through municipalities in times of economic downturn. What garners attention, however, are disasters. New York had its share. We had our trials, and we developed ideas and initiatives to deal with them.

.　　.　　.

In January 1990, only a few weeks after I was inaugurated, a Haitian woman claimed that she was beaten without provocation by a Korean grocer in Brooklyn in a dispute over plantains and peppers. The shopkeeper denied the claim, saying that the woman had not paid for her purchase and had begun flinging the produce at her. Hospital records indicated that the Haitian woman had a scratch on her face. (Third-degree assault charges against the shopkeeper were eventually dropped.)

There is a short list of activists known to the black community to whom individuals often repair in an effort to settle a grievance. Many of these folks are clergy, as the church in many areas functions as both house of worship and community center. The woman first approached Rev. Herbert Daughtry, pastor of the House of the Lord Pentecostal Church in Boerum Hill, Brooklyn, who was known to actively advocate when a wrong had been perpetrated. She complained of her abuse and said that blacks were routinely treated badly at the establishment, the Family Red Apple. This is a widely held feeling in the New York and national black community; the sense is that in many establishments and environments we are not being treated with the respect given others of different races. Reverend Daughtry and a group of ministers visited the grocery store on the woman's behalf. "We found the owners rather hostile," the reverend recalls. "Rather arrogant. I guess the only reason why we didn't do anything, I just had too much on my plate." The woman ultimately found another activist, Sonny Carson, and persuaded his group, the December 12th Movement, to take on her cause.

I had had a run-in with Carson at the National Black Political Convention in 1972, and although we had paid his organization to get out the vote in the mayoral election, Sonny Carson had his own agenda. The Haitian Economic Development Association, a black community group, organized a boycott of the Family Red Apple and another Korean-run establishment across the street that had harbored one of the Red Apple employees who had been pursued by African American customers during the original disturbance. Carson and his group took that street action and ran with it. The boycott ostensibly concerned only the supposed mistreatment of the single Haitian individual, but by implication this was a demonstration against racial disrespect and the encroachment into the black community of outside entrepreneurs who "took money out of the neighborhood." African American ownership of businesses in the African American community was a major issue. Meanwhile, Koreans had begun opening greenmarkets in so many parts of the city that their successful stores were fast becoming ubiquitous. This conflict between customer and proprietor became a physical metaphor for historical anger and a myriad of discontents. One boycott leader said, "The stores have become a symbol of what has happened across this city in terms of the lack of recognizing the humanity of black people. It was not an isolated incident. And people are realizing that it doesn't have to be tolerated." The boycott was news—initially, unsubstantiated rumors flew that the Haitian woman had died of her injuries—and Rupert Murdoch's *New York Post* and others sold newspapers by fanning the flames of controversy.

"Our approach had always been, number one, responding in a productive way toward the community, with a view toward reconciliation. That's how Reverend King approached controversies," says Reverend Daughtry. "We're not trying to make enemies, we're trying to get a circle that will rope people in. We just want them to deal fairly. But [Carson and his organization] came in, and they wanted to shut the store down. So it generated tensions. There were no negotiations. They took a very hard line." One flyer read: "The question for Black folks to consider is this: Who is going to control the economic life of the Black community? This is the 1990s. People understand that this struggle we are presently engaged in is a continuation of our historical struggle for self-determination."

The boycott took off. Picketers manned their lines daily, and the scene became hostile and raucous, with racial epithets flying. Police were called in, and the picket line became a place of strong contention, to the point where State Supreme Court justice Gerald Held issued a temporary restraining order requiring boycotters to remain at least fifty feet from the stores. The NYPD did not enforce that injunction, pending our appeal that the police ought to be allowed to use their discretion in this matter; in the department's estimation, a closer proximity allowed both protest and safety. When the judge ordered the cops to enforce his order, we as an administration and I as a black man were then roundly criticized for coddling the violent crowd—which was largely African American—and implicitly for allowing an unruly black mob to run wild. It was not true, but nevertheless we took quite a beating.

We attempted to mediate the conflict quietly, but our attempts came to naught. Even though on a typical day there would be three or four picketers outside the store, when word leaked that Bill Lynch had brought lawyers from the two sides together in an effort to come to an understanding and it appeared that they had developed a settlement that would satisfy all parties, somehow that day there would be forty picketers shouting at the cameras. Then the media would arrive en masse, because tempers flared and that made for good television, and the process of encouraging an end to both the boycott and its causes would be made infinitely more difficult.

Not long after the incident, a young Vietnamese man who lived three blocks away was beaten by about ten black men because they thought he was Korean, which gave rise to public conversations in the press about race relations in New York and beyond. "What the press tried to do, and to some extent succeeded [in doing]," says Reverend Daughtry, "was tying all of that into a blacks-against-Koreans, blacks-against-Jews, blacks-against-everyone [story] . . . and so . . . [they] poured more fuel under the cauldron. They were very irresponsible; in this very tension-packed time, they would not try to diffuse, but in fact enhanced the flames."

I was the first black mayor, folks were expecting this not to happen on my watch . . . and it got out of hand. Other Korean grocers began to give financial support to the boycotted store owners, while many blacks found the grievances persuasive. "They look at you as though you are a thief," a boycotter told CBS News. And because Carson had no intention of settling the dispute—the longer it survived, the more widely he and his ideological pronouncements would gain attention—there was no end in sight.

The New York City Commission on Human Rights led our efforts to end the conflict. At my direction, Commissioner Dennis deLeon tried to convince leaders of the Haitian community to ask for an end to the boycott, but the *New York Times* reported that the effort failed "partly because the boycott has taken on a life of its own."

We established a task force of African Americans and Asians to study the boycott and black-Korean relations, headed by Laura Blackburne, a lawyer and president of the Institute for Mediation and Conflict Resolution. The task force studied lending practices to minority applicants as well as ways to improve relations between the community and the proprietors. Still, the boycott and the street action went on for months. Ms. Blackburne was criticized for being overly sympathetic to the African American position. I was criticized for not crossing the picket line and ending the boycott by example.

I was prepared to personally mediate the dispute, but I suspected my presence would not have helped at that juncture. I told the *New York Times* that some felt I had a special ability to sway the opinion of African Americans, but in this instance I believed that my participation would do more harm than good. I put Bill Lynch in charge, and he was working diligently. Bill did excellent work throughout this ordeal. At around the same time, another situation arose involving a Korean merchant and a black customer in Queens, and Bill and his people solved it in a day and a half.

More important even than this particularly difficult civic moment was the state of racial affairs in the city. The trials of Yusef Hawkins's attackers in Bensonhurst were occurring and, coupled with the boycott, occasioned a significant conversation about the continuing issue of race. In a twenty-five-minute speech crafted with great skill by my speechwriter John Siegal—carried live in its entirety from City Council chamber by four television stations and excerpted live and on tape by several others—I exhorted clergymen and politicians to urge their communities to "join in an affirmation of tolerance and respect."

Some people thought that confrontation was superior to conciliation. I disagreed. "This city is sick of violence," I said. "We're aching, and we must heal the pain. My administration will never lead by dividing. At the same time, and in the same spirit, we will never allow any group or any person to turn to violence or the threat of violence to intimidate others, no matter how legitimate their anger or frustration may be. Whatever happened in that incident did not warrant this sort of ongoing intimidation. Boycotts can be an appropriate and effective response," I said, "but this one is not, and the vast majority of the people in that community know it. . . .

"I've already seen far too much pain and far too much hate in my lifetime. I challenge all of the people of this city to reject these calls to bigotry, because if the bigots succeed in spreading their poison it's nobody's fault but our own. . . . I call upon all involved to set aside their intransigence, to come in, to sit down, to settle this, and to settle it now. . . . My personal commitment is absolute. I will bear any burden and walk any mile—and I am confident that we will be able to settle this situation through mediation and conciliation. We're going to quit tearing ourselves apart—and begin the long, hard work of sewing our city back together. We must absolutely, categorically reject the despicable notion of group guilt. We abhor those who preach it, and we must be mindful that predictions of violence and anger tend to be self-fulfilling. . . . But whatever the outcome, as we have so many times over so many years, we must repress our rage, channel our energies, and come together to make this tragedy transforming. . . .

"Right now, each of you must look into your own hearts, in your own families. Look honestly at yourselves—and your own communities—and ask whether you can be swayed by prejudice, and what you're going to do about it. Because no matter how much government can do, government cannot substitute for the content of our character."

The Council chamber was filled with five hundred invited political, business, labor, church, and community leaders, and I was particularly pleased that, when I said that the media must try to foster tolerance and be more respectful when reporting stories involving race, I received a twenty-second standing ovation from the chamber audience.

I instructed the city's Commission on Human Rights to begin a survey of the real needs of community-based businesses and to step up its efforts in communities to find tensions and stop problems before they started. I offered several initiatives that I felt would help reduce racial tension, including a study on discrimination in bank lending, a combined group of district attorneys and law enforcement to focus on gangs, an anti-bias strike force, and a "prejudice prevention" curriculum in the schools.

My speech was well received, but still the boycott continued. The press was unrelenting, and Ed Koch suggested that if he were mayor he would walk right in and buy something and personally break the boycott. One can only imagine the effect that action would have had if he had still been in office.

I respectfully disagreed. I felt that negotiations were called for, and that it would be improper of me to take a side in this dispute. I would proudly walk into the store and seal the deal once an agreement that we had brokered had been reached. The idea was to stand, like President Clinton clasping the hands of Yitzhak Rabin and Yasir Arafat, over a fact and symbol of conciliation.

Unfortunately, that deal was not forthcoming. Sonny Carson was skillfully intransigent, and it wasn't until a Brooklyn grand jury declined to indict the shopkeeper, we lost our appeal of the court order, and the Family Red Apple owner sold the business to another Korean that I finally did go to the store and make a purchase. Whatever may have happened there in January—and there remained some dispute about what did happen—forcing those shopkeepers out of business amounted to cruel and unusual punishment. "Some of those involved have refused to participate in a way that would allow it to come to an end," I told the *Times*. "They wished only to beat these store owners into submission and to force them out of business. And this is neither reasonable nor acceptable."

Why had I finally decided to go to the store? "I think that we've gone to the ultimate limits of trying every way known to man to try to get people to be reasonable. There are some folks who don't want a resolution."

It may well be that I waited an overly long time to take this step, but I had faith in the court system and in the rational ability of people to come to satisfactory conclusions among themselves. I may have been wrong on both counts.

. . .

The Happy Land Social Club at Southern Boulevard and East Tremont Avenue in the Bronx was like hundreds of other venues around New York—an illegal gathering place for people, often minorities, looking for some sense of community. This particular club was a hangout for those of Honduran descent, but it was not unique. Often these establishments were poorly maintained, haphazardly run, and in violation of many city laws. Happy Land had been cited for such building code violations as no fire exits, alarms, or sprinkler system, and it was ordered closed in November 1988. However, the Fire Department had not followed up, and the club remained open. On the night of March 25, 1990, an employee's jilted boyfriend was ejected by a bouncer after an argument, returned angry, poured gasoline in the hallway and on the only staircase leading to the second floor (not so much a staircase as a pull-down ladder with handrails, of the kind one often sees leading to an attic), lit two matches, and set the club ablaze.

The fire exits had been sealed to prevent people from sneaking in and avoiding the cover charge, so there was no escape. Fire engulfed the hall and doorways, and smoke filled the club. Three minutes after receiving the alarm, Ladder Company 58 arrived on the scene. It was 3:44 AM, and the street was quiet. Usually on a Saturday night the street would be ringing with loud music as people danced to the club's DJ. "There were no screams. There was no sound at all," a firefighter later told the *New York Post.* Inside, as their hoses shot water into the hallway, firefighters saw several bodies on the steps. They may have thought their grisly night was through. Then they went upstairs.

When I arrived, I was briefed on the situation; then the firefighters gave me fire gear, and we walked inside and climbed to the second floor. One man had been close enough to a window to jump. Of those who were upstairs drinking and dancing, he was the only person to survive.

No one in that room died from burning—they perished from smoke inhalation. Asphyxiated. The floor was filled with bodies stacked like cordwood, fallen over each other in their attempt to reach safety. We had to step over them. No one had burn marks. Young people in their Saturday night best sat at tables and along the bar as if they were exhibits in a wax museum. A young man still had a drink in his hand; the fire had made the floor uncertain, and the liquid sloshed in his glass when I moved toward him. I stared at his face, I could not look away. I was seared by the vision. Human mannequins. Death masks. Smoke hung in the air and was undisturbed by a single movement, a terrible stillness. I moved slowly; the room held sixty-nine bodies, and I didn't want to disturb the dead. It was awful. Just so awful.

I found myself at the bottom of the ladder, but I could not leave. "I want to go back up," I told Jules Martin, the head of my security detail. "I don't ever want to forget this as long as I live." I climbed once again to the second floor. These were sons and daughters, clean-cut kids out for a nice night. In minutes I would have to comment to the press, but in this moment I could not think as the mayor alone, I could do nothing except stand still and observe the fullness of the silence. Each one of these young people could have been my child.

In an odd coincidence, March 25, 1990, was the seventy-ninth anniversary of New York's deadliest industrial disaster, the Triangle Shirtwaist Factory fire. Both involved young immigrants. The Triangle fire was the catalyst for a major overhaul of New York's fire codes, and there was work to be done to prevent this modern catastrophe from recurring. A few days later, we drafted legislation that would allow the city to shutter immediately any eating or drinking establishment ordered closed in violation of fire or safety codes. Happy Land had stayed open sixteen months after being found wanting, and people died as a result; I was determined this would not happen again.

One would have thought this to be an unassailable idea, but we were quickly challenged by representatives of various ethnic communities saying, in effect, "This is the only place we can hang out, this is all we have; we should not be burdened with restrictions." We remained steadfast. Our position was, "Life is far more important than that." A less stringent bill had died in the City Council a year earlier. We would not allow such a fire to occur again. I will always remember those faces.

. . .

Brian Watkins, his parents, brother, and sister-in-law were classic US Open tourists. They had come to town from Provo, Utah, to see the tennis matches in the fall of 1990—this was their fifth family trip to the event—and while in the city they also saw the Mets at Shea Stadium and *Cats* on Broadway. They were going downtown to have dinner in Greenwich Village when they were mugged on the E train subway platform by a gang of teenage thugs from Queens. The gang slashed Mr. Watkins with a box cutter and kicked Mrs. Watkins to the ground when she tried to help him. Brian, twenty-two years old, a former Idaho State University scholarship tennis player, and a former Boy Scout, came to his mother's aid and was stabbed in the chest with a four-inch "butterfly" knife. He chased the assailants up the subway stairs until they disappeared into the street and he collapsed. The gang went dancing at Roseland that night with the money they had stolen. Brian died in St. Vincent's Hospital at 10:46 PM. This was a terrible tragedy, a young man killed in front of his family.

How does one respond to such a despicable act? First, acting on a tip, the NYPD immediately captured some of the killers while they were still inside Roseland; they arrested the rest of them later at or near their homes in Queens. Seven gang members were convicted of the murder and sent to prison. I was, of course, tremendously concerned for the family and for the safety of the city, and I expressed my upset and my condolences. The fact that the Watkins family had been to New York to attend tennis matches, with which I was associated, rather than a basketball or football game or a theater event, served as easy kindling for a firestorm of complaints about my administration's handling of the very serious issue of crime, starting with my tone. The editor of the *New York Post* opined, "We are in a war, are we not?" and demanded that I act like a Wild West sheriff out of an old television show like *Gunsmoke*. He suggested that I show the electorate the private self with which, he said, insiders were familiar: "a man with strong opinions, a sharp temper, capable of angry words and much more than the courtly figure we see on television." I do have a temper, and I am not above calling someone out if I feel he or she has let us down on the job. I have been known to say loudly, "I am surrounded by assassins!" My operative phrases were often "I want more and better from every living ass!" and "If I tell you a flea can pull a plow, then hitch him up!" Apparently the *Post*'s editor was taking issue not with my policies but with my comportment. I was, of course, extremely concerned that a visitor to our city had been murdered, but I was also quite distressed at the shallow yet incendiary nature of his comments.

As mayor, I had followed one bellicose talker in the office who had worn out his welcome, and it was not my style to confront a problem with bombast. I had seen styles that I did not wish to emulate. I had seen styles that, frankly, were not so great, albeit popular at the moment. For all his loud remarks, Ed Koch had presided over a nonstop escalation of New York's crime rate and handed this mess to me on his way out the door. In my inaugural address, I had promised to be "the toughest mayor on crime the city has ever seen," but I preferred finding solutions to yelling about the problems. I had immediately presented proposals designed to raise revenues in order to put more police on the streets, but the *Post* in its infinite wisdom had screamed "Dave, Do Something!" on its front page and codified its complaint. The *National Review* wrote, "Politically, the first victim of the media fallout has been Mayor David Dinkins, who was urged to abandon his habitually serene demeanor and show a little fury. There is something absurd about such advice, as if rug chewing will make the streets safe. Yet there is also justice in the anti-Dinkins backlash, for he owed his election to a conviction among liberal-minded whites that only the election of a black man to the mayoralty could appease the city's seething pathologies. Those who sow delusion reap frustration."

Putting aside the clear anti-urban bias evidenced by the phrase "seething pathologies" and the concept of appeasement substituting for government, a black man was not necessary to bring down crime; sound policies were, and we had them. We would increase the size of the NYPD and bring about the first decrease in across-the-board New York City crime in almost forty years. Safe Streets, Safe City saw to that. In my last two years in office, crime throughout the city dropped in all seven FBI index crime categories for the first time in nearly four decades. In my four years, those crimes declined by 15 percent. Crime in the subways declined even more dramatically, by 36 percent over the course of my mayoralty. We established the Stop the Violence Fund, which gave out 1,377 grants to 847 neighborhoods for community anticrime programs. We established the first computerized stolen vehicle recovery system in New York City to track stolen autos and deter car theft. The city received $500,000 from a contract with the LoJack Corporation, which installed tracking devices in police patrol vehicles, trained police officers, and maintained the systems. We enacted the toughest local gun control laws in the nation, and I was a leading advocate for national gun control legislation, including the Brady Bill. I was proud to stand with President Clinton at the White House as that bill was signed into law. We doubled the city's domestic violence prevention program, which provided law enforcement intervention and immediate social services to families in which domestic violence had been reported. As a result, more cases of domestic violence were addressed by police in participating precincts. We increased the number of emergency domestic violence shelter beds to over 1,100 and developed comprehensive nonresidential services— including counseling, advocacy, referrals, and legal assistance. We developed the legal basis that was used to get the squeegee guys off the streets. And we put 6,500 more cops in uniform.

And yet, popular perception would have it that New York was the Wild West when I was mayor. Popular perception would be wrong.

While we were developing the information and strategy to put Safe Streets, Safe City and these other programs into practice, I was routinely criticized for my "serene demeanor." "Courtliness" became a code word for "inaction," yet I was both courtly and active. I have always maintained that my manner of speech, my choice of language, is deeply ingrained in my personality. I believe a mayor should appear in a certain fashion; there is a dignity to the job that should be recognized and promoted, and New York deserves that dignity. That doesn't mean that I didn't get angry, but I am who I am. No one has ever suggested that I care any less than others about the best interests of the city. If I used language that suggested great displeasure—if I said, for example, "I feel great displeasure"—I felt it behooved the press to report that I was, in fact, highly angry. The reporters knew me, they had experience of my choice of words, and they could easily have reported that the mayor was outraged, whether I mentioned the word "outraged" or not. The story is not a public official's language, it is his actions. My actions spoke loudly.

And for my part, perhaps I should have learned to express my fury in more easily reported terms.

.　　.　　.

I was in Japan leading a city trade mission the day in February 1993 when the World Trade Center was bombed by terrorists. Several men had conspired to build a bomb, rented a yellow Ryder van, drove it into the building's parking structure, set the timer fuse, walked out, and blew the place up. They intended to knock one tower into the other and bring both down. Fortunately, that effort failed, but six people lost their lives, more than one thousand were injured, and parts of the building were decimated. And yet there were those who found time to say, "How dare the mayor be away while they're bombing the World Trade Center!"

I made plans to return to New York immediately, and I established a command post in my hotel room to monitor news reports as I was preparing to leave. The video was horrifying. It was a miracle that more people were not injured. In the meantime, it was vital that in my absence the city be in firm hands.

I have said time and again that I value the skills and reliability of the people with whom I worked in government; they came into their jobs highly qualified and enthusiastic, and when put to the test they delivered. This was an instance in which my faith and trust in my staff was richly rewarded. It was established protocol that when I was out of the city, First Deputy Mayor Norman Steisel was in charge. In my absence, it was his job to coordinate the city's response in case of emergencies. That day he coordinated the rescue operation between the Police and Fire Departments; Emergency Services, which at the time was under the aegis of the Department of Health and Hospitals; the Department of Environmental Protection (because the explosion was at first thought to have caused the release of PCBs); and, once the dust settled so to speak, the Buildings Department. Norman brought me up to speed.

I was also immediately in touch with Police Commissioner Ray Kelly, who briefed me with as much up-to-the-minute information as was available. (This was before cell phones were in wide use, and the communication necessary to keep me current was more arduous.) While Norman was coordinating the agencies, Kelly's cops were at the forefront, running into the buildings and coordinating the physical rescue.

At first we did not know the extent of the casualties or the facts of what had transpired. The bomb had cut the World Trade Center's main power line, including the emergency lighting system, and smoke had billowed up the fire stairs as high as the ninety-third floors of both towers. Because there was no emergency power to run the ventilation system, the stairwells were pitch-black and filled with smoke, trapping everyone on the higher floors. With no power, people were stuck in elevators, and many were injured by smoke inhalation. The NYPD and NYFD coordinated to evacuate the building, but because the emergency power system was inadequate and the basic design of the ventilation system was not sufficiently functional, the effort took four hours.

While others in a similar position might have headed for the nearest camera, Norman did not feel that need. He coordinated police commanders, fire officers, environmental officials, and others in the rescue effort—the Police and Fire Departments had been feuding over turf for years—and did so successfully, openly, and with candor, as one would expect from as no-nonsense a man as Norman. He also coordinated with state officials. While at the outset we did not know this was a terrorist attack, there was the possibility that it might be, so Norman also contacted the Clinton White House. New York had been attacked, the country at large was implicitly in danger, and by words and deeds he made clear that the city was under control.

In the bombing's immediate aftermath, city officials, including Steisel and Kelly, were working out of temporary headquarters in the Vista Hotel next door to the site. As they stood around a conference table, a Port Authority engineer approached Deputy Commissioner for Public Information Paul Browne and said, "Can you tell the police commissioner that this floor could give way at any moment?" Browne told him, "You can make that announcement yourself right now—here's a bullhorn!" They moved promptly to the lower level of the World Trade Center.

An NYPD bomb squad detective and a graduate of Brooklyn's Automotive High School, Donald Sadowy, identified a piece of scrap metal as the differential from the truck's transmission, and it was carefully carried from the wreckage like a body. From this scorched metal the NYPD was able to figure out the vehicle's identification number, which they traced to a rental agency. It turned out that the bombers had returned to the rental shop in an attempt to reclaim their $225 deposit. The case was broken wide open.

In the first hours, Steisel and Kelly appeared on local and national television to calm fears. This was not a boiler explosion; there was more to the story. We didn't know exactly what that story was, but it was clear that something significant and dangerous had happened, a planned event, and it was important to make clear to the nation not only that we had an effective operation but that we had the situation in hand. Some in this position might have seized the media opportunity and posed for the cameras as though they had control of the situation; we actually had that control.

With Norman Steisel at the helm, the city was in excellent hands, and he was highly and rightly praised for his work. The *New York Times* called him "the pre-eminent figure in [Dinkins's] inner circle of advisers at City Hall." He found himself being applauded in restaurants. Norman performed exquisitely.

Among our immediate tasks upon my return was the restoration and maintenance of the Lower Manhattan area around the World Trade Center. We offered city loans and grants to encourage local businesses to bring their commercial activities quickly up to speed, and we leveraged the phone companies to make the restoration of their service a priority. I created a task force, chaired by Steisel, and took a strong position in compelling the New York Port Authority, which ran the WTC, and Gov. Mario Cuomo to make the towers conform to New York City building and fire codes. (When it was constructed in 1973, the complex had been exempted from these provisions by Gov. Nelson Rockefeller because of budget considerations.) After significant negotiation, improved lighting, ventilation, and other systems were installed in the towers' stairwells and concourses.

Our efforts proved crucially important on September 11, 2001, when two hijacked airplanes were crashed into the towers. The structural changes and new safety systems, installed at my insistence, arguably saved many thousands of lives. Thirty thousand people got out. The 9/11 Commission reported that the evacuation

> was aided greatly by changes made by the Port Authority in response to the 1993 bombing and by the training of both Port Authority personnel and civilians after that time. Stairwells remained lit near unaffected floors; some tenants relied on procedures learned in fire drills to help them to safety; others were guided down the stairs by fire safety officials based in the lobby. . . . Rudimentary improvements, such as the addition of glow strips to the handrails and stairs, were credited by some as the reason for their survival. The general evacuation time for the towers dropped from more than four hours in 1993 to under one hour on September 11.

I found this extremely gratifying.

. . .

On June 6, 1993, Peter Johnson, my friend and one of my closest advisers, received a call from a quirky NYPD detective, Brian Mulheren, who had been on the force going back to the days of Mayor Lindsay and used to ride around the city in what Peter called a "tricked-out Lincoln Town Car with every radio imaginable, which he bought himself." Detective Mulheren was something of a personal emergency management unit who would call up in the middle of the night and alert me when a cop had been shot or a firefighter had gone down or there was some unusual unrest or disturbance. That night he informed Peter that the US Park Police were reporting that Asians with guns had been sighted on the beach in Queens. Peter called and woke me.

"*What?!*"

"The report is, there are Asians with guns out in the Rockaways. That sounds a little insane, but they may be coming from a ship that's run aground."

"It sounds like that movie *The Russians Are Coming, the Russians Are Coming!*"

I hurried to the site with the head of my security detail, Jules Martin. We found a living nightmare. A Chinese freighter, the inaptly named *Golden Venture,* with thirteen crew members, had indeed run aground approximately five hundred feet from shore. The ship's captain had tried to navigate the waters circuitously without being detected, as his cargo included 286 immigrants from China whom a gang of smugglers was trying to introduce illegally into this country. The ship was not sinking, but the people on board had panicked and poured over the sides, jumping from the decks into the deep, cold water. It was after midnight, pitch-black, and many had drowned. Police and Fire Department helicopters hovered overhead, their bluish searchlights scanning for survivors. When I arrived, bodies were strewn on the beach and I found pockets of people huddled together on the ground for warmth. Commissioner Ray Kelly, Norman Steisel, and Fire Department chaplain Father Mychal Judge were on the scene. The city provided blankets and clothing for the survivors. Local Fire Department and Hatzolah EMS trucks were parked in front of the dunes, taking in the injured, their red emergency lights churning.

Bodies were washing up, and people were still dragging themselves out of the water, their clothes clinging to them, stumbling ashore. New York City had a limited water rescue capability, with only a small number of police harbor launches, but the Coast Guard also did not have significant assets available for deployment in the New York area. Steisel recalls that "Ray and I got into a huge jurisdictional fight with the local Coast Guard guy," because the agency was forced to send to Providence, Rhode Island, for helicopters. "We were unhappy that they couldn't get assets there more quickly," he says.

One of the immediate tasks was to establish a remote morgue and a process for identifying the dead and the living. The NYPD was having difficulty communicating with the survivors; most seemed to be from the Fujian province, but our interpreters spoke only Mandarin Chinese. (Since that time, the city has widened its range of interpreters.)

But when I arrived, what I saw most was people in need. These men and women, huddled and shivering, needed human contact. I moved forward. "Don't go near them," I was advised. "They may have tuberculosis. They will need to be quarantined." I could not allow that to deter me. I spoke no Chinese, and they spoke no English, but I tried to console them in tone and in presence. These folks were being smuggled into this country by human traffickers; I do not know how often anyone had spoken to them in a kindly way. I hope I was able to help them in some small regard.

Once it was determined that these were immigrants attempting to enter the United States illegally, the Immigration and Naturalization Service (INS) was notified, the US attorney arrived, and what had begun as an NYPD/NYFD rescue was transformed into a federal operation. Having survived a crossing that began in Thailand, stopped in Kenya, and circumnavigated the Cape of Good Hope, the boat's surviving passengers were remanded into custody and sent to prisons around the United States. I was particularly proud to see Elizabeth Aivars, my administration's director of the Office of Immigrant Affairs, arrive to assist the survivors. I do not know who contacted her, but I was pleased that she was out there protecting the interests of these immigrants. They may have been illegal, but they were human.

·   ·   ·

An unsettling truth about New York City in the 1990s was that the level of mistrust and misunderstanding among races, ethnicities, and economic strata was extremely high. In difficult economic times, people often protect themselves and their families more stringently than they would when their first concern isn't money and security. This self-involvement was particularly manifest among the city's youth, who were being squeezed educationally and culturally and as a result were less well prepared to enter the workforce than the generation before them. I was, of course, concerned about the African American community, but I saw the trend developing among all New Yorkers.

We needed to step back and see the gorgeous mosaic, to understand one another, or else we would be doomed to a lifetime of civic blindness. It sounds utopian, but I felt it was necessary to invest in our young people now so they could develop into great New Yorkers of empathy and common experience in the future. I wanted city-sponsored programs that would foster amity and grassroots participation; solve tensions in the city's neighborhoods; use the government to benefit the citizens of the city, both now and in the future; and train New Yorkers in conflict resolution. The program we developed to build bridges of trust and understanding among our multitude of communities was the Increase the Peace Volunteer Corps (IPVC), or in the phrase coined by its founder Peter Johnson, Increase the Peace.

Increase the Peace was run from the mayor's office by Executive

Director Robert Sherman. During its two and a half years of operation, it trained and worked with nearly 1,500 volunteers, of a multitude of ages, races, and backgrounds, who supplied their input, time, and focus and were taught how to use government agencies to avert local intergroup crises.

We developed a network of neighborhood first responders, what we would call truth-tellers. We trained them and gave them phone numbers to call and liaisons within the police precincts; we also enabled them to go into the neighborhoods as leaders and calm people in times of potential civil unrest and say, "You need to hear the facts." We could not afford crises like the one that would happen later in Crown Heights, when a rumor spread that Hatzolah would not take the Cato children to the hospital because they didn't want to soil their ambulance with black blood. That rumor would add fuel to a fire we would be trying to put out. It was untrue, so obviously untrue, but if some in the community wanted to believe it, we needed the capacity to get out in the neighborhoods and say, "No. Didn't happen. I'm a black guy, I'm Dominican, I live here, I'm telling you: didn't happen!"

People of all races worked together to implement several creative projects, all designed to improve relations citywide. We supported summer programs in local parks that aimed to break down their segregated use, including youth video "speakouts" on race relations that were viewed by hundreds of people; these projects also included playground cleanups, street fairs, and festivals. In Jamaica, Queens, IPVC spearheaded a campaign along with local institutions to reduce racially motivated attacks by largely Caribbean American customers on Asian American small businesses. Arrest numbers, usually especially high during the Halloween season, were reduced in 1992, as were tensions in the community, which had reached an all-time high. In Staten Island, often characterized as New York's most conservative borough, IPVC members sponsored the first-ever public forum following the brutal bias beating of a gay man. The meeting was attended by two hundred people and was widely reported in the local press. In selected high schools, IPVC members took groups of twenty students of various ethnic backgrounds on a series of field trips to each other's cultural institutions, with the aim of promoting greater appreciation and understanding of their respective cultures. In high schools where highly publicized racial incidents had taken place, IPVC members and adults from the surrounding neighborhoods actively engaged students on issues of intergroup relations.

In addition to these initiatives, citywide task forces were formed to address fifteen key issues, including a black-Jewish dialogue group that met on a monthly basis for close to two years. A theater group called Theater for a Greater Peace, formed by forty-five IPVC members, wrote and produced a play about neighborhood racial tension, *My Enemy, My Brother*, which was performed to excellent reviews in community centers and even had an off-Broadway run. A women's issues task force arranged art shows and discussion meetings and cosponsored a major conference with the New York City Commission on the Status of Women on the many roles of women as peacemakers in homes, communities, and the city.

IPVC took a two-pronged approach: municipal sponsorship and involvement, and personal transformation through finding common ground with members of ordinarily segregated groups. The more visible the public-sector leadership and the more sustained the work of individuals, the more widely effective the program was. The model of people working across race and class lines to improve civic life can change the neighborhood and the community-wide climate in very concrete ways.

When I announced Increase the Peace's formation, I said, "I cannot help but think how sad Dr. King would be to know that in New York in 1991 the mob that had to be restrained was not wearing hoods but came from the 'hood, and that the man of God they lynched was not a black preacher who gave a fiery talk but a Jewish divinity student out for a quiet walk. And although I am proud to be an African American, I am the mayor of all the people of our city, and I will seek in every way I can to help all New Yorkers lift themselves up without pushing anyone else down."

Once the operation was up and running, a twenty-four-hour telephone line for Corps members was installed in my office, and I met with volunteers on a regular basis. Those were among the most rewarding moments of my job.

And so, in the incendiary summer of 1992, when the acquittal of the police officers who beat Rodney King occasioned riots in Los Angeles, San Francisco, Las Vegas, Atlanta, Seattle, Pittsburgh, and Philadelphia and brought on civic unrest in many other cities around the United States, New York was blessedly untouched. The *New York Times* referred to it as "That Weird Day." One public official recalled, "I had never seen anything like the fear that was in this city that afternoon. It was like Godzilla was in New Jersey and was coming into New York." *Times* columnist Bob Herbert wrote, "Rumors were racing through the city's streets like lit fuses." A riot was supposedly planned for Times Square at 5:00 PM, and suburbanites began streaming out of the city by the tens of thousands. A Manhattan office worker told Herbert, "It was eerie. The city was clearing out and it was the middle of the afternoon. All anybody wanted to do was get safely home. It was like the apocalypse was coming."

Demonstrations began erupting in Greenwich Village, midtown, Harlem, and other locations, and some people were advocating violence. Bottles and rocks were being thrown, windows were broken, but Bill Lynch and I made up our minds that we would not allow these events to tear the city asunder. We met with the NYPD command, community activists, and local clergy and mapped out strategy. As well as our community assistance units, Increase the Peace volunteers fanned out, gathering information, debunking rumors, and playing a vital role in keeping the city together. For my part during that day of potential difficulty, I took to television and radio and urged calm not only to the people of the city but to the media in its coverage of the events. I walked the streets of Harlem and kept city offices open late as an example to merchants who had begun closing early in fear of possible trouble. Bill Lynch told Herbert, "We contacted all of our youth and recreation programs, put them on alert and kept them open late so there were places where kids could go."

And it worked: Westchester had riots, but New York had none. Even the *New York Post* acknowledged our performance, with a big front-page headline "Dave, Take a Bow." Gov. Mario Cuomo said, "He was elected, in part, as a person who could help calm a threatened city, and he did that." Cardinal John O'Connor, with whom I had had my difficulties concerning the St. Patrick's Day parade, praised my "sensitivity and prudence." I was gratified that when I traveled to Queens and some white neighborhoods of Brooklyn several days later, people came up to me in the street and on the subway and thanked me for keeping New York calm. After twelve years of Ed Koch, it wasn't written that the city would remain so. *New York Newsday* called me "Mayor Cool."

. . .

Judge Milt Mollen devoted two years to being deputy mayor for public safety, and when he left my administration I threw him a reception at Gracie Mansion. He had done such a splendid job that I and many others wanted to thank him for his service as he left to engage in the field of arbitration mediation. The law enforcement agencies presented him with gifts, and those in attendance applauded and showered him with praise. It was a lovely June evening. As Milt and his wife were leaving, I said, "Wait a minute, I want to talk to you." He and I walked downstairs, where I often held private planning sessions with Bill Lynch, Peter Johnson, and others. Judge Mollen was flush with good feeling from the fine social event that had just ended. I told him I had another important job that needed the right man. "I want you to investigate the police department."

Michael Dowd and five other NYPD officers had recently been arrested by Suffolk County detectives, who would not ordinarily operate inside the city but had entered because the Suffolk County district attorney on Long Island had placed a wiretap on a drug dealer out there and picked up a conversation with Dowd, who was a loud-mouthed guy. Six police officers in one arrest was unusual. Individual cops sometimes go wrong, but six at a time was more than worrisome. Public interest was starting to build, prodded by and at the same time encouraging coverage from the media. Police malfeasance is always press fodder. The question "What's going on in the police department?" is eternally loaded. With this as a background, I asked the judge to investigate. Was this an isolated incident, or was it indicative of a more widespread situation? How deep was the corruption, and if it was deep, how deep?

He said, "I can't do it. I signed a three-year contract, I've taken on obligations in private enterprise, I can't do it." I told him, "I don't care how you construct it, but I want you to oversee this." I was quite insistent. Judge Mollen had the stature, experience, and integrity to perform this investigation better than anyone in New York. Having performed so admirably in facilitating the expansion of the NYPD, he also had a reservoir of goodwill within the department, which would be necessary to delve behind the cops' legendary Blue Wall of Silence.

He said, "Let me think about it."

The judge's wife, family, and friends were united in their response: "What, are you crazy? Investigating the Police Department? You can't win. You'll get killed! If you're effective, the police will hate you. If you're ineffective, the public will think you're a faker." In the end the judge could not say no to the opportunity, to the responsibility, or to me.

Judge Mollen came back with the concept of a commission structure, in which he would be chairman and oversee its workings while leading a nonpartisan group of unimpeachable civic leaders in the task. In July 1992, I issued an executive order, and it was under way. There was no question that Rudy Giuliani was going to run against me again, and the independence of this commission and the integrity of the process both had the potential to play a major role in the race. It was vital that the panel not be criticized for being political. Not only was the creation of a nonpartisan investigatory organization the right thing to do, but Judge Mollen also felt it would keep Rudy off balance and, with his prosecutorial background, eliminate the possibility of him claiming the entire enterprise was simply a political setup. The judge simultaneously insulated the commission and selected highly qualified commissioners, all distinguished men. The commission consisted of two Republicans, two

Democrats (Mollen was one of the two Democrats), and a member of the Liberal Party.

Republican Harold Tyler Jr. had been a federal judge for thirteen years, nominated by President John F. Kennedy, and deputy attorney general of the United States under President Gerald Ford; at the time he was heading a major law firm.

Republican Roderick Lankler had a background in law enforcement, having been a stalwart prosecutor and ultimately chief of the Trial Division at New York County district attorney Frank Hogan's office, as well as New York State special prosecutor for the investigation of corruption in the New York City criminal justice system, before going into a highly successful private practice.

Herbert Evans, a Democrat who had been the New York State chief administrative judge, had worked with Judge Mollen and earned his trust and respect. He was a partner in the law firm of Shea & Gould, a founder of the civic organization 100 Black Men, and a member of the State Commission on Judicial Conduct, the agency responsible for disciplining judges. I knew and liked Judge Evans.

Judge Harold Baer Jr. had served as executive director of the NYPD's Civilian Complaint Review Board, headed the US Attorney's Chief Criminal Division, been an adjunct professor at New York Law School, and won election to the New York State Supreme Court on the Liberal Party ticket and served for ten years. He was in private practice but resigned to work on the Mollen Commission.

All the commissioners had substantial positions; when Judge Mollen asked them to waive salaries and work pro bono, they all agreed. They then went looking for a first-rate, nonpolitical staff that would get paid.

Judge Mollen received a call from Manhattan district attorney Robert M. Morgenthau, recommending a very capable fellow who had recently left his office to go into private practice. (Judge Tyler was also very close to Morgenthau, who had worked for him.) Morgenthau said the man, Joseph Armao, had run the rackets bureau and won convictions against members of the Lucchese crime family and the mobbed-up painters' union. Judge Mollen said, "Well, if he just went back into private practice, what makes you think he'd be receptive to an offer from us?"

"I think he might."

Joe Armao arrived for his interview, and Judge Mollen found a man he would characterize as a bulldog with enormous intellect. Armao had grown up in Howard Beach, Queens, graduated from Columbia University summa cum laude, received a scholarship to Oxford, where he received his master's degree with honors, and come back and graduated cum laude from Harvard Law School. He liked law enforcement and had spent seven years in the Manhattan DA's office. It turned out he was interested. Armao was quickly named chief counsel to the commission and hired at a salary that was generous for government pay but nowhere near what he could have been making in private practice.

Chosen as deputy chief counsel was the impressive candidate Leslie Cornfeld, who left the firm of Paul Weiss to join the commission. Judge Mollen considered it important to put a woman in one of the highest positions of significance on his commission. Brian Carroll, a retired police lieutenant who had investigated the fish market, historically controlled by the Mafia, was named chief investigator. He impressed immediately as well. Judge Mollen's former chief of staff Katie Lapp had been named criminal justice coordinator. He called and said, "Katie, we need a budget for our operation."

"What do you need?"

"I really don't know, but let's start relatively small. Let's start with a million dollars."

"Fine."

"What about office space?" he asked. The judge's business offices were headquartered on the eighth floor at 345 Park Avenue.

Ms. Lapp said, "I'll have either the commissioner or deputy commissioner of real estate call you. They handle that." The call came, Judge Mollen stated the commission's approximate needs, and the real estate commissioner said she would get back to him. A few days later, he got the call. "I've got a great spot for you, Judge."

"Where is it located?"

"345 Park Avenue. Eighth floor."

Judge Mollen had no difficulty imagining the headlines. "Park Avenue Commission." "Lazy Judge Walks Across Hall to Investigate Cops."

"Isn't there some space that the city has that's not being utilized?"

After she did some more research, she told him, "Yes, there's 17 Battery Place."

At the end of the first year, the commission had used only $800,000 of its $1 million budget. Katie Lapp called the judge and asked, "What do you want me to do with the surplus?" He said, "Give it back."

"Give it back?"

He said, "Yeah, give it back. We didn't use it."

"That's unheard of!"

You may have read stories in the past stating that if there are unused funds as the end of a budget year approaches, agencies will go out and buy television sets, or computers, or furniture. They will do something, but they will always use the money. It is almost against governmental religion for an agency to return money once it has been allocated.

The judge said, "No, Katie, we didn't use it. Give it back." The commission had a two-year term. "We'll work on our needs for the second year." Judge Mollen realized that, with the city's finances in an uproar, money was an issue. He put together a good staff, but he did it as reasonably as he could.

Judge Mollen was on the phone with Chief Counsel Joe Armao and Chief Investigator Brian Carroll daily. His first major dictate was that they needed to produce consistent, concrete results in order to indicate continuing accomplishment. It was important not only to move forward but to appear to be moving forward. At the outset the investigators found corrupt cops here and there, but soon they were informed of a situation in the Thirtieth Precinct in West Harlem, where an officer named George Nova was allegedly corrupt. Everybody knew he was corrupt, they were told, but no one had been able to catch him. A number of complaints had been lodged with the Internal Affairs Bureau against Nova, but they always came back unsubstantiated. District Attorney Morgenthau had investigated him for four years and had been unsuccessful. One day Armao and Carroll went to see Judge Mollen. They said, "Judge, we think there's a possibility we can get Nova, but here's what we have to do. There's this thing called the food stamp scam."

A recipient of food stamps is not permitted to use the government-issued scrip to purchase liquor or tobacco, only food. That's why they're called food stamps. However, there are several ways in which people try to game the system. Often a recipient will bring $100 worth of stamps to a local bodega or grocery store and exchange it for a discounted amount of cash. With this cash, they then go out and buy a bottle or cigarettes or worse. This black market economy undermines the social usefulness of the entire food stamp program as well as serving as one conduit for city residents to buy drugs. It is a widespread practice, and it is illegal.

Mollen Commission investigators had had Nova under surveillance for some time. On most workdays, Armao and Carroll explained, he would enter a small bodega on Amsterdam Avenue, stay there quite a while, and leave without carrying groceries. Clearly he was at that location for other purposes. The investigators figured the bodega was a payoff place. They said, "If we can nab this bodega owner and find out he's running a food stamp scam, we'll arrest him and flip him." In order to make this arrest, however, the commission had to involve federal authorities. The food stamp program is a federal program, the stamps are distributed by the US Department of Agriculture, and if Nova was going to be arrested, it would have to be by the US Attorney's Office.

Judge Mollen was aware of the sensitivities and jealousies of law enforcement officers. After Armao was hired, the judge arranged meetings for the pair with the five district attorneys in the City of New York, the US attorneys from the Eastern and Southern Districts, the assistant director of the FBI in charge of the New York region, and the assistant director in charge of the Drug Enforcement Administration. Judge Mollen had very strong views about cooperation among law enforcement agencies and worked hard to develop a good working relationship among the NYPD and the FBI, the Drug Enforcement Administration, and the State Superintendent of Police. Previously there had been little cooperation. Petty jealousies abounded, and little information was exchanged. That was historic. The FBI's unwritten slogan was supposedly "We only take information, we never give information." The judge, however, had developed relationships with Jim Fox, the head of the FBI in the New York region, as well as with US attorneys Mary Jo White and Andy Maloney, DEA head Bob Riden, and staff at the Internal Revenue Service and other agencies.

At these meetings, the judge would introduce Armao and then, knowing how jealous each of these officials was of his or her own prerogatives, would say, "Now look, when we conduct our investigations, if we have information that indicates that any one of you is already investigating them, we will pull back. We'll let you know what we have and we'll pull back. I also want you to do the same thing. If you're doing an investigation and it involves police corruption, I want you to discuss it with us, and we'll decide whether it's more effective for us to handle it or for you to handle it."

Internal Revenue was particularly important because the judge wanted IRS records to demonstrate that these cops were living on a scale high above their salary.

An understanding was reached that was ultimately very helpful.

The food stamps investigation was approved, and sure enough the owner made a buy. He was arrested, brought in, and agreed to cooperate. Nova, it turned out, was getting paid off, and he rolled over. After that, the cops fell like dominos, one after another. The results were devastating. Ultimately, thirty-three cops were arrested in one precinct, the Thirtieth, which came to be known as the "Dirty Thirty."

The Mollen Commission was historic. In its summary, the commission said, "We find . . . shocking the incompetence and the inadequacies of the department to police itself. . . . From the top brass down to local precinct commanders and supervisors, there was a pervasive belief that uncovering serious corruption would harm careers and the reputation of the department. . . . The department allowed its system for fighting corruption virtually to collapse. . . . One commanding officer encouraged illegal searches and arrest charges as a means of bolstering his unit's performance record."

The corruption was not systemic, I was happy to note, but nevertheless widespread. The commission found that "the problem of police corruption extends far beyond the corrupt cop. It is a multi-faceted problem that has flourished in parts of our city not only because of opportunity and greed, but because of a police culture that exalts loyalty over integrity; because of the silence of honest officers who fear the consequences of 'ratting' on another cop no matter how grave the crime; because of willfully blind superiors who fear the consequences of a corruption scandal more than corruption itself; because of the demise of the principle of accountability that makes all commanders responsible for fighting corruption in their commands; because of a hostility and alienation between the police and community in certain precincts which breeds an 'Us versus Them' mentality; and because for years the New York City Police Department abandoned its responsibility to insure the integrity of its members."

The report said: "Corrupt cops did not just stumble upon opportunities for corruption, they sought them out." Rather than arresting dealers and shutting down the drug trade, they faked police raids and robbed stash houses and bag men, sometimes violently, seizing large amounts of cash. They called this operation "doin' doors." They engaged in the practice of "collars for dollars," making numerous arrests in order to garner more overtime pay and earn promotions to coveted assignments. They perjured themselves in court, resulting in the dismissal of many cases that would otherwise have been sound. Particularly damaging was the effect that corrupt cops would have on the entire community policing program we were attempting to put into place. If the community questioned the integrity of the cop on the beat, it would not alert him or her to crime on the street, and this distrust would deeply affect the ability of the police to pinpoint potential crime problems before they developed.

There was some good news. The Mollen Commission expressed fundamental optimism in the fact that the vast majority of New York City police officers were honest and hardworking and served the city with skill and dedication. It found that, as a result of the commission's work, the department's leadership now had "a determined commitment to fighting police corruption."

The commission held two weeks of public hearings that brought much of the widespread miscreance to the public eye. History, however, can be unkind. Although I created the Mollen Commission, I was leaving office when it issued its findings in December 1993, and its complete report including corrective prescriptions in July 1994. The "Dirty Thirty" busts took place in April 1994. I had fully expected to preside over these successes.

My successor, Mayor Giuliani, had appointed Bill Bratton, who had served in my administration as commissioner of the Transit Police, to be commissioner of the NYPD. Bratton has a great sense of the dramatic. At the precinct house arrests of the first of the "Dirty Thirty," he personally took the badges off the chests of two officers, ultimately retiring the shields so that no other officers would carry the dishonor.

Judge Mollen is rightly proud of his work. History is often created in the aftermath, and it is important that Judge Mollen and everyone on his commission be credited properly.

11

Net Gain

The debate about the role of government over the last forty years has not proceeded in the right direction. Too many perceive government as ineffective and intrinsically corrupt and believe that only the private sector can solve societal problems and manage social responsibilities well. Years ago, when many of the people who ultimately worked in my administration were attending graduate school, all of those who chose to concentrate in government had burning causes. Some wanted to deal with discrimination, others with the issue of police brutality, still others with affordable housing; their interests were diverse, but every one of them came to my administration with a devotion to service. Many students today pursue careers in the financial services rather than public service, earning MBAs and law degrees, while graduate education in the public sector has become a default selection for young folks who are not certain of what they want to do. In addition, because people do not perceive government as a critically important part of their lives, we do not always have the best and the brightest sitting at the helm. President Clinton understood the role of the Federal Emergency Management Agency (FEMA), for instance, and its vital function in assisting people in times of dire need. Under President George W. Bush, the position of administrator of FEMA became a political plum and went to International Arabian Horse Association commissioner Michael Brown, who did a heckuva job. Fortunately, President Obama has re-empowered the organization. When I teach my students at Columbia University these days, I tell them that I hope they will have an interest in public service, and I always say that public service includes both politics and government; when practiced properly, I believe, politics and government do indeed fall within that realm.

I entered the office of mayor with a vision of what I wanted to do with the city in trying times. My idea of government held that the viability of the city was intimately connected to the viability of its neighborhoods; how would government respond to individual neighborhoods? My director of operations, Harvey Robins, took this idea to heart.

Harvey graduated from George Washington University in 1968. Washington, DC, burned each year he was in school, which informed his choice of careers. These were extremely political times, and given that George Washington was within walking distance of both the White House and the Reflecting Pool, many civil rights and antiwar demonstrations were also within his immediate world. Harvey earned a graduate degree in government at the University of Pittsburgh and a doctorate in government and in public policy from Union Institute in Vermont. He is one of those people who stayed the course.

Robins worked for Mayor Koch in the Office of Management and Budget, then joined social services and ultimately rose to the position of first deputy, the number-two person, at the Human Resources Administration, at the age of thirty-eight. People would say about him, "Well, Harvey's so young. He's a young Turk. You gotta give him a little room, you gotta give him a wide berth, but he really has good instincts."

Harvey was given great responsibility at a young age, ranging from overseeing programs for the homeless to handling the issue of child abuse, to dealing with food stamps and welfare, and he got away with more than most. The AIDS crisis had only just begun in the mid-1980s, and amid the hysteria some individuals were hesitating to visit welfare centers to fill out their applications for fear of coming in contact with AIDS sufferers and contracting the disease. As a result, some who were entitled to benefits were going without. Recognizing this problem, social workers approached Harvey and said, "We need to create a special program for AIDS clients." He in turn asked the health commissioner, "Is this a program that you would prefer to do rather than me?" and was told, "No, no, no, if you want to do it, you do it." Robins and the social workers investigated and found that AIDS clients were being required to run through a gauntlet of lines, in different bureaucracies, in order to access welfare or food stamps or housing benefits. Not only were AIDS patients in desperate need, but they were being shunted from place to place by the very institutions that were supposed to serve them.

With this information, Robins and the social workers developed a case management program under which individual caseworkers would be assigned a specific number of clearly designated AIDS patients. Harvey went to the Office of Management and Budget for approval and was told by its deputy budget director, "Well, these people are going to die in three months anyway, we're not going to approve it." Undeterred, he returned to his office and said, "We've got approval. Let's go." Harvey recalls:

"Having decided to pursue a career in government service, shaped by the 1960s, I had hoped that I would be able to make choices and take risks for those who had no voice. The AIDS initiative is an example of this opportunity."

The civil service union was initially opposed to the program, as they believed that consolidating the work and multiple service tasks under each caseworker would result in jobs being lost. He told them, "Get over it. This is an epidemic in its early stages; this is not about jobs, this is about improved services, and your caseworkers are the front line." (As the caseload grew and the demand for case managers increased, the union's concern was dropped.) He did not require workers to join the AIDS program—it was entirely voluntary—and it is a tribute to New York's caseworkers that there were more volunteers than cases.

They served 647 clients the first year and kept meticulous notes on the specific needs of, and caseworker staff's response to, each client so that Harvey could present an informed request for future funding in the following budget cycle.

After a year, Robins approached Mayor Koch and said, "Look, I gotta tell you something. I don't want the deputy mayor in the room, I don't want the budget director in the room, I need a one-on-one." Koch agreed. With both pride and trepidation, Robins presented his results. Koch rose from behind his desk and said, "You made one mistake." Harvey figured, that's it, I'm done. Koch said, "You shoulda told me last year. I would have embraced this."

"But, Mayor," said Robins, "I didn't have the data. I have the data now."

It should be noted that the program continues today, some twenty-five years later, and serves more than thirty thousand HIV and AIDS clients annually.

Housing for the homeless was at the time also guided by the Human Resources Administration. Only Harvey and the agency's procurement director knew the suggested locations of the proposed shelters, and they would canvass neighborhood sites in the middle of the night. Robins remembers, "The Mayor used to beat me up all the time: 'You can't do this, you have to have a process!' I told him, 'If we have a process, we'll never open a shelter, and there are people who are lining up for them!'" If he did not create the term NIMBY (the catchphrase encapsulating the resistance of some people of means to the introduction of housing or services for the poor into their neighborhoods), Harvey created scenarios for its use.

Robins also spent a year working for schools chancellor Richard Green, rising to the position of deputy chancellor for finance and administration at what was then the Board of Education and is now the Department of Education. Mayor Koch, budget director Paul Dickstein, and Bobby Wagner, who was chairman of the Board of Education at the time, told him, "You'll have the title of deputy chancellor for finance administration. Your first assignment is to tell us how many people are at central headquarters of the Board of Ed." No one knew, it was one of the great mysteries of city government. "And then you'll begin to dismantle it," they told him. The Board of Education was well known as a large drain on the city's finances, with many unnecessary expenses hidden in its budget. He said, "I'm on, but only under the condition that some of the money that we save goes back to the schools. I don't want it to be just a pure gap closer for the city." He was told this sounded like a fair deal.

Harvey literally did a desk audit. His staff moved from desk to desk collecting signatures every time each person at the Board of Education signed for his or her paycheck. Armed with this information, he analyzed the board's productivity and proposed cutting 1,800 jobs. When Chancellor Richard Green died of asthma, his successor, Joseph Fernandez, asked Robins to stay on, with yet another mandate. Fernandez told him, "You can't leave me unless you give me another six hundred cuts, because on my first day I want to announce that what you started under Chancellor Green continues."

Harvey had made a conscious decision never to participate in the electoral process beyond voting; he did not write a check to any candidate, and he never campaigned. He felt, "If they want a manager they'll hire me, if they don't they won't. I don't want to be appointed on the basis of my politics, I want it to be based on my work." Robins did not think he had a chance of landing a job in my administration, so he was quite surprised to receive a phone call from Norman Steisel, saying, "If you want to be the director of operations, there'll be no transition committee. If you want the job, it's yours." He certainly did want it.

The Board of Education is located at 110 Livingston Street in Brooklyn. Harvey told the chancellor, "I gotta go back across the river." Out of a continuing sense of duty, however, he worked the first eight hours of that day for Chancellor Fernandez and during the second eight hours participated in his first budget meeting with me at Gracie Mansion. Another of Harvey's notable cost-saving achievements was the elimination of chauffeurs for all board members. This did not sit well with some but was a budgetary and symbolic victory. At the press conference announcing his appointment, a reporter asked me, "Well, Mayor, are you going to ask him to do the same here?" I said, "Yes, but not my vehicle."

Several billion dollars needed to be eliminated from the city budget, and Harvey's job was to be a significant factor in the making of those choices. Revenues had fallen in the tail end of my predecessor's tenure, and though Koch had made cuts, he had not made enough.

Whenever there's a recession, city revenues fall because of the downturn in the economy. The city is extremely dependent on Wall Street and the real estate market; when Wall Street starts to teeter, New York City takes the fall. Every real estate transaction has an associated tax; some of that revenue goes to the city, and some goes to the MTA for transit. If developers are not constructing new buildings, not only is there a decrease in payments for material and labor, but the income from taxes on these transactions is decreased as well. Any disruption of this lifeblood of tax revenue has a huge ripple effect across the government. Other administrations, preceding and following my own, chose to satisfy Wall Street first and hope the economic benefits would trickle down to the remainder of the city. Wall Street's well-being was of vital importance to New York, and I had a group of advisers who tackled the Wall Street issues and responded to those concerns. My concerns were economic and social, and I saw it as my job to walk through that fire so we could have it both ways. The fact that New York City had fewer dollars did not mean we ought not be concerned about spending those dollars wisely.

Within the Office of Operations, Harvey Robins adopted this larger vision and considered the services that were being provided to neighborhoods and the best way to provide them. I felt strongly that every neighborhood in the city should receive its fair share of services and that we should eliminate what had been a de facto policy of being more attentive to some neighborhoods than to others. In this way alone we would be reinventing government. Our model for delivering services involved answering the question: is this the most cost-effective means to our end? If we found the city restricted in its ability to deliver, was there another means to achieve the desired results? For instance, could we create public-private partnerships? Sometimes this meant restructuring, sometimes consolidating, and sometimes investigating services that spanned several bureaucracies and demanded coordination and responsibility. Whether it was having the Sanitation, Transportation, Parks, Police, and Buildings Departments combine forces to make the parade route safer for the public when Nelson Mandela visited or making the city shine for the 1992 Democratic National Convention, Harvey was the man for the job.

Many in my administration strongly believed that certain programs were bedrock for the city's physical, moral, intellectual, and spiritual well-being. For Youth Commissioner Richard Murphy the priority was the Beacon schools; for Deputy Mayor for Human Services Cesar Perales it was public health; for all of us the concept of community was bedrock. For Harvey Robins it was libraries.

Libraries, Robins felt, span the ages. Use of each individual facility varies by day and by time of day; the elderly are not likely to frequent the buildings while kids are running around, however quietly, so they sit and read while the children are in school. Parents might arrive a little later in the day, with or without their offspring. On weekends, working people might use library computers to network for jobs or help their children with homework. As Commissioner Murphy said about the Beacons, Harvey didn't care what went on under the roof. The library system had 205 branches spread citywide throughout every neighborhood in New York's five boroughs, and every one of them, he felt, should have an individual emphasis and focus, from the selection of books to the variety of reading programs, because each neighborhood had its own personality. Harvey was insistent. Of course, it wasn't hard to sell me; this was what I wanted to do as well.

New York City public libraries are not simply repositories for books and magazines; they serve greater purposes. They are safe havens for some people who have few places to go to escape the dread of the streets. I recognize this is not the libraries' mandate, but let's live in the real world and recognize the ancillary benefits of places of education. For some poor folks the library is the only place their kids have to go in the winter to get warm because it's cold at home. Forget studying, just be warm. In the summer as a child in Harlem, I remember we used to hang out on the fire escapes. In summer the libraries are cool. For many children that was it—there was no place else.

In much the same way we insisted that health care clinics and Beacon schools be open at night and on weekends to serve all New Yorkers, we addressed the issue of library hours. Faced with cutbacks and the necessity to eliminate not only fat but muscle and bone from the city's budget, the concept had been put forward to save money by curtailing library time. I felt this was a bad idea.

Harvey researched the issue and found that in 1901 when Andrew Carnegie offered New York City $5.1 million to create a branch library system throughout the five boroughs he mandated that it be open seven days a week, seventy hours a week, ten hours a day. Libraries, Carnegie said, were for the "industrious and ambitious; not those who need everything done for them, but those who, being most anxious and able to help themselves, deserve and will be benefited by help from others."

In 1947 the city had cut public library availability to six days a week. It had fallen further since. When I came into office, Robins sent his staff to visit each of the 205 branches and report what the current hours actually were. "Why did you take staff time?" I asked. "Why couldn't you just ask the libraries to send you their schedules?"

"If it was literally inked on the glass of the door," he told me, "I believe that number more than what they would give me on a sheet of paper."

When the information arrived, he appeared at my door. "Racism is alive and well," he said. "We have four different library systems: New York, which covers Staten Island and Manhattan, then we have Queens, then we have the Bronx, and then we have Brooklyn."

The Jamaica branch on Queens Boulevard, for example, was open three days a week. Five miles up the road, in Forest Hills, libraries were open every day except Sunday. "What we need to do," he said, "is to fill the cup to get everybody up to five days, and the following year everybody to six days, and the third year to seven. Then we'll worry about reaching Carnegie's goal of ten hours a day and enough books and materials." Harvey's version of the Carnegie vision was to make it unnecessary to have a schedule on one's refrigerator to know when the library was open. In the simplest terms, this was his ideal library system: no one should need a schedule. We formulated a plan to accomplish this goal.

Libraries in the school system are often the first program excised from the budget when a principal is faced with the need to cut back. "Well," the principal figures, "we have to have somebody teaching English, and someone teaching math." From that perspective, I suppose it makes sense; one has to cut somewhere. With school libraries being eliminated, however, the city's public system became even more important. The question was: could we get the funding? Harvey said, "Don't worry. We'll get the money."

Harvey's research had revealed the cost of revitalizing the city's library system to be approximately $47 million. Having been trained in the Office of Management and Budget, he was a demon budgeter, and through decreases in Police and Fire Department overtime and other judicious savings—from asking, as I have mentioned, questions such as "Do we need an annual report in color?" "Do we need another driver?" and "Do we need all these trips?"—he found what we truly needed. "The budget director wasn't too happy with me going line by line through his budget," he recalls.

I convened a meeting of the deputy mayors downstairs at City Hall. I began by asking them to consider what they would do if they found a pot of $47 million. Where would they spend it? I went around the room encouraging discussion, and in these intramurals each deputy mayor had a good use for such funds. Then I invoked the Lincoln Rule.

One immediate problem encountered was that library budgets were City Council member items: each borough president could decide where to spend his or her money. Queens borough president Claire Shulman was extremely invested in libraries and yet was allocating funds unequally between poor and middle-class neighborhoods. Harvey said, "Claire's going to be very upset with you. She's going to say, 'I'm not going to get as much as some of the other boroughs because I've already invested in libraries for the last ten years.'" To which we replied, "Well, God bless you, you've done God's work. You've made a good choice."

Claire was indeed upset, but we did get the money, and for the first time since 1947 libraries around the city were open six days a week.

.　　.　　.

Several of our lasting contributions to New York's cultural life were created in preparation for our hosting of the Democratic Convention: Fashion Week, Restaurant Week, and Broadway on Broadway. Much like infrastructure or new housing constructed when a country hosts the Olympics, these civic advances served the community far beyond their initial purpose. Henry Miller, the CEO of New York '92, the nonpartisan organization that managed the city's hosting of the event, developed these ideas, and for more than twenty years they have stood the test of time.

The purpose of Fashion Week, originally called "New York Is Fashion," was to publicize and promote the city's $14 billion-a-year fashion industry, which employed 180,000 people, including 100,000 apparel workers, designers, illustrators, stylists, models, and marketing people. In an effort to involve our visitors, we invited the convention's main audience of delegates, Democratic Party officials, and their families to mingle with fashion industry executives under a huge tent on the Great Lawn in Central Park. The initial show brought together established and up-and-coming designers and was broadcast on the Sony Jumbotron in Times Square. Sponsored by the International Ladies' Garment Workers Union, the Fashion Institute of Technology, and New York '92, the show was funded by the union, American Express, and several Seventh Avenue fashion houses. What began as a single promotion grew into a semiannual event attracting over 115,000 attendees to each fall and spring showing in tents in Bryant Park; the total estimated one-week economic impact on the city in 2008, according to the New York City Economic Development Corporation, was $391 million. Now called Mercedes-

Benz Fashion Week, this staple of the fashion world has added to New York's already estimable cachet.

Restaurant Week was a similar inspiration, created in coordination with restaurateur Joe Baum and Tim and Nina Zagat of the *Zagat Guides*. Ninety-five of New York's world-famous restaurants offered a three-course lunch for $19.92. Not only did this extravagant bargain entice convention visitors, but the surge of customers expanded the restaurant business throughout the city. People visited establishments they might not have been able to afford otherwise, and they chose to return after excellent experiences. The program was such a success that it continued annually, the price increasing a penny a year—$19.93, $19.94 . . .—and participating establishments being added until 2006, when the price jumped to $24.07 for lunch and $35.00 for dinner. This is still a remarkable bargain for high-quality New York City meals. By the summer of 2011, more than three hundred restaurants participated during the two weeks of Restaurant Week.

Broadway on Broadway was conceived as a Democratic National Convention welcome party and turned into a free outdoor concert attended by fifty thousand people in Times Square. A high-energy presentation of singing and dancing selections performed by the casts of current and upcoming musicals, it was designed as free entertainment for our guests and the city at large. The extravaganza worked so well that it has since been incorporated into Broadway tradition. Held each September, Broadway on Broadway presents musical numbers and features appearances from almost every show on Broadway as well as sneak peeks at shows about to open. It attracts consistently good-sized crowds each year in what is a very large and showy advertisement for the upcoming Broadway season.

As the *New York Sun* noted:

> The short-term economic impact of the 1992 Democratic National Convention was estimated at the time to be more than $300 million. That represented a ten-fold return on the cost of

hosting the Convention. But New York created events for that occasion with lasting value, and the return on that investment continues to benefit all New Yorkers to this day. The economic impact of those events . . . runs easily into the billions. No other host city has created events with lasting benefits that come anywhere close to New York's.

.   .   .

Times Square had gone straight to hell. Through a combination of difficult economic times and civic neglect, what had been a central New York urban attraction filled with Broadway theaters, gaudy neon-lit movie houses, and hidden-treasure record stores had over the course of a generation fallen past hard times and directly into cultural devastation. Strip clubs and pornography shops abounded. Stories were rife about roving bands of young toughs terrorizing tourists and cops needing to patrol 42nd Street between Seventh and Eighth Avenues three abreast in order to feel safe themselves. One of the priorities of my administration was to reintegrate Times Square into the civilized world of New York.

Carl Weisbrod joined my administration after overseeing the effort to revitalize Times Square for several years as director of the 42nd Street Development Project, a state entity. Not long after I was elected, the State of New York condemned the land and took possession of six of the nine historic theaters on 42nd Street in preparation for the area's redevelopment. This was vital. A nonprofit organization, The New 42nd Street, was established to oversee the development of the neglected midblock theaters and begin to restore the area to something approaching its former glory. However, even with this economic opportunity, no improvement of significance to the entire area was going to take place unless a developer with financial wherewithal could be found to take charge. There were inquiries, but the economy was still struggling after the stock market crash in 1987, there was a high corporate office vacancy rate, and new office development—which was going to be the economic driver of the restoration—was simply not taking place, certainly not in such a notoriously dangerous location as 42nd Street. How could we resuscitate this fallen giant?

Several in our circle had connections to the Walt Disney Company and very much wanted to replace the seedy, squalid urban crime center with its antithesis. What could be more symbolic than getting Disney to participate? Getting Mickey Mouse to come to Times Square?

How would we approach Disney? One of the architects we were using in Times Square, Robert A. M. Stern, later dean of the Yale School of Architecture, was on the Disney board of directors. Stern reviewed the project and professed at a Disney board meeting that the organization really ought to think about Times Square, that it was worth a shot. Disney itself, after a significant fallow period, was in the process of a corporate reinvigoration and starting to think of urban areas as the centers for its entertainments, as opposed to the suburbs, as had been its strategy in the past. The concept of having a live theater, especially in New York, began to make sense to the company. The cross-marketing possibilities were excellent; the company could develop its film and musical proper-ties into Broadway shows and own the theaters in which those shows would be produced. Clearly this was a good idea, as the success of *The Little Mermaid, Mary Poppins, The Lion King, Aida, Beauty and the Beast,* and *Tarzan* can attest. We approached Disney at the right time, and the Disney people started to work on it.

They were very tough. They essentially said, "We're Disney—we can do whatever we want. You're damn lucky to have us. You negotiate by giving us what we want or forget about it."

They wanted to be able to buy a theater, and they wanted a very low-cost loan so they could pay for it. They wanted a guarantee that the envi-ronment around 42nd Street would be such that the Disney brand would fit comfortably and not be embarrassed. For instance, the sex businesses had to be removed by certain dates, and another major theater had to open on the block by another deadline. Furthermore, they wanted the right to cancel their commitment if these conditions were not met.

The New Amsterdam Theater, home of the Ziegfeld Follies, had potential. Built in the Art Deco style in 1903, it was a beautiful landmark theater. It had good bones but was a real mess. The New Amsterdam had never degenerated into a porno theater, but it was in horrible, dilapidated condition. Inside, it smelled like urine and cats. The Nederlander Organization, one of the big Broadway producers, had purchased the property in 1982 but was not prepared to finance the substantial renovation necessary to bring it back to life. After some negotiation, Nederlander had essentially told New York City and State, "We don't want it. We can't do anything with it on this block. Take it. Just pay us the bare minimum."

Carl Weisbrod recognized that to attract Disney to Times Square we would be best advised to present them with a sweetheart deal. Such an arrangement would be controversial; although New York's many business organizations wanted a high-profile tenant to anchor the area, none would be pleased if we, in effect, gave away the store. In a very clever fiscal negotiating maneuver, Weisbrod developed an offer based on the Disney demands and before taking it to Disney presented it to the three major Broadway theater chains: the Shubert Organization, the Nederlander Organization, and Jujamcyn. Carl can be extremely conversational. He told each of them, "Look, here's the deal."

As he expected, each organization declined. Shubert's Gerald Schoenfeld, himself quite a conversational fellow, said, "Here? On 42nd Street? Forget about it. I'm not gonna do it, I don't care what kind of loans you give me." With these definitive rejections in hand, we went in and made the deal with Disney, which was pleased with the opportunity.

Our discussions took place over the course of my term, and those negotiations finally bore fruit. They were by no means easy, and they continued into the final days of my administration. I had planned on being mayor during groundbreaking and presiding over the restoration of Times Square. Sadly, this was not to be. Nevertheless, it was very important to me and to many in my administration that this deal be signed before we left office; we could only control what we saw in front of us, and anything left until January 1 would be subject to the whims of the next administration. Of course, Disney wanted to see the deal signed while I was mayor as well. With all of us wanting the memorandum of understanding consummated, we worked furiously that last week. On Friday, December 30, 1993, the deal was delivered by Carl for signature by Deputy Mayor for Economic Development Barry Sullivan.

"And sure enough, after that all the theater owners squawked," Weisbrod recalls. "They wanted 42nd Street improved, but they really didn't want Disney on the block, because Disney wasn't part of the club. So they said, 'This is outrageous! This is a sweetheart deal!' I said, 'Look, I offered it to you; this is the same exact deal.' And ultimately Disney did have a profound impact on making that block what it is today."

.　　.　　.

In 1992 the large and influential financial institution Morgan Stanley was seriously considering moving its corporate headquarters to Stamford, Connecticut. The company had an option to buy a substantial plot of land in the downtown area on which to build. Of course, this was of tremendous concern to us. The economic issues that had loomed before I entered the race had only worsened in the months after I had been elected. The city relied on the revenue derived from its major corporate citizens to provide services to run its financial engine. We needed the taxes on profits, wages, and bonuses of everyone from the corporations themselves to their highly paid executives and their middle managers, secretaries, and mail room employees, to the ancillary businesses connected to each of these institutions: the companies that provided their copy machines, the neighborhood coffee shops that served them lunch, the upscale restaurants, the furniture and office suppliers that did business in the companies' wake. We were concerned that a move by Morgan Stanley could create a domino effect that might induce JP Morgan, Merrill Lynch, and the other major players in the financial world to depart the city as well. The effect would be staggering, profoundly affecting the city's bottom line. A financial services subsidiary of the First Chicago

Corporation took one thousand jobs to Jersey City, and only after serious negotiations were we able to prevent four of the city's five commodities exchanges and Prudential Securities from doing the same.

Morgan Stanley had concerns about its future with us. Crime was certainly a graphic issue, but the company's chief concern was recruitment. It was having a hard time convincing top talent from around the world to come to New York City. "How do we get the quality workforce we need?" they asked. To their way of thinking, if they located in Stamford, they would be only an hour and a half from the city, they could attract executives and office workers who would enjoy life in the suburbs, and they would be safe from the danger that, so the story went, was everywhere in New York. I had heard they had already made the deal. One typically arrogant Morgan Stanley banker told us, "Forget about it— the train's already left the station."

Yet we were negotiating. Everyone in City Hall recognized that if an industry leader as distinguished as Morgan Stanley departed, not only would we lose the company's 4,100 jobs and estimated $2 billion in annual economic activity, but it would be a terrible symbol for the city. We wanted to make clear to the entire corporate world that New York was where businesses did their best business, where the giants and the leaders chose to headquarter themselves. Carl Weisbrod took the lead for us. Along with the New York City Partnership, he organized a meeting with Morgan Stanley's chairman, Richard Fisher, and brought to the table some of New York's most notable citizens.

It became almost a matter of survival. Cardinal John J. O'Connor was in attendance, as were Senator Daniel Patrick Moynihan, Senator Al D'Amato, and Congressman Charlie Rangel. The scene still, to this day, brings tears to my eyes. We presented a united community of smart, distinguished business, political, and cultural leaders, one after another, very gravely and passionately telling Dick Fisher, "We love this city. You have an obligation to stay in this city." Our arguments were factual and emotional. In suburbia, we argued, the pencils hit the desk at 5:00 PM as people headed for the door. New York had a superior talent pool, an intense concentration of business services, and communications and transportation centrality. The city was home to a preponderance of their potential clients, with whom they could interact face to face, a significant advantage. We had culture and opportunity and were at the heart of the workings of the world. The Rev. Timothy Healy, head of the New York Public Library and a Jesuit priest, said eloquently, "They've been burying New York for decades now. They've tried to say New York is dead, but they've never produced a body . . . and they never will."

Fisher was listening. Finally, Pat Moynihan faced him directly. "Let me just make this clear," said the senator. "I'm the chairman of the Senate Finance Committee. My friend and colleague over here, Charlie Rangel, is the ranking member of the House Ways and Means Committee. If you leave the city, you're dead."

Dick Fisher as much as blanched. He said, "Well, I'm going to have to think about it."

A week later, the same banker who had told us the train had left the station said, "All right, let's negotiate a deal. Just keep the cardinal out of it."

Morgan Stanley was projected to pay $911 million in combined city and state taxes over the next ten years. We agreed to freeze the city's general corporate tax rate for the coming four years and offered tax breaks and financial incentives totaling almost $40 million. I found this a modest investment given the company's importance to our financial future. Morgan Stanley ultimately bought two vacant buildings in Times Square and helped lead that area's economic revival. They are good New York citizens, and their headquarters remain exactly where they should be.

Our plan to restore and rebrand Times Square was a striking success. Financial institutions now crowd the area, as do newly built hotels and restaurants and theaters, drawing business traffic and tourists in record numbers. In 2012 *Crain's* magazine reported on findings by Cushman & Wakefield: "In the rankings of top retail strips in the Americas, Fifth Avenue still reigns supreme. It is followed by three other New York shopping magnets: Times Square, Madison Avenue and East 57th Street,

which took second, third and fourth place, respectively. They were followed by Beverly Hills' Rodeo Drive." In hindsight, it looks obvious: of
course tourists and entertainment-related companies would flock to
Times Square—it has historically been the crossroads of the world. At
the time, however, given the depths to which the area had fallen, this was
radical thinking. The traditional economic development community was
singularly focused on improving Manhattan through the financial services sector alone. Midtown was going to be a "one-trick pony." Granting
incentives to the tourism and entertainment industries was unheard of,
except for convention center/sports arena developments.

Yet here we are, more than two decades later and despite the conventional wisdom, with Times Square beating all but Fifth Avenue, and
performing well beyond Rodeo Drive, as the best retail spot in the United
States—thanks in large measure to implementation of the economic plan
created by my administration.

.   .   .

Among our most pressing concerns during New York's fiscal difficulty was the threat that major institutions would leave us for the tax
breaks and various incentives offered by other cities around the country.
The Morgan Stanley encounter had been intense, and now we were concerned about losing the Girl Scouts of America. We were also concerned
about losing the United Nations! It is not written anywhere that the
United Nations has to be in this country, much less in New York City.
When New Yorkers discuss the UN, they are likely to complain about
the diplomats who refuse to pay their traffic tickets and things of that
nature, and they don't see much beyond that. One of my predecessors
even said that we should level the United Nations and make it a parking
lot. I had a different attitude.

I was also extremely concerned about losing the US Open Tennis
Championships.

The US Tennis Association (USTA) franchise, which runs the annual

US Open, is more economically valuable to the city than the Yankees, the Mets, the Knicks, and the Rangers combined. Those franchises are culturally significant and play many games in their individual venues, but since the average New York sports fan already resides in the metropolitan area, most fans attending those games either live in the city, drive in, or take public transportation. A family of four may drive to the stadium, pay for parking, pay for their tickets, buy hot dogs and beer and souvenirs, and return home. The US Open, on the other hand, attracts tourists from around the world. They come to New York for a week, they rent hotel rooms, they eat in restaurants, they go to the theater. We are comparing a $400 family outing of people who already live in the area—and who, if they go to the Bronx or Queens, may never make it into Manhattan—to 700,000 people, perhaps half of whom are coming from out of town, each spending between $5,000 and $10,000. Imagine having the World Series or the Super Bowl or the Final Four in the same place, year after year, and running, not for a week or a weekend or one day, but for two full weeks. That is the impact of the US Open on the economy of New York City. It is colossal. To lose it would have been devastating.

·   ·   ·

I am known for being a tennis fan. I played ping-pong when I was growing up in Trenton, and I messed around with tennis in high school and college, but I really didn't know how to play. Bill Hayling, Les's brother who became a doctor and ultimately delivered Joyce's and my children, was the first to put a racquet in my hand. I didn't even hold it properly. But in 1974, when tennis became all the rage, I got bitten by the bug, and I have been crazy about it ever since.

I understand that it is relatively unusual for an African American my age to have a devotion to this particular sport—stereotype would have me be a baseball or basketball fan—but I enjoy tennis, I speak the King's English, and I willingly wear a tuxedo when the occasion calls for it; if these traits are unsettling to anyone, so be it. One might deem these preferences aspirational, as my generation of African Americans, denied a smooth path into American life, made physical, intellectual, and cultural integration an important goal. One might roll that over in the mind. The media and others have often focused on these attributes, as if to imply that I am somehow attempting to live above my station. No, these are simply choices I have made based on the man I am. Or it may simply be that I like tennis, proper diction, and formal wear.

In one of his books, the first black Wimbledon/US Open/Australian Open tennis champion Arthur Ashe said, "If you want to see what a tennis player should look like, go look at Charlie Pasarell." Pasarell was trained in his native Puerto Rico by coach Welby Van Horn, and in 1974 and again in 1975 I went to Van Horn's Connecticut tennis camp and learned how to play. The instruction did not so much raise my game— as I had none to begin with—as create it. I continue to play tennis five times a week even to this day, and I have a list of sixty-four friends, men and women, to whom I send a weekly email blast to fill my rotation of partners. We play a spirited game. It is one of my consuming passions.

I like and admire tennis players, including Roger Federer, Rod Laver, John McEnroe, Monica Seles, Serena Williams, and Ilana Kloss, who plays in my game. A former number one–ranked doubles player and current commissioner of World Team Tennis, Kloss is also Billie Jean King's life partner. There would be no women's professional tennis without Billie Jean. She is a remarkable woman, an inspiration particularly to women in sports, but also to all of us. I had the honor to share a court with Billie Jean and was pleased and proud to be on the USTA Board of Directors when we voted to name the USTA National Tennis Center after her.

But most of all, I would be remiss if I did not mention my admiration for Arthur Ashe, a beacon of honor on the court and off. I was in Madison Square Garden during a match in which a shot at Arthur's end was called out by the umpire in the chair. "No," Arthur informed him, "that was good." A rare occurrence indeed. He was such a gentleman. That's the way he was taught by Dr. Robert Walter Johnson, the "godfather" of black tennis.

I am friendly with the whole McEnroe family—father, mother, and their sons Patrick, Mark, and John. I was having dinner out one evening when John's wife Patty came over and told me, "My father-in-law is upstairs celebrating his birthday with the family and some of his law partners, and they'd love for you to join us." I went upstairs to find two or three dozen people in the party. They asked me to speak, and I talked about my love of tennis and the National Junior Tennis League, an organization co-founded by Arthur Ashe that encourages tennis participation in poor neighborhoods and the inner cities throughout the United States. I said, "Over time, nationwide, perhaps millions of youngsters have come through the program. A handful become world-class players, like John and Patrick." (Their brother Mark said, "What am I, chopped liver?") "A greater number attain a degree of proficiency so they can get college scholarships, and given what it costs to go to college these days, that's important. But more important to me is that nationwide, over a period of forty years, millions simply become better people through tennis."

.   .   .

In negotiating with the USTA, one needed to understand its internal politics. The organization is divided into seventeen geographical sections, and according to its constitution, voting power is based upon the number of registered USTA members residing in each section. In the early 1990s, there was a movement afoot to take the US Open out of New York. Chicago and Atlanta were the leading alternative sites, with some consideration being given to locations in Connecticut, Westchester, and New Jersey's Meadowlands. Understanding the workings of the USTA, one had to be extremely concerned. We were negotiating to keep the Open in town, but there was significant support within the association for a move.

As someone involved in the tennis world, I was aware of the USTA's internal workings. At that time the players were challenging the governing bodies controlling the Grand Slam tournaments in an effort to increase their portion of the revenues. Tennis had a checkered history of financial dealings with its players, having come late to professionalism, and there was considerable interest among the pros in creating their own tour. Golf, a game and industry with a similar social and cultural background, was controlled not by the United States Golf Association but by the Professional Golfers' Association, the players. If the US Open paid $30 million to the participants out of $120 million in profits, the players asked, why couldn't they organize their own tour and make the profits themselves? The Association of Tennis Professionals (ATP) hired President Jimmy Carter's former chief of staff, Hamilton Jordan, to assist in the creation of just such a tour.

If the USTA abandoned the New York market and moved the tournament elsewhere, what might New York do? Well, the USTA owned neither the land on which the tournament was played nor Louis Armstrong Stadium, the Open's premier court; these were city properties. If the US Open was no longer being played there, why couldn't the city negotiate with the ATP and the Women's Tennis Association and create a new Grand Slam event on the spot? I met with Mr. Jordan to discuss the possibilities. This gave us considerable leverage as our negotiations with the USTA intensified as well.

Professional sports as a moneymaking industry was in its infancy in the 1970s and early 1980s. Even when USTA president W. E. "Slew" Hester moved the event from the historic West Side Tennis Club to expanded facilities in Flushing Meadows in 1978, the Open wasn't an instant financial success. Within three or four years, as the tennis craze took hold and lucrative television contracts were negotiated, the USTA quite suddenly developed significant earnings. What would the organization do with this capital? An expanded tennis center at the site of the US Open was high on its list of priorities.

This was not immediately good news for us. First, a new tennis center would demand a large expanse of land, and New York City did not have an adequate new site to offer. Second, a stadium that cost $300 million to build in New York could have been built in Chicago for around

$100 million and in Indian Wells, California, for $50 million. There were union issues and materials issues to contend with, but that was only a 20 percent factor. The major drawback to new construction was that if the new facilities were to remain in Flushing Meadows, they would have to be built on landfill, which would have to be made not to sink and settle. Such construction was extremely expensive.

In the interim, the USTA felt that it needed to build four more practice courts in Flushing Meadows—plain old-fashioned tennis courts. In the 1980s, one could build an individual asphalt court for between $25,000 and $30,000, but in its wisdom the USTA spent $2.2 million on four practice courts with a fence. Building on a landfill, its engineers found, was like building the courts in water: before contractors could even lay down a footing, they had to build a structure that could support it, they had to create a deck. The construction was obviously very expensive. Between the cost and the politics and the difficulties with the players, if from 1985 to 1990 one had asked a professional oddsmaker, "What's the line that the USTA will stay in New York?" I think you would have gotten, at best, a 50-50 bet. Maybe 7 to 5 against.

We began negotiating with the USTA, which was represented by David Markin, the Checker Motor Company CEO who had just finished a term as the organization's president. (His father had created the company that manufactured and supplied the city's iconic Checker cabs.) Traditionally the city had been represented in these sorts of negotiations by the Parks Department, because the land on which the tennis grounds sat was Parks Department land. However, that department did not have the expertise to negotiate complicated economic development agreements, so Norman Steisel called in Carl Weisbrod, at that time the president of the New York City Economic Development Corporation, to lead our team. Carl's mandate was to negotiate and come back to me with a deal, and he performed admirably.

There are two major reasons why stadium deals are rarely advantageous for municipalities. First, they often begin with a threat to leave by an existing franchise—"We are going to pull up stakes, and you will no longer be perceived by America as a major league city"—followed by a demand: "In order for us to remain, you must build for us a new, state-of-the-art stadium, renovate or create modern infrastructure around this edifice, and establish a business environment in which we can thrive. We will take all the revenue—including but not limited to parking, concessions, and ticket sales—while you earn only a highly negotiated rent and the taxes on the substantial revenue we earn. And since you own the facility and the grounds on which it stands, it is your responsibility to maintain them; as the building and surroundings age and require repair, we will pay for none of it. That's the deal. Take it or we're leaving."

Second, stadiums have historically been located in downtown areas, the center of urban environments, and aside from game day, most of the time they are dead. A football stadium is used approximately nine days a year—ten or eleven if a team is fortunate enough to get into the playoffs. (Teams don't even practice in these stadiums; they usually train at facilities in the surrounding suburbs, which are more than willing to trade civic funds for proximity to the major leagues.) Baseball stadiums are open eighty-one days a year and closed the rest. A casual stroll around any major league facility in the off-season will confirm the utter solitude of a building without a team. In some respects, these facilities are a blight on the urban environment, except around game time.

In this case, however, we were dealing with an organization that had a striking willingness to negotiate. New York was clearly established as the center of the American tennis world, and among the USTA's primary goals was the expansion of the sport itself and the elimination of New York City as a stop on any tour the players might put together. The association wanted to grow the sport and needed a shining arena in which to showcase it. New York clearly possessed that potential, particularly as the base for much of the nation's media companies, particularly all three major television networks. The deal was sufficiently expansive that there was room for give-and-take on both sides, and while other sites were being considered, the city and the USTA set about to fulfill each other's needs. The negotiations were hard but not acrimonious, and Weisbrod felt that the USTA was exceptionally generous in understanding the city's position.

Rather than demand that the city spend several hundred million dollars to build the new facilities, the USTA agreed to pay for the construction of the entire stadium. The land would continue to belong to New York, and the city would own the stadium as well. However, instead of sticking the city with what could be a sizable bill, as in other stadium deals, the USTA agreed to maintain the stadium as well. And it would be open to the public on a paying basis. The US Open Tennis Center would become a tennis hub, a gathering place for the city's players. Lessons would be taught, games would be played, a community would be encouraged. The courts would be open. Unlike Yankee Stadium, Shea Stadium (and now Citi Field), or Madison Square Garden, eleven months of the year any member of the public with a court fee could play tennis where the pros played. The effect on the sport itself would be profound. I perceived the USTA to be remarkably prescient in this regard.

Louis Armstrong Stadium, which the new facility would replace, was originally the Singer Bowl, erected for the 1964 New York World's Fair and home to a series of music concerts, including those by Jimi Hendrix and Janis Joplin. The new venue would seat 23,500 and might serve in a similar capacity, and a clause was negotiated that stated that the proceeds of any paying events scheduled during times when there were no tennis tournaments would be split evenly between the city and the USTA. The city would pay for improvements to the roads around Grand Central Parkway, which were needed in any case. The USTA would receive all parking revenues, which were significant only during the two weeks of the Open. We also agreed to support tax-exempt bonds so that the USTA as bondholders would pay a lower interest rate. The city, state, and federal governments would lose a very modest amount of money in taxes, perhaps $100,000.

Often the municipalities in stadium deals are paid a percentage of net earnings. This leads to the unseemly spectacle of corporate ownership throwing the kitchen sink into the expense list (one construction worker to hold the chair, one to screw in the lightbulb), deducting it from revenues, and presenting the city that built their stadium with revenue streams that trickle rather than flow. One heard this in the press as it covered city disputes from time to time with George Steinbrenner or the folks out at Shea over the amount of rent due from the Yankees and Mets, respectively. Rather than allow that to happen, we negotiated a deal in which the USTA paid New York City an annual rent of $400,000, which would rise incrementally, *plus 1 percent of the gross.* As revenues have grown, this deal has become extremely and increasingly lucrative.

There were ancillary issues. Flushing Meadows Park was huge—it encompassed four or five different community boards. One of the great multicultural parks in the city, Flushing Meadows was used daily by Asians, Latinos, Caucasians, African Americans, the poor, everyone from relatively low-income people to the fairly well-off. It was close to middle-class neighborhoods like College Point, blue-collar white neighborhoods like Maspeth, and Latino neighborhoods like Corona. The park was so inviting that people would travel to spend time there. Many Pakistani and Indian families who did not live in close proximity used it fully nonetheless. Because it was a large and very much a family park, many felt that they had a stake in it. This became an issue when we declared the intention to eliminate a Flushing Meadows pitch-and-putt golf course in order to accommodate the needs of the tennis center.

Although it occupied a tiny section of the park, the pitch-and-putt course, we came to find, was much beloved. Local residents complained to their legislators, who complained to us. Here we were, building a huge stadium to generate substantial revenue at a time when the city desperately needed it, revenue that would increase as the years progressed, and a pitch-and-putt was standing in the way. One would think this could have been easily resolved, but in New York State a city government cannot simply appropriate parkland, even to lease it to a responsible commercial tenant, without getting approval from the State Legislature. The entire tennis center development project had to go through the public approval process, be the subject of hearings, and be discussed before the various community boards. Betsy Gotbaum, whom I was proud to have appointed to be the first female commissioner of the Department of Parks and Recreation, secured the support of the local legislators to de-map the parkland and was vital in facilitating this process.

There was, as there always is with any public project in New York, a degree of contentiousness. The neighborhoods were upset; they wanted the pitch-and-putt course relocated, they wanted free tennis lessons for neighborhood residents, they wanted reduced prices for seniors and children when the complex was open to the public, they wanted a cap on the fees charged for court time. Their list of demands was extensive. Ultimately, we found another location within the park for the pitch-and-putt course, we accommodated several community requests, and the issue was resolved.

The major bone of contention hanging over the entire deal, however, was the issue of flyovers. Louis Armstrong Stadium and the entire US Open Tennis complex lay directly in the flight path of LaGuardia Airport. During takeoff and landing, planes regularly flew over the courts, rocking the area with a noise that would rattle one's insides. The tradition of tennis demands silence at key moments, both for decorum's sake and to allow the players to concentrate. The screaming jet engines during matches were more than disconcerting—they were extremely disruptive. Conversations were forced to cease, and more to the point, players could not hear the ball hitting the court or coming off their racquets, which affected their ability to gauge its power and fashion their response. The noise affected the game itself; it affected who won and who lost.

The players were unhappy with the USTA over the game's economics to begin with. When they learned that a new US Open Tennis Center was planned to stay in Flushing, they complained bitterly, particularly eight-time finalist and three-time winner Ivan Lendl, who said, essentially, "Either solve this or we're out of here!" USTA representatives told Carl Weisbrod, "The facility would be cheaper elsewhere. We will admit, we would rather keep the Open in New York, but ultimately we are dependent on the players. If we cannot get peace and quiet from LaGuardia, the players will not come to the tournament and we will have to move." For all the economics, this was the one overriding issue. They as much as told us, "Look, we want to do this, but we can't be locked into a deal where the planes are going to fly and our players are going to boycott this event. It's just not going to work for us."

Claire Shulman was the newly elected borough president of Queens, the home of Flushing Meadows Park. Nick Garaufis, a young attorney in her office, was helpful in contacting the appropriate people within the Federal Aviation Administration (FAA), with whom we held several extensive conversations. (Garaufis went on to become the FAA's chief counsel and is now a federal judge.) We explained our position and asked that they change the offending flight paths, if not universally, then during the two weeks in which the Open was played.

We were extremely fortunate. It developed that the flight path that brought planes over the stadium was not the one actually favored by the FAA. A safer pattern preferred by the agency had the aircraft coming in and out from the north and east, over Long Island Sound. However, pressure was being brought to bear on the FAA by federal elected representatives protecting the suburbs: planes were being routed over Queens only because these politicians did not want them disrupting their constituents on Long Island and in the bedroom communities of Connecticut. The thinking was that if you fly over a park, you disturb fewer people than if you fly over a neighborhood. Residents of Queens might see it another way.

Hearing our concerns, the FAA was happy to say, "The city insists! The US Open is so important to our economy that we must respond! Great!" They agreed to reroute the planes for the entire duration of the Open. We were very pleased to bring a positive response to the bargaining table; the players would be satisfied, and it appeared not only that the Open would remain in New York but that we would be the beneficiaries of a wonderful new athletic facility.

Sadly, the USTA was not satisfied at all. While they appreciated the immediate statement from the FAA, they wanted a long-term commitment in writing, which the FAA, in order to maintain its own options, was not willing to make; the FAA would give us assurances and commit its best efforts to us, but it could not bind its successors to such a policy. The USTA expressed concern that succeeding mayors might not be so solicitous of the association's feelings and might not lobby the FAA so hard the next time such a problem arose. Having been locked into a long lease and invested half a billion dollars in a facility, they would be utterly lacking in leverage. More than the agency's assurances, they wanted a firm commitment that the FAA was not going to change its mind. Failing that, they demanded a stronger commitment from us.

This was the point at which the negotiations became difficult. Carl Weisbrod met with David Markin in Markin's posh apartment on Fifth Avenue in the 70s, where the USTA demanded a default provision—the right to walk away from our contract in the event of a specified number of flyover incidents. Markin told Carl, "There will be a deduction from the rent for flyover violations, particularly during the semifinals and finals, other than for reasons of safety." (All of us understood that safety concerns such as weather conditions or security held primacy over issues of sound level at the Open.)

"This is outrageous," Weisbrod told him. "We're never going to agree to this. This is totally outrageous!"

"We can't live without a penalty," Markin said.

"We can't commit to something we don't control!" Carl responded. "We can't give you a penalty. We'll do our best, we'll commit to best efforts, but we can't commit to suffering a harm if we don't control it. We don't control this! The FAA controls this, we don't, and we're not going to agree to this!"

Negotiations became nasty. Carl said, "We are immovable on this issue. I don't care if it's ten cents, I'm not gonna even present this to the mayor." At that point he stormed out. The men stopped speaking to each other. The silence lasted several days. Finally Weisbrod told them, "Look, I'm not even going to deal with this issue until I know it's the only one left on the table." When the two sides had finally agreed upon every other outstanding point, Carl walked into my office and said, "Mr. Mayor, I think we're pretty much there with this USTA lease, except for one modest issue, which is this flyover thing. The USTA is insisting on a penalty, and honestly, Mr. Mayor, my view is that they're not going to agree to this without one."

I was quite clear in my response: "No damn way."

"I think it's a deal-breaker," he told me.

"It can't be." I sent Norman Steisel and Judge Mollen back in there with Carl, who said, "All right, guys, see if you can change it." They returned the next day and told me, "Look, this is a problem, and here's why this is a problem. They really want to permanently hold the next mayor and the next mayor and the next mayor's feet to the fire. We eliminated the default provision, but the best we could all do was negotiate a cap on the penalties in any one year." That maximum was $325,000. The base rent was $400,000.

I spoke with David Markin personally. He was a hard-bargaining, hard-driving guy, fierce but fair. I tried to explain the impossibility of the City of New York being made responsible to pay the USTA several hundred thousand dollars annually as a result of a decision in which we had no part. "Politically," I told him, "how am I going to explain that we're going to pay you if a plane flies over a damn tennis match?!"

"It's a deal-breaker," he said.

"Dave, you're killing me!" I told him.

"It's a deal-breaker."

Finally we acquiesced; we needed the Open, and we felt that the FAA had our back and the penalty provision would be rendered moot. But the problems were far from over. The deal required the approval of what seemed like everyone in public service: the legislature had to approve the alienation of the parkland; the federal government had to affix its approval because federal money had been involved in the creation of the park itself; and the entire plan had to go through the laborious public approval process before the borough community boards, the Queens borough president's office, and ultimately the City Council.

In the heat of the 1993 mayoral campaign, there was great pressure on many City Council members to oppose this plan. The race was too close to call, and officeholders had to make choices as to which candidate was the one with whom they wanted to curry favor. To mollify detractors and speed the process we made the ready-to-sign lease available to the City Council. This was unprecedented; the executive branch of New York City government simply does not open its books to the legislative. The City Council's responsibility in a parks case such as this was simply on the land-use side. They had no power over the economic deal; that was the mayor's prerogative. Given the controversy and public misstatements and wrong statements, however, we took this unprecedented action, even though our outside counsel and many in the administration disapproved.

At its hearing, the City Council got to ask David Markin, who turned out to be quite a good witness, all manner of questions concerning the lease. Ninety percent of the members didn't have the faintest idea what they were talking about. Nevertheless, it was as if there were fifty-one lawyers in the room questioning Markin, who managed, despite the fact that he has a temper, to maintain his cool throughout. One member asked how many gay people were included on the USTA board of directors. Markin said, "How do I know? I don't ask people if they're straight or gay."

"Well, how many stated gay people are on the USTA board of directors?"

Markin didn't know, and that was the end of that. Ultimately, the City Council gave its assent as well.

After two years of negotiation and government approvals, we had a deal. During any single year, a breach of a specifically defined quiet would cost the city a maximum of $325,000, but the new US Open Tennis Center would be built, including a new stadium and fifteen new courts. The USTA would pay $172 million for the expansion, the city would add forty-two acres of parkland to the site, and the US Open would remain in New York for twenty-five years—with a series of incremental rent increases and options that could extend the lease to a total of ninety-nine years. The USTA would maintain and operate the center, the public would have access to it, and the city would own it.

I postponed the signing of the lease once because borough president Claire Shulman and City Council speaker Peter Vallone were not available to stand by my side that day. I finally signed with them sharing the glory and standing in support in December, two weeks before I would leave office. Parks commissioner Betsy Gotbaum and Norman Steisel's chief of staff, Ellen Baer, were extremely helpful in getting the site prepared quickly so construction could begin on my watch and mitigate against Rudy Giuliani reversing the deal, as he had promised he would do during the mayoral campaign and indeed attempted to do when he was elected. He tried to scrap the deal! Needless to say, the agreement was sound, the USTA stood its ground, and the Open continued with much success in spite of Rudy's objections.

In 2010 the city had an estimated economic impact from the tournament of $756 million, up from $420 million in 2001 and $145 million in 1991. It's the best-attended annual sporting event in the world and a real showcase for the city, viewed by 85 million people in the United States and broadcast to 188 countries worldwide. The flyover penalty remains $325,000, but in nearly two decades it has never been brought into play. Mayor Bloomberg visited my radio show and on the air called the contract that my staff and I negotiated "the only good athletic sports stadium deal, not just in New York, but in the country."

I have been privileged to sit on the USTA's board of directors. I was very vocal in promoting the naming of the center after Billie Jean King, one of the sport's greatest players, the person who single-handedly saved women's tennis, and a pioneer in equalizing the economic and social treatment of not only women tennis players but of women around the world. The USTA has proposed building, at an estimated cost of $500 million, an expanded facility with the capacity to sell an additional 10,000 tickets for each of the Grand Slam tournament's first several days. It is a big deal.

I recognize that there is a long list of deserving people for whom a court or building could be named at the Tennis Center, which is why I was so supremely moved and proud when, in recognition of my efforts to expand the game of tennis in New York and guarantee that the US Open would have a place to call home for decades to come, the suggestion was made by my friend and tennis proselytizer Skip Hartman to name the plaza directly in front of the East Gate entrance to the center, the David Dinkins Circle.

Skip and I had met in the mid-1970s during an effort to bring tennis to low-income black and Hispanic inner-city children. Not only did he attempt to bring me some recognition at the US Open, the man saved my life. I had previously had a minor heart attack in 1985, and in 1996, when Skip and I were playing together at Hilton Head Island, South Carolina, I suffered another incident. Skip doesn't like to play doubles because he likes to run. I always tell him, "If I'm your partner, you get to run a lot." So we were playing doubles, and it was hot, and I felt something was wrong. Serious tennis players don't quit in the middle of a game. Maybe at the end of a set, if not the whole match, but not in the middle of a game. I said, "I gotta sit down." I took a seat courtside and fainted. I was out for five or ten seconds. When the doctors examined me, they concluded I had three or four blockages and needed a triple-bypass operation. Joyce was in New York, and during that time Skip Hartman became my protector. If anybody came anywhere near me, Skip wanted to know, "Where's your board certificate? Are you board-certified?" Skip was zealous and would not leave my side.

I wanted to go home to my own doctors but was told, "You can't fly." The question then became, where would the surgery be performed? I was given a list of hospitals reachable by ambulance and picked Charleston, because the surgeon was reputedly the third-best in the country and because I knew the mayor, Joe Riley. (In one campaign I supported Joe before I knew whom he was running against. "I should tell you," he said, "my opponent is black." "A black Republican?" I said. "Screw him!")

It develops that the Medical University of South Carolina was one of the best hospitals in the country, and the surgery was successful. When Joyce flew down, Skip stepped away, but his care and caring was vital to my survival, and I am extremely grateful.

The USTA accepted Skip's suggestion in 2008, and David Dinkins Circle is the gateway through which hundreds of thousands of tennis fans pass each year to attend the US Open and during the fifty other weeks of the year to play their personal matches. In 2008 a dedication ceremony was held, and I was gratified to see many friends gathered in the plaza that brings together so many things that I love. I love the tournament, I love the sport, and I love the city. I am deeply grateful that my name will forever be associated with the Billie Jean King USTA Tennis Center and the US Open. It is a true honor.

12

Mandela

Nelson Mandela was coming to New York.

Mandela was a genuine hero. He was also my personal hero, a transcendent symbol of freedom. He had the capacity to lead people. He truly had the courage of his convictions. He was a lawyer and an activist, a very smart man who, knowing that if he was captured he would be convicted of treason, nevertheless fought a system that was ruining his people. He believed, against overwhelming odds, that he was going to one day succeed. And he was ready to die for his beliefs. There may have been people who were his equal in modern history, but I would dare say no one was ever greater.

In the first year of my mayoralty, this was not a universally held view. His image as a world statesman had not yet been burnished. In fact, Mandela and the African National Congress (ANC) were perceived by some in positions of power to be part of the international communist conspiracy. The ANC was a revolutionary organization fighting South Africa's apartheid government. In 1962 the CIA, whose director at the time was George H. W. Bush, is said to have tipped off the South African security police, and Mandela was captured, tried, and sent to prison. After twenty-seven years of hard labor for sabotage and armed revolt against the white regime, Mandela was released on February 11, 1990. Through a campaign of organizing and information, the efforts to win his freedom grew into a worldwide movement, with many countries boycotting or imposing economic sanctions against the government of South Africa to end apartheid and bring about his release. Minus these sanctions, he would still be in jail. A mere four months into his freedom, friends in his country were organizing a six-week, fourteen-nation tour to celebrate this triumph, raise funds, and encourage the continuation of economic sanctions against the white regime that had imprisoned him.

Harry Belafonte, who is a god in South Africa and a celebrated civil rights leader and entertainer here in the United States, was instrumental in planning the American leg of this tour, along with Bill Lucy, the secretary-treasurer of the American Federation of State, County, and Municipal Employees (AFSCME), AFL-CIO, president of the Coalition of Black Trade Unions, and the most powerful African American in the US labor movement. They and others were organizing an event in Washington, DC, but weren't certain which city would have the honor of welcoming him to the United States. He was scheduled to visit eight cities while he was here. We knew Harry and Bill, they were close friends, and we got involved in the negotiations.

Someone might have made the argument for going to the nation's capital first, but George H. W. Bush was now president. He was no great fan of Mandela, and his administration had not been particularly forceful in opposing apartheid. Bill Lynch had the notion that Mandela should arrive in New York City. "Works for me," I told him. It was a stroke of genius. We said, "New York. We'll give him a *real* party!"

The idea took hold, and Bill was thoroughly involved in every aspect of bringing it to fruition. Ultimately, the decision was made: New York City would be this great man's first stop in the United States. Harry Belafonte, Cleveland Robison of the United Auto Workers, and I were co-chairs of the Nelson Mandela New York Anti-Apartheid Welcome Committee.

Mandela and his wife, Winnie, would be staying with me and my wife, Joyce, in a guest suite at Gracie Mansion. Gracie is not a spacious home and includes only three main bedrooms. The Mandelas might have had more commodious accommodations at one of New York's many five-star hotels. Nevertheless, I thought it was important that they be accorded the honor and respect of New York and reside with us in the mayor's official residence; it was the right thing to do, and I wanted this visit to be perfect.

I surveyed the room where they would be staying and said to my bride, "I think he is too tall for this bed." In my mind Mandela was ten feet tall. Joyce said, "He'll fit." Of course she was right.

·   ·   ·

On June 20, 1990, Nelson Mandela flew from Canada to New York, arriving at Kennedy International Airport. The plane was two hours late, but when he finally touched down, I was truly moved to be in his presence. The city of New York literally rolled out a red carpet for him, and he was most gracious in receiving a line of fifty that included Gov. Mario Cuomo and Gov. Jim Florio of New Jersey, then stepped beyond it to greet several hundred supporters who had massed behind us. "It is a source of tremendous joy and strength for us, my wife, our delegation," he said, "to be received with such a rousing welcome by the people of the city. . . . Join us in the international actions we are taking. The only way we can walk together on this difficult road is for you to ensure that sanctions are applied." This was why he was here, and I could not have agreed more.

In fact, a week earlier, I had drafted a bill that would give New York City the most stringent anti-apartheid sanctions in the United States. I was a longtime opponent of apartheid and had made this a key element in my mayoral campaign. Now I was going to keep my promise. There was some movement in Congress to reconsider the sanctions, which were intended to force the South African government to abandon its racist policies, but sanctions were the ANC's main leverage and I could not abide any attempt to curtail them. Under my bill, the city would not contract with companies or banks that had business ties to South Africa. We would rate banks according to their efforts to exert pressure on the South African government to end apartheid and give our business to those with the highest ranking. We would make strong efforts not to invest the $43.1 billion in city pension funds in companies doing business there. This bill passed, and over the years our sanctions were effective. Large companies doing business in South Africa, like IBM and 3-M, and others seeking to do business with the city were clearly influenced. There was a lot of money to be made in New York, and lucrative contracts would go only to those companies that stood with us. These sanctions would remain in effect until there was tangible, fundamental political change, the cornerstone of which would be a democratic South Africa and the destruction of apartheid as South Africa's law of the land.

We had a full first day prepared for Mandela. A visit to Boys and Girls High School in Brooklyn, followed by a ticker-tape parade on Lower Broadway and up the Canyon of Heroes and a welcoming ceremony at City Hall. Why a ticker-tape parade? Because Nelson Mandela was a man of stature. Not everybody gets that parade. Look at a short list of people who have been deemed worthy: Teddy Roosevelt, Charles Lindbergh, Admiral Richard Byrd, Jesse Owens, Winston Churchill, Dwight Eisenhower, Charles de Gaulle, John F. Kennedy, Pope John Paul II; the Apollo 11 astronauts who walked on the moon; the World Champion New York Yankees and New York Mets; and Vietnam War veterans. Nelson Mandela deserved his place among them.

Fifty thousand people were at the airport and lined up along the route in Queens. Things take time in New York, and our forty-car motorcade plus State Department security personnel, led by two dozen police motorcycles, with police helicopters hovering overhead, was running late. It was suggested that because we were behind schedule, maybe we should skip Boys and Girls High. Lynch said, "Nope, they'll be waiting."

And sure enough, they were. The Parks Department had set up a stage on the school's Fulton Street football field, and the kids were yelling and screaming. "Mandela! Mandela!" There must have been ten thousand people on the field and in the stands to hear and see him. In school and at home they had learned he was a hero, and here he was in front of them. At that moment we knew we were on to something. "We in South Africa have always known that we have loyal friends among the people of New York," Mandela told the crowd, "but we had no idea that we were perceived with such love and warmth!" As we were leaving, hundreds of kids ran alongside the car, whooping and hollering as they sent him off. His security detail was a little perturbed, but Mandela loved it. He just loved it.

We drove through the streets of Bedford-Stuyvesant, East New York, Fort Greene—all African American neighborhoods—and police estimated that 100,000 people were lined up, sometimes four-deep, cheering wildly. On the other hand, the *New York Times* reported that in a white neighborhood in Queens, "one man with a video camera held his hand in front of the lens with a finger raised, so that the motorcade became the background for an obscene gesture."

Because of concern for his safety—the worry was that white South Africans might have a hit out on him—the NYPD built a secure vehicle with a clear bubble top in which Mandela could see and be seen as he rode up Broadway. A similar vehicle had been crafted for Pope John Paul II and dubbed the Popemobile. So we had the Mandelamobile. Ticker tape is obsolete—it's all computerized now, there are no more tickers!— so confetti made of computer printouts rained on us. The NYPD estimated the crowd at 400,000, but to me it looked like at least a million.

Standing at a lectern in front of City Hall, Mandela said some kind words, praising me as New York's first black mayor, which I greatly appreciated. Then he told a packed crowd, "Apartheid is doomed. South Africa will be free. The struggle continues." Bill Lynch, sitting a row behind him, broke down in tears.

It was a day of tremendous significance. A genuine African freedom fighter was welcomed as a hero by the people and the city of New York. And it wasn't just black folks; on the drive from City Hall to Gracie Mansion, people on the Upper East Side were standing three- and four-deep to catch a glimpse of this man. He was received as a statesman throughout his American tour, and I would argue that we set the tone for the rest of the country.

Mr. Mandela was seventy-one years old, fresh out of prison, and had already toured several cities in Europe just prior to his arrival in New York. By the end of the day he appeared to tire noticeably. Meetings with black journalists and South African exiles were canceled, and what had been planned as a twenty-two-person formal dinner became an intimate meal with Mandela, his wife Winnie, my wife Joyce and me, our children Donna and David Jr., our granddaughter Kalila, and Bill Lynch. Bill doesn't remember what we talked about. "I have no idea," he says. "I was in such awe, they could have been talking about Mickey Mouse." I recall talking with Mandela at length. You never know for certain what a person is about until you sit with him or her comfortably. I was pleased, but not surprised, to find that there was an absolute and total lack of bitterness in the man. *Well,* you might think, *he just behaves that way in public—in reality he's an angry fellow.* No, he is a man of grace. Strong-willed—you don't last twenty-seven years in prison the way he did without strength of purpose—but calm and completely focused on the task at hand. What he and others accomplished in South Africa demonstrates to me that one day there will be peace in the Middle East.

Personally, I was thinking, *This mayor stuff is pretty good!* I had been in office only a couple of months, and here I was sitting over coffee with the great Nelson Mandela.

The next day Mandela got up and went for a walk. This was his custom—he got up early in the morning and took a walk. The concept being that if he had done it in prison on Robben Island, he could do it anywhere else. It just happened that he was walking the streets of New York. The Secret Service went crazy running after him. "Mr. Mandela!" Maybe the special agents thought New York's streets weren't safe, but we knew better.

Mandela had another full day. He was interviewed by Ted Koppel, a crackerjack journalist, for ABC's *Nightline*. Mandela had long been criticized by some for his membership in the South African Communist Party, and Koppel tried to use that to get him in a corner. Mandela would not be intimidated and calmly responded by saying, in effect, that the Communists "were the only ones that helped us. Next question." I found that very impressive.

The demands for his time were plentiful: ministers, politicians, school-children, all wanted to be in his presence. Songwriters wanted to sing him their songs. Organizations of all stripes wanted to honor him and share his visibility. "The greatest amount of lobbying I've heard about," said one of my senior advisers, Ken Sunshine, "is from folks in Brooklyn and folks in Harlem. It's a traditional rivalry." Harlem and Brooklyn had put that rivalry aside during my campaign, but there was no way to please every-one. Mandela would speak at an ecumenical service at the Upper West Side's Riverside Church, and we decided to hold a rally at 125th Street and Lenox Avenue, followed by an event at Yankee Stadium.

The tour was in part a fund-raiser for the children of South Africa, and at Riverside Church Mandela received a check for $200,000, ear-marked for South African schools, housing, medicine, and refugee assis-tance. "We have risen up on the wings of angels," he said. "We have walked and not fainted. Our destination is in sight. Our victory will be your victory!" He had people literally dancing in the aisles.

In Harlem the streets were jammed with 200,000 celebrants. Folks were hanging out of windows. The emotion was almost physical, you could feel it in the air. It was an absolute exaltation of everyday people. Racial pride at its best. Mr. Mandela used soil brought over from the black township of Soweto to plant a tree to honor black children who had been killed by South African authorities.

And here's how politics works. Several speakers had been scheduled, including me and Congressman Charles Rangel. Some of Harlem's black nationalists, who had been active in the anti-apartheid movement, fig-ured that they were the true representatives of the people and thought they were going to take over 125th Street. They had been given one speaking place in the program, but they had a former Black Panther who was himself newly released from prison, and they were going to upstage us and showcase him. This is the kind of crap some of these guys would pull from time to time. But Bill Lynch had a good relationship with all of them, and he would not be intimidated. Bill said, in so many words, "This is my mayor, now all of you back off." Congressman Rangel got hold of the microphone, introduced me, and a crisis was averted. The crowd was chanting "Viva Mandela! Viva Mandela!" I introduced him.

Mandela looked out over this massive crowd and told them that he and the ANC had been following the struggles of the people of Harlem for thirty years. He said he felt "a kinship of solidarity. . . . Harlem signifies the glory of resistance."

"Sojourner Truth . . . ," he intoned.

"Dr. Martin Luther King Jr. . . .

"Marcus Garvey . . .

"Paul Robeson . . .

"Rosa Parks . . .

"Adam Clayton Powell. . . ."

At each incantation the crowd erupted.

He was standing at the corner of 125th Street and Lenox Avenue, which only two years earlier had been renamed for . . .

"Malcolm X!"

"There is an umbilical cord that ties us together," he said. "My only regret is that I am unable to embrace each and every one of you." He ended by crying, "Death to racism!" The crowd was in a frenzy.

.   .   .

We'd had some difficulty booking Yankee Stadium for the big rally. Yankees owner George Steinbrenner refused to let us use it. He never quite came out and said it, but my impression was that he thought the community would get in there and tear the place up. We talked about holding the event at a stadium on Randall's Island, but that was too small. Madison Square Garden was out of the question; it held only twenty thousand. Ken Sunshine, who had had a successful career in the music industry, contacted promoter Ron Delsener, who was representing Billy Joel. Joel had scheduled a three-night stand at the Stadium and had rented the place outright. In one of the great magnanimous gestures in rock-and-roll history, Billy Joel let us have one of his nights and also donated the staging and equipment. So now we had Yankee Stadium, and there was nothing George Steinbrenner could do about it.

We sold the place out. Seventy-five thousand people. A lot of money was raised that night. There were performances by Judy Collins, Richie Havens, Tracy Chapman, and calypso legend the Mighty Sparrow. Many speeches were given, including by Bronx borough president Freddy Ferrer and Harry Belafonte. I addressed the crowd.

Jesse Jackson wanted to speak. He had run for president two years earlier and carried New York City in the New York primary. He had accompanied the Mandelas to Riverside Church earlier in the day. Jesse is a dynamic and powerful speaker, and there is little doubt the crowd would have loved him.

Harry Belafonte would have none of it. There is a tension between the two men that exists to this day—certainly it was evident that day at Yankee Stadium. Bill Lynch was part of the organizing and program committees and friendly with both men, but Belafonte ran the Yankee Stadium program. Earlier in the day there had been a cordial disagreement between them right on the steps of Gracie Mansion. Jesse was trying to get in, and Harry just let it be known, "Not gonna happen."

After hours of music and speeches, when Mr. Mandela finally came onstage the place was rocking. People had seen news reports from South Africa of crowds chanting "Amandla! Amandla!" and had taken the call as their own. Many thought it meant "freedom" or "victory." In fact, *amandla* is the Zulu word for power. Even better. The chant shook the Stadium.

Mandela was moved by the reception. He spoke about apartheid and the need for continued sanctions. He spoke about the commonalities of our peoples. He ended his speech by saying, "The people of New York, we admire you, we respect you, and, above all, we love you."

I walked over and, in front of the entire screaming crowd, placed a Yankees jacket—blue and white, with the NY logo over the heart—across his shoulders. I put a Yankees cap on his head. He beamed and said to the crowd, "You now know who I am. I am a Yankee!"

The photo of Nelson Mandela in the Yankees jacket and cap was transmitted all over the world.

The next day George Steinbrenner called and said, "I'll pay for the event!"

. . .

Bill Lynch convinced me that we ought to go to South Africa. New York was leading the way with our insistence on maintaining economic sanctions, and negotiations that would ultimately result in South African national elections had begun. We wanted to create a "sister cities" effect— take some of New York City's health, housing, police, and education commissioners, as well as business and religious leaders, and team them up in preparation for the day when their South African counterparts would take over the government. This was not a junket but the pursuit of a business opportunity. Not only would it be socially and morally positive, but it would redound to New York's economic benefit when South Africa did finally change governments and went looking for people with whom to do business. The ANC would remember who stood by them.

Lynch wanted to rent an airplane and create something of a New York–South Africa Express, but the cost was high; rather than have New York City foot the bill, I asked that the trip be privately financed, that each of the travelers pay his or her own way. Although reservations were made and schedules put in place, we could not raise sufficient funds, and that plan ultimately did not materialize. A month later, on an extremely scaled-down budget, a group of us—including Carl McCall, president of the New York City Board of Education; Betty Shabazz, Malcolm X's widow and director of institutional advancement at Brooklyn's Medgar Evers College; Herbert Daughtry, pastor of Brooklyn's House of the Lord

Pentecostal Church; health commissioner Dr. Margaret A. Hamburg; NYPD deputy inspector Jules Martin; Lee Dunham, owner of several McDonald's franchises in Harlem; and a contingent of press—flew to South Africa via Al Italia. We would stop over in Rome, where we had arranged an audience with the pope, and fly from there to the South African capital of Johannesburg.

When we touched down outside the Italian capital, we were escorted into the center of the city by a motorcade flanked by police motorcycles. While New York's City Hall is an impressive edifice, the piazza on Rome's Capitoline Hill was designed by Michelangelo. We walked on a red carpet up a long column of stairs flanked by a phalanx of heraldic trumpeters costumed out of Cecil B. DeMille. We lunched with the mayor of Rome and dined later that evening with the area's governor. Speeches were delivered, and gifts exchanged. I was pleased to be so honored, but I didn't take it entirely personally; the mayor of New York is accorded rare privilege and respect in faraway lands.

I had never been to Rome. I visited the Trevi Fountain and dropped in three coins.

While a papal audience had been on our original itinerary, we learned that the pope would not be available when we actually came to town. This was unfortunate but not unexpected; I suspect it had something to do with my decision earlier that year to march with gays and lesbians in New York's St. Patrick's Day parade.

Everything is connected. In 1991 the issue of gay and lesbian rights was unavoidable—at least for me. The St. Patrick's Day parade is one of New York City's major events, and for the first time a gay organization applied to march under its own banner. The Ancient Order of Hibernians, which organized and ran the parade, refused to accept them. The Hibernians could not prevent gays and lesbians, Catholic and otherwise, from marching. Because of the Freedom of Assembly Clause of the Constitution, they could do nothing about it. What concerned the parade organizers was that they and the Church did not want to implicitly condone homosexuality by authorizing an openly gay entity to participate.

Negotiations got under way with representatives of the Hibernians in one room and a representative sample of gay activists in another. Bill Lynch and our director of European-American affairs, Debra Pucci, shuttled back and forth trying to put together an agreement. Finally, they got everybody in the same room, and an arrangement looked imminent. The negotiations were down to specifics: where they would march, what kind of banner, with whom. Things were getting closer and closer. Imagine: an agreement between such divergent parties on so important and visible a stage. This would be unprecedented!

Then the Hibernians received a call from John Cardinal O'Connor, the Roman Catholic archbishop of New York and head of the New York archdiocese. One of their leaders left the room to take the call. When he came back, it was all over. No deal.

Nothing was ever stated in the open, but it was Lynch's impression that the word was out: the archdiocese would be "displeased" if the parade officially included gays. Within a couple of minutes, the negotiations were disbanded.

I suppose I could have stayed away, either in boycott or out of an unwillingness to offend some of my constituents. But I refused to stand idly by; history tells us that one should not be silent in the face of persecution. In a display of amity, Division 7 of the Ancient Order of Hibernians, the midtown Manhattan chapter, invited the Irish Lesbian and Gay Organization (ILGO) to participate with them. ILGO is usually a pretty loud bunch, and I agreed to join their group of around two hundred. I began my march on Fifth Avenue, a block from St. Patrick's Cathedral. It was not a pleasant journey.

Fifth Avenue at St. Patrick's is the epicenter of the parade, and every year it is crowded to overflowing with the faithful and the curious, and sometimes the drunk and the belligerent. Historically, people pour in from Long Island, New Jersey, Connecticut, and all five boroughs to participate and partake. Nor do I make the assumption that everyone was Irish. I saw signs reading GAY SEX, NO WAY and ONE-TERM DINKINS. The booing started as soon as I arrived, and the crowd got ugly. As I began to walk I heard people call out, "You're a disgrace!" "This isn't your parade!" "Nigger!"

When we reached the cathedral, Cardinal O'Connor did not come down to greet us as he had done with other mayors in the past, so I climbed its steps and greeted him. He was not smiling. We exchanged a perfunctory embrace, said a few words, and I returned to the march. The booing continued for the forty blocks I walked. I responded to it by vigorously waving a shillelagh.

When we crossed Central Park South, we were doused with beer. The *New York Times* described it as an "arc of liquid" raining down on us. I saw it in slightly less poetic terms. My police escort quickly opened umbrellas to protect me. Then it got worse. Full cans of beer flew over my head. Not empties, full cans. If they had hit someone, they could have caused real injury. The vitriol was unceasing. I imagined it was like marching in Birmingham, Alabama, during the civil rights movement. I had known there would be deep emotions about gays marching and me marching with them, but I did not anticipate this. Whether or not one agrees with gays and lesbians, they are God's children and should be treated as such. What kind of a coward would throw a full beer can into a crowd?

Two men, five blocks from one another, were arrested and charged. Cardinal O'Connor's response was telling. He said, "I asked people that there be no violence, either oral, physical, or even mental. That's not what we're about. We don't return disrespect with disrespect." Yet he was not the one being disrespected.

His response to the gay marchers? "I don't determine who will march."

Some years later, Deputy Mayor Barry Sullivan tried to reach out and improve the relationship between our administration and the archdiocese—to very little avail. He was told, "If he just hadn't marched past the cathedral!"

I don't know this to be true, but the assumption I make is that the archdiocese let the folks in Rome know that they'd be just as happy if the pontiff didn't reschedule. And newspapers make their choices; although

I had been received like a head of state by the mayor of Rome, the head-lines back home read, "Pope Snubs Dinkins."

· · ·

One would have thought that our trip to South Africa would be roundly praised. The apartheid government was so clearly on the wrong side of the moral equation, and the history of the United States is so heav-ily invested in the pursuit of liberty, yet we faced significant criticism from the press and some high-ranking members of government. In a remarkably graceless moment, New York's senior senator, Alphonse D'Amato, told reporters, "Maybe if he wants to go over there on a long sabbatical and let someone else run the city, we'd be better off."

I found this clearly to be race-baiting—sending the first black mayor of New York back to Africa?! D'Amato was far too astute and calculating a politician for this to have been a casual slip of the lip—and I said so immediately. Rudy Giuliani added his opinion: "I would not find those comments offensive."

Bill Lynch did. He told the papers, "The senator is treating us like a bunch of jungle bunnies." This caused serious political difficulty for all of us. Bill ultimately apologized. "Senator," he told D'Amato, "I shouldn't have been such a smart-ass." D'Amato, on the other hand, refused to acknowledge the obvious. It was in this atmosphere that we left New York. I to this day have a hard time understanding the resistance to our making this trip.

As guests of the ANC, we arrived in South Africa with hope and expectation. The front page of the main black newspaper, the *Sowetan,* ran a picture of me with the headline, "Welcome Home, Comrade." We were not granted an appointment with the acting president, Gerrit N. Viljoen, who was in charge while President F. W. de Klerk was traveling that week, although I cannot say this was a surprise; we had enacted sanctions, I was in their country speaking forthrightly against apartheid, and we were guests of the ANC, which was trying to remove them from power. We met with South African business executives, visited former ANC leader Oliver Tambo in the hospital where he was under care, spoke with peace groups, and toured the townships.

One afternoon we were running late, as often happens. We were supposed to visit a small village, and someone said, "Maybe we'll skip it and catch up to schedule."

"No, no," I said, "they'll be waiting."

And they were. When we arrived, we found an array of cookies and sodas—it might have cost the equivalent of a month's worth of food there. For us. I encouraged the townsfolk to share in it. What seemed like the whole village was dancing and singing, "Keep the pressure on!" This was the slogan for the movement to continue the sanctions. "Keep the pressure on!" I was very glad we had come.

Several political parties were competing for control of the country, and it was important to me that, despite the fact that I was the ANC's guest, I not show favoritism to one at the expense of the others. I was there to facilitate and encourage change; South Africans themselves, I felt, should be the ones deciding which specific changes were best for the country. And the trip was a success; we made important contacts, and I came away with a far greater understanding of the economic, political, and social dynamics of South Africa than I'd had when I arrived.

One of the highlights of that trip was a conversation I had at the home of South African novelist and Nobel Prize winner Nadine Gordimer. "I'm going to ask you something hard, and I hope it's not going to upset you," Ms. Gordimer told me. Already I admired her candor. "I find, having been coming back and forth between the States now for years, that there's more separation now between black and white than there was some years ago, even among the small circle that I move in, of writers, journalists, TV people, and people in the arts. We mix much more here under apartheid on that kind of level than they do."

"That's quite an indictment," I said.

"It's a terrible thing to say, but this is my experience," she told me. Ms. Gordimer had significant bona fides. A white South African, she was noted for her anti-apartheid works and political activism on behalf of the ANC. She was a woman of true perception whose opinions I respected.

I was surprised to hear this. My impression of apartheid from afar did not include this level of contact between the races. And she was right: I was aware of the growing racial insularity in America. I tried to find an explanation. "You know what I think it may be," I said. "When I was a child, and that's a long time ago, but when I was a child, if you came into an area with strangers, you very deliberately . . . tried to integrate. And then there came a time still later in my experience when you came into a room, a conference or whatever, you would seek out the other African Americans and say: 'What's happenin'? We need a caucus.'

"And so today there may be greater awareness of the heritage each of us has, which I think is a good thing." When I was growing up, the image of Africa held by many in the black (at the time known as the Negro) community—in fact, in America as a whole—came from books and Hollywood with such works as *Tarzan of the Apes*. That had changed. I mentioned that my being elected mayor of New York was a sign of progress, "because, if nothing else, many of us who are African American have come to have some confidence in our own abilities."

The term "African American," I said, was gaining wider use in the United States as a sign of respect. We no longer defined ourselves simply by our color; we were increasingly conscious and proud of our heritage. "It's what we use and how we describe ourselves."

"But the fact is," she told me, "you're all Americans."

Yes, but black Americans were often made to feel less equal than others in our country. I honored the pride and concerns of Jews for Israel, the Irish for Ireland, and other ethnic groups for their native lands, but often the feelings were not reciprocated. "So I'm perplexed when folks seem not to understand my concern and desire for South Africa," I said. "I really cannot understand it."

"No, but you see, I think your desire and concern for South Africa surely go beyond that," she said. "I don't think you have to be an interested party, so to speak, to be against racism."

"I hasten to agree with you," I said. "This is not a black and white issue; it's human rights."

"But isn't it difficult to get people to see it like that?" Ms. Gordimer asked. She was asking about my vision of the future.

"Well," I said, not unaware that I was surrounded by journalists as I spoke, "we will get them to see it when we convince enough writers and editors and publishers and those who control the mass media, when they are persuaded, then that's what the story will be because that's how the story gets out."

The one group we did not meet with was the white ruling National Party. The South African government had an embassy in New York, and although they wanted to meet with us to discuss our economic policies, we refused to allow them into City Hall. Apartheid was in and of itself a disqualifier, and we refused to meet with them. That is, until just as we were leaving their country.

We got a call from the United States ambassador, William L. Swing. Was I still at the airport? Yes, I was. Well, he told me, Pieter Willem Botha would also be there. The former South African prime minister was arriving by plane from outside the country shortly and would like to meet with me. Was I amenable? It would be below the radar; there would be no official imprint of our conversation, just an informal meeting between two men. Ambassador Swing would appreciate it if I would accede.

I knew about Botha. He had been the official face of apartheid. As prime minister, he had defied international opinion and isolated his country rather than initiate any change in its racial policies. "South Africans will not allow themselves to be humiliated in order to prevent sanctions," he had said. "We do not desire and we do not seek it, but if we are forced to go it alone, so be it." Although he had been the South African government official to authorize contacts with Mandela, he refused to negotiate with the ANC and almost personally brought on the economic sanctions that were now doing so much damage. He had suffered a stroke two years earlier and been forced to retire. He had left grudgingly. Why did he want to see me?

I agreed to find out.

We met in a conference room at the Johannesburg airport. In addition to Botha and myself, there were two of his aides and Bill Lynch. Lynch described it as Sugar Ray Robinson meeting Jake LaMotta. Or Joe Louis versus Primo Carnera.

Botha was a very large man. He towered over me, and his bulk was substantial. The first thing he did was offer me a drink. One of his assistants brought in a tray of what appeared to be bourbon, or its South African equivalent. I accepted. Botha poured a highball glass full for himself and downed it. Then we got down to business.

"Mandela is playing the sanction card," he told me quite forcefully.

"That's the only card he has to play," I answered.

"It is harming our country. You must lift the sanctions!"

One sees news reports of formal negotiations around large tables staffed with aides and seconds. This was not such a negotiation. Far from it. "If you get the ANC or Mr. Mandela to agree to lift sanctions," I told him, "we will lift sanctions."

"He is harming our country," he repeated.

"I understand your point, Mr. Prime Minister. I will tell you again: if you convince Nelson Mandela to lift sanctions, we will be glad to oblige. Failing that, we intend to maintain our position—for the good of South Africa."

"Mr. Mayor," he bellowed, "I am a South African!"

The meeting was short. Neither of us budged. Finally, Mr. Botha left the room to return to Johannesburg and I boarded the plane for America.

New York's sanctions were particularly effective. We were among several cities in the United States to make such a municipal decision, and it is one of which I am extremely proud. "New York City's sanctions are meaningful because there are major corporations that find them inconvenient," a State Department official said. "The ANC would be giving a signal" if it encouraged us to lift them. William Moses, an analyst with the Investor Responsibility Research Center in Washington, DC, said that our actions would have an effect on the thinking of cities like Los

Angeles, Boston, and Chicago, plus states like Massachusetts and California, which had imposed sanctions of their own.

And yet, our position was not without controversy; there was always pressure. Several people whose opinions I respected—from the unions, from business, from government—told me, "Dave, I know you think you're doing the right thing, but by denying the country the ability to do business, you're really hurting the very people you want to help." I remained steadfast.

Several months later, in May 1992, Bill Lynch received a call from David Rockefeller, at the time the chairman of the International Advisory Board of Chase Bank. Rockefeller and I always had a very respectful relationship. He was a Republican and had been instrumental in my administration, landing Deputy Mayor Barry Sullivan at a time of heightened economic anxiety. This was important. The city was in difficult fiscal times, and here we got a Rockefeller Republican coming on as deputy mayor for finance and economic development. That gave us a boost and showed those in the business community, who had their suspicions about a liberal Democrat from Harlem, that we were serious about our approach to business and not to be taken lightly. Chase had done significant business with South Africa prior to our sanctions and clearly wanted to resume those profitable ventures. Rockefeller met with Bill Lynch in the basement of City Hall and told Bill that we needed to lift the sanctions. He said quite directly, "Mandela wants the sanctions lifted."

David Rockefeller was a powerful and respected man, and although I had not heard such a change in directive from Mr. Mandela, I took David's words very seriously. The next day Bill Lynch was on a plane to South Africa, along with Percy Sutton, corporation counsel Peter Sherwood, and finance commissioner Carol O'Cleireacain to get the facts. The decision to make this trip was tactical. If the delegation could meet with Mandela himself and return with a signed document in hand, there would be no confusion regarding his intentions and no further discussion of the matter.

In Johannesburg they met with ANC international representative

Thabo Mbeki and deputy president Walter Sisulu, who had been in jail with Mandela. In two days the second round of talks was scheduled to begin among South Africa's nineteen political parties—the Convention on a Democratic South Africa—which would ultimately lead to the establishment of an interim government, followed by national elections that would change the direction of the country entirely. Lynch and our delegation received an audience with Mr. Mandela at ANC headquarters. He told them directly, "Do not lift sanctions!" New York's economic heft was a heavy bargaining chip for the ANC. Not content with a verbal directive, which might be questioned or denied, Bill asked for and received a handwritten, signed letter from Mandela saying this directly: do not lift sanctions.

We remained resolute.

Mr. Mandela visited New York again in August 1992, during the Democratic National Convention. I was proud to bring a delegation of the country's mayors to Gracie Mansion to meet him. Although it must have been ninety degrees and muggy in ways that only New York gets in August, Mandela stood outdoors on the back porch and delivered an hour-long speech about apartheid and freedom and the economics of sanctions. I thought a couple of the mayors were going to faint. Mandela was, once again, relentless in pursuit of his goal!

I was also pleased that week to introduce Mandela to Bill Clinton and Al Gore, who were being nominated to head the Democratic ticket. The two presumptive nominees recognized that they were in the presence of greatness, and Mr. Mandela was glad to meet the responsive men who he felt would soon be the leaders of the free world. All were suitably gracious, and Mandela was invited to attend the convention. What an impression he would have made! But Mandela respectfully declined to attend. At first I thought, *Hey, you're supposed to be with us. What do you mean you don't want to go to our party?!* In my admiration, I somehow forgot that he was a statesman. Mandela was my friend and hero, but he was also a leader who might have to work with the other side and therefore could not demonstrate partisanship. Again I appreciated his political skills.

I developed a comfortable relationship with Nelson Mandela. He stayed at Gracie Mansion once again and spent some time sitting at an old-fashioned writing desk signing autographs for my children and grandchildren. I am a great believer that people reveal themselves in the way they respond to children, and I am pleased to say that Mr. Mandela showed himself to be the best of men in that regard.

.   .   .

In 1993, shortly after I left office, I was asked by the ANC to travel to South Africa to serve as one of many official observers of that country's first free elections. I was, of course, honored by the selection, and I agreed instantly. Having just completed a grueling campaign and endured a difficult loss, I was ready to be uplifted. The old regime had crumbled, and it appeared that Mandela, having endured all those years in prison and a lifetime of abuse, might finally ascend to the South African presidency. Bill Lynch had preceded me and gone on the stump with him, working to get the ANC elected in Pretoria, Durban, and the country's rural areas and mountains. He had witnessed Mandela travel to the white Afrikaners' farmland—these people were supposed to hate him!—and seen him turn their resistance into belief. If Bill had anything to do with it, I felt Mandela's election was secure.

We visited Bishop Desmond Tutu's residence, which was modest, and Oliver Tambo's, which was magnificent. We went to Bishop Tutu's church and heard him preach. The building was substantial; the crowd was sizable, a couple of hundred at least, and jubilant. Bishop Tutu, it turned out, was a hell of a preacher!

We stayed at the home of Walter Sisulu and visited with Mr. Mandela at his house in Soweto. On election day a group of us traveled to a polling station and found it rather empty. With time on my hands, I perused the ballot and found it to be quite different from what I was used to in America. First, the design was complicated, not a simple list of candidates' names and parties. It made Florida's butterfly ballot look like a study in simplicity. Then there was a photograph of each candidate printed directly on each ballot! For a moment I was taken aback, but then it occurred to me that this was to assist those voters who were not able to read. Still, it was quite a shock the first time I saw it. We waited for voters to arrive in great numbers.

Nothing was going on, at least not at that polling place, so three or four of us climbed into the car and drove to another, looking for action. A few miles down the road we found some.

As we arrived we witnessed a phalanx of vehicles and television cameras and lights and people standing around with tape recorders and pencils in their hands. What were they so excited about? First in line to vote was Bishop Tutu. He cast his ballot in the box, then jumped in the air and let out a joyful noise.

"Wheee!"

This, to me, was the sound of freedom.

.   .   .

It is testament to the grace and power of the man that, upon his election as president of South Africa, Mr. Mandela invited his captors, his *jailers!*—the men who had been physically responsible for the minute details of his incarceration, separate and apart from the people on high in the government—to attend his inauguration. Such forgiveness! I also attended and was standing near Gen. Colin Powell when South Africa's air force performed a flyover of the grandstand. The former chairman of the Joint Chiefs of Staff looked up at the planes streaking by and said, "They're all his!"

South Africa's future was hopeful but not secured. So many wrongs would not miraculously be cured the day Mandela took office. So many expectations would not be met even in one wonderfully symbolic term. No one was more aware of that than I. But there was enormous work to be done, and a country to heal. I had faith in the men who would try. Who but Mandela and Bishop Tutu could have conceived and created a

Truth and Reconciliation Commission? White or black, you could come before the commission and confess to dastardly "politically motivated" acts committed during the apartheid regime, and if your story was accepted, you would be granted amnesty and accepted back into a new and civil society. Can you imagine if someone had suggested such a commission in lieu of the Nuremburg trials after World War II? We'd have had World War III!

When Mandela retired after one term as president, at the age of eighty-one, he remained a presence for good. I continue to find him an inspiration.

13

Crown Heights

I was raised in a time when blacks and Jews were natural allies. The civil rights movement was populated by a large percentage of blacks and Jews who recognized parallel concerns and fought side by side for racial and social justice. I was a founding member of the Black-Jewish Coalition, an organization dedicated to fostering understanding between the communities and moving forward with progressive proposals. I am proud to have always been counted among the friends and allies of the State of Israel and have always spoken out for her security and survival. In 1975, along with Percy Sutton, who conceived the notion, I was a founder of BASIC—the Black Americans to Support Israel Committee. At the time, I, along with a number of other prominent African Americans, condemned the United Nations' "Zionism Equals Racism" resolution in a full-page advertisement in the *New York Times*. In 1985, after President Ronald Reagan made the appalling decision to pass over a concentration camp and honor the war dead by visiting a cemetery in Bitburg, Germany, where forty-nine members of the Nazi Waffen-SS were buried, I was one of three black Americans—the others were comedian

Dick Gregory and the chairman and editor-in-chief of the *Amsterdam News*, Bill Tatum—who traveled to Munich with members of the American Jewish Congress to visit another gravesite. Some of the Jewish members in our group had not set foot in Germany since 1939 or 1940, and for them the trip was extremely traumatic. We visited the graves of members of the White Rose, an organization of young Germans, mostly students, some of whom had been executed simply for handing out leaflets criticizing the Nazis. These were very brave young people, and I found myself extremely moved by their sacrifice.

In October 1985, Black Muslim minister Louis Farrakhan was scheduled to speak at a rally at Madison Square Garden. Minister Farrakhan, a particularly polarizing presence in New York due to his anti-Semitism, was to preach allegedly on political and economic self-determination for blacks (a worthy topic for discussion). But more to the point, Farrakhan had within the past year defined Judaism as a "dirty religion" and called Adolf Hitler a "great man." Some Jewish leaders called for the black community to repudiate him. I had spoken out against racism by whites against blacks, and I found it particularly abhorrent for a black man, who should have known better, to expound virulent racism as well, yet within our community there was significant discussion of how to deal with Minister Farrakhan. His bigotry was intolerable, but some found the question of the proper response to be complex. Bill Tatum wrote in the *Amsterdam News*, "In many ways, black leadership is being placed between a rock and a hard place in terms of their response to Farrakhan and his cleverly devised messages. On the one hand, he preaches love of blacks for themselves, self-help, economic independence and the survival of our communities. Interspersed with this message of survival there is also a message of hate—hate toward Jews." Black leaders, Bill wrote, were "finding it difficult to articulate their abhorrence of Farrakhan's hate while supporting his message of hope."

Abdul Wali Muhammad, managing editor of the Nation of Islam's publication *The Final Call*, said, "I would like to see how much Jewish money is put into advertisements in the *Amsterdam News*."

Having been slighted or ignored by people in power for most of their adult lives, some black leaders bristled. Congressman Charlie Rangel said, "It's easy to come down heavy on Farrakhan, but I just hope that this is not coming to the point where, if blacks in South Africa have to carry a passbook to go from place to place, that black Americans have to carry their last statement refuting Farrakhan. I would not, if someone said Jesus Christ is a phony, go around asking Jews to sign a statement to condemn him."

"There is a lot of concern among a lot of blacks that they don't want to be told what to do," Charlie said, "notwithstanding the fact that they probably would have done it anyway."

I was New York's city clerk at the time, running for Manhattan borough president, and along with a number of the city's civic, religious, and political leaders, I chose to stand outside the Garden and speak about Farrakhan. I felt it was important that New Yorkers hear what I had to say.

"Living in a free society, as we do," I told the small crowd that had gathered, "presents us with a clear obligation to face the wrongs in our community and to speak out against them. Recognizing this responsibility, and in light of Minister Farrakhan's visit to New York, I must say that I find his blatantly anti-Semitic remarks offensive, and I condemn them.

"One of our most precious American rights is free speech," I continued. "Minister Farrakhan, like all Americans, has the right to his opinions. But when those opinions express racial prejudice and bigotry, we cannot be silent, for in this climate, silence can often suggest assent.

"While I unquestionably condemn Minister Farrakhan's statements of bigotry and hatred, I believe it is incumbent on us all to look at the deeper reasons why many rational, good people have found his message so appealing. Minister Farrakhan preaches of power and hope; his is an uplifting message of new ideas for economic development and a better future. To a population that has long and disproportionately suffered from crime, unemployment, and all the woes that accompany poverty, this message can be a strong elixir. But we must be vigilant in remembering that no good can come of prejudice. A call for power and pride couched in terms of racial and religious bigotry can never offer true hope. That hope can only come from building coalitions among our diverse cultures, as we have worked to do in New York City. New York is unique: a fragile quilt of many cultures, religions, and peoples whose contributions enhance and enlighten us all. Two such distinct groups— the black community and the Jewish community—have been important catalysts in the formation of a broader coalition, a coalition that is working hard to improve the quality of life in our city. Realizing that an attack on any religion threatens all religions and an attack on any people threatens us all, we shall not be deterred from building our own coalition and working for common goals."

I was proud of the address, but I do not have a long list of people who applauded me for speaking that day. From time to time I hear some in the black community say, "You let the white man run you." That is not what happened. I simply felt that there are times when folks are supposed to stand up and say something, and that's what I did.

During Minister Farrakhan's oration to the crowd in the Garden he talked about "those silly Toms" who "run out and do their masters' bidding."

"I am saying, brothers and sisters," Farrakhan preached, "the reason why a David Dinkins—now listen, he's my brother and he's getting heavy, heavy to carry—the reason David Dinkins would do that is because they don't fear us. They fear white people. What I'm suggesting to black people is that leaders have to begin to fear the people that they say they represent.

"When the leader sells out to people, he should pay a price for that," he said. "Don't you think so? Do you think the leader should sell out and then live?" The crowd shouted "No!" Farrakhan responded, "We should make examples of the leaders!"

Tapes of that speech were sent to Mayor Koch, who said, "The life of David Dinkins was threatened by Minister Farrakhan, in my opinion."

I was at first unwilling to believe that my life might be in danger. I certainly didn't want to express whatever fears I might have in public; there was a widely recognized unwillingness in our community to demonize a black leader and give the press an opportunity to criticize us all, plus I didn't want to show fear to the Black Muslims who might want to harm me. But some nut in the fourth row might take Farrakhan's clarion call as marching orders, which, frankly, is what I think happened to Malcolm X. So when asked by the press whether I was afraid for my life, I said, "No comment."

Mayor Koch sent the tapes to NYPD commissioner Benjamin Ward, who immediately ordered police protection for me. I was persuaded by Ben, who was a good friend, to accept his offer of some security measures. I was running for borough president and was spending considerable time speaking in public during the race, which some thought left me vulnerable. I had a small detail travel with me for several months. Clearly, I survived.

.   .   .

The Crown Heights riots of 1991 and I are linked inextricably in New York City history—so much so that I have no doubt it will lead my obituary in some newspapers. At the time there were as many versions of events as there were witnesses, and some details are still in dispute to this day. The account of what happened presented here is based on my reflections on those times, as well as conversations with colleagues from inside and outside my administration.

Let me be clear about one thing: there is a pervasive myth that the police were instructed to restrain themselves from preventing the black population from running in the streets. Or that somehow we were counting on inclement weather to hold down the violence. People seem to think the cops were told, "Hey, let them vent." To be absolutely clear: there was no order given, there was no unstated code, there was no tacit understanding, there was nothing anytime or anywhere that authorized the police not to do their jobs, to stand down, to allow the black community to attack Jews and create mayhem. I expected and relied upon the NYPD to restore order in Crown Heights without fear or favor. After I determined that their strategy and resource allocation was failing, I ordered them to rethink and reset their tactics. I demanded quick and decisive action the first night in a meeting with the NYPD top brass at the Crown Heights precinct house, at Kings County Hospital and throughout the event and I continued to expect and demand the police to succeed in preventing more harm from coming to the city and its people. In many ways, the Police Department failed and the buck stopped with me, the mayor.

.   .   .

In the early twentieth century, Crown Heights was a posh residential neighborhood characterized by the stately brownstones built along its major thoroughfare, Eastern Parkway. By 1950, the neighborhood was 89 percent white, approximately half of whom, 75,000, were Jewish. In 1957 an influx of people of color from Jamaica, the West Indies, and the American South brought the black population to 25 percent, or approximately 25,000 people. At that time there were thirty-four large synagogues in the neighborhood, from Reform to Hasidic.

Crown Heights was home to an Orthodox branch of Hasidism, the Chabad-Lubavitch, which originated in Russia and was a presence in Brooklyn in the 1920s but really took root in 1940 when the Grand Rabbi (Rebbe) Yosef Yitzchak Schneersohn bought a mansion at 770 Eastern Parkway. His home became the spiritual and political center of the Lubavitcher community. A decade later, Rebbe Schneersohn's son-in-law, Menachem Mendel Schneerson, succeeded him as rebbe and moved into the mansion.

While the Lubavitcher roots in the community grew stronger in the 1960s and 1970s, many assimilated Jews moved away, part of the "white flight" fleeing the crime and poverty that afflicted so many urban neighborhoods throughout the country. Rebbe Schneerson counseled his followers to stay, and despite the fact that the overall Jewish population had decreased, the Lubavitchers remained a potent social, cultural, and political presence in Crown Heights. Over time, more people of color from the West Indies moved into the area, and by 1990, when I became mayor, the population was 65 percent African Caribbean, 15 percent African American, 10 percent Hispanic, and 8 percent white, with other ethnicities comprising the rest.

A number of issues contributed to the misunderstandings, tensions, and conflicts that arose between the Lubavitchers and blacks in Crown Heights even before the night of August 19, 1991, when the riots began. Put simply and painted in broad strokes, blacks felt that the Lubavitchers were receiving more than their fair share of police protection and city administrative attention. Lubavitchers felt that the black population was being protected and coddled by that same police and administration. The level of communication between the two communities was poor and resentments festered. I found this more than unfortunate.

The Hasidic lifestyle was highly circumscribed, and they felt that their enclave deserved to be treated appropriately. Because of religious restrictions, they didn't drive on Saturdays and arrived at their synagogues on foot; it was therefore important to each Lubavitcher to be within walking distance of his or her synagogue. They didn't want to cross Eastern Parkway, a large and busy six-lane boulevard that includes a sizable median, and believed that, as an accommodation, the surrounding streets should be shut down to traffic. However, the Crown Heights black community had no such cultural or religious restrictions; Saturday was the day those folks went out to do their shopping, and they needed to use their cars.

Overcrowding only compounded the tensions. The Lubavitchers were committed religious families, dedicated to educating their children, performing acts of charity, and joyfully spreading Jewish life, religion, and culture. The Hasidic culture encouraged large families, and many in the Jewish community sometimes had six, seven, eight or more children. Typically, two young families would start out living in a two-family house, and by the time one family had expanded such that they needed larger accommodations and moved out, the other would have grown sufficiently to take over the entire unit. But the Lubavitchers were unwilling to move to surrounding neighborhoods because they felt that doing so would dilute the community and put a strain on anyone faced with extended walks to attend their house of worship.

I should also point out that it was not unknown that Rebbe Schneerson could be counted on to deliver the Lubavitchers as a highly valuable voting bloc when the mayoral, gubernatorial, senatorial, and state legislative and judicial races were run, and that the Hasidic community could be counted on for its loyalty if it was treated well. Mayor Ed Koch even assigned the Grand Rebbe his own police car, which sat across the street from the Lubavitchers' central building at 770 Eastern Parkway twenty-four hours a day. This was unusual in New York, where other religious leaders did not routinely receive such around-the-clock police support, though the Lubavitchers believed that Cardinal John J. O'Connor was so protected and that the Grand Rebbe deserved the same. It was also aggravating to many who, having been victims of crime, felt that the law enforcement manpower ought to have been more equitably distributed in the community.

Let's just say that on the warm evening of Monday, August 19, 1991, Crown Heights was a very angry, very divided neighborhood.

Twice a week, the Grand Rebbe, then eighty-nine years old, was driven to a cemetery in Queens to visit his wife's and father-in-law's gravesite, accompanied by his motorcade and a police escort. On this night there were three cars. On its way home, the line of vehicles drove through an intersection and the light changed. Twenty-two-year-old Yosef Lifsh, with three other people in his station wagon at the end of the motorcade, ran the light. Lifsh apparently thought he had the right of way because of the police escort, similar to driving in a funeral procession when the string of cars travels as one to and from the gravesite. At 8:20 PM, Lifsh ran the light. He collided with another vehicle and lost control of his car, which jumped the curb and hit two little children—seven-year-old Gavin Cato, the son of Guyanese immigrants, and Angela Cato, his seven-year-old cousin—who were playing on the sidewalk. Both the New York City Emergency Medical Services and the Jewish community's private Hatzolah ambulances were called immediately. A huge crowd gathered quickly, and while at least one of the people in the car was reportedly helped away by an unknown African American, the crowd set upon Yosef Lifsh. The Hatzolah ambulance arrived first, and Lifsh was put in it, possibly for his protection. The two children were still on the ground, pinned beneath the station wagon. Gavin died at the hospital, and Angela was severely injured.

At that point the crowd simply erupted. Moments later, the city ambulance came and took away the Cato children. The anger over the accident and the perception of preferential treatment for the culpable driver when he was put into a Jewish ambulance while a dying child was pinned under a car on the sidewalk, combined to spark a riot. Black men and women ran through the streets looking for vengeance. Rumors ran rampant, including one that said the Jewish ambulance had come and taken away the Jew and left the blacks to die. There were anti-Semitic outbursts as more and more people took to the streets.

Three hours later, approximately twenty young black men shouting "Get the Jew! Kill the Jew!" surrounded a twenty-nine-year-old Australian rabbinical student named Yankel Rosenbaum and stabbed and beat him. Rosenbaum was visiting New York to research his dissertation. He was unaware of the accident. Before being taken to the hospital, Rosenbaum identified sixteen-year-old Lemrick Nelson Jr. as the one who stabbed him.

I received word that there had been an incident, that there was a riot going on, and that Yankel Rosenbaum was at Kings County Hospital. I went to visit him immediately. He was a man who had been set upon by a mob, and I felt it incumbent on me as mayor, for personal as well as obvious political reasons, to express my concern for his well-being. As I stood at Yankel Rosenbaum's bedside, I could see that he was in pain. His eyes seem to cry out the question: why me? I reassured him, took his hand in mine, and we spoke about his studies. Police Commissioner Lee Brown stood at the other side of his bed, and the deputy mayor for public safety, Judge Milton Mollen, stood at the foot. A nurse entered the room, and Judge Mollen asked, "How's he going to be?" She told him, "He has wounds, but we're going to take care of him. He'll be all right." His doctors said that although his wounds were serious, they expected him to survive. I was relieved. I have visited the hospital bedside of other crime victims, police officers injured in the line of duty, friends, and family; it is never easy or pleasant.

That night the young man died. The emergency room doctors at Kings County Hospital had failed to detect a chest wound on his left side, did not document his vital signs, and did not order a chest X-ray in a timely manner. Although the doctors tried to save him, Yankel Rosenbaum bled out internally. He should have survived.

After leaving the hospital, I continued inquiring into what had happened in Crown Heights and what was being done about it. Rioting was taking place in the streets of Brooklyn. This had to be stopped. There was no discussion of specific tactics, any more than a president would discuss infantry squad troop movements with his generals. I demanded and expected that the situation would be resolved. The New York Police Department was the best in the world at controlling riot situations, and I tasked them with creating order. There was no reason to believe they could not handle this.

Hurricane Bob made its way up the Eastern Seaboard the same week and passed by Brooklyn the morning of August 19. The weather had been stormy all day, and the streets were still wet. The summer youth employment program prematurely ended a week early because of lack of funds, and Crown Heights community organizer and head of the Crown Heights Youth Collective Richard Green found himself with many young people back out on the street. Summer jobs were crucial in keeping young people out of trouble. Now there were no more summer jobs.

Sometime after midnight word reached the Seventy-First Precinct that Yankel Rosenbaum had died. Loesch told Green, "Rich, we're having a lot of problems on Eastern Parkway. Do you mind going out there and seeing if you can cool them down? There are a lot of young people. I'll have one of my officers take you out there." Green agreed.

The precinct was at New York Avenue and Empire Boulevard. Green and Brooklyn assemblyman Clarence Norman were driven to Eastern Parkway between Kingston and Albany Avenues, about four blocks away. By the time they arrived, the Hasidic youth had learned of Yankel Rosenbaum's death and were congregating there. A large and angry crowd of black youth had come down as far as Eastern Parkway and Albany Avenue. Only a city block separated them, and the situation was tense.

The police were not prepared for a violent confrontation: they were not outfitted with riot gear, and they did not even have their sticks, as many had been on duty at Wingate Field at a Bobby "Blue" Bland and B.B. King show in the Martin Luther King Jr. concert series run by my friend, then-state senator Marty Markowitz. This had begun as a summer night without a hint of trouble, they were not properly armored for the occasion, and the streets were becoming very crowded, very rough.

Assistant Police Chief Thomas Gallagher was the senior police commander on the scene. Gallagher deployed his cops and a pair of squad cars along Albany Avenue, creating a makeshift demilitarized zone between the black youths and the young Hasidim. The cars were equipped with public address systems that were used in attempts to calm both sides. Gallagher gave Richard Green the bullhorn and said, "You talk to the crowd. Just let them know what's going on, that they're gonna investigate the killings and everything's gonna be on track and we just gotta get off the street tonight, and tomorrow morning everything will be back on track."

Green first tried to engage the Hasidim. They were extremely agitated, having just learned of Yankel Rosenbaum's death. Green asked to hear their feelings, asked them to define their problems. A lot of shouting ensued. Green told them, "Let's get this thing under some kind of control. You head on home. We're gonna go up there and do the same thing to the black youths, try to get them off the street, and let's see if we can sort this whole thing out tomorrow morning." He was not greeted with enthusiasm.

Having run the summer youth program and been a presence in the black community for many years, Green did a little better with the black youth. He spoke to many one on one and gave them the opportunity to air grievances in an atmosphere in which they felt they would be heard. This was not often so in that community. He told them the same thing he told the Hasidim: "You know what? Tomorrow morning bright and early, we're gonna have some answers for you." He was not greeted with enthusiasm there either.

However, the DMZ held. Chief Gallagher did the best he could to prevent the situation from worsening. He certainly was provoked. Although the police were without protective gear or batons, one minute the Hasidic youths would advance and they would have to push them back, and then the next minute the black youths would advance and they'd have to push them back. One officer was hit by an object thrown from the crowd and knocked out cold. He lay on the ground, but the crowds were so close and dense that he could not be moved. The cops moved to scatter everyone, but Chief Gallagher kept them in check, thus preventing the action from spilling onto other streets. Over the course of four days, 152 courageous police officers were injured, trying to bring order to Crown Heights.

They held the line. The police presence remained in place until around 2:30 in the morning. Chief Gallagher and his force were able to dissipate the crowd, after which he began to pull his cops back. Meanwhile, a squad car had been set ablaze by a crowd of rioters on Troy Avenue, a block over.

On the morning of August 20, Al Sharpton introduced the Cato family on the steps of City Hall, where they conducted a press conference. Sharpton, having come into the city from his home in New Jersey, was a controversial and highly visible leader in New York. It was no surprise to learn that he had received a phone call from Carmel Cato, father of Gavin, asking him for representation. Of course Sharpton accepted. I sent word that when the press conference had concluded I wanted to meet the Cato family in City Hall and offer my sympathies. Reverend Sharpton swooped them away without complying.

We established the auditorium at Public School 167 as our center of operations. Our community efforts at understanding and reconciliation between the groups flowed from that building. We brought in representatives from the social service agencies, including Youth Commissioner Richard Murphy and Human Resources Administration Commissioner Barbara Sabol, the "people commissioners" who were responsible for dealing with large groups of individuals. School was out, so we set them up in individual classrooms. Police were on-site, and parents could come and find out where, when, or whether their children had been arrested. At the same time the police department did its work to enforce the law and bring order.

It was our belief that in times of difficulty it is best to gather both sides together so that each has the chance to hear the other, with the goal of understanding and reconciliation. With that in mind, we invited both the black and the Jewish community to meet at the school and air their grievances. The meeting did not go as we had hoped.

I remained at City Hall in the morning while my trusted deputy mayor Bill Lynch presided. A rumor spread overnight that Angela Cato had died. We had received no such indication, so Lynch got on his cell phone in the middle of the auditorium and called Kings County Hospital. He spoke to Dr. Kildare Clark, a black doctor in charge of the trauma unit, and said, "Give it to me directly. Is she okay?" He was told that she was stable. Her death, like a lot of what had fueled the rioters, was a false rumor.

Yet the rumor ruled and things got ugly very quickly. Several African Americans made what Lynch considered to be anti-Semitic statements against the Jews, accusing them of taking money out of the black community, stealing from them at the stores they owned, and charging exorbitant rents as landlords. It ran the gamut of the economic and social grievances that had been building for decades. They said that the circumstance of Gavin Cato's death was only one grievance among many in a lifetime of preferential treatment they felt the Jewish community had received.

When the Lubavitchers tried to speak, the atmosphere deteriorated even further. Their feeling was that crime was on the rise in Crown Heights, that the black population was being treated with too much leniency by the police, that they did not feel safe in their own neighborhood, and that the same black people who had rioted in the streets the night before and killed Yankel Rosenbaum were responsible for this ever-present danger. The blacks in attendance loudly took offense, and the meeting became a shouting match. The meeting was no longer about Gavin Cato being hit by a car or Yankel Rosenbaum getting stabbed in the street; this was about how the two communities living next to each other felt about one another. When Bill Lynch tried to moderate what was becoming an extremely hostile confrontation, the Lubavitchers accused him of not giving them the opportunity to speak. The morning session broke up with no peace and no reconciliation.

Herbert Block, assistant to the mayor and my liaison to the Jewish community, inquired of the Lubavitcher community whether there would be a funeral for Yankel Rosenbaum. If there was, I certainly wanted to participate and pay my respects for this innocent student whose hand I held in the hospital. We were told by several people in positions of authority that his body had been brought to a funeral home and would be transported to his native Australia later that day, that the hearse carrying his body would be merely passing in front of the Chabad Lubavitch headquarters on Eastern Parkway on the way to the airport, and that there would be no funeral or ceremony and my appearance would not be appropriate.

It turned out that the body was carried through the streets by a caravan of mourners, that there was a substantial and lengthy public ceremony, and that speeches were made and various public officials did attend. The *New York Times* reported that it "soon became a forum for Hasidic leaders to denounce Mayor Dinkins's handling of the situation and what many called an unprovoked attack on Jews incited by black 'agitators' from outside Crown Heights." Of course I would have participated had I been given the opportunity. The fact that I was excluded was further indication of the deep divide in the community. As a man and as the mayor of the City of New York I wanted to offer condolence. I found the refusal to accept my solidarity to be deeply troubling.

I needed to put an end to the violence immediately. There were those who counseled me not to negotiate with anyone who might be representing those who were rioting in the streets. I told them, "I will talk to anyone. I'm trying to restore peace." I met with the black leaders first because I feared we were heading into our second night of violence. Bill Lynch called Al Sharpton, who said, "I'm here with the [Cato] family."

And so, on the afternoon of August 20, Al Sharpton and I met in Brooklyn, and I told him, "I don't care what anybody says, we need to sit down and stop this violence." With Sharpton's assistance, Lynch had convened a meeting at the Restoration building, a Bedford-Stuyvesant community center, and I traveled there with him.

In the room were many of the older militants who were instrumental in the violent street actions. I was joined by Lynch, First Deputy Mayor Norman Steisel, Judge Mollen, and Commissioner Brown, among others. Perhaps five parents of people who had been arrested were present as well. A significant amount of yelling and screaming occurred, mostly over the fact that many blacks and few Jews were in jail. A rabble-rouser whom people called Mother Africa said, "Y'all locked up two hundred blacks, there's only two Jews there!" They wanted me to let everyone out of jail. I told them, "Give me the facts. I don't want to hear 'discrimination,' I want the facts!" They kept on screaming.

At one point I went to the men's room, and Sharpton followed me. "Let me tell you something, Al," I said. "They can scream and yell, but I'm not giving people a free pass out of jail, and I'm not going to let people tell me don't talk to you all. So you all be fair, I'll be fair. But I'm not letting some kid who committed any violence out of jail."

Sharpton told me, "Got it."

Later that afternoon, I visited PS 167. I wanted to hear more of what the people of Crown Heights had to say, and I wanted to tell them what their government was doing. I felt it was important that I try to convince the young people who were rioting in the streets that there were better ways of having their voices heard than burning police cars and causing civil unrest. All it would result in was violence, then arrest and pain for them, their families, and the city of New York. I felt it was important that the parents of Crown Heights hear this as well. Before I arrived, a group of demonstrators had marched on the Seventy-First Precinct station house.

Commissioner Brown looked at them and said, "Hey, these are a bunch of kids. These are kids!" My reaction was, "But they are kids who ran up and down Eastern Parkway carrying milk cartons filled with rocks, which they threw at the school and also at Lubavitcher headquarters, where a homemade Israeli flag was burned." Kids or not, we needed order.

I met with the street leadership, mostly young men in their teens and early twenties. They were extremely angry. There were obscenities and provocations, but mostly they said that they weren't getting their fair share, they felt they had no possibilities, no present and no future. They complained about the Jewish landlords who, they said, were "screwing" the community. They complained of petty instances of disrespect that they took to heart. Many were indignant, demanding to know why the driver Yosef Lifsh had not been arrested. I felt that at least by hearing them out we were moving in the right direction.

They complained about their treatment by police. "Your family can't come find you. . . . My homeboy got arrested, and they took him to Bushwick, or they took him to Coney Island, and they asked him who was the sixteenth president of the United States and he couldn't answer. . . . One girl got arrested, had a small fracture in her foot, and they took her to Long Island because she had a warrant out in Nassau, she just disappeared." My staff took notes, and we told them we would look into their grievances. I knew, however, the anger was just too deep.

Bill Lynch felt that transparency was good for government, so rather than hold these meetings entirely in private or restrict access, after some time and conversation had elapsed we allowed television camera crews to film them. We wanted to get our message to the city and felt that we could make use of the media for this purpose.

Wrong. Once reporters were allowed in, the kids played to the cameras. What had been a heated conversation devolved into an overheated confrontation. I encouraged them to talk *to* their neighbors instead of *at* them, but that message was not heard. What appeared on the evening news that night had very little to do with what had gone on inside the room for most of the session; sadly, the cameras made it look like the entire black community of Crown Heights was totally out of control.

Later, outside on the school's steps, I spoke through a bullhorn to a crowd of around five hundred people in the wet afternoon.

"Will you listen to me for just a minute, please," I asked.

"No!" the crowd responded.

"I care about you—I care about you desperately!" I said.

"Arrest the Jews!" they shouted back.

I have great faith in the law and told them that the matter of Mr. Lifsh would be presented to a grand jury, which would determine what the charges should be. This was not at all satisfying to some in attendance. They wanted an eye for an eye. "In the meantime," I told them, "it's very important to understand that we will achieve nothing with violence."

.   .   .

Though I was denied the opportunity to be present at the ceremony memorializing Yankel Rosenbaum, I was equally determined to pay my respects to the family of Gavin and Angela Cato on their loss. It was the right thing to do. The Cato family home was on President Street, a few blocks away, and we had planned to walk through Crown Heights and show the media and the people in the neighborhood that the streets were safe. Commissioner Brown met me in the principal's office and said he wanted me to wear a helmet for safety. I said, "There's no way in hell I'm going to wear a helmet to walk the streets of New York!"

Several months earlier, Safe Streets, Safe Cities, our program to add at least a thousand new cops and empower countless kids, had been instituted. Richard Green's Crown Heights Youth Collective had been funded to run a thirty-day training program designed to take young people off the streets and encourage them to assume leadership roles in their community. He directed another program called City Sports that ran track and field and basketball programs for hundreds of kids, not only in Brooklyn but all over the city, using facilities like the gym at Medgar Evers College. His organization ran programs for more than 1,500 young people. These programs were helpful to those who participated in them, and they had the added benefit of providing jobs to people in the community who became counselors, trainers, and mentors of these kids. Green had a good group of young people under his aura and influence and offered them hope, training, opportunity, and jobs. He called on these street leaders, who stood in sharp contrast to the violent ones who had run rampant the night before. These were the kids with whom he hit the streets that evening at PS 167.

I was surrounded by these kids of all different ages and sizes, all saying, "Yo, you wanna go to the Catos' house? We gonna walk you over there. If they're gonna throw anything, they're gonna have to hit us first."

The police believed there were guns in the crowd. They had a specific number of guns they believed were present. Lynch said, "He's not gonna walk around there. We're not going to put him in that kind of danger." A compromise was reached. I would be driven to the corner of Utica Avenue and then walk down the block to the home. We got in a car and drove against traffic down President Street.

Prior to my arrival, several of my staff had done some advance preparations. The Catos' apartment was small, so they decided we would meet next door in a two-story house at the home of a friend of theirs. A large group of angry, shouting demonstrators filled the block.

It was starting to get dark, and as far as the police and the community were concerned, when it got dark, "everything goes on the other side," as Richard Green puts it.

There is some disagreement, even within my circle, about whom the violence was directed toward. First, the car in which I was riding drove against traffic down President Street surrounded by plainclothes police running alongside, which may have looked to the people in the demonstration like a frontal assault. Richard Green rode with me to the house and was standing next to me after we got out of the car, and as he sees it, I was attempting to speak to the crowd and could not be heard. Bullhorn or no, my words were not carrying to the crowd in the street over their shouting. Green says that they moved forward en masse to get closer to me when the police, seeing an approaching crowd of irate people, pushed to keep them back and me safe. Another squad tried to move the young people who were standing on the other side of the street. In response to that, Green says, the people pushed back and started to throw things. Not at me, he insists, but at the cops. "They weren't trying to stone him, they were trying to hear," Green recalls.

Many people saw it differently, including my head of security, Deputy Inspector Jules Martin. As he remembers it, I stood on President Street amid the shouting, angry crowd. Commissioner Brown and I attempted to speak, and all of a sudden bottles began to fly through the air toward us. A bottle went whizzing past, landing between me and Judge Mollen. In the crush and tumult, Mollen was pushed out of the way from the oncoming bottle. According to Inspector Martin, there wasn't one projectile thrown accidentally to the right or left, they were all well aimed at me. He grabbed me with both arms and pushed me inside the house because, if I had simply stood there, I would not have been a hero, I would have gotten hurt, and his job was to keep me safe.

We climbed the stairs inside the family friend's home and met quietly with Gavin Cato's father and immediate family (his mother having not yet arrived from Guyana). I expressed my sincere condolences for this senseless tragedy. The children had been playing, they had done nothing wrong, and one of their young lives had been cut short. I assured them that I would do everything in my power to make sure that justice was served. When I was told that Gavin's mother was still in Guyana, I said I would make inquiries into getting her into the country immediately. Brooklyn congressman (now New York's senior senator) Chuck Schumer was helpful in this regard. One of the youth groups from Manhattan Valley picked her up from the airport the next day and brought her to Crown Heights.

My conversation with the Cato family ended amicably, and it was time to leave; I was scheduled to meet with Jewish community leaders later that evening. But there was still an extremely volatile situation downstairs, and the police were concerned for my safety. My security team looked for a back exit but found that a fence bordered the property. There was some discussion about breaking it down. I said, "No, I came in the front door, I'm going out the front door. I'm not some sneak thief. I'm not leaving over or through any fences." I walked down the stairs and stood outside with Carmel Cato and his family and attempted to hold a brief press conference—the media was swarming—to tell everyone that we had had a good talk, that they should go home, and that we would continue to see that justice was done.

The crowd surged. The police moved the people back in an effort to protect me; the young people did what young people do, which is to push back (at the cops, Richard Green maintains, not at me), and then they continued doing what they had been doing all day, which was throwing rocks and bottles at the police. The cops reacted, grabbing and swinging and pushing, and the demonstrators threw more stuff at them. As we were moving through the crowd and then racing toward the cars, members of our group were kicked and jostled by the crowd.

I was driven from the melee on President Street to the Lubavitcher headquarters on Eastern Parkway, where we met in a large room. I also told the group assembled there that I was determined to see that justice was done and that they would be given maximum police protection. They were understandably angry that one of their young men had been killed. They too were dissatisfied with the conduct of the police, who they felt were not being sufficiently vigilant or proactive in protecting their community from rioters. The Jewish people, as I knew well, had a long and terrible history as victims of oppression and injustice.

I received reports from the field that things weren't as bad as they seemed, that the streets were quieting down, that the situation was being handled properly. I took that as very good news.

The NYPD high command had met the morning of August 20 to plan strategy for that day. Commissioner Brown, patrol leaders, and the borough commanders of Brooklyn North and Brooklyn South were involved in meetings with the community. A large detail of cops was assigned to Crown Heights. Nevertheless, at some point Commissioner Brown's car was stolen. Then there was a call for a 10-13, Assist Police Officer. That is a very big deal because it indicates an officer is already hurt or in serious danger, and Ray Kelly, who was not in the chain of command in these proceedings and as yet had had no operational role, jumped in his car and responded. Kelly had previously been commanding officer of the Seventy-First Precinct but for some reason had not been asked by Brown to participate in the response. When he arrived, Kelly said to Commissioner Brown, "Do you want me to get involved in this?" Brown said yes.

It was already late in the day, and when Kelly visited the Seventy-First Precinct, he was not happy with the way things were organized. He thought the place was "somewhat in disarray." As far as he was concerned, rosters were insufficient and cops were not being properly deployed. He changed headquarters from the Seventy-First Precinct to the Sixty-Seventh.

That evening a large group of young black men congregated on President Street, and another group gathered on Utica Avenue. By now, the cops were prepared. They were outfitted in riot helmets and in possession of their batons. A large force had been mustered, and helicopters hovered overhead. As night fell, small skirmishes broke out in both areas. Richard Green was walking President Street, talking to the young people as he often did, in an attempt to help maintain order, when one of the youths looked him in the eye and said, "Mr. Green, I suggest you get out of here tonight."

"Why do you say that?"

The young man said, "It's gonna get hot out here. . . ."

Green returned to the precinct house and told the officer in charge, "These youths are really, really angry, and I think we've got to find a way to cool them out, 'cause it looks like they're gonna clash." The officer said to him, "Thank God we have Officer Rain coming in tonight." They were hoping that, along with their efforts, a rainstorm would discourage people from committing violence in the street. Tuesday night it did indeed start to rain.

The Department of Traffic loaned Green one of its yellow vans equipped with a bullhorn, and he commenced driving around the neighborhood, talking to the young men, telling them, "Go back to your stoops, go back to your buildings, stay off of this block." The van came in handy.

Commissioner of Youth Services the late Richard Murphy wore a thick beard and was also walking the neighborhood, talking to whomever he could reach in an attempt to do some good. He was engaging in true hands-on diplomacy. During this tour, Murphy walked into the middle of a crowd of African American teenagers, apparently thinking that, since as youth commissioner he was familiar with the scene, he had no reason to run and hide. Much to his surprise, they began to harass him. Driving by, Green and several others intervened, pulled Murphy into the van, and got him out of there. The young black men were preparing to beat him up; they thought he was a Hasid.

The rain came, but the city's temperament was no cooler. Kids, some not even in their teens, were throwing rocks and running away. Groups of young people set stores ablaze. Windows were broken, and people all over Crown Heights, but particularly in the Jewish community, were afraid for their lives. The police arrested many young people, but they did not go in there swinging. They arrested these kids but did not beat them. We received a report that eight cops had been hit by shotgun pellets fired from the rooftops. I went to Kings County Hospital again, this time to visit the officers who had been injured. More police were deployed, mostly on foot, but there did not appear to be a successful strategy in place, and their force of numbers did not effectively control the streets. Brooklyn rioted, and we did not have it under control. The situation became so stressful that Bill Lynch went temporarily blind.

We commandeered a private room in the hospital, and I told Commissioner Brown, "How dare you let it get this way! I want every officer that can be sent to Crown Heights to be there tomorrow. If you have to use horses, add the horses. Why don't sergeants have radios? I want it all! Patrol cars, uniforms. Everything that you need to maintain peace. We're not gonna have this any longer!" The commissioner did not argue; he said he would see to it.

Again, I made it clear: there was no excuse to let people vent and create mayhem, no invitation for cops to stand down, no permission given to allow blacks to attack Jews. Far from it. Instead, I demanded quick and decisive action to restore order and protect all New Yorkers.

Mario Selvaggi, who had succeeded David Scott as chief of patrol when Scott was promoted to chief of department, has acknowledged that the NYPD did not react quickly enough to stem the violence, and that it was only on Wednesday, August 21, after rocks and bottles were thrown at me and shotgun pellets injured eight police officers, that "we saw then and there that we had to adjust and change our tactics." That was the police plan. It was not mine. But I made the decision to change their plan.

"A lot of law-abiding citizens were reacting to some of the rumors," Selvaggi told the *Times*. He said the cops were aware of the African American community's emotions triggered by the traffic accident and the rumors that the driver had been treated before the Cato children. "We didn't want to overreact so that the original incident was forgotten and the police became the issue."

At 7:00 AM on Thursday, August 22, Commissioner Brown and First Deputy Commissioner Kelly met with the Brooklyn borough commanders. Explanations were demanded. "Why weren't there cops on the roof?" Kelly asked. Because it was dangerous, he was told. This was no reason. "Why weren't the streets closed off?" Because people had to get to work. None of this made any operational sense.

The *New York Post* ran a full-page, heart-wrenching photo of a young boy crying in a Crown Heights street beside a fallen man in a dark suit. A Hasid's large hat lay in the foreground. The headline read: "Blacks, Jews and Cops Battle in the Street. DAY OF HATE." None of this was acceptable.

I called Commissioner Brown and again demanded answers. There was no reason to believe the NYPD couldn't handle and contain this situation, no matter how out-of-hand it got. I told Brown several times during this affair, "Look, I'm not a police professional; it's your job. The NYPD is the best department in America. Do your job!" Clearly what had been attempted had failed. "Are you locking people up?" I asked.

"We're looking at the type of charges that can be brought."

"Well, what about freaking riot?! Why don't we start with that!" I exploded. "Whatever you are doing ain't working! Now get it together!"

The *New York Times* quoted a rabbi saying, "When we were children, pogroms were only words in history books. Unfortunately, we in this neighborhood have seen a pogrom with our own eyes." The *Times* quoted another Crown Heights resident calling me "the first mayor who made a pogrom against Jews in America."

I was shocked, outraged, and extremely hurt by these characterizations. A pogrom is an organized, official massacre of an ethnic group. I had not sponsored this riot, I had not condoned it. Indeed I had tried everything I knew how to do to prevent it and then stop it. And yet the venom toward me continued. A poster appeared on walls in Crown Heights saying that I had instructed the police not to take action, with a picture of me under the bold block letters WANTED FOR MURDER. Two weeks later, on the op-ed page of the *New York Times,* A. M. Rosenthal wrote a column headlined "Pogrom in Brooklyn." For almost two decades Ed Koch continued to describe it as a pogrom. They both should have known better. These were riots, terrible acts conducted by felons, but they were not state-sponsored terrorism, and the accusation that I was a Jew-hater, a bigot, and a murderer was especially outrageous, painful, and despicable. Nobody in the government directed the cops to let blacks attack Jews; nobody ever indicated a desire that that would be the case; nobody said, "Let the blacks vent." How could they believe, even for a second, that we would do such a thing? I was the guy who stood up to Farrakhan's threats, who stood over graves in Germany, who had traveled to Israel that same year in support of Jews under attack. And now this.

But my feelings could be left for another day. We needed to stop this madness immediately. Under Kelly's command, the NYPD devised a plan by which they were able to cordon off the streets with police vans at each end, isolating rioters and then arresting them. They added mobility, bringing in more vans and adding fifty mounted police to the area. On Thursday night when the rioters tried to continue their lawlessness, they were locked up in such numbers—there were more than one hundred arrests—that the police used the Armory as a processing center. With this plan in operation, the situation was finally brought under control. The rioting did not simply peter out; under aggressive policing, it ceased.

In the debriefing afterwards, Ray Kelly recommended some changes to training techniques and tactical planning to deal with such disorders. A year later, when I named him NYPD commissioner, he was in the odd position of making recommendations to himself, and in the NYPD's new *Disorder Control Book* he accepted them all.

Yosef Lifsh was not held legally responsible for his role in Gavin Cato's death. A grand jury failed to indict him despite the issue of running a light. Legal notes provided to reporters covering the grand jury proceedings explained that, "just losing control of a car by itself is not criminal negligence under the law. . . . The fact that death or injury resulted by itself is not criminal negligence under the law." The black community was incensed. Within days, Al Sharpton traveled on his own authority to Israel, where Lifsh had migrated, in an attempt to serve him with a summons for a planned wrongful-death civil suit.

Despite being identified by Yankel Rosenbaum as his attacker, Lemrick Nelson Jr. was acquitted of charges of murder as a hate crime. I continue to fail to understand that verdict. Several years later, Nelson finally admitted to the stabbing; he was convicted of violating Rosenbaum's civil rights and incarcerated. He served his full ten-year sentence. In 2005 New York City agreed to pay $1.25 million to settle a lawsuit brought by Yankel Rosenbaum's family charging negligence in his death.

Some in the Jewish community believed that I ought not to attend Gavin Cato's funeral. I challenged them, saying not only that my presence was necessary in order for the city to unite and recover from these difficult times, but that I would encourage them to join me at the service. To their credit, some accepted the invitation. Then they discovered that Al Sharpton was giving the eulogy. Of course they objected. I told them, "I've known Al since he was sixteen. He's not going to say anything irresponsible."

Sharpton and his followers had decided to march from the church in which the funeral was to be held to the cemetery, a distance of about a mile and a half. Violence had shaken the neighborhood all week, and now they were going to march through it carrying a body. The scene was tailor-made for an explosion.

I sat in the first row at the service, my mayoralty being judged by what might occur. Brooklyn street militant Sonny Carson and his followers were situated on one side of the church. Sharpton delivered an incendiary eulogy that served to inflame passions that one had hoped would cool. He said, "The world will tell us [Gavin Cato] was killed by accident. . . . It's an accident to allow an apartheid ambulance service in the middle of Crown Heights. . . . The issue is not anti-Semitism; the issue is apartheid."

As the congregation was gathering behind the hearse and preparing to march to the cemetery, I hugged Carmel Cato. As I moved to the car waiting to return me to City Hall, I spoke with the officer in charge concerning the day's security precautions and police deployment in yet another situation fraught with potential difficulty. "Mr. Mayor," he said, "we've got everything set." I looked at Sharpton and firmly stated, "I'm not worried about violence." I said, "Am I, Al."

And so ended a Crown Heights chapter almost as hard to revisit as it was to experience. Of course I wish it never happened. But I never did, nor will I start now, blame anyone else for what occurred on my watch. Most importantly, of greater moment than any discussion of police tactics or racial and religious politics, I want to honor the lives of Gavin Cato and Yankel Rosenbaum, two young people who died needlessly and far too soon. I mourn each. Their deaths were the true tragedy of Crown Heights.

14

Race Against Rudy

My run for reelection essentially began when Kiko Garcia got shot on July 3, 1992.

Jose "Kiko" Garcia was an immigrant from the Dominican Republic living in Washington Heights. Police officers in the street said they saw him in possession of a firearm and tried to arrest him. Attempting to surround and disarm Garcia, they cornered him in the lobby of an apartment building—"You don't want to chase them down the street, they usually run faster than you," then–Deputy Police Commissioner Ray Kelly said. "You can second-guess this, but this is done all the time." In a struggle, the police shot and killed the man. Members of the community who said they witnessed the incident professed that Garcia was unarmed and possibly unconscious when shot. Police said that they found a gun on the man, but that it showed no fingerprints. Kelly called the officer "aggressive, active, and good" and questioned the witnesses' credibility.

The NYPD had been the focus of complaints of aggressive behavior and other charges from various groups of citizens. I was in favor of establishing a civilian-run Civilian Complaint Review Board, which did not endear me to the cops, who historically have bridled when asked to be policed by anyone but themselves. Having maintained calm during the Rodney King riots, I visited Washington Heights that afternoon in an attempt to ward off the possibility of trouble. I met with and expressed sympathy to the family of Kiko Garcia, who had just lost a son, assured them there would be an investigation into the matter, and said the city would pay for Garcia's body to be flown to the Dominican Republic for burial, as had been the city's precedent for indigents. I spoke for fifteen minutes on Spanish-language radio in an effort to keep the peace.

A few hours later, a demonstration led by the local City Council member, Guillermo Linares, descended into violence. Rumors flew that the officer was a bad cop, that he had taken drugs and money from drug dealers. NYPD investigators had been aware of these prior allegations, and Ray Kelly challenged anyone who made them to step forward, but no one did. The crowd seethed. The *New York Times* reported that people turned over cars, set fire to at least six automobiles and an abandoned building, threw bottles from windows, and ran amok over a forty-square-block area. The newspaper reporter wrote that "bands of 50 to 100 people ran through the streets, kicking over garbage cans, lighting fires, and shouting 'Killer Cops' and 'Justice' in Spanish." One man died during the violence as he was being pursued by police for throwing bottles from a building rooftop. At least fifteen others were reported injured. The night was an urban horror story.

Later, Garcia's police file was leaked to the press, and it was revealed that he had a record of drug convictions. After a thorough investigation, the men who apprehended him, including the officer who shot him, were cleared of all charges, and a grand jury failed to indict them. Although a group massed to demonstrate when the grand jury's decision was announced, I advised them, "Frustration, disappointment, or anger will not be tolerated as excuses for engaging in destructive behavior. Those who would engage in violence should remember that they hurt themselves and their own community most of all."

Many cops were furious with me over my immediate expression of condolences to the Garcia family, feeling it displayed favoritism toward him and a bias against the police. I had no such bias, yet the perception festered. On September 10, 1992, a few months after the shooting, I addressed a roll call of police officers in Washington Heights at the Thirty-Fourth Precinct house in an attempt to change their minds. As I was commending them for standing "between good citizens and lawlessness," I was interrupted by police officer Thomas Barnett, the Patrolmen's Benevolent Association union representative, who said, "I believe you're an honest, sincere, caring man, but what you did that day still leaves a sour taste in our mouths. . . . You lived in this neighborhood. You know what it's like here."

"Of course," I said.

"This is a dangerous place, and what you did that day was bad," he told me.

"What is it that I did that day that was bad?"

"When you went and confronted that drug dealer's family, you left a sour taste in all the officers' mouths."

"What do you mean I confronted? You mean I comforted them."

"Yes."

"So did the cardinal." Cardinal John J. O'Connor had visited the neighborhood and expressed his condolences as well.

"He's wrong too, but you're here now."

"No, no, no, no, no."

"That's our feeling."

"I understand that's your feeling, but you're wrong."

Our exchange lasted ten minutes. I felt this was unheard of, a mayor directly challenged by a police officer. No mayor would have stood for it, and some I knew would have been irate that the authority of the office was disrespected. Nevertheless, I engaged the officer. "I'm older than I guess anybody in this room," I said, "and I've been around a long time. People die in riots, you know. Sometimes there are police officers who die in riots." If they really thought that to comfort a family was to take sides against the police, "that's bullshit," I told them.

"That's the way it looked to us," he said.

Now I was agitated. I was responsible for putting six thousand more cops in uniform, for raising their pay, for expanding the department the prior two years while almost every other city agency—including health and education—took large budget hits during the pervasive fiscal crisis. There were no cuts for cops. I said often and in public that after fiscal stability, public safety was our foremost concern. Where was the recognition by the union or the officers?

"Where is it that I am the enemy of the police officers? . . . [I am] the one who has stood up and produced more for this Police Department than anybody in recent years. Now, you may continue to feel the way you do until the day you die and the day I die, but, sir, you are wrong. You are dead wrong. And so I am going to continue to do what I think is right."

Several days later, the police themselves rioted.

Upset over a wage dispute and my support for the Civilian Complaint Review Board, ten thousand off-duty cops converged on Lower Manhattan. Six thousand demonstrated peacefully. The others went out of control. The *New York Times* reported that four thousand police officers "swarmed over barricades, blocked the entry to City Hall, and later marched onto the Brooklyn Bridge, where they tied up traffic for nearly an hour." They were stomping over cars and running wild. I was not in my office at the time, but my staff had a bird's-eye view of the riot, and Ray Kelly, whom I had just appointed acting NYPD commissioner after Lee Brown's abrupt resignation, could see it from his office at One Police Plaza.

Many were drunk, and many were outright racist in their behavior. The crowd of police officers, almost entirely white, all of them men and women who were assigned the responsibility of protecting and serving all of New York's people, carried signs reading, MAYOR, HAVE YOU HUGGED YOUR DEALER TODAY? and HEY DINKINS, WE'LL PAY FOR YOUR FUNERAL. Another sign read NO JUSTICE, NO POLICE. The most egregious read, DUMP THE WASHROOM ATTENDANT and DINKINS SUCKS, with, as *Newsday* reported, "a shaded-in drawing of a face with 1960s-looking afro hairstyle and large lips."

Two black Brooklyn City Council representatives were abused during the riot. Una Clarke, a petite woman, was forcibly stopped by a beer-drinking off-duty officer, in uniform but without a badge, while trying to cross Broadway. "I showed him my credentials," she told *Newsday,* "and he said, 'I don't care who the f——k you are, you are not going across the street.'" The officer said to his sidekick, "This nigger says she's a member of the City Council."

Another black Brooklyn City Council woman, Mary Pinkett, was frightened when her car, stuck on the Brooklyn Bridge because of the riot, was rocked and shaken by off-duty cops. A Channel 2 cameraman, John Haygood, had the word "nigger" shouted at him by demonstrators. One officer, who asked not to be identified, told *Newsday,* "Dinkins is just afraid we're going to go on a rampage shooting all of his black people. That shows how much respect he has for cops."

Chief of Patrol David Scott, a black man and the highest-ranking uniformed officer in the department, was booed when he urged the crowd to stop mobbing the steps of City Hall. The *Times* reported that some on-duty officers encouraged the protesters. The demonstration (really more a brawl or riot) lasted two and a half hours.

Newsday columnist Jimmy Breslin reported:

> The cops held up several of the most crude drawings of Dinkins, black, performing perverted sex acts. A sign said, "Dinkins, We Know Your True-Color: Yellow Bellied."
>
> And then, here was one of them calling across the top of his beer can held to his mouth, "How do you like the niggers beating you up in Crown Heights?"
>
> Now others began screaming, "Crown Heights! How was that?"
>
> "Now you got a nigger inside City Hall. How do you like that? A nigger mayor."

And they put it right out in the sun yesterday at City Hall. We have a police force that is openly racist.

This behavior has no place in New York's streets, homes, or anywhere else, let alone being perpetrated by our police. If some officers would use racial slurs and yell "Niggers!" in full view of cameras, the public, and their superior officers, then I feared how they would behave when they were out in the streets. They behaved like hooligans. It was dangerous for our city for such people to have a badge and a gun. Any responsible public official would condemn it. Rudy Giuliani, not yet a candidate for mayor but clearly waiting for his opportunity, chose to stand on a flatbed truck with the president of the Patrolmen's Benevolent Association, Phil Caruso, and egg on the demonstrators.

"The mayor doesn't know why the morale of the New York City Police Department is so low," he exhorted the crowd. "He blames it on me! He blames it on you! *Bullshit!*" The cops cheered. The *Times* reported that Giuliani "derided Mr. Dinkins's claim that he had been tough on crime and supportive of the police, repeatedly [saying 'bullshit!']." Giuliani listed my policies and after each one shouted, "Bullshit!" (Despite the large number of eyewitnesses, Rudy, for his part, insisted he only said the word twice.) Rudy Giuliani was out there all but inciting the police to riot. Gesturing with his fist, he shrieked into a microphone, "The reason the morale of the Police Department is so low is one reason and one reason alone: David Dinkins!"

After Giuliani started to catch hell in the press for his profanity and his actions, he tried to backtrack without actually apologizing. Several days later, he claimed I was "perpetrating a fraud" about his activity during the riot. "When he apologizes for that," Giuliani said, "when he has the wisdom and the sense to apologize for that, then other people can apologize to him for things." Giuliani, who apparently has some difficulty apologizing for anything, even had the gall to claim (through a spokesman) that he was trying to keep the protest from becoming even more raucous.

Would the cops have acted in this manner toward a white mayor? No way in hell. If they'd done it to Ed Koch, he would have had them all locked up. I called for the police to handle the situation and assigned Ray Kelly to investigate. This appears to have been a wrong decision. Somehow, according to the NYPD, the Internal Affairs cameras that were documenting this demonstration were in the wrong place—"Bad positioning," Kelly now says, though with ten thousand cops in the street, almost anywhere would have been a viable position. Only eighty-seven cops could be identified, and only forty-two of them faced departmental charges. It strains credulity. Nobody ever paid a price for their behavior during the demonstration. Outrageous, absolutely outrageous.

.   .   .

We thought that good government was good politics. Those of us in and around my administration were never adroit at cultivating credit for our civic accomplishments, and with our difficult and sometimes contentious relationship with the press, our failings were written large and often exploited by those who opposed us, but our successes seemed often to be buried, if not ignored altogether. We had a good record on which to run. In the face of soaring rates of homelessness and AIDS infection, the crack epidemic, and a deep recession caused by a Wall Street and real estate collapse, we had:

- Created Safe Streets, Safe City and shepherded it successfully through the legislature, expanding the NYPD by 6,000 cops, including 1,400 more to come in February 1994
- Implemented community policing and increased the number of officers walking the beat by over 500 percent
- Reduced the crime rate in all seven of the FBI crime index categories for two consecutive years after decades of increases
- Enhanced anticrime efforts for the elderly and improved services for crime victims

- Enacted the toughest local gun control laws in the nation
- Kept the city's credit rating strong and prevented it from being downgraded
- Cut overtime spending, kept the budget balanced, and delivered it on time for four consecutive years
- Achieved labor settlements below the rate of inflation
- Expanded the USTA National Tennis Center using no taxpayer money, while generating more economic benefit for the city of New York than the Yankees, Mets, Knicks, and Rangers combined
- Launched the revitalization of Times Square by negotiating and executing the original agreement that brought the Walt Disney Company to Forty-Second Street
- Invested $2 billion in housing, either the building of new structures or the rehabilitation of dilapidated ones, for homeless or low-, moderate-, and middle-income New Yorkers, beginning the revitalization of neighborhoods that had long been left for dead
- Decreased the homeless population significantly
- Built the Beacon schools—thirty-seven community centers with after-school programming, located in neighborhood public schools, which kept tens of thousands of kids off the street
- Closed the budget
- Opened the libraries
- Created Communi-care and Medicaid Managed Care and established the Primary Care Development Corporation to expand primary and preventive health care in underserved communities
- Created the city's first needle exchange program, which helped significantly reduce the spread of AIDS
- Established the city-state collaboration that led to Hudson River Park
- Preserved the historic colonial-era African Burial Ground in Lower Manhattan
- Purchased key upstate environmental properties and created a long-term plan to preserve New York City's watershed, maintaining

water quality and averting the future need to build water purifi-
cation plants, saving the city between $5 billion and $8 billion in
capital construction costs and $300 million in annual operating
costs

- Launched the largest municipal recycling program in the United
States
- Kept the city calm during times of riot elsewhere
- Created the Increase the Peace Volunteer Corps and made toler-
ance and respect among all groups a top administration priority

Bill Lynch had resigned from his deputy mayorship to run the campaign. We felt that our black-Latino-labor coalition would hold, that the
base would turn out, that New Yorkers would be open and receptive to
hearing about our good work keeping the ship afloat in perilous seas,
and that we would win.

I was running for a second time against Rudolph Giuliani. A confi-
dential 450-page "Vulnerability Study" commissioned by his campaign
laid out the candidate's problems and his putative solutions. For instance,
the document carried advice on how to "humanize the candidate." Recognizing "Giuliani's arrogance and self-righteousness," it advised him to
"fight a natural tendency to sound trident [*sic*] and shrill."

As to the issue of race, in a chapter entitled "Practicing the Politics of
Racial Polarization" the study said, "Simply put, Dinkins won't have to
work hard [at] painting Giuliani as a racist." No wonder. Pointing to the
incident when comedian Jackie Mason called me "a fancy schvartze with
a mustache" during the 1989 campaign, the study continued: "Giuliani
has trouble getting his story straight about the Mason flap." And then,
"The Giuliani campaign's race-baiting did not end with Jackie Mason
remarks. Less than a week after Mason leaves the campaign, the Giuliani
campaign purchases a racially polarizing ad in a Yiddish-language newspaper linking Dinkins to Jesse Jackson." In response to these obvious failings, the Vulnerability Study advised Giuliani to call me, through Bill
Lynch, "the real racial polarizer," playing the race card while seeming

shocked at accusations of his own culpability. The study was so brutal that, according to Giuliani biographer and *Village Voice* writer Wayne Barrett, the candidate ordered all copies collected and destroyed after the initial distribution. (Clearly one survived.) It was going to be that kind of a campaign.

We put together a policy advisory board in an effort to frame our accomplishments properly and inform the electorate. Ester Fuchs, a highly intelligent professor of political science at Barnard College, was brought in, as was her colleague Phillip Thompson and my friend and adviser Peter Johnson. Theirs would be a struggle as my opponent sought to emulate Richard Nixon's "Southern strategy" and use racial politics to pick off various constituencies within the Democratic Party in order to beat me. Primary among them were Jewish voters, a potent and concentrated bloc that turned out consistently and, because of Crown Heights, seemed particularly available.

Jewish voters had been my strong supporters in 1989, on merit, but now the Orthodox in particular were strongly against me, and no amount of factual reasoning seemed to have an effect. The belief that I had discouraged the police from protecting Jewish citizens from black rioters was pervasive in the Orthodox community, particularly in Brooklyn but all over the city as well. As hard as I tried, I could not make significant headway in combating this clear falsehood, and a lie told over and over can sometimes become accepted truth. Barbara Fife, well respected in the Jewish community, spoke on my behalf with several groups in Brooklyn and Queens and found the experience troubling. "You just couldn't get to the second sentence," she recalls. "They were so angry. You couldn't talk about the positive things we had done in their communities or the relationships the mayor had had. They couldn't get past Crown Heights. The yelling and anger was palpable."

While we were focused on the day-to-day of governing, we did not focus strongly enough on the Giuliani candidacy or respond to its attacks. Giuliani had clearly chosen to divide people along racial and religious lines in his effort to win the mayoralty. He used the extremely charged word "pogrom" in describing Crown Heights and my part in it, consistently and often. I found this shameful, a violation of honor, and extremely telling about the man himself, but unfortunately his efforts proved successful.

With race as its subtext, the Giuliani campaign emphasized Crown Heights and crime, with the "squeegee men" personifying the latter. That there were only seventy-five such men in the city didn't matter—it was the image that was paramount. The Giuliani campaign astutely realized that what mattered was not so much crime itself as the *perception* of crime, and they attempted to lay the blame for this lowering of the quality of life on me and my time in office. Having no jobs and nowhere to go, homeless people were by-products of the economic downturn, but they became a symbol of the degree to which New York had fallen. In fact, crime was down, homelessness was down, and safety had risen during my administration, but perception often takes time to catch up to reality and the image stuck. There was a First Amendment issue—could we simply sweep these people away?—but Ray Kelly's office and our attorneys found applicable law, and the police were in the process of getting the homeless off the street while the election took place. They were gone by inauguration day. In his book *Turnaround,* NYPD commissioner Bill Bratton said, "Ironically, Giuliani and I got credit for the initiative."

.   .   .

A report on the Crown Heights riots, commissioned by Gov. Mario Cuomo, was released in the middle of the campaign. Questions have been raised as to why such a report was commissioned at all and what the governor's interest was in responding to such a local issue. Some have suspected that the reason was political: a gubernatorial race was on the horizon. I was in a meeting that day with Mario when he said to me, "I watered it down. It would have been a lot worse if I had not." It's hard to see how that could have been. The Girgenti Report, named after Director of Criminal Justice Services Richard H. Girgenti, who compiled it, was harshly critical of Police Commissioner Lee Brown and, while not holding me personally culpable, lay responsibility at my feet. It happened on my watch, but I did my best to control it. I told Mario, "If you, me, and a bear are in a fight, Governor, help the bear."

My relationship with Governor Cuomo played a more significant role in this election than one might expect. Common wisdom has it that I lost my reelection because of Crown Heights. I believe we lost because of Staten Island and the issue of secession.

Though it has become slightly more diverse in the decades since, Staten Island's population in 1990 was 80 percent white and widely acknowledged as more politically conservative than the other four boroughs. It is connected to the rest of the city only by the Staten Island Ferry and the Verrazano-Narrows Bridge and is culturally distinct from the rest of New York. In 1993 Staten Island residents' widespread concern was that they were being forced to shoulder a disproportionate burden of the city's serious financial problems. They felt no kinship to the Bronx; no one was talking about Fort Apache, Staten Island. They did not want to pay for their commute to and from their jobs in Manhattan; they wanted passage on the Staten Island Ferry to be free. Frustrations were mounting, and they wanted out.

In simple terms, they felt they were paying more to New York City than they were getting from it. "If Sanitation costs X, and Police Y, and Fire Z, and you add them all up, is that amount of money less or greater than what we pay in taxes?" If the answer is in the negative, it would suggest that they would do better by themselves. (New York City feels much the same about its relationship with New York State, and legislative battles erupt constantly in attempts to balance fees and services.) From this disgruntlement a movement for secession developed.

The borough president of Staten Island, Guy Molinari, commissioned a study and found that, when one factored in the establishment of a governing infrastructure, the numbers did not in fact favor secession. The study found further that secession was not legally permissible. Staten Island was part of New York City; it participated in the city's debts as well as its assets and could not be sheared off. If I take a mortgage on my house—if you loan me $100,000 with my house as collateral—I can't then take off the roof and sell it to someone else; the whole house is mortgaged. Clearly, secession would not stand up to a legal challenge, and New York City would challenge any attempt on the part of any of its boroughs to duck out on its obligations.

New York City was created by actions of the State Legislature, and all changes to its fundamental makeup require legislative approval. A referendum was requested from that body, but I contended that it should not be permitted unless the city issued a home rule message supporting it, which the city would not supply. I certainly was not in favor—first, because of the aforementioned legal objections, and second, for frankly self-serving political reasons. Though a popular local referendum would guarantee an extraordinarily high and motivated voter turnout, of itself a good thing, because Staten Island was a Republican stronghold, those voters were highly unlikely to vote for me.

I was quite comfortable in the belief that the issue would never make the ballot. The State Senate would pass the referendum bill because the GOP controlled that body and the possibility of creating a new Republican city of several million people would be hard for them to resist. But the State Assembly was under Democratic control, and I was certain that Speaker Mel Miller would organize and easily defeat it. A challenge would be issued, the clear illegality of the request would be made manifest, and that would be that.

The bill passed. I did not know then and do not know now why. The times were not as highly partisan as they are now, but any party allegiance would have mitigated against this bill seeing the light of day. Why would Democratic Assembly representatives make the election of a Democratic mayor of New York more difficult and less assured? Perhaps each representative thought, *Why should I take the hit? The governor's only going to veto it*. I did not have an answer.

The question then became: will Governor Cuomo sign it?

I said, "No way." Keep in mind, Mario Cuomo is a great orator and a legal scholar. He was considered by some as a likely nominee for a seat on the Supreme Court of the United States. Why on earth would he sign a bill that made no sense legally, made no sense politically, made no sense any kind of damn way? Why would he sign this? "Let the people decide"? That's nonsense. There are some issues that are simply not up for public discussion. This was one of them; the legal issues were clear.

Mario signed it.

Why?

I am aware that he and I had only a cordial relationship during the time I was in office, and as I described it in our encounter over the Girgenti Report, it was sometimes less than cordial. On occasion I would call the governor on city business, and before responding he would have someone on his staff call Norman Steisel to find out what I wanted.

Many people have theories on the matter. I do not believe he let the bill pass because he liked Rudy Giuliani. Some feel that Mario was still nursing hard feelings over the decision of Harlem's black elected officials to back Koch over him during his candidacy for mayor in 1977. Others feel that he was more concerned with his own electoral outlook than with assuring the election of a Democratic New York City mayor, that he did not wish to alienate voters whose support he might need in the near future. He may well have been aware that his electoral chances were more perilous than widely believed. Only a few years earlier, he had had a plane sitting on the tarmac ready to take off if he decided to file the papers necessary for him to run for president, yet he was defeated in his bid for a fourth term by George Pataki in the gubernatorial election a year after my run.

As my mayoral race progressed it also became clear that we had some challenges regarding our base, the black electorate. We understood that people would not be as passionate about my second run as they were about my first. This was no longer a historic election; a black man had been elected mayor, that milestone had been reached, and the fervor originally felt in black neighborhoods had been replaced with a more complex set of dynamics. There may have been a sense that, *Well, he'll win again, I don't have to work as hard to get him there, I don't have to come out and vote.* The same misperception of crime that afflicted the broader New York population was at work in the black community as well. I had been elected, in some part, because people felt that as a black man I would have a greater effect on their lives than someone who was not so deeply knowledgeable about their trials and needs, and when crime did not appear to abate as quickly or effectively as desired, there may have been a disappointment beyond reality. One plays the expectation game—if expectations are high, even good results seem wanting; if expectations are low, even the most modest results appear tremendous. The expectations of my mayoralty in the black community were elevated almost to the mythical, and when, because of economics and because of the requirement that I be mayor of all New York, I did not fully deliver on these dreams, I was held accountable.

We faced a quandary. The African American community felt that I had not delivered, and the white, Jewish, and Hispanic communities believed that I was delivering too much to the black community; they discredited my accomplishments, while the African American community felt that I had not done enough to honor my commitments. The Latino community criticized me for not being sufficiently attentive to its needs. We often responded by appointing another Latino commissioner to our inner circle, signifying that we were including them in the planning and development of the city. It seemed the politically adept thing to do. On reflection, however, Lynch feels that we would have done better to increase services where the effects would have been felt by the rank and file, who, after all, were the ones who would come out to vote.

We were trying to run a coalition campaign while at the same time fortifying our base. It was important to me that we not focus entirely on the African American community. I was sensitive to the criticism that I cared only about being the Mayor of Black People; that way lay division, loss of amity, loss of the election. I was not altogether joined in this notion by the people around me. Al Sharpton recalls a night not long after the Girgenti Report came out, near the end of the campaign:

"Our thing was, we wanted to fight fire with fire. I remember a very infamous meeting we had at the Park Lane Hotel with Bill Lynch, Dennis Rivera, Ken Sunshine, Jesse Jackson, and I. We were arguing that we wanted to go after Cuomo, and we wanted to do all this, and Jesse and I were rah-rah-ing. We felt that Mario Cuomo had politically timed this and had made a deal with Giuliani—this was our feeling—and we wanted to go after him and rile up the base to come out. We was at the Park Lane 'cause Jesse was staying there, compliments of [SEIU Local] 1199, and we were in Jesse's suite. And I mean, it was one of those three-hour, knock-down-drag-out meetings. We were saying, 'We can't sit by and let them just hit us like this! We're taking too many shots, this is black and white, we gotta fight it like that!' Jesse was saying, 'We need to hit the housing projects, we need to put out fliers. Dennis, you need to buy ads!' Dennis was on the phone, he was planning this media blitz.

"But it was race-tense. I mean, I'm being honest. We were going to say, 'Since they want to make it a race fight, we gonna make it a race fight.' We had this great gutter plan. We probably would've had the biggest race war of the century in the city, we were that mad. 'Cause you gotta remember, we felt betrayed by Cuomo. It's bad when you fight your enemies; it's worse when you feel your friends have turned on you. So it was real personal to all of us. Dennis had the machinery to go, Jesse and I were going to hit the streets and the churches. I mean, we had everybody in the room to do it, but Lynch would always say we had to have his blessing, it was his call. And the only thing we wanted, probably, was to get the meeting over with before [Dinkins] got there. We would have been off to the races!

"So midway through the meeting the mayor arrived, and he sat and listened to us. And he stood up there that day, in the living room, and he says—I'll never forget—'I do not want a divisive campaign. I'd rather lose with dignity than to go to their level to win. I'm not going to do that,' and killed the whole plan.

"We couldn't believe he wasn't gonna let us do it. Jesse was beside himself. Dennis started talking Spanish to himself!

"He wouldn't do it. It was him. I ain't gonna argue with him. He said, 'I'm not gonna do that.' He calmed us down, but I don't think he ever convinced any of us."

But the topic of race did not go entirely undiscussed. President Bill Clinton came to town to help in my reelection effort and told a packed fund-raiser, "Too many of us are still too unwilling to vote for people who are different than we are. This is not as simple as overt racism," he explained. "It's not that simple. It's this deep-seated reluctance we have, against all our better judgment, to reach out across these lines."

On election day, I traveled the city with Jesse Jackson. At a street rally in Brownsville, Brooklyn, I told the crowd, "We've all waited for things in our lives from time to time. We waited for freedom and it came. We waited for the right to vote and it came. The right to vote is blood-soaked."

I reminded them that they had "voted over time for those who did not look like you," but urged that no one be criticized for "voting for someone who *does* look like you!"

I earned a bunch of "*Amen!*"s for that one.

The race was very tight on election eve. Polls were going either way, though it was true that the "Bradley Effect"—coined after Mayor Tom Bradley of Los Angeles lost in his 1982 bid for governor of California despite being ahead in the polls—did obtain: some white Democratic voters were unwilling to admit to pollsters that they had not voted for a black candidate and said that they had. We repaired to the Sheraton to await the results.

As Al Sharpton recalls, "Jesse and I came up, and Peter Johnson came in, and Bill Lynch took the mayor in the bathroom and went down the count and said, 'It looks like we're not gonna make it.' Jesse and I were in the bedroom, and he came out and he says, 'Well, we gotta go down to the ballroom' [to concede]. Then he went and talked to his wife, and [former NAACP president] Hazel Dukes was sitting in the living room, started crying like a member of the family.

"As we were waiting all to go downstairs, someone came by to congratulate him and Mark Green [who had won the race for public advocate]. I was pissed. I looked at Mark Green, and I said, 'How does all the whites on the ticket win and he loses?' And the mayor says, 'Al, congratulate him.' He made me shake Mark Green's hand. We was standing in his suite, at the Sheraton. We was pissed. The whole Democratic ticket won, but him. And his whole thing was, we gotta calm everybody down.

"When we got to the ballroom, people were furious, and he had that same calming thing. He did not want his legacy to be that he was bitter. And I don't know what he said to Joyce that night, but I never saw him chafe from that. It made us feel like we had to live up to his standard. If he'd had just one wrinkle on his forehead, we probably would have felt justified going nuts, but he wouldn't do it."

.   .   .

Of course I was upset that I lost my bid for reelection. There was so much work left to do, and I would not have the opportunity to bring my ideas to fruition. The class of new cops about to hit the streets would be instrumental in continuing the decrease in crime that we had worked so hard to create. There were people to house, businesses to encourage, Times Square to see rejuvenated, and the USTA National Tennis Center to see expanded. "We will help Rudy," I told the crowd. "Our city is in his hands. We must help him be as good a mayor as he can be.

"My friends, we have made history. Nothing can ever take that away from us." My life as mayor would be over shortly, I told them. "Mayors come and go, but the life of the city must endure. We must all reach out. Never forget that this city is about dignity. It is about decency."

I had won the 1989 election by approximately 2 percent of the vote. I lost in 1993 by the same margin. Approximately 10 percent fewer people voted in the second election. There are five registered Democrats for every one registered Republican in New York City. When asked why I lost, I used to say, "Why do you think?" I did not want to say it out loud, but it's time. Now I say, "Racism, plain and simple."

Staten Island turned out heavily for secession and Giuliani. Black turnout was way off, and we had no surge of voters in places where we expected and needed them. Lynch says, "We didn't go black enough." We had registered tens of thousands of new voters in Harlem, which had given us great hope, but our get-out-the-vote effort fell short, and few came to the polls. We lost a lot of black votes in Brooklyn. Surprisingly, from the first election to the second, the Jewish vote stayed about the same.

And so my incumbency was coming to an end. As I had told the *New York Times,* "What's important here in general is not to, quote, 'be politically right.' What's important is to do the right thing. And that does take some courage and conviction. I understand the whole business of form and substance and whatnot. You can get out the smoke and mirrors and do things and, hell, Ronald Reagan was damn good at it. But that did not make him right. And I'm not going to be a part of that kind of crap."

Postscript

The morning after the election we held a press conference at City Hall. Throughout election day we had received many rumors and complaints that white off-duty police officers were intimidating voters at the polls—asking things like "Do you have your driver's license on you?" "Have you ever been arrested?" "Are you a citizen?"—and driving potential voters away. We did not have documentation, but we were getting similar calls from around the city, and I believed them. As word got out, people were very angry. We held the press conference to air these complaints and put them on the record, knowing that ours was only anecdotal evidence, that true or not the charges would be denied, and that the election had been decided nonetheless. In this country we don't have coups and revolutions, we have elections. I said, "The people have spoken. . . ." But the next morning I looked at my bride and I said, "You know what, we've got less than sixty days to get out of Gracie Mansion, find a place to live, a means to pay the rent, and simultaneously transition an entire government in a responsible, professional way, lest they say, 'You let those people in and see what they did.'"

Bill Lynch, Norman Steisel, and all the other deputy mayors and commissioners had the same problems as I. They had to pay rent and tuition and all the continuing expenses of living in New York. But, to a person, they were magnificent.

And I was lucky. Percy Sutton called and said, "You want to do a radio show with WLIB?" (His company owned the station.) I said, "Hell yeah." I was on for two hours a week, live, and they paid me a lot of money. Then I heard from Vernon Jordan. "Ron Perelman's gonna call," he said. "He'll ask to see you. See him." I said, "Okay." Perelman was a very wealthy New Yorker, a mover and shaker with a wide variety of business interests.

"He'll make you an offer. Take it."

"All right."

Sure enough, Ron Perelman called, he came to Gracie Mansion, he brought his executive assistant Richard Halperin with him. We sat down and had coffee, and he offered me a position as a consultant with an office and a secretary and a seat on the board of directors of one of his boards, which I held for eight years.

Peter Johnson said, "You ought to teach at Columbia University." I said, "I can't teach at Columbia, I haven't practiced law since 1975." He said, "No, SIPA—the School of International Public Affairs. You'd be good at it. You'd speak and have guest lecturers." Peter negotiated with the president of the university and the dean of the college and kept saying things like, "He's a former mayor, he's gotta have an office. He's a former mayor, he's gotta have. . . ." I have been there since 1994 and am presently teaching a course called "Practical Problems—Urban Politics."

I had the good fortune of having a lot of friends. That's what got me elected in the first place: friends. I did not come from money. I did not make a point of amassing a fortune; I preferred to serve. I would never have been able to survive if it had not been for these same friends.

There is also family.

I have always liked kids. They are literally and figuratively our future, and I would often prefer to spend time with children in their guileless-ness than with some adults and their stealth. When I was in office, some-times it got me in trouble with the press, who are always looking for more of a mayor's time. One day we were in a big hurry, and my press secretary cut off a session with a pack of reporters by saying, "Sorry, he doesn't have any more time, we're late going to Brooklyn."

"One more question!"

"No, I'm sorry, we're late."

So we went rushing out, and there on the City Hall steps were some children, awed by the environment or just getting their first sense of the grandeur of government. I stopped to play with them.

The reporters got mad! How dare I play with kids when the fourth estate was not done with me? I guarantee you, I had more effect in those few minutes with the children—they will remember talking to the mayor—than the press did in the creation of that day's reportage.

.   .   .

My son, Davey, graduated from Case Western Reserve with a degree in communications and earned a fellowship to its graduate school for speech communication. As part of this fellowship, he won a position at the local NBC affiliate. Within a year, he returned to New York as the assistant to a producer at ABC Sports, a job that suited his interests perfectly. Davey worked at ABC for several years, and then briefly at Inner-City Communications as an assistant to Chairman Percy Sutton. When an ABC Sports colleague moved to CBS, Davey was offered a promotion and put on the fast track to a job as a network producer. At the age of twenty-eight, he was producing, a fine accomplishment considering the paucity of African American producers and directors at the network level, then and now. Davey tells me that while there are at present more African Americans on camera than ever before, people tend to be comfortable with the folks they know, and the number of minorities and women at the production, executive, and corporate levels of that business remains limited. Referrals are infrequent, and the avenues for opportunity remain quite narrow, he says; the ratio one sees on camera does not extend to the top decision-makers.

Davey has done well for himself. After working with promoter Bob Arum, contributing to Olympic and concert coverage, and producing college football and basketball with ESPN, he is now senior vice president and executive producer at Showtime and spending most of his working hours producing boxing telecasts for that cable network. I could not be more proud.

And we are playing tennis together! Davey did not have the access, opportunity, or inclination to play the sport when he was younger, but when he neared the age of forty, he picked it up as a means for the two of us to spend more time together and have a hobby in common. I thought this was a wonderful gesture, and I surely do enjoy playing with my son. I am told that my game is sound—big forehand, good strategist, move people around the court, very competitive, make line calls accurately and honestly. One day Davey finally beat me, and when we told his mother she said, "You let him win." I did not, but I was happier than he was at the result!

I also fully believe that people demonstrate their true character during athletic endeavor. For example, Davey and I were on one side of the court, playing against a friend who will remain anonymous and someone younger still. We were talking a lot of smack, as is customary on these occasions—nothing vulgar, nothing overtly insulting, simply an informed estimation of one another's athletic prowess and the relative likelihood of each other's success . . . with examples—and it came to pass that my adversary really drilled me at net. I did not think anything of it, these things happen in the heat of competition, but apparently this close-range assault did not sit well with my son. He waited for the next opportunity and then banged a heavy forehand off the man's hip. Got him good.

There is a tennis convention that demands, in times such as these— a ball hits the net cord and rolls to one's advantage; a shot gets away from a player and strikes another—that the perpetrator acknowledge his benign intentions by raising his hand or racquet in a gesture of amity and saying "Sorry." Davey said the word and made the gesture. When he turned toward the baseline, he saw me chuckling.

"Why are you laughing?!" he said.

Well, of course I knew he did it on purpose. "That's just the first one!"

I told him. "That's just to get even. Now I have to hit him one more time!"

Before I could avail myself of the opportunity, Davey got him again. This time I was near tears; I couldn't see I was laughing so hard and had to hide my face lest my opponent think I was laughing at him. (To be clear, I do not sanction or encourage retaliatory on-court violence or expressions of improper sportsmanship. But I was so amused that my loving son would feel the need to exact a pound of flesh on his father's behalf . . . and then another!) I kept repeating under my breath, "That's my Little Fella!"

The guy didn't go near me the rest of the day.

Donna married Jay Hoggard, a talented jazz vibraphonist and composer, and worked as a visiting nurse and in a prenatal program for a community health center while their children, Jamal and Kalila, were young. My son-in-law Jay has played with vibraphone masters Lionel Hampton, Milt Jackson, Tito Puente, and Bobby Hutcherson; toured with Kenny Burrell, Dr. Billy Taylor, and many others; guested with the Dizzy Gillespie Big Band; and is now an adjunct associate professor of music at Wesleyan University, where for fourteen years he has been director of the school's jazz orchestra.

My daughter earned a degree from the Columbia University School of Nursing and did postpartum work on an obstetrics floor. As their children grew Donna decided to go back to school and get her master's. I encouraged her to study at Wesleyan, where her husband had faculty privileges. "It's free," I reminded her.

"They don't have what I want, Daddy," she told me.

Donna earned her master's in social work from the University of Connecticut and is now a clinical social worker. This is her third academic degree; Joyce and I tell her she collects them. She is a good person, she truly cares about people, and I am very proud of her.

And unlike her brother, she has contributed to the grandchildren pool! Her son Jamal was barely more than a toddler when I became mayor, but we sat him in the big chair behind my desk, and I have pleasant memories of him careening around Gracie Mansion. Her daughter

Kalila, as an infant, bounced on Nelson Mandela's knee! Both of my children remind me that I am much more doting as a grandfather than I was as a father. I suppose that is not unheard of. If either of my grandkids dropped a quarter into a sidewalk grate, I would gladly give them another.

Jamal and Kalila are both computer-literate. Jamal graduated from the University of Massachusetts at Amherst with a degree in communications. Kalila, a disciplined and organized student, graduated from Columbia University with a double major in political science and anthropology. She is interested in international relations and in possibly working for a nongovernmental organization or the State Department. Like her mother, she is bright enough to do whatever she sets her mind to. She is Granddaddy's Cupcake.

My bride has tolerated me all these years and been at my side through thick and thin. We celebrated our sixtieth wedding anniversary on August 30, 2013. I say to Davey, "Your mother makes good children." He tells me, "Well, Dad, you're half right," but he never says which half! Davey refers to Donna as "the Golden Child." They love each other, and of course we are extremely proud of both of them. And thank God they love and truly care about their parents! I love children, and I love our children most of all.

·   ·   ·

When I was privileged to serve New York City as mayor, not infrequently the press would surround me and fire questions. I would give what I felt was an appropriate response, and they would say, "You mean, in other words. . . ." My response was, "No, not in other words; in the words I've just given you."

There will be no other words. These are the words.

·   ·   ·

Postscript

I leave you with this:

In 1889 there was a big flood in Johnstown, Pennsylvania. Now this really happened, you can look it up in encyclopedias. The dam above the town gave way, and 20 million tons of water came down and more than two thousand people lost their lives. There was a wooden railroad trestle that had been constructed by the Pennsylvania Railroad Company. Some people clung to it and thought they'd be saved, but debris piled up along the trestle, friction caused a fire, and they too perished. So this really was a tragedy of immense proportion, the Johnstown Flood.

A man survived this ordeal, lived to be a hundred and five. He was a good person, and when he went to heaven he found out there is a custom in heaven that when your turn comes you step forth and tell of a momentous event in your life. This man knew that he would be an instant celebrity in heaven; after all, he had survived the mighty Johnstown Flood.

Finally his turn came. He strode down the center aisle toward the lectern, confident in the knowledge that within a matter of seconds everyone in heaven would know who he was, for after all, he had survived the mighty Johnstown Flood, this tragedy of immense proportion. As the man passed an angel, the heavenly representative reached out and touched him on the shoulder. The angel said, "I think you should know that Noah is in the audience."

Acknowledgments

I want to tell *our* story and what *we* did, because it is WE. Where there was a screwup, I'll take the heat. But we got a lot of extraordinary work done, and I cannot emphasize enough the comfort I found in knowing so many people cared about me and the job we were trying to do. I had the good fortune to have had a mayor's office, and a borough president's office before that, both filled with bright, trustworthy, honest, hardworking people. They were not simply trying to feather their nest or improve their status—their dedication and devotion made a tremendous difference—and they have gone on to do even more good work.

First Deputy Mayor of Intergovernmental Affairs Bill Lynch Jr. is founder and CEO of the consulting firm Bill Lynch Associates. There is no better group of political strategists in New York. Period.

First Deputy Mayor Norman Steisel is president and CEO of EnEssCo Strategies.

Peter Johnson Jr., trusted senior adviser who served without pay during my mayoralty, is now a partner at the law firm Leahey & Johnson and an analyst at Fox News.

Speechwriter extraordinaire, Anita Kawatra, who worked with me for ten years, became my chief of staff and adviser at Columbia University and is now adviser to the chief executive officer and head of communications and investor relations at Prothena Biosciences.

Deputy Mayor for Planning and Development Barbara Fife retired recently after having been director of external affairs at Baruch College's School of Public Affairs.

Office of Management and Budget Deputy Director Barbara Turk is now senior fellow at Community Resource Exchange.

Carol Banks did not serve in my administration but is now my assistant and project coordinator at the Columbia University School of International and Public Affairs.

Deputy Mayor for Health and Human Services Cesar Perales is now the secretary of state of New York.

Dennis Rivera was president of Local 1199. In 1996 that organization merged with the Service Employees International Union. He is now senior adviser to the president of SEIU, the largest labor union in the United States, representing more than 2.2 million members.

Elie Tatum, a high school student volunteer during my administration, is today publisher and editor in chief of the *New York Amsterdam News*.

Ester Fuchs, a professor of political science at Barnard College and adviser to my second mayoral campaign, is now professor of public affairs and political science at the Columbia University School of International and Public Affairs.

Counsel to the Mayor George Daniels is now a judge in the US District Court, Southern District of New York.

Deputy Chief of Staff Greg Fawcett is now CEO of the political strategy/technology/development firm Politics-360.

Harold Ickes was a senior adviser to both my mayoral campaigns. He is now president of the Ickes & Enright Group, a government affairs firm headquartered in Washington, DC, and co-chair of the labor and government affairs departments of the law firm Meyer, Suozzi, English & Klein.

Director of Operations Harvey Robins retired recently as director of strategic planning and operations at the Edna McConnell Clark Foundation.

Corporation counsel O. Peter Sherwood was appointed to the New

York State Court of Claims in 2008 and upon assuming that office was given an additional assignment as an acting justice of the Supreme Court, New York County, Commercial Division.

Howard Rubenstein was then and remains founder and president of Rubenstein Associates, a New York–based public relations firm.

Jim Hanley was then and is now New York City commissioner of labor relations.

Director of State Legislative Affairs John Bozzella is today a senior executive at the New York–based private equity firm Cerberus Capital Management.

John Siegal, issues director, 1989 deputy campaign manager, chief speechwriter, and criminal justice counsel under Deputy Mayor Milton Mollen, is now a partner in the law firm Baker Hostetler.

Deputy Inspector Jules Martin, former commanding officer, Municipal Security Section, Intelligence Division, New York Police Department, who headed my security detail, is now vice president, global security and crisis management, at New York University.

My first chief of staff, Ken Sunshine, is now president of the multifaceted public relations agency Sunshine Sachs.

Laura Hart held several posts during my administration, including special assistant for external affairs on the New York City Commission on Human Rights, and director of media relations of the DNC Convention host committee. She is now a documentary filmmaker.

Mark Benoit was my director of scheduling in both the Manhattan borough president's office and at City Hall (1987–1991) and was special assistant to the campaign manager for the 1993 reelection effort. Since that time, he has been a political consultant on thirty-two campaigns, including managing Anthony Weiner's 2005 New York City mayoral campaign and New York State comptroller Tom DiNapoli's successful 2010 election effort.

Maxine Griffith, director of planning and development and economic development in the office of the Manhattan borough president and an appointed planning commissioner during my time as mayor, is now executive vice president for government and community affairs and special adviser, campus planning, at Columbia University.

Judge Milton Mollen, deputy mayor for public safety, principal labor negotiator, acting mayor for cable television, and chairman of the Mayor's Commission to Investigate Allegations of Police Corruption (the Mollen Commission), is presently a member of the Mayor's Advisory Committee on the Judiciary, which reports to Mayor Michael Bloomberg its recommendations for mayoral appointments to the criminal and family courts. He is of counsel to the law firm of Herrick, Feinstein LLP. Judge Mollen also continues to serve, by appointment of a federal judge, as investigations counsel to Local 282 of the Teamsters International (the union once controlled by John Gotti and the Gambino crime family). He has, since 2004, continued to serve as ethical practices counsel to the International Longshoremen's Association and as special counsel to the Roofers Trust Fund.

Nancy Wackstein, director of the Office on Homelessness and SRO Housing, is now executive director of United Neighborhood Houses of New York.

Nick Balamaci, deputy chief speechwriter, is now a communications executive in New York.

Patrick Gaspard, Special Assistant to the Deputy Mayor (Bill Lynch) for Intergovernmental Affairs, served as the White House political director under President Barack Obama and is now executive director of the Democratic National Committee.

Richard Green, who was so extremely helpful during the Crown Heights situation, is now chief executive of the Crown Heights Youth Collective, Inc.

Assistant Press Secretary Ruby Ryles is director of public relations for Kingsborough Community College, Brooklyn, part of the City University of New York (CUNY) system.

During the time of my borough presidency and mayoralty, Skip Hartman was president of HCK Recreation, Inc., volunteer president of the New York Junior Tennis League (NYJTL), and volunteer president of the Sports & Arts in Schools Foundation (SASF). Today he is chairman emeritus of NYJTL, CEO of SASF, and still president of HCK. He remains an avid tennis player, New York City indoor tennis entrepreneur, and civic leader in the development of inner-city youth programs.

Herbert Block, whom I met when he was a high school student and who served as my assistant at City Hall, particularly as a liaison to the Jewish community, is now assistant executive vice president of the American Jewish Joint Distribution Committee and a member of the US Commission for the Preservation of America's Heritage Abroad in the Obama administration.

New York Police Commissioner Ray Kelly is once again leading the NYPD. I have never once called him "Commissioner." We are both former Marines, and I am pleased to address him as "Colonel."

Carl Weisbrod, president of the Economic Development Corporation in my administration, is now a clinical professor of real estate at New York University and a partner at the boutique real estate advisory firm HR&A Advisors.

Arnie Segarra, the director of the mayoral advance team and my "body man," is retired.

Basil Paterson and I were partners in the law firm Paterson, Michael, Dinkins and Jones until I was elected borough president of Manhattan. We had known each other for many years prior to being elected in 1965, I to the New York State Assembly and he to the New York State Senate. Our wives were in a bridge club together. When I was redistricted out of my Assembly seat, I joined Basil's law firm. Basil is now a partner in the law firm Meyer, Suozzi, English & Klein and co-chair with Harold Ickes of its labor department. They represent over forty trade unions, and Basil is personally counsel to the United Federation of Teachers and the American Federation of Teachers.

Dr. Leslie Hayling and I go way back. We grew up together. He was in my wedding, and I am godfather to his son, Dr. Leslie Hayling Jr. I have known his wife, AC, almost as long. Les was a Tuskegee Airman. He is a successful dentist in Trenton, New Jersey, and quite the storyteller.

Rev. Dr. Herbert Daughtry asked to be acknowledged as my longtime friend, supporter, and admirer. Reverend Daughtry is national presiding minister of the House of the Lord Churches; founder and chairman of the Downtown Brooklyn Neighborhood Alliance; chairman emeritus of the National Black United Front, National Religious Leaders of African Ancestry, African People Christian Organization, and African American Clergy and Elected Officials.

Robert Rubin, one of my economic advisers and co-senior partner and co-chairman, Goldman, Sachs & Company, during my administration, went on to serve as US Treasury secretary under Bill Clinton and is now co-chairman of the Council on Foreign Relations.

Commissioner of Protocol Judith Rubin is now chairman of the board of Playwrights Horizons, a not-for-profit theater in New York City.

I have known Rev. Al Sharpton since he was a teenager. I did the legal work necessary to incorporate the National Youth Movement, an organization he founded at age sixteen to fight drugs and raise money for impoverished children in the inner cities. He has matured and mellowed over time, and I am pleased with his television work on MSNBC.

My childhood friend Fred Schenck is the former deputy undersecretary, US Department of Commerce; former senior vice president, Resorts International; and former vice president, Cunard Line. He is presently a management consultant. Fred was the best man at my wedding and I at his. He is David Jr.'s godfather.

I also want to acknowledge people who contributed their talents to my administration but have not been involved with the creation of this book:

Bill de Blasio, Marcia Smith, Betsy Gotbaum, Victor Kovner, Diana Hoffman, Regina Morris, Gordon Campbell, Dr. Marjorie Hill, Richard Murphy, Prema Mathai-Davis, Sally Pinero, Ellen Baer, Michael Schlein, Sandy Frucher, Dennis Walcott, Victor Gotbaum, Carol O'Cleireacain, Michael Geffrard, Fritz Alexander, Michael Jacobsen, Mindy Tarlow, Jim Dumpson, June Christmas, Billy Jones, Catherine Abate, Martha Hirst, Floss Frucher, Margaret Hamburg, Irwin Redlener, Lee Jones, Albert Scardino, Phil Michael, Arthur Levitt, Reg Lewis, Donald Kummerfeld,

Acknowledgments

Jim Harmon, Roger Altman, Dall Forsythe, Nicholas Katzenberg, Cliff Wharton, Rudy Rinaldi, Lew Rudin, and Jack Rudin.

.   .   .

If it weren't for Len Riggio, there would be no book. The CEO of Barnes & Noble Bookstores, Len served as finance chairman on my second mayoral campaign and is a dear friend. Despite everything else on his plate, Len nonetheless has been insistent from day one that there be a book, that we had an important story to tell, and he has done all that is humanly possible to bring it about. Len has a remarkable heart. His philanthropy in building and giving away two hundred houses in New Orleans after Hurricane Katrina stands as a testament to his generosity of spirit.

My collaborator, Peter Knobler, worked long and hard gathering stories and insights from the many people who contributed to this book and crafting my voice on these pages. He is a lifelong New Yorker who is in touch with the soul of the city, and I appreciate his efforts. We both thank Esther Newberg of ICM for bringing him to this project.

Robert Kimzey performed ably as editor and Cynthia Buck made many improvements as copy editor. They played an important role in shaping this book..

Thanks to Ian Wehrle, Nadine Wolf, and Joycelyn Furginson for their transcribing.

As always, I am deeply indebted to my wonderful, beloved family—my bride Joyce, my children David Jr. and Donna, and my grandchildren Jamal and Kalila. Their love makes everything possible.

Index

Index

PublicAffairs is a publishing house founded in 1997. It is a tribute to the standards, values, and flair of three persons who have served as mentors to countless reporters, writers, editors, and book people of all kinds, including me.

I. F. Stone, proprietor of *I. F. Stone's Weekly,* combined a commitment to the First Amendment with entrepreneurial zeal and reporting skill and became one of the great independent journalists in American history. At the age of eighty, Izzy published *The Trial of Socrates,* which was a national bestseller. He wrote the book after he taught himself ancient Greek.

Benjamin C. Bradlee was for nearly thirty years the charismatic editorial leader of *The Washington Post.* It was Ben who gave the *Post* the range and courage to pursue such historic issues as Watergate. He supported his reporters with a tenacity that made them fearless, and it is no accident that so many became authors of influential, best-selling books.

Robert L. Bernstein, the chief executive of Random House for more than a quarter century, guided one of the nation's premier publishing houses. Bob was personally responsible for many books of political dissent and argument that challenged tyranny around the globe. He is also the founder and was the longtime chair of Human Rights Watch, one of the most respected human rights organizations in the world.

·   ·   ·

For fifty years, the banner of Public Affairs Press was carried by its owner Morris B. Schnapper, who published Gandhi, Nasser, Toynbee, Truman, and about 1,500 other authors. In 1983 Schnapper was described by *The Washington Post* as "a redoubtable gadfly." His legacy will endure in the books to come.

Peter Osnos, *Founder and Editor-at-Large*